Banking and Finance Series

Accountancy

Banking and Finance Series

Accountancy

by

Roger Bryant, *M.Sc, B.Sc (Econ), FCA, FIB*
Senior Lecturer in Accounting,
Huddersfield Polytechnic

Graham & Trotman

First published in 1985 by

Graham & Trotman Limited
Sterling House
66 Wilton Road
London SW1V 1DE

Graham & Trotman Inc.
13 Park Avenue
Gaithersburg
MD 20877, USA

ISBN 0 86010 567 9 (softcover)
ISBN 0 86010 584 9 (hardback)

British Library Cataloguing in Publication Data

Bryant, Roger
Accountancy.———(Banking and finance series)
1. Accounting
I. title II. Series
657 HF5635

ISBN 0-86010-584-9
ISBN 0-86010-567-9 Pbk

Production Services by Book Production Consultants, Cambridge

Typeset in Great Britain by The Castlefield Press, Moulton, Northants
Printed and bound in Great Britain

Contents

Series Foreword

The *Banking and Finance Series* has been written for students who are preparing for the Associateship of the Institute of Bankers. The structure of the series follows the syllabus closely. Although the emphasis is on the Institute of Bankers' examinations the series is also relevant to students for other professional examinations such as the different Accountancy Bodies, Chartered Secretaries, Diploma in Public Administration, undergraduate business courses, BTEC, BEC, HND, DMS, Stock Exchange courses, Association of Corporate Treasurers, Institute of Freight Forwarders, Institute of Export.

May 1985

Brian Kettell
Series Editor

This book is dedicated by Roger Bryant to his mother

Acknowledgements

The author is indebted to the following for permission to reproduce previously published material:

The Chartered Association of Certified Accountants for reproduction of past examination papers and material from articles by the author which first appeared in *The Student Newsletter*.

The Centre for Interfirm Comparisons for reproduction of the pyramid in Chapter 9.

The Institute of Chartered Accountants in England and Wales for reproduction of Accounting Standards and material which first appeared in continuing professional education courses, of which the present author was Joint Technical Author.

The Institute of Bankers for reproduction of past examination papers, and material from articles by the author which first appeared in *The Journal of the Institute of Bankers*.

He is also grateful to John Argenti for permission to summarise in Chapter 14 sections of his book *Corporate Collapse: Causes and Symptoms* (McGraw Hill).

Preface

The study of Accountancy is an important component in the education of anyone engaged in the affairs of business. That this should be so is hardly surprising, for the role of accounting is to record, interpret and report the use of scarce and valuable economic resources. In order to make the process more valuable the results of this activity are expressed in monetary terms, hence the common misconception that accountancy is about "money". It is more correct to say that it is about the things that money will buy. However, the process is not without problems, some due to the need to report annually the results of events lasting over several periods, and some due to the changing value of money over the years. It is hardly surprising therefore that the users of accounts have found it more and more difficult to understand the pictures portrayed by accounts in recent years, or that accountants have found it more and more difficult to reduce the complexities of modern business to statements of convenient simplicity. The consequence is that it now takes some skill to be able to understand and to interpret a set of accounts. Such skills have to be acquired, hence the need for books such as this which attempt to help in the process.

In the modern world there are many users of accounts each having their own particular needs. It is hoped that there will be something of interest to anyone interested in accounting within this book. However, it has been written with the particular needs of the banking community in mind. Thus it should be of particular use to the practising banker and to those who wish to discover what a banker needs to know about accounts. More specifically it has been written to meet the needs of those who are preparing for the examinations of the *Institute of Bankers*. The contents cover the syllabus of the *Accountancy Examination of the Banking Diploma Stage 2*.

In preparing for examinations in Accountancy it is essential to read and to digest a number of key principles and rules. These are tested under examination conditions by requiring candidates to complete practical questions based on those principles and rules. To meet this requirement efficiently and accurately requires a good deal of practice. It is not therefore sufficient merely to read and to digest the contents of this book in preparing for the examination. In addition, candidates should practise the skills needed in the examination room by attempting suitable questions based on the contents of the book. With this in mind a companion *Questions and Answers Revision Guide* has been prepared. This contains a large selection of questions organised to match the chapters of this book, including many drawn from past examination papers of the Institute of Bankers.

In preparing this book I have drawn on ideas obtained from a wide numbers of sources over many years. It is now impossible to remember where all of them have come from. However, I undoubtedly owe a debt of gratitude to many past and present colleagues and students. In preparing this text I have received particular help and encouragement from Brian Kettell, Alan Munroe, and from Mrs J. Tayles, who typed part of the manuscript. Lastly, I must thank my wife, Jayne, and my children, Katie and Simon, for their considerable support, patience and understanding over the months which I have devoted to authorship.

August 1985 *Roger Bryant*

Chapter 1

Introduction to Accountancy

The most widely quoted definition of Accounting is that given by the American Accounting Association:

> "The process of identifying, measuring, and communicating economic information to permit informed judgements and decisions by the users of the information."[1]

This might at first sight seem an unduly complicated approach to the subject. However, after obtaining only a slight knowledge of accountancy it soon becomes obvious that in the modern world the provision of useful and reliable information about business concerns and their transactions is bound to be a complex subject. Traditionally accounts were prepared only with the shareholder in mind, and were restricted to a balance sheet, showing the position at the end of the trading period, and later a profit and loss account showing the results. However, as society has become more complicated many other groups have developed an interest in the financial affairs of business enterprises. As a result it has often been found that traditional accounts do not meet the needs of all of the various users. In recent years therefore the accountancy profession has been obliged to re-examine its practices and procedures. A great deal of time and effort has been expended in attempting to determine:

- who are the principle users of accounting information;
- what are the information needs of the major users;
- which transactions should be reported in financial statements;
- how these transactions should be measured, and the results communicated.

Several areas have caused particular problems. These include:

- reporting the effect of changing prices in a period of rapid inflation;
- showing the investment in intangible assets, such as goodwill and in assets with indeterminate lives, such as research and development;
- presenting the results of long-term contracts, where the benefits accrue over several years;

[1]. *A Statement of Basic Accounting Theory* (The American Accounting Association, 1966).

- disclosing the impact of items which distort the results of a single period, and are not expected to occur frequently in the future;
- showing the effect of changing exchange rates where a company operates at home and overseas.

For the users of accounts the discovery that accountancy is not an "exact science" may have been disconcerting. However, it is essential to appreciate the nature of the problems in order to understand the solutions and the extent to which reliance may be placed on accounting information. An objective of this book is to explain the topics which figure most prominently in "identifying, measuring and communicating business transactions," and to outline the way in which the accountancy profession in the United Kingdom has tried to provide information which will "permit informed judgements and decisions by the users of accounts." In doing so special attention is paid to the needs of bankers. However, the debate on accounting practice is a continuous one and the procedures discussed are always liable to develop and change over the years.

A sound starting point for such a venture is a consideration of the users of accounting information and of their needs. This chapter continues with an outline of the way in which the finance function is organised in order to meet these needs and of the main financial statements prepared in order to do so.

THE USERS OF ACCOUNTING INFORMATION

Company law requires every company to lay accounts before its members at least once in every accounting reference period, which in practice means once a year. Statute also recognises the right of certain creditors to receive accounting information. However, until recently the regulations governing the provision of information largely ignored other groups having an interest in the progress and state of affairs of companies. This omission was identified by the Accounting Standards Committee at an early stage and accordingly a committee was appointed to identify the principle users of accounts and their needs. The findings of this committee were published in a document called *The Corporate Report.*[2]

The committee accepted that there is an implicit responsibility on all organisations whose activities significantly affect others to provide information about their activities. Those chiefly affected by corporate entities and having a reasonable right to such information were classified by the committee into seven main groups.

(1) The Equity Investor Group

This group includes the present shareholders of the entity, and potential

Although the report was prepared by a sub-committee of the Accounting Standards Committee it was never adopted as standard policy. Nevertheless, it has had a substantial impact on the content of company accounts in the years since it was published.

shareholders or investors in it. The information needs of such owners or potential owners includes a requirement for information to assist in reaching trading decisions, in deciding whether or not to subscribe to new issues of shares and in reaching voting decisions at general meetings. The decision-making process generally involves making comparisions with earlier years and with other companies. In particular, investors will wish to make judgements concerning likely movements in share prices (including by private sale in the case of smaller firms), likely levels of future dividend payments and management efficiency. In addition the group will be interested in the economic stability and vulnerability of the reporting entity, and especially during periods of rapid rises in prices, investors need information about the internal cash generating processes of the entity.

(2) The Loan Creditor Group

This group includes not only holders of long-term securities, such as debentures and loan stock, but also short-term lenders such as the banks. The information needs of loan creditors are similar in many respects to the needs of equity investors. They will wish to assess the economic stability and vulnerability of the borrower, but unlike equity investors they are primarily concerned with the risk and consequences of default. If the restrictive covenants in Articles of Association, debenture deeds, or loan agreements commit an enterprise to maintain working capital or liquidity within certain limits, loan creditors may look to the financial statements to confirm that these restrictions have been observed. Short-term loan creditors are likely to be especially interested in ascertaining the levels of liquid assets, and in estimating cash flow in the immediate future, the realisable value of assets and the priority of various claims.

(3) The Employee Group

The right of employees to information arises from their personal ties with the employer. The reporting entity has a responsibility for the future livelihood and prospects of its employees and possibly its past employees through pension payments. The employee group needs information for evaluating performance, and objectives, including employment plans; estimating the future prospects of the entity, including its capacity to pay remuneration and predicting future levels of employment; assessing the position and prospects of individual establishments within a group. Much of this information will be made available to the trade unions as representatives of employees.

(4) The Analyst-Advisor Group

This group consists of analysts and advisors working for members of the Stock Exchange, banks, competitors, and the press. These experts use accounts in a more sophisticated manner than those to whom they report, and thus require more detailed information to be given.

(5) The Business Contact Group

As the name implies, this group includes all those whom the reporting entity deals with in its business operations including regular customers, suppliers, trade creditors and even competitors and business rivals. The business contact group needs information in order to estimate the future prospects of the entity and to predict future levels of production. For example, suppliers and creditors would be interested in the ability of the entity to pay for goods and services supplied, as well as the ability to repay any outstanding amounts owed. Also customers need information concerning the current and future supply of goods and services offered, prices and other product details and conditions of sale. Competitors and business rivals seek information in order to enhance their efficiency, possibly through investment in, and even acquisition of, other firms. Although many organisations prefer their competitors not to know about their activities, a free flow of information is generally regarded as essential for the market to operate efficiently.

(6) The Government

For the government, company accounts are an important source of the statistical information essential for the formulation of economic and industrial policy. In addition accounts provide the basis for levying business taxation, and for checking compliance with many legal obligations and requirements.

(7) The Public

This group includes taxpayers, ratepayers, consumers and other special interest groups such as political parties. Their rights to information, it is argued, arises not from a direct financial or human relationship with the reporting entity, but from the general role played in society by economic entities.

The corporate report did not deal with the internal uses of accounting information. The needs of *management* are mainly met by internal reports, but corporate reports act as a feedback on management action in meeting the company's objectives. Also the corporate report offers management an overall view of the company, rather than the individual areas in which particular members of a management team are located. The detailed information requirements of management and the way in which these are met is the subject of Chapters 8–12 of this book.

ORGANISATION OF THE FINANCE FUNCTION

The nature of the finance function in each business is likely to vary according to the characteristics of the organisation concerned, with a large firm employing many staff in this area organised into several departments, and a small concern relying on its auditor to provide essential accounting services. Figure 1.1 shows a typical division of duties in a large manufacturing firm. It can be seen that four main functions exist: financial accounting, management accounting, auditing and the treasury function. At the summit of the internal organisation is the *Finance Director* who is responsible for supervising the staffing and organisation of the finance function, determining policy in this area, and providing the board of directors with crucial advice on the financial aspects of its deliberations. As a member of the board of directors the finance director owes a collective duty to the shareholders with the other members of the board. In a few instances the finance function is not represented at board level, and it is true to say that this is often a matter of some concern to investors and creditors. In some large organisations the day-to-day responsibilities of a Finance Director are undertaken by the Financial Controller, or Chief Accountant, with responsibility for overseeing both the financial and management accounting functions.

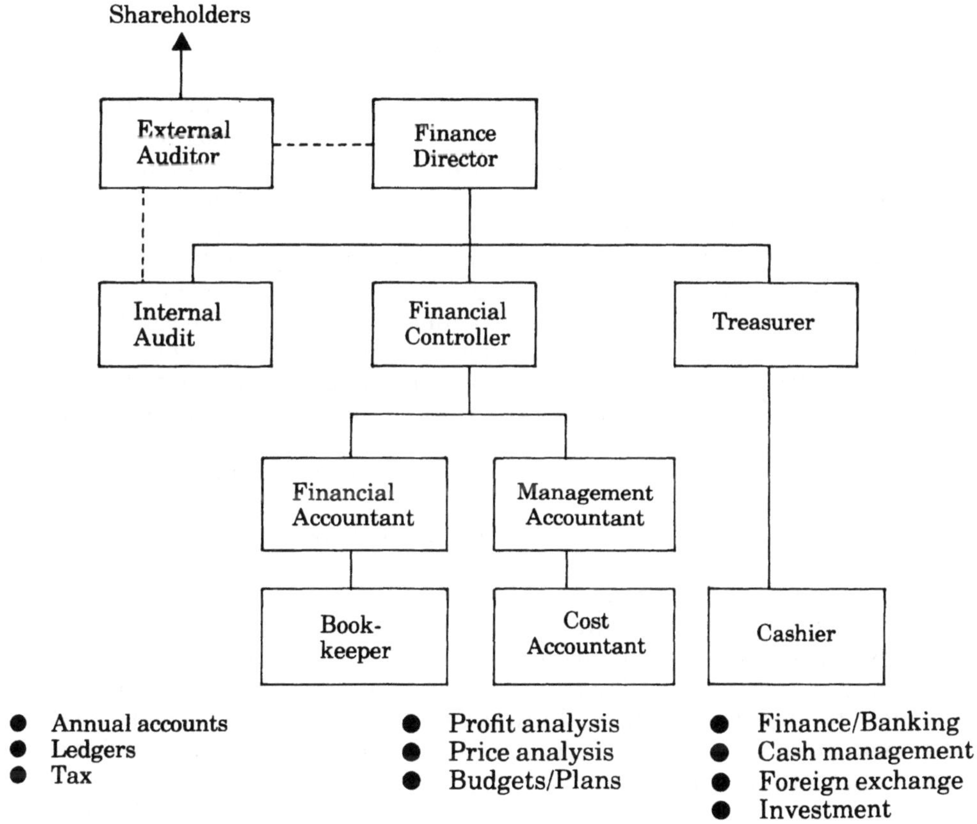

Figure 1.1 Organisation of the Finance Function

FINANCIAL ACCOUNTING

Financial accounting consists of two main operations; keeping the basic accounting records of the business and preparing accounts once a year or more frequently if required. Much of the detailed work is today undertaken using computers, but the *Financial Accountant* remains responsible for designing the system, monitoring it in operation and using the output to prepare accounts in accordance with any relevant legislation.

The routine tasks of classifying transactions, checking that they have been properly processed, and reconciling the books with external evidence is usually undertaken by a *Bookkeeper*. In small firms the bookkeeper continues to be responsible for entering the transactions in the books of account. In most organisations the Financial Accountant is also responsible for negotiations with the Inland Revenue concerning the charge for corporation tax, although in this he may receive expert advice from specialists in the company's firm of auditors. Only the very largest firms have special staff responsible solely for tax accounting.

MANAGEMENT ACCOUNTING

Management accounting comprises the preparation and reporting of information to management regarding the detailed operations of the company in order for decisions to be taken over pricing, control of costs and expenses and the composition of the product portfolio. The control and management of the system is in the hands of the *Management Accountant* who will supervise the detailed work of the *Cost Accountants*. The Management Accountant will generally be responsible for the preparation of the annual budget and for monitoring the extent to which actual outcomes correspond with the budget. Most importantly he will be responsible for collating explanations for departures from plan, subjecting them to critical examination, and reporting on his analysis to management. The Cost Accountant will prepare detailed analyses of the costs associated with aspects of the production process, and will be responsible for estimating and monitoring performance.

TREASURY FUNCTION

The treasury function may be described as the process of seeing that the business has the funds available to meet its liabilities as they fall due. However it also consists of ensuring that the business makes the best use of the funds at its disposal. Thus the *Treasurer* will be responsible for raising all forms of finance ranging from share capital to short-term bank loans, and also for seeing that surplus funds are deposited securely for a suitable period at the most competitive rate. Where the firm operates internationally, the job of treasurer assumes a further dimension. The firm is able to raise finance in a variety of capital markets around the world, but becomes subject to the risks associated with changes in exchange rates. In most small firms the job of Treasurer is undertaken by the Financial Accountant, with routine operations undertaken by a *Cashier*, responsible for controlling cash and banking transactions.

AUDITING

Auditing It is the role of the *External Auditor* to report to the shareholders on whether in his opinion the accounts laid before them show a true and fair view and comply with the Companies Act. In order to make his report he carries out detailed tests on the accounts and on the underlying books. In a large firm the volume of testing can be considerably reduced if the company has a sound system of internal control. The Auditor then designs his tests to establish whether the system is operating as intended and to ensure that the accounting records are accurate and complete. In many large firms a key aspect of the system of internal control is the presence of an *Internal Auditor* who reports to a key member of the management team on the reliability of the records, and on any other aspects which are of concern. It is desirable that the internal auditor reports to an official who is not personally involved in maintaining the accounting records, and that he has access to the Managing Director on matters of major importance.

In a small firm it is unlikely that there will be an internal auditor, and the internal control system will depend on the close involvement and supervision of the directors. In many such cases the external auditor not only performs the audit function, but is also responsible for preparing the financial accounts, maintaining statutory books such as the register of members, calculating and negotiating tax liabilities, and providing general financial advice.

This book is concerned mainly with the accounts of limited companies. Such organisations must fulfill certain minimum accounting requirements. They must keep specific accounting records, they must prepare annual accounts, those accounts must comply with the detailed provisions of the Companies Act, must show a true and fair view and must be audited. Today many firms, including quite small ones, use computers for basic record keeping.

However, many business organisations are not incorporated as companies but are run as personal enterprises or as partnerships. For such businesses there are no statutory rules governing the books which they must keep and the accounts which they must prepare. However, these firms are likely to be asked to produce accounts by the Inland Revenue and by banks as soon as they wish to borrow money. Thus bankers will frequently receive accounts for which the detailed rules covered in this book do not apply. Nevertheless, whenever an accountant is asked to produce accounts which show a *true and fair view* he must apply the basic concepts and conventions developed by his profession if the figures he prepares are to be sound and reliable.

Thus, although this book concentrates on company accounts, it is important to appreciate that the principles on which they are based apply to all forms of business organisation, even though they are not mentioned specifically in this book.

THE FINANCIAL STATEMENTS

The annual report of a company is now a complicated and lengthy document consisting of several important statements, the larger the firm, the longer the report tends to be. The quality and quantity of information disclosed tends to vary considerably from company to company. For companies quoted on the Stock Exchange the publication of the annual report is a vitally important public relations exercise.

CHAIRMAN'S STATEMENT

The purpose of the Chairman's Statement is to give the shareholders and other readers of the annual report up-to-date information about the company's progress, performance and prospects. It is not required by law, and is only likely to be found in the reports of companies listed on the Stock Exchange. For such companies it is a useful source of information and will serve to explain much of the information appearing in the accounts. However it should be read critically, and it will often prove useful to read the comments of investment analysts and press commentators at the same time.

THE DIRECTORS' REPORT

A Directors' Report is required by law and must show the information laid down by the Companies Act 1985. The purpose of this document is to give information about the business which the legislators consider it essential for the shareholders to receive. This includes a fair review of the development of the business, as well as details of dividends proposed, changes in the fixed assets, details of the current market value of land and the names of directors. The report must also state the principle activities of the business and any changes therein. The auditor is now required to check whether the information given in the director's report is consistent with the accounts. A full list of the information to be given in the director's report is shown on p. 110–111.

THE AUDITOR'S REPORT

The auditor is required to report to the shareholders on whether the accounts show a true and fair view and comply with the Companies Acts 1985. He must also be satisfied that proper books of account have been kept, that adequate returns have been received from branches, and that the accounts are in agreement with the books. If he does not obtain all of the information and explanations he requires then he must say so in his report. Where he disagrees with the view shown in the accounts or is unable to substantiate certain amounts then he must qualify his report. It is important to realise that the auditor is only required to express an opinion on the basis of the examination he carries out. He does not certify that the accounts are correct although many people refer to the auditors report as a certificate.

There is no definition of the phrase "true and fair view" in the Companies Act. In practice it is usually taken to mean that the accounts have been prepared with reasonable accuracy using the concepts and conventions generally accepted by accountants. Moreover that the amounts are shown in a way which is relevant and meaningful so that items which are insignificant are omitted and items which deserve prominance receive it, this operation being done without bias on the part of the person preparing the accounts.

THE PROFIT AND LOSS ACCOUNT

The purpose of the profit and loss account is to match all on the relevant costs against the revenue of the period. The main objective of accountants is to ensure that the profit figure shown in the accounts is soundly based and reflects the results of the ordinary activities of the business, thus permitting meaningful comparisons from year to year. The profit and loss account which appears in the statutory accounts of a company need only show certain items required by law. However, it is necessary for every firm to prepare a detailed profit and loss account in order to calculate the result for the year. In the case of a small firm the detailed profit and loss account is usually made available to bankers.

THE BALANCE SHEET

The balance sheet of a company is required by law to show the state of affairs of the company at the balance sheet date. However it is important to appreciate that in accordance with the conventions used by accountants it shows items at historical cost, subject to optional adjustments to show property and sometimes other fixed assets at current value. Current assets which have a value below cost are written down to net realisable value, and fixed assets must be written down where they sustain a permanent loss of value. Nevertheless, accountants do not claim that the balance sheet is a statement of value showing the true worth of the assets, let alone the value of the business. In particular the fixed assets are shown at cost or revaluation less accumulated depreciation, but this figure is not intended to be a valuation. Rather it is the residual balance arising from the allocation of the cost of using a fixed asset to the profit and loss account over its expected useful life. Furthermore it is important to remember that most intangible assets, despite having considerable commerical value, do not figure in company accounts. Thus whilst a balance sheet is a useful starting point for the valuation of a business it is not itself a statement of value. Moreover the balance sheet shows the account balances at the end of a single day's trading in each period; it says nothing about the position at other times of the year, which may have been considerably different.

The main headings for the items to be shown in a company balance sheet are now laid down by law and are shown on pp. 100–103.

THE NOTES TO THE ACCOUNTS

Much of the detailed information shown in a modern set of accounts is given in the form of notes to the main statements. This information is of the following kinds:

- headings in the balance sheet and profit and loss account which may be combined and shown as notes to the accounts in order to improve their presentation;
- information regarding departures from the rules laid down in the Companies Act which are required in order to show a true and fair view. Particulars of such departures, the reasons for them and their effect must be given as notes to the accounts;
- supplementary information required to be given as notes to the accounts by the Companies Act (see App. 1 for a full description);
- information required to be given as notes to the accounts by Statements of Standard Accounting Practice or the Stock Exchange Listing Agreement.
- information which the company considers should be given as a note to the accounts in order that they show a true and fair view and give the reader all of the information which is needed in order to comprehend the results of the company and of its state of affairs.

Although the notes do not make lively reading it is important to remember that they are an integral part of the accounts and contain much vital information.

THE STATEMENT OF SOURCE AND APPLICATION OF FUNDS

In accordance with standard practice, which is discussed in Chapter 2, all companies should include a statement of source and application of funds in their accounts. This statement is not required by law. The objective of a funds statement is to show the manner in which the operations of a business have been financed and in which its financial resources have been used. It highlights the change in working capital and especially the movement in net liquid resources. It does not show the gross receipts from turnover but starts by showing the profit achieved before tax, and effectively links the balance sheet of the previous period with that at the latest accounting date. For this reason it should perhaps be described as a statement of change in financial condition; a phrase more commonly used in the USA.

OTHER STATEMENTS APPEARING IN ANNUAL REPORTS

Statistical Analysis of Shareholdings

Many quoted companies include a statement showing the composition of its body of shareholders. This is usually broken down by size of holding and also by type of holder. It is always interesting to see the extent to which the company is owned by individual shareholders, rather than financial institutions.

Five or Ten-Year Record

All quoted companies include a table of key accounting figures covering the last few years. This provides a useful insight into the recent history of a company, beyond that obtainable from the comparative figures shown in the annual report.

Statement of Value Added

Value added statements were advocated by the committee responsible for the Corporate Report and now figure in the reports of about 30% of the largest companies. The committee stated: "The simplest and most effective way of putting profit into proper perspective vis-à-vis the whole enterprise as a collective effort by capital, management and employees is by presentation of value added. Value added is the wealth the reporting entity has been able to create by its own and its employee's efforts. This statement would show how value added has been used to pay those contributing to its creation."

OTHER STATEMENTS ADVOCATED BY THE CORPORATE REPORT

In addition to the value added statement the Corporate Report suggested that the following additional statements should be included in annual reports:

(a) An employment report showing the size and composition of the workforce relying on the enterprise for its livelihood, the work contribution of employees and the benefits earned. This report would assist users in assessing the performance of the entity, evaluating its economic function and performance in relation to society, assessing its capacity to make reallocations of resources and evaluating managerial performance, efficiency and objectives.

(b) A statement of money exhanges with government showing the financial relationship between the enterprise and the state.

(c) A statement of transactions in foreign currency showing the direct cash dealings of the reporting entity between this country and abroad.

(d) A statement of future prospects showing likely future profit, employment and investment levels.

(e) A statement of corporate objectives showing management policy and medium-term strategic targets. This statement would assist users to evaluate managerial performance, efficiency and objectives.

Whilst not discouraging companies from disclosing additional information the government has expressed the view that most of this information is now required by statute in the directors report and accounts: special provisions have been introduced within employment legislation governing the provision of information to employees. In recent years only a minority of firms have provided the additional statements advocated in the report, although a number have voluntarily provided information on their general dealings with society in a *social report*.

THE INTERRELATIONSHIPS OF THE FINANCIAL STATEMENTS

Although the financial statements consist of three principal separate documents and related notes, it is important to appreciate that each statement is related to the others. A change in the position shown by one will automatically result in a change in the others. It is vital to understand the way in which the statements are related to gain a proper appreciation of the nature of a firm's financial affairs. The position will be demonstrated by reference to Figure 1.2 which shows each of the main financial statements in simplified form.

The Profit and Loss Account and the Balance Sheet. The profit and loss account shows the surplus or deficit arising when the sales revenue of the period is matched against the cost of goods sold and the relevant expenses. After taxation has been taken into account and dividends paid, or provided for, the remaining profit is added to the share capital and reserves in the balance sheet. Not all of the expenses of the period will have been paid for in cash during the period, and taxation and dividends may remain to be paid in the following period. Each of these items will change the disposition of assets and liabilities within the balance sheet.

The Funds' Statement. In order to help the users of accounts to identify the changes which have taken place, and to demonstrate their impact upon the liquid resources of the business, a funds' statement is prepared. This

PROFIT AND LOSS ACCOUNT

	£
Sales	xxx
Cost of Sales	(xxx)
Gross Profit	xxx
Expenses – including:	
Depreciation	(xxx)
Net Profit	xxx
Taxation	(xxx)
Dividends	(xxx)
Retained Profit	£ xxx

BALANCE SHEET

	Year II £	Year II £	Year I £	Year I £
Fixed Assets		xxx		xxx
Current Assets				
Stocks	xxx		xxx	
Debtors	xxx		xxx	
Cash	xxx		xxx	
	xxx		xxx	
Current Liabilities				
Creditors	(xxx)		(xxx)	
Net current assets		xxx		(xxx)
		xxx		xxx
Other Liabilities		(xxx)		(xxx)
		£xxx		£ xxx
Capital and Reserves				
including:				
Profit retained	xxx			xxx
	£xxx			£ xxx

FUNDS STATEMENT

		£
Funds from operations		
Net profit		xxx
Depreciation		xxx
		xxx
Other funds		xxx
Total sources		xxx
Applications		
Fixed assets	(xxx)	
Taxation	(xxx)	
Dividends	(xxx)	(xxx)
Change in working capital		£ xxx
Stocks	xxx	
Debtors	xxx	
Creditors	xxx	xxx
Change in liquid resources		xxx
		£ xxx

Figure 1.2 Financial Statements — Simplified

statement also takes account of the profits made by the company, but does so before use is made of them to pay taxation and dividends. The statement shows the way in which profits are reduced by charges not involving the payment of cash in the current period and makes an adjustment for this amount. In practice the funds generated by business operations may be much higher than the level of profits. The funds' statement then shows the effect of any other sources of funds received by the business and the total available for use during the year. The latter amount is detected by changes in the long-term liabilities of the business and from the sale of assets. The statement identifies the way in which the funds are employed to acquire fixed assets, and to pay dividends and taxation. Changes in the balance sheet also reveal the overall movement of current assets including stocks and debtors, and the extent to which these have been offset by additional trade credit. The end result of these movements will be to alter the level of liquid resources in the balance sheet.

The nature of the relationships discussed briefly here will be considered in more depth later in the book, when we shall also consider the way in which the full flows of funds during the year, rather than the net effect, may be reviewed and controlled. This discussion is left until Chapter 10.

ACCOUNTS AND THE BANKER

Although accounts are produced essentially for the shareholders of the company wide use is made of them by a number of other users. Amongst these other users bankers are amongst the most important; their chief interests being to gain an insight into the financial strength of a business. In many respects accounts are significantly deficient in this area. The need to provide statements of stewardship to shareholders and to minimise the scope for subjectivity in financial reporting inevitably limits the usefulness of annual reports for assessing lending propositions. Equally the need to present statements on a going concern basis undermines the usefulness of accounts as a basis for gone concern valuations. However despite these limitations financial accounts remain the best, possibly the only, independently verified statement of the assets and liabilities of a business produced on a regular basis, and the only independently attested confirmation of the annual trading performance. For this reason they will remain an important aspect of the analysis for lending decisions. In order to use financial accounts effectively, and to avoid being misled by their limitations, every lending banker must be aware of the principles on which accounts are prepared, and of their inherent limitations.

Unfortunately it must also be recognised that the accounts prepared for smaller businesses do not always meet the high standards expected of them. This is especially true of smaller companies and unincorporated businesses, whose accounts are often prepared with more thought of the demands of the Inland Revenue, than of the need to show a true and fair view. In many cases the accountant is forced to rely upon the representations of the owners of the business regarding the contents of the accounts. Frequently the whole process is considerably delayed, and in recent years many companies have failed althogether to deposit accounts with the Registrar of Companies. As a result of these deficiencies the banker often finds it impossible to obtain reliable information from customers with reasonable promptness. Accordingly the banker is forced to place more emphasis on other components of the lending decision including the taking of adequate security for money advanced. Nevertheless these shortcomings do not justify the rejection of all accounting information. The banker should persuade his customers to provide sound and timely accounts for two reasons: the taking of strong security is never an adequate substitute for reliable and up-to-date information on the performance and position of a business: secondly it is clearly in the interests of the businessman himself that he has access to reliable information about the progress of the firm, especially if it is to grow and to prosper.

THIS BOOK

The content of this book has been arranged with the needs of bankers and banking students in mind. Chapters 1–7 deal with financial reporting, and is devoted to explaining the principles on which accounts are based, and their inherent limitations. Chapters 8–13 are concerned with the use of accounting information for decision-making, and particularly with its use in bank-lending decisions. The basis for all relevant and reliable accounting information is a sound system of bookkeeping. However it is beyond the scope of this book to describe the double entry system which is normally employed in order to achieve this objective. Readers who wish to pursue this subject are referred to the suggested reading at the end of this chapter.

In this chapter we have considered the main users of accounts, the organisation of the accounting and finance function, and the principal components of the financial statements prepared by businesses. In the next two chapters we examine the accounting principles and rules which have been established for dealing with such complex areas as the valuation of stocks and work-in-progress, the treatment of research and development expenditure, and the amortisation of tangible and intangible fixed assets. The regulations described have been laid down by two sources of authority on accounting matters; the Accounting Standards Committee, in the form of Statements of Standard Accounting Practice, and Parliament, in the form of Companies Acts. Chapter 4 deals with the treatment of taxation in company accounts, and Chapter 5 with the way in which information must be disclosed in the accounts of companies in accordance with legal requirements. Many organisations comprise not one, but several companies; such firms are obliged to prepare accounts which show the affairs of the business as if it were one entity. Group accounts are the subject of Chapter 6. The first half of the book concludes with a discussion of the complex problem posed by the changing price levels of recent years. For over a decade the accountancy profession has been attempting to produce a system for dealing with the effects of changing prices on accounts. Several proposals have been introduced and tried, but none has won sufficient support to become established. Chapter 7 examines the problem and the proposed solutions, including the latest statement from the Accounting Standards Committee, ED35 (now withdrawn).

The second half of the book, dealing with accounting for decision-making, begins with a description of the use of accounting ratios in analysing accounts. Chapter 9 deals with the use of internal management accounts by companies, and its relevance for lending bankers. The chapter is concerned with three main issues: assessing the plans of the business, evaluating its progress and performance, and resolving problems as they arise. In practice the immediate cause of the failure of most firms is an inability to meet their liabilities as they fall due, rather than their failure to make profits. For this reason the ability to plan and to control the working capital requirements of the firm and the flow of funds within it is an essential component of effective financial management. This area is dealt with in Chapter 10. The next two chapters deal with the topic of capital budgeting, which consists of two elements: investment decisions, which commit large sums of money for considerable periods of time, and the financing decisions made to support them. The book concludes with chapters dealing with the valuation of companies, and the accounting implications of liquidations, reorganisations and recontructions.

FURTHER READING

There are numerous introductory books on accounting of which that by Wood, which concentrates on the technical aspects, is the best known. The book by Parker provides a simple introduction to the subject, and that by Nobes an insight into the theory of accounting. The texts by Edwards and Mellett, Egginton and Clemens and Dyer all provide treatments aimed at the banker. The books by Carsberg and Hope, and by Lee provide a useful introduction to some of the most significant recent developments in accounting, whilst that by Samuels, Rickwood and Piper will prove useful to those wishing to extend their knowledge of accounting beyond the level covered by this book.

R. H. Parker, *Understanding Company Financial Statements* (Penguin, 2nd ed., 1982).
F. Wood, *Business Accounting* (Longmans, 4th ed., 1984), 2 vols.
C. Nobes, *An Introduction to Financial Accounting* (George Allen and Unwin, 2nd ed., 1983).
J. R. Edwards and H. J. Mellett, *Accountancy for Banking Students* (The Institute of Bankers, 1983).
D. A. Egginton, *Accounting for the Banker* (Longmans, 1977).
J. H. Clemens and L. S. Dyer, *Balance Sheets and the Lending Banker* (Europa, 5th ed., 1977).
T. Lee, *Company Financial Reporting* (Nelson, 2nd ed., 1982).
B. Carsberg, and A. Hope (eds.), *Current Issues in Accounting* (P. Allen, 2nd ed., 1984).
J. Samuels, C. Rickwood and A. Piper, *Advanced Financial Accounting* (McGraw-Hill, 1981).

Chapter 2

Accounting Principles and Practice I

INTRODUCTION

Few of the items appearing in the accounting records of a business can appear in the financial statements as they stand. Many require interpretation in order to determine whether they arc, for example, assets or expenses, both of which appear as debit items in the ledger. Furthermore, it is frequently the case that an item will only in part constitute an expense of one period, with the balance representing an asset which may be used in succeeding periods. It is the role of the accountant to allocate such items in a way which will ensure that the accounts show a true and fair view. Such an operation is by no means straightforward for in most cases the manner of allocation will be determined by expectations about future events, such as the life of a piece of plant or the success of a new development.

In order to guide the accountant in this task various principles and rules have been developed. Until the 1970s this process was informal with individual accountants making up their own minds on the most suitable treatment for particular items. In doing so they were guided by what they had learnt as students and by guidance statements from the professional bodies, but at this time were no definitive rules to follow. However, this situation could result in widely differing approaches to the same item being applied by accountants all claiming to have followed "best practice". The problem was compounded by the fact that the extent of disclosure of the accounting policies adopted often did not permit even well informed observers to predict the approach taken by the accountant concerned.

As a result of several "accounting scandals" in which the inconsistency of acceptable accounting practice was highlighted the accountancy profession established a committee in order to lay down definitive rules in the future.[1]

See footnote on next page.

The work of this committee, named the Accounting Standards Committee (ASC), forms the main topic of this chapter and the next. However, in 1981, as a result of the United Kingdom's membership of the European Community, a new Companies Act was introduced which also specified certain accounting principles and accounting rules. There are thus two sets of rules which overlap, and to a certain extent support each other. In this book each set of rules will, as far as possible, be considered as a whole. The next two chapters are therefore based on accounting principles and rules derived from two sources, the Accounting Standards Committee and the Companies Act.

In addition to laying down a framework of accounting principles and rules, the Companies Act also contains standard formats governing the content and layout of company accounts. These formats, and the rules governing their operation are dealt with in Chapter 4.

THE ACCOUNTING STANDARDS COMMITTEE

During the 1970s the Accounting Standards Committee began to issue a series of Statements of Standard Practice designed to narrow the areas of difference and variety in accounting practice and to increase the level of disclosure of the accounting bases adopted. In its first decade of operation the Committee issued 19 statements and several proposed statements (termed exposure drafts). A full list is shown in Table 2.1. These statements describe "methods of accounting approved by the member bodies for application to all financial accounts intended to give a true and fair view of the financial position and profit or loss" shown in a set of financial statements. Members of the professional bodies which support the Standards programme are expected to observe the standards if they assume responsibilities in respect of financial accounts, and apparent failures to do so may be investigated by the disciplinary committee of the relevant professional body. The standards are not intended to be a comprehensive code of rigid rules, and alternatives are to be used where it is necessary in order to give a true and fair view. In such cases members are required to disclose significant departures from standard

[1] The most serious incident and probably that having the most effect occurred when, during a takeover bid in November 1967, Associated Electrical Industries forecast profits for the year of £10m. After a struggle the bid by the General Electric Company was accepted. However, when the accounts of AEI came to be prepared it was found that far from making a profit, the company had sustained a loss of £4.5m. The two largest firms of Chartered Accountants in the United Kingdom at that time were commissioned to investigate the cause of the "discrepancy". Their report stated:

"The appraisal of stocks, contracts, and a number of other matters involves the exercise of judgement; they are not matters of precision. Broadly speaking, of the total shortfall of £14.5m we would attribute roughly £5m to adverse differences which are matters substantially of fact rather than of judgement and the balance of some £9.5m. to adjustments which remain matters substantially of judgement."

Largely as a result of the controversy surrounding the case, the Institute of Chartered Accountants in England and Wales set up the Accounting Standards Steering Committee which later became the Accounting Standards Committee.

practice, to give an explanation, and to quantify the effect of the departure where it is practicable and not misleading.[2]

As a result of a review of the standard-setting process it was announced in 1983 that the committee would begin to issue a new category of final pronouncement named Statements of Recommended Practice (SORPs). A SORP will be issued when a need is seen for a pronouncement on a specific topic, but the subject does not meet the criteria for an accounting standard, i.e.

- a matter of major importance affecting the generality of companies;
- applicable to all accounts intended to give a true and fair view.

Although companies will be encouraged to comply with SORPs compliance will, unlike standards, not be mandatory. Thus there will in future be a hierarchy consisting of legal requirements for accounts, accounting standards and SORPs. A sub-category of SORPs is to be introduced called "franked SORPs". These will generally relate to topics of limited application, for example a specific industry. The work on the franked SORPs will generally be undertaken by a working party from the industry concerned, but its work will be overseen and subject to review by the ASC. The final approved document will be published by the industry concerned.

Although the development of Accounting Standards was undertaken by the independent professional accountancy bodies, the programme had the general support of the government. It was felt that greater progress, particularly in response to new developments, would be made if the professional bodies were allowed to determine the rules of accounting with the government lending statutory support through Parliament where necessary. This approach was followed until 1981 when the government was compelled by the United Kingdom's membership of the European Community to incorporate certain basic accounting principles and rules into the Companies Acts.

THE ACCOUNTING REQUIREMENTS OF THE COMPANIES ACTS

There are now two sets of overlapping rules in operation derived from the Companies Acts and from Accounting Standards. In preparing their accounts companies must follow both sets of rules, the statutory ones because the law specifically requires compliance with a Schedule of the Companies Act (as amended), and Accounting Standards because the Act requires accounts to show a true and fair view, which in most cases requires the application of

[2] Explanatory Foreward to Statements of Standard Accounting Practice. The ASC was originally established as a Steering subcommittee of the Institute of Chartered Accountants in England and Wales. It was later reconstituted as a subcommittee of the Consultative Committee of Accountancy Bodies with representatives of all the major accountancy bodies on the committee. In 1980 the committee began a review of its achievements over the previous decade and in response to certain criticisms made, changed its composition to include members in practice in industry and commerce, users of accounts, and the public enterprises, and an academic member of the profession. The individual accountancy bodies represented on the committee remain responsible for issuing standards to their members and for monitoring their implementation.

standard practice. In the main the provisions are identical or at least compatible. Where standards require additional information to be shown then this must be done. Similarly where statute permits several approaches to an item but the standard is more restrictive, then the standard prevails because of the requirement to show a true and fair view.

Prior to 1981 the regulations governing company accounts were contained in the Companies Act of 1948, although important changes were made by the Companies Acts in 1967, 1976 and 1980, as well as by a host of other statutory items. The detailed provisions governing the content of company accounts were contained in Schedule 8 to the 1948 Act, which was replaced in full in 1967. When it became necessary to amend UK law in order to meet European Community requirements this was done by amending the 1948 Act. Thus Schedule 1 of the Companies Act 1981 was inserted in the 1948 Act with the old schedule being retained as Schedule 8A. The Schedules were renumbered 4 and 9 respectively in the C.A. 1985.

In view of the complex nature of the various provisions and especially of the need for frequent cross references it was decided to consolidate the provisions in a new Act of parliament by statutory instrument. Power to undertake this reform was contained in the 1981 Act. Thus in 1985 a new Companies Act was introduced, which consolidated, but did not change the provisions of company law. The Companies Act 1985 came into force on 1 July of that year. Thus within the text where reference is made to "The Companies Act" it may be taken to mean:

- The Companies Act 1948 as amended by subsequent legislation up to 1983; and/or
- The Companies Act 1985

Where a reference is required to any other pieces of company legislation a specific reference is made.

THE FUNDAMENTAL CONCEPTS AND PRINCIPLES OF ACCOUNTING

In recent times much discussion has taken place concerning the basic concepts and ideas which underly accounting practice. Although important, these ideas were often not defined, and it has been necessary to determine the principles from an analysis of accounting practice. Inevitably there has been much confusion especially concerning the use of terminology. The Accounting Standards Committee discussed the matter in the second statement issued, and highlighted four fundamental concepts as being of particular importance. Later the Companies Act 1981, laid down that all companies must apply these concepts in preparing accounts, and made reference to a further principle not dealt with in SSAP 2. However before discussing these fundamental concepts it is necessary to mention other concepts which underly all accounts, but are not dealt with in SSAP 2 or the Companies Act.

Under the *entity concept* the affairs of a business are regarded as quite separate from those of its owners. In the case of a company this is a legal fact

Table 2.1
Accounting Standards

No.	*Topic*	*Issued*	*Included in 1985 syllabus of Inst. of Bankers*
1.	Accounting for the Results of Associated Companies	Jan 1971	Yes
2.	Disclosure of Accounting Policies	Dec 1971	Yes
3.	Earnings per share	May 1972	No
4.	Accounting treatment of Government grants	May 1974	No
5.	Accounting for VAT	May 1974	No
6.	Extraordinary and Prior Year Adjustments	May 1974	
	Amendment	Sept 1975	Yes
	Amendment	Aug 1978	
7.	(Provisional CPP Accounting)		No
8.	The Treatment of Taxation under the Imputation		Yes
	System in the Accounts of Companies	Sept 1974	Yes
	Amendment	Jan 1978	
9.	Stocks and Work in Progress	July 1975	Yes
10.	Statements of Source and Application of Funds	Sept 1975	Yes
11.	(Accounting for Deferred Taxation)		No
12.	Accounting for Depreciation	Jan 1978	Yes
13.	Accounting for Research and Development	Jan 1978	Yes
14.	Group Accounts	Oct 1978	Yes
15.	Accounting for Deferred Taxation	Dec 1978	Yes
16.	Current Cost Accounting	April 1980	Yes
17.	Accounting for Post Balance Sheet Events	Sept 1980	No
18.	Accounting for Contingencies	Sept 1980	No
19.	Accounting for Investment Properties	Nov 1981	No
20.	Foreign Currency Translation	April 1983	No
21.	Accounting for Leases	Aug 1984	No
22.	Accounting for Goodwill	Dec 1984	No
23.	Accounting for Acquisitions and Mergers	April 1985	No
Exposure Drafts Outstanding			
28.	Accounting for Petroleum Dev. Tax	March 1981	No
32.	Accounting for Pension information in Company Accounts	May 1983	No
33.	Accounting for deferred tax	July 1983	No
34.	Pension Scheme Accounts (SORP)	April 1984	No
36.	Extraordinary Items and Prior Year Adjustments	Jan 1985	No
37.	Accounting for Depreciation	March 1985	No

with the organisation having a legal personality quite separate from its members or shareholders, although in practice the directors of a small company may have difficulty in appreciating this fact and in keeping the company's assets separate from their own. In the case of a partnership the liabilities of the firm become the personal liabilities of the partners, as they are in the case of a sole trader, and its profits are taxed as the personal profits of the partners. However in each case accountants regard the affairs of a partnership and the business of a sole trader as separate from their personal affairs and transactions. Thus when a sole trader removes cash from his business it is regarded as a debt owed to the business unless formally recognised as a withdrawal of capital. If the business acquires an asset such as a car then it is regarded as belonging to the business, rather than the individual, and will be included in the balance sheet of the enterprise. If the asset is eventually withdrawn from the business for personal use, then its value must be removed from the accounts and, unless paid for by the owner, counts as a withdrawal of capital.

As a result of the recognition of the existence of the business as an entity separate from its owners, it becomes possible to recognise and record transactions between the business and its owners, whatever the legal status of those transactions. This feature leads naturally to the duality concept which is discussed below.

The *duality concept* recognises that just as transactions involving the owners and the business itself have a dual aspect so indeed do all transactions. A sale on credit involves the recognition of a sale and the creation of a debtor. The purchase of a fixed asset for cash affects both the level of fixed assets and the total of cash held by the business. The dual nature of these transactions makes it possible to establish a system of separate accounts for each type of transaction in which each is recorded by a double entry.At this point it is important to appreciate that it is the duality of business transactions which makes such a system possible.

ACCOUNTING CONCEPTS UNDER THE COMPANIES ACT AND SSAP 2

The first statement by a professional body in the UK of the broad basic assumptions which underlie the financial accounts of business enterprises was made in Statement of Standard Accounting Practice No 2, entitled *Disclosure of accounting policies* which was issued in November 1971. This statement singled out four fundamental concepts for special mention:

(1) the going concern concept;
(2) the accruals concept;
(3) the consistency concept;
(4) the prudence concept.

It was pointed out that the standard was not an attempt to develop a basic theory of accounting, and that such an approach would include many more propositions than the four fundamental concepts referred to,[3] and it was noted that:

> "The main difficulty in applying the fundamental accounting concepts arises from the fact that many business transactions have financial effects spreading over a number of years. Decisions have to be made on the extent to which expenditure incurred in one year can reasonably be expected to produce benefits in the form of revenue in other years and should therefore be carried forward, in whole or in part; that is, should be dealt with in the closing balance sheet, as distinct from being dealt with as an expense of the current year in the profit and loss account because the benefit has been exhausted in that year."

[3] In 1980 the ASC commissioned a report by Professor R. A. Macve on the development of such a basic theory of accounting "A Conceptual Framework for Financial Accounting and Reporting."

A decade later the Companies Act 1981 incorporated certain basic principles in Schedule 1 to the Act, and laid down that "the amounts to be included in respect of all items shown in a company's accounts shall be determined in accordance with these principles."[4] The Companies Act referred to five principles, whilst SSAP 1 had cited four, but all of those used by the latter also appear in the Act.

In describing them below reference will be made to the name used in the standard, the requirements of the Act, and the explanation given in SSAP 1, where appropriate.

The going concern concept "The company shall be presumed to be carrying on business as a going concern." This means that it is assumed that the enterprise will continue in operational existence for the foreseeable future, and in particular that the accounts assume no intention or necessity to liquidate or curtail significantly the scale of operation.[5]

The consistency concept "Accounting policies shall be applied consistently from one financial year to the next." This is a vital prerequisite if accounts of succeeding periods are to be meaningfully compared.

The concept of prudence "The amount of any item shall be determined on a prudent basis, and in particular:

(a) only profits realised at the balance sheet date shall be included in the profit and loss account[6]; and
(b) all liabilities and losses which have arisen or are likely to arise in respect of the financial year shall be taken into account including those which only become apparent between the balance sheet date and the date on which it is signed on behalf of the board of directors."

SSAP 2 explains that revenue and profits should not be anticipated but should only be recognised by incorporation in the profit and loss account when realised in the form of cash or other assets, the ultimate cash realisation of which can be assessed with reasonable certainty. Provision must be made for all known liabilities, where necessary on the basis of a best estimate in the light of the information available. This approach, of always recognising losses but only taking account of *realised* profits, is sometimes referred to as the concept of "conservatism" and arises from the desire of accountants to err on the side of caution, rather than risk over-stating the assets of a business in its accounts.

The accruals concept "All income and charges relating to the financial year to which the accounts relate shall be taken into account, without regard to the date of receipt or payment." This concept relates to the procedure of matching

[4] Companies Act 1981 Sch. 1, para. 9.

[5] Bankers often examine accounts with the objective of determining the value of the assets on the basis of the business being a gone concern. It is important to remember that the accountant uses a totally different assumption, viz. that the company is and will remain a gone concern. See Chap. 14, where this topic is considered in greater depth.

[6] See Chapter 5 page 125 for a discussion of the meaning of the term "realised profit."

revenue and costs which lies at the heart of the accountant's approach. SSAP 1 states "Revenue and profits dealt with in the profit and loss account are matched with the associated costs and expenses by including in the same account the costs incurred in earning them."

The standard notes, at times, the accruals concept will be in conflict with the prudence concept, a point which will be discussed in detail later in this chapter. In such cases the prudence concept prevails.

Separate valuation of items "In determining the aggregate amount of any item the amount of each individual asset or liability that fails to be taken into account shall be determined separately." This accounting principle has no parallel in SSAP 1, but is nonetheless assumed by accountants in preparing accounts. In practice it means that when stock is valued at the lower of cost and net realisable value, this basis must be applied to each item of stock rather than all of the stock being valued on each basis, aggregated, and the lower figure of the two taken. The result will be that by valuing each item separately surpluses on some items will not be able to compensate for deficits below cost on others. As a result the overall stock valuation will be lower. This principle can be derived from the prudence concept, for to offset surpluses against deficits in this way would be to anticipate profits on the surplus items.

The Companies Act states that if it appears to the directors that there are special reasons for departing from any of the principles stated above in preparing a company's accounts they may do so, but particulars of the departure, the reasons for it and its effect shall be given in a note to the accounts.

Materiality One important idea applied by accountants that is not defined in either SSAP 2 or in the Companies Act is that of materiality. This has been described as the process by which accountants omit the many small and trivial items which are likely to confuse the readers of accounts if they are included. The Companies Act states that amounts which are immaterial may be disregarded for the purposes of Schedule 8, and departures from Standard Accounting Practice need not be disclosed unless their effect is material. Auditors are advised to regard an item as material if knowledge of the matter would be likely to influence the user of the financial statements. "Materiality may be considered in the context of the financial statements as a whole, the balance sheet, the profit and loss account, or individual items within the accounts. In addition, depending upon the nature of the matter, materiality may be considered in relative or absolute terms."[7] Thus if a consignment of stock and the related creditor were omitted from the balance sheet the materiality would be judged in terms of the effect on the balance sheet, whereas the omission on either the creditor or the stock alone would affect the profit figure and must be judged in relation to this as well. Where items must be disclosed by statute, for example, directors' emoluments, their absolute size is material without reference to the size of the balance sheet total or of the profit for the year.

[7] Auditing Standard, *Qualifications in Audit Reports*, paras 20–23.

ACCOUNTING BASES AND ACCOUNTING POLICIES

SSAP 2 suggests that the fundamental concepts of accounting lead to the development of "accounting bases" which are defined as "the methods which have been developed for expressing or applying fundamental accounting concepts to financial transactions and items". For example it refers to the various methods of stock valuation and of accounting for the depreciation of fixed assets which are generally accepted by accountants. It explains the purpose and limitations of accounting bases as follows:

> "In the course of practice there have developed a variety of accounting bases designed to provide consistent, fair and, as nearly as possible, objective solutions (to the problems of allocating transactions which straddle on more than one financial period). Accounting bases provide an orderly and consistent framework for periodic reporting of a concern's results and financial position, but they do not, and are not intended to, substitute for the exercise of commerical judgement in the preparation of financial reports. Where a choice of acceptable accounting bases is available judgement must be exercised in choosing those which are appropriate to the circumstances and are best suited to present fairly the concern's results and financial position; the bases thus adopted then become the concern's accounting policies. The significance of accounting bases is that they provide limits to the area subject to the exercise of judgement, and a check against arbitrary, excessive or unjustifiable adjustments where no other objective yardstick is available."

In order to apply the accounting bases companies adopt "accounting policies" which are defined as "the specific accounting bases judged by business enterprises to be most appropriate to their circumstances and adopted by them for the purpose of preparing their financial accounts." SSAP 2 requires the disclosure of the accounting policies followed for dealing with items which are judged material or criticial in determining profit or loss for the year and in stating the financial position. The explanations should be disclosed by way of a note or notes to the accounts and should be clear, fair and as brief as possible. As is noted in Chapter 5 the accounting policies adopted by the company must now be disclosed by statute.

ACCOUNTING RULES

The Companies Act also lays down two sets of Accounting Rules which are to be applied in preparing a company's accounts:

(i) Historical Cost Accounting Rules;
(ii) Alternative Accounting Rules.

The historical cost rules largely follow existing accounting practice, whilst the alternative rules permit the practice of revaluing assets and allow inflation adjusted accounts to be prepared as the *statutory accounts* of a company. Where a company prepares a *supplementary statement* to its accounts in accordance with SSAP 16, these rules do not apply.[8] However, where the SSAP 16 accounts replace the historic cost accounts then the Alternative Accounting Rules must be followed.

[8] See Chap. 7.

The Act states that the amounts to be included in respect of assets of any description referred to in the Act may be determined in accordance with the Alternative Accounting Rules, thus three possibilities exist:

(1) *Pure Historical Cost Accounts* – in practice rare in the UK;
(2) *Historical Cost Accounts subject to the revaluation of certain assets* (in accordance with the Alternative rules) – which is the most common practice;
(3) *Inflation Adjusted Statutory Accounts* – which is exceedingly rare.

In discussing the presentation of items in the accounts the two sets of accounting rules and the requirements of Accounting Standards will be considered together. The key points of each and any contrasts with accounting standards are summarised in Table 2.2 on pp. 44–45.

In applying the accounting principles outlined above it is often found that conflict arises between particular concepts. As has been mentioned, the accruals principle often conflicts with the prudence principle. Nowhere is this conflict better illustrated than in the topics which will be dealt with in the remainder of this chapter: the valuation of stocks and work in progress, the valuation of long-term contracts and the treatment of research and development expenditure.

STOCKS AND WORK-IN-PROGRESS

THE SIGNIFICANCE OF STOCK VALUATION

In discussing the accruals concept earlier in this chapter it was noted that the idea of "matching" costs and associated expenses lay at the heart of the accountant's approach to calculating the financial results of a business. The valuation placed on stocks and work-in-progress has a vital part to play in this process. Indeed, as a leading text book on auditing notes, the valuation of stocks and work-in-progress "is likely to have more effect on the trading results than any other item in the accounts."[9] Before discussing regulatory requirements in this area it is worthwhile considering this point in more depth.

In order to calculate profit under the accruals concept it is necessary to ascertain the cost of each item that is sold, including any related expenses. This figure can then be matched against the revenue derived from sales to give gross profit. Subsequently the overhead costs for the period can be ascertained and deducted to find the net profit. In theory this procedure could be applied item by item, and all of the individual gross profits aggregated. However this procedure would be extremely time-consuming and is not used in practice.[10]

[9] V. R. V. Cooper, *Manual of Auditing* (1st ed.).
[10] It is worth noting that the introduction of Electronic Point of Sale accounting making use of bar coding on products and laser recognition offers the prospect of matching individual cost and sale amounts to determine gross profit. However this technology does not apply in all circumstances, and particularly not to the especially difficult area of valuing work-in-progress in manufacturing companies.

Invariably the alternative method of deducing the cost of sales from the amount of stock is employed instead. Under this approach the closing stock is ascertained and its value deducted from the total for purchases (including any opening stocks) to give the cost of sales. As can be seen from the layout below if the value of stock is wrongly stated the profit figure will also be incorrect.

Example: The Significance of Stock Valuation

	£'000
Opening stock	400
Purchases	2,000
Less	
Closing stock	550
Cost of sales	1,850
Sales preceeds	2,350
Gross profit	500

The value of the cost of sales is found by deducting the cost of closing stock from the total of purchases and opening stock. If the cost of closing stock was calculated incorrectly the gross profit would be wrong. For example if the cost of closing stock in this example should have been £600,000 instead of £550,000 as shown, then the profit figure would have been only £450,000.

The importance of stock valuation is heightened by the difficulties which arise in practice in determining the value at which the stock should be shown. In a simple world it would be possible to identify which stock remained at the year end and to ascertain the invoice price of each item. However, in the real world matters are complicated by the following considerations:

(1) Items are not easily identified once included as stock, and a rule of thumb must be utilised in order to determine which costs relate to the stock held at the year end.

(2) Some items are unlikely to realise their cost when sold because of deterioration, damage, obsolescence or changes in market conditions. In accordance with the prudence concept the loss which will be incurred when the items are sold must be recognised as soon as the firm is aware of it rather than when the goods are sold. This process requires an estimate to be made of the proceeds of sale and of related costs.

(3) Many firms are involved in manufacturing rather than in simply merchandising goods, and must match the costs of manufacture and the purchase cost of raw materials with sales revenue. In such cases the costs incurred on incomplete goods and on goods manufactured but not sold must be excluded from the cost of sales and carried as stock. In order to achieve this objective estimates must be made of the amount of stock at various stages of completion and of the costs incurred in bringing the stock

to its present location and condition. Inevitably this procedure is complicated and involves the exercise of considerable judgement.

Determining the amount at which stocks and work-in-progress is shown generally involves two distinct operations:

(1) *Counting and identifying the stock* – where necessary noting the stage of completion and any obsolete, slow-moving or deteriorating stock.
(2) *Valuing the stock* – in accordance with the accounting policies adopted by the company.

In a large company records will usually be kept of stocks of raw materials and components and of finished goods. In some cases the records will also cover work-in-progress at various stages. In such companies checks must be made from time to time to determine that the stock records are accurate (a continuous stock counting system), but this need not be at the year end. The advantage of this approach is that stock quantities may be derived from the records whenever it is necessary to prepare accounts.

In a small company such a system will not be cost effective and it will be necessary to count stock whenever it is intended to prepare a set of accounts.[11] This method is known as a periodic stock count and is the most common method in practice.

Once the stock has been counted and identified it is possible to value it, deriving the relevant costs in the following ways.

- Raw materials – invoice price;
- Work-in-progress – invoice price of raw materials; *Plus* appropriate proportion of overhead costs to bring stock to present location and condition.
- Finished goods – invoice price of raw materials; *Plus* appropriate proportion of overhead costs to complete production.

The calculation of the appropriate proportion of overhead costs can be an extremely complicated process and will be considered in more depth below. However, first it is necessary to consider the various methods available in order to calculate the appropriate invoice price.

STOCK COST ALLOCATION METHODS

It was noted above that the cost of raw materials, and part of the cost of work-in-progress and finished goods is derived from the invoice price. In an ideal world this would be the price quoted on the invoice relating to the goods concerned. However, in practice it is often not possible to determine which goods in stock actually relate to which particular invoice. For example, a quantity of oil for resale will be a mixture of various consignments. Furthermore, even where it is possible to determine the actual price, the cost

[11] In companies preparing regular management accounts without the benefit of a full cost recording system it is often the practice to estimate stock for accounting purposes. However it is desirable in such cases to count the stock periodically, and essential in order to prepare the annual statutory accounts.

of doing so is often unwarranted. Accordingly various rule-of-thumb methods are used to estimate the price of stock. In a period of stable prices the method chosen will not materially affect the resulting figure. However, where prices are altering, as happens in a period of inflation, the result obtained will vary according to the method chosen. This is an important point because, as we have seen, the value of stock has a direct impact on the level of profits. The Companies Act refers to three basic methods each of which will be described below.

First In First Out (FIFO). Under the FIFO method it is assumed that the first item taken into stock is the first to leave. Thus it is assumed that sales are made from the earliest stock purchased, and therefore it is from the earliest invoice that the price is taken for the matching process. The consequence of this approach is that the last items of stock purchased must be the items in stock at the end of the period. The great advantage of this feature is that it is not necessary to calculate the value of stock each time a sale is made, but merely to ascertain the amount of each item in stock at the end of the period, and to allocate invoice prices sequentially starting with the last until all of the stock is accounted for.

Example

A company has 765 units of component No. 134/5678 in stock at the year end; the last few invoices for deliveries of this component towards the year end were as follows:

		Units in Stock (FIFO)
12 October	150 units at £5.35	—
28 October	80 units at £5.40	65
7 November	200 units at £5.40	200
23 November	150 units at £5.50	150
2 December	200 units at £5.45	200
11 December	150 units at £5.50	150
		765

Under the FIFO approach invoice prices are allocated starting with the delivery on 11 December until all the closing stock is accounted for, within the delivery on 28 October. The balance of the latter delivery and all of that of 12 October are included within the cost of sales figure and are matched with sales.

Because of the simplicity of the FIFO method it is the most widely used within the United Kingdom, but it does have the property of placing the highest value on closing stock during a period of rising prices. The consequence of this is that a larger deduction will be made from the purchases total to obtain the cost of sales. Because the latter will be lower the profit figure will be greater. As we shall see later the appearance of an inflated profit figure can be somewhat misleading in calculating the amount that a company can afford to distribute to its shareholders, whilst maintaining its operating capacity.

Before leaving the FIFO method it is necessary to emphasise two points:

(1) During a period of falling prices the use of the FIFO method will have an opposite effect and will tend to understate profits. It is important to

appreciate, that the tendancy of FIFO to overstate profits only occurs in *a period of rising prices* for the goods concerned.

(2) In order to minimise stock losses through physical deterioration, and any other cause, companies generally circulate stock so that the first in is, in practice, the first out. If the physical movement of stock, and the method of valuation are synchronised that is useful, but it is not a prerequisite of the use of the FIFO method by accountants. No attempt is made by accountants to determine whether the movement of stock in practice corresponds exactly with the assumption used in the method of stock valuation.

Last in First Out (LIFO). The application of the LIFO method of stock valuation is based on the opposite assumption to that used in FIFO, so that the goods sold are assumed to be those last received into stock, and those remaining in stock are those first received. The method is rather more complicated to apply than the FIFO method because account must be taken of a reduction in the level of stock brought forward, with replacement stock valued at its actual cost in subsequent valuations.

Example

A Company holds stocks of material B during the year to 31 December 1983.

	Purchased	*Units*	*Price*	*Balance*
Opening stock	1978	100	£2.00	100
Issue	1.3.83	50		50
Purchase	1.4.83	100	£3.00	150
Purchase	1.6.83	100	£3.50	250
Issue	1.7.83	150		100
Purchase	1.9.83	100	£3.75	200

At the end of the year there are 200 units in stock. However, as can be seen, under the LIFO assumption this balance must comprise the following purchases:

1.9.83	100	at	£3.75
1.4.83	50	at	£3.50
1978	50	at	£2.00

The issue of 50 items on 1 March 83 was made from opening stock reducing the year end quantity to 50. The issue of 1 July 83 is made from the purchases of 1 June 83 (100) and from that of 1 April 83 (50), leaving a balance of 50 from this purchase for stock.

Had the FIFO method been used the final stock would have been valued as follows:

1.9.83	100	at	£3.75
1.6.83	100	at	£3.50

The effect of using the LIFO method of valuation is, in this case, to value the stock at £650, whilst the FIFO method gives a value of £675.

Because the LIFO method gives a lower stock value in periods of inflation, and as a result lower profit figures, it is often claimed to be useful as a way of accounting for the impact of rising prices on the cost of replacing stock. However, the side effect is that the value placed on stock appearing in the balance sheet is unlikely to reflect the cost of stock held. Over a period of time the value will become increasingly out of date. As can be seen in the example above the closing stock includes some units purchased in 1978 at a cost of £2.00 compared with a final price of £3.75. In the United Kingdom the LIFO method is not acceptable to the Inland Revenue, has been deemed unsuitable by the Accounting Standards Committee.[12]

Weighted Average Cost (or Price) (WAC or AVCO). The Weighted Average method effectively combines features of both the FIFO and LIFO methods, by calculating the average price of stock after each receipt and using this price in order to price issues from stock and the closing balance. As the method is relatively simple in operation it is incorporated in the example below, rather than being dealt with separately. The only technical point to note being that issues from stock make no difference to the average price, which can only change when items are added to stock at a price different to the average. It is sometimes claimed that the weighted average method is superior to the FIFO and LIFO methods, because it is less severe in its impact on the profit and loss account and on the balance sheet in a period of inflation. However, it is complicated to apply for a firm which does not maintain continuous stock records showing stock values, and it does not really provide a satisfactory figure for stocks or for cost of sales in a period of rising prices. This topic will be considered again when the subject of accounting for inflation is considered in Chapter 7. Before considering an example showing each of the three methods of stock valuation discussed so far, it should be noted that companies operating sophisticated management accounting systems may value their stocks using predetermined standards. Where these standards are close to the actual cost of stock during the year they will be acceptable for valuing stock at the year end. This subject is considered in more depth in Chapter 9.

Example

A company buys and sells units of product X during the month of January. Calculate the cost of sales, profit and closing stock using each of the following methods:
(i) first in first out (FIFO);
(ii) last in first out (LIFO);
(iii) average cost or weighted average price (AVCO).
Stock movements during January were as follows:

Date	*Transaction*	*Units*		£
2	Purchased	200	at	1.00
5	Purchased	200	at	1.10
14	Sold	250	at	1.50
21	Purchased	150	at	1.20
31	Sold	100	at	1.55

[12] SSAP 9 *Stocks and Work-in-Progress* – Appendix.

Solution

(i) FIFO Method

Date	*Additions*	*Withdrawals*	*Stock*	*Analysis*
2.1	200 at £1 £200	——	200	200 at £1
5.1	200 at £1.10 £220	——	400	200 at £1 200 at £1.10
14.1	——	250–200 at £1 50 at £1.10 =£255	150	150 at £1.10
21.1	150 at £1.20 £180	——	300	150 at £1.10 150 at £1.20
31.1	——	100 at £1.10 =£110	200	50 at £1.10 150 at £1.20
Total	£600	£365	——	£235

Note

Under the FIFO method it is not necessary to keep detailed records such as these. The closing stock must have been drawn from the last two consignments priced at £1.20 and £1.10. In reverse chronological order these prices are allocated to the 200 units in stock until the balance is accounted for.

(ii) LIFO Method

Date	*Additions*	*Withdrawals*	*Stock*	*Analysis*
2.1	200 at £1	——	200	200 at £1.00
5.1	200 at £1.10	——	400	200 at £1.00 200 at £1.10
14.1	——	250–200 at £1.10 50 at £1.00 =£270	150	150 at £1.00
21.1	150 at £1.20	——	300	150 at £1.00 150 at £1.20
31.1	——	100 at £1.20 =£120	200	150 at £1.00 50 at £1.20
Total	£600	£390	——	£210

Note

Under the LIFO method it is necessary to identify the consignment from which each withdrawal is made. At the end of January the stock balance is the same as after the first delivery but only 150 units of the original consignment remain. The remainder is assumed to be part of the delivery on 21st of the month, all of the items delivered on 5 January having been allotted to the sale on the 14th.

(iii) AVCO method

Date	*Additions*	*Withdrawals*	*Stock*	*Cost* £	*Average cost per unit* £
2.1	200 at £1 £200	——	200	200	1.00
5.1	200 at £1.10 £220	——	400	420	1.05
14.1	——	250 at £1.05 =£262.50	150	157.50	1.05
21.1	150 at £1.20 £180	——	300	337.50	1.125
31.1	——	100 at £1.125 =£112.50	200	225	1.125
Total	£600	£375	——	£225	1.125

Note
Under the AVCO method it is necessary to calculate the average cost of stock each time a consignment is received. This is easily done by adding the cost to the consignment of the total value of stock and dividing by the new total number of units. Future deliveries are made at the new average cost.

Profit and loss account

Method of valuing stock		*FIFO*		*LIFO*		*AVCO*	
		£	£	£	£	£	£
Sales 350 units							
250 at £1.50	375						
100 at £1.55	155						
	——		530		530		530
Purchases							
200 at £1.00	200						
200 at £1.10	220						
150 at £1.20	180						
	——	600		600		600	
Closing stock		235		210		225	
		——		——		——	
Cost of goods sold			365		390		375
			——		——		——
Gross profit			165		140		155

As can be seen the profit is £25 lower using the LIFO method. Under conditions of rising prices this is always the case. The AVCO method always gives a result between the FIFO and LIFO methods, but it will not usually be equally between, depending on the pattern of stock movements and price changes.

STOCK VALUATION UNDER THE COMPANIES ACTS AND ACCOUNTING STANDARDS

The Companies Act 1981 laid down a new series of rules for valuing stock, which must be applied in conjunction with SSAP 9.

The fundamental rule governing the valuation of stocks is that all current assets are to be shown at the lower of purchase price or production cost and net realisable value. Thus whenever stocks are valued using the methods and bases described below, a check must be made to see that the figure so obtained is not in excess of net realisable value. This term is defined in SSAP 9 as:

> the actual or estimated selling price (net of trade but before settlement discounts) less:
> (a) all further costs to completion; and
> (b) all costs to be incurred in marketing, selling and distributing.

The Act requires purchase price to be determined by adding to the actual price paid any expenses incidental to its acquisition. Production cost is to be determined by adding to the purchase price of the raw materials and consumables used the amount of the costs incurred by the company which are directly attributable to the production of that asset. The Act states that companies *may* include:

> (1) a reasonable proportion of the costs incurred by the company which are only indirectly attributable to the production of that asset, but only to the extent that they relate to the period of production; and
> (2) interest on capital borrowed to finance the production of that asset to the extent that it accrues in respect of the period of production (subject to disclosure as a note to the accounts) but *may not* include distribution costs in production costs.

(This contrasts with previous practice where distribution costs were allowed to the extent that they were incurred to bring that stock to its location at the balance sheet date, as might be the case where a company operates from several different sites.)

The Act allows several methods of allocating cost:

- First in First Out;
- Last in First Out;
- Weighted Average Price;

and any other method similar to these methods.

The method chosen must be one which appears to the directors to be appropriate to the circumstances of the company. Where the resulting amount is materially different from the replacement cost of the stock the difference must be disclosed in a note to the accounts.

Stocks under the alternative accounting rules may be shown at current cost, with any surplus or deficit arising from the use of this basis being passed to the revaluation reserve. In this case there is no requirement to show the comparable amount under the historical cost accounting rules or the difference between historic and current cost.

STANDARD ACCOUNTING PRACTICE: STOCKS AND WORK-IN-PROGRESS (SSAP 9)

The approach required by the Companies Act is generally consistent with Standard Accounting Practice as laid down, but conflicts on a number of significant points, which are explained below. SSAP 9 requires stocks and work-in-progress to be stated at the lower of cost and net realisable value, but defines cost as follows:

> "that expenditure which has been incurred in the normal course of business in bringing the product or service to its present location and condition. This expenditure should include, in addition to cost of purchase such costs of conversion as are appropriate to that location and condition."

These costs are defined thus:

Cost of purchase comprises purchase price including import duties, transport and handling costs and any other directly attributable costs, less trade discounts, rebates and subsidies.

Cost of conversion comprises:
(a) costs which are specifically attributable to units of production, i.e. direct labour, direct expenses and sub-contracted work;
(b) production overheads;
(c) other overheads, if any, attributable in the particular circumstances of the business to bringing the product or service to its present location and condition.

The *production overheads* referred to above are defined as: "overheads incurred in respect of materials, labour or services for production, based on normal levels of activity, taking one year with another". It is noted that for this purpose each overhead should be classified according to function (e.g. production, selling or administration) so as to ensure the inclusion in cost of conversion of those overheads (including depreciation) which relate to production, notwithstanding that these may accrue wholly or partly on a time basis.

Regarding the basis for allocating costs the Appendix to the standard states:

> "in practice it is rarely practicable to relate expenditure to specific items of stock and appropriate methods must be used instead. The method chosen should provide the fairest practicable approximation to 'actual cost'. Standard costs should be reviewed to ensure that they bear a reasonable relationship to actual costs during the period. LIFO and base stocks (see p. 39) will rarely be acceptable under this criteria."

In the Appendix to SSAP 9 a number of other pertinent points are made.

Abnormal conversion costs such as exceptional spoilage and idle time should be excluded from cost.

> Where firm sales contracts have been entered into for the provision of goods and services to the customers specification, overheads relating to design and marketing and selling costs incurred before manufacture may be included in arriving at cost.
>
> Costs of general management and of service departments are not directly related to the cost of conversion and should therefore be excluded from cost of stocks and work in progress, unless they can reasonably be allocated to the production function.
>
> Allocation of overheads should be based on a normal level of activity.
>
> Where a company's management accounts are based on a marginal costing approach it will be necessary to calculate and adjust for appropriate overheads relating to the cost of conversion.[13]

The Standard also lays down certain basic disclosure requirements covering the accounting policies which have been used in calculating cost and net realisable value. It also requires companies to sub-classify their stocks in a manner which is appropriate to the business so as to indicate the amounts held in each of the main categories. In many cases this will be achieved by using the headings in the standard balance sheet format.[14]

DIFFERENCES BETWEEN THE ACT AND THE STANDARD

The Companies Act 1981 brought a certain amount of confusion to the area of stocks and work-in-practice by using some different terminology and setting slightly different rules from those found in SSAP 9, which was issued three years earlier.

(1) The Act uses the term "costs indirectly attributable to" whilst the standard uses the term "overheads" to refer to those costs which are not directly attributable to the production of particular items. Examples of such costs include factory power, light, heat, rent and rates. However, neither the Act nor the Standard attempts to define the meaning of the terms used (perhaps wisely), and in practice some variation exists in the way in which individual firms use them in their internal accounting. It is essential that in preparing their statutory accounts firms are consistent in classifying costs, but users of accounts should bear in mind the possibility that different firms may use different definitions.

(2) The Act states that firms *may* include indirect costs attributable to the production of stock and work-in-progress. However SSAP 9 *requires* the inclusion of production overheads where these are part of the cost of production. Since the introduction of the Standard some firms have refused to follow this practice and have received a qualified audit report.

[13] See Chap. 9 for a description of marginal listing principles.

[14] Before the introduction of this standard it was common practice to describe stocks as being shown at "the lower of cost and net realisable value". This information was of little value to analysts of accounts and allowed companies to use various definition of cost without needing to state that a change in accounting policy had taken place.

Therefore it seems that in order to achieve a true and fair view companies must follow SSAP 9, and include appropriate overheads notwithstanding the Act does not *require* their inclusion.

(3) The Act allows firms to include interest on capital borrowed to finance the production of stock related to the period of production. In the past the accountancy profession has not accepted this practice in relation to short-term items, and is unlikely to do so in the future notwithstanding the permission given in the Act. With reference to long-term work-in-progress (taking more than a year to complete) the Standard states:

> "In ascertaining cost of long-term contract work-in-progress it is not normally appropriate to include interest payable on borrowed money. However, in those infrequent circumstances where sums borrowed can be identified as financing specific long-term contracts, it may be appropriate to include such related interest in cost, in which circumstances the facts should be clearly stated."[15]

LONG-TERM CONTRACT WORK-IN-PROGRESS

In addition to dealing with stock and work-in-progress SSAP 9 also deals with long-term contract work-in-progress. The treatment of this topic has highlighted one of the most significant conflicts between the Act and Standard Accounting Practice. A long-term contract is defined in SSAP 9 as:

> "a contract entered into for manufacture or building of a single substantial entity or the provision of a service where the time taken to manufacture, build or provide is such that a substantial proportion of all such contract work will extend for a period exceeding one year."

The problem with such contracts is that application of the prudence concept might be held to require that profit is only taken when the contract is complete. However, if such an approach were adopted some companies would only show profits, albeit large ones, occasionally when contracts were completed. Accordingly the view is expressed that it is appropriate to take credit for ascertainable profit while contracts are in progress subject to:

(a) not doing so until the contract is reasonably advanced;
(b) the outcome of the contract is reasonably certain; and
(c) making prudent provision for variations in profitability.[16]

Standard practice is laid down as follows:

> "The amount at which long term contract work in progress is stated in periodic financial statements should be cost plus any attributable profit, less any foreseeable losses and progress payments received and receivable. If, however, anticipated losses on individual contracts exceed the cost incurred to date less progress payments received and receivable, such excesses should be shown separately as provisions."

The standard introduces the following definitions:

[15] For a more detailed consideration of the relationship between the Companies Act 1981 and SSAP 9 see J. G. Chastney "Statute and Standards in conflict on Accounting for Stock" in *Accountancy* (July 1982).

[16] Not all companies engaged in long-term contracts have readily accepted the practice required by SSAP 9, regarding it as imprudent to anticipate profit on a long-term contract in any circumstances.

Attributable profit: that part of the total profit currently estimated to arise over the duration of the contract (after allowing for likely increases in costs so far as not recoverable under the terms of the contract) which fairly reflects the profit attributable to that part of the work performed at the accounting date. (There can be no attributable profit until the outcome of the contract can be assessed with reasonable certainty).

Foreseeable losses: losses which are currently estimated to arise over the duration of the contract (after allowing for estimated remedial and maintenance costs, and increases in costs so far as not recoverable under the terms of the contract). This estimate is required irrespective of:

(a) whether or not work has yet commenced on such contracts;
(b) the proportion of work carried out at the accounting date;
(c) the amount of profit expected to arise on other contracts.

Example

A company is engaged on a long-term contract worth £10m. which is 90% complete. Expenditure to date amounts to £8m and further costs to complete the contract are estimated at £1m.

	£	£
Contract price		10,000
Expenditure to date	8,000	
Remaining costs to complete	1,000	9,000
Estimated profit		1,000
Profit to date at 90%		900
Less profit already taken		300
Profit for year		600

In practice various methods are used to estimate the extent to which the contract is complete including work done, work certified by independent architects, and work invoiced. The standard does not lay down a standard method to be followed on this point, but it does require the method used to be fully disclosed and followed consistently.

Where a company is engaged in a loss-making contract the standard requires a full provision to be made for the amount of the eventual loss.

Example

		£
Contract price		10,000
Expenditure to date	9,000	
Remaining costs to complete	3,000	12,000
Estimated loss		2,000

Disclosure in Financial Statements The accounting policies which have been used in calculating cost, net realisable value, attributable profit and foreseeable losses (as appropriate) should be stated.

In relation to the amount at which long-term contracts are stated in the balance sheet there should be stated:
(a) the amount of work in progress at cost plus attributable profit less attributable losses;
(b) cash received and receivable at the accounting date as progress payments on account of contracts in progress.

LONG-TERM CONTRACT WORK-IN-PROGRESS AND THE COMPANIES ACT 1981

The treatment of long-term contracts required by SSAP 9 does not follow the accounting rules laid down in the Act for disclosing current assets: the latter not permitting the inclusion of profit earned to date in the value of a current asset. This has caused some difficulty in the accounting profession which at the present is unresolved. However, it would appear that the treatment of long-term contracts in the way required by SSAP 9 can be justified by the requirement to show a true and fair view, and to depart from the requirements of Schedule 8 where the special circumstances of the company require it.

BASE STOCKS

Where a company deals in products having a volatile price the valuation of stocks might have a destabilising effect on the annual profit figure. Accordingly such companies often use a base stock method of accounting. SSAP 9 defines the method thus:

> "the calculation of the cost of stocks and work in progress on the basis that a fixed value is ascribed to a predetermined number of units of stock, any excess over this number being valued on the basis of some other method. If the number of units in stock is less than the predetermined minimum, the fixed unit value is applied to the number in stock."

SSAP 9 suggests that the base stock method is not normally suitable as a method of stock valuation because it does not give a stock value which provides the fairest possible approximation to the expenditure actually incurred. However, it is generally accepted that in some cases it is necessary to use the method in order for the accounts to show a true and fair view. Similarly it is often used to value tools, jigs and comsumable stores. The Companies Act allows the use of this method, which is referred to as "assets included at a fixed amount" but only where:

(1) The assets are of a kind which are constantly being replaced.
(2) Their overall value is not material to assessing the company's state of affairs.
(3) Their quantity, value and composition are not subject to material variation.

This provision will not apply to those companies who use base stocks as their main method of stock valuation. Such companies will need to rely on the true and fair provisions in order to comply with the Act. In such cases the company will also need to value the stock on one of the acceptable bases proposed by the Act to enable them to show particulars oif their departure from the Act, the reasons for it, and its effect.

RESEARCH AND DEVELOPMENT EXPENDITURE

The main reason for including a discussion of the treatment of research and development expenditure in this chapter, is that like stocks and work-in-progress the topic highlights the application of the acccurals concept and illustrates its frequent conflict with the concept of prudence. The accruals concept would seem to require expenditure on research and development to be carried forward and matched against the resulting revenue. However the prudence concept requires such expenditure to be written off as incurred because of its highly speculative nature.[17] Because of the immensely damaging effects of applying the wrong treatment the Accounting Standards Committee devoted SSAP 13 to the topic.

SSAP 13 Accounting for Research and Development makes the point that the: "terms 'research' and 'development' are currently used to cover a wide range of activities. Classification of the related expenditure is often dependent on the type of business and its organisation. The dividing line between such categories of expenditure will often be indistinct and particular expenditure may have characteristics of more than one category."

The following definitions are used in the standard.

"Research and development expenditure means expenditure falling into one or more of the following broad categories:

(a) Pure (or basic) research: original investigation undertaken in order to gain new scientific or technical knowledge and understanding. Basic research is not primarily directed towards any specific practical aim or application;
(b) Applied research: original investigation undertaken in order to gain new scientific or technical knowledge and directed towards a specific practical aim or objective;
(c) Development: the use of scientific or technical knowledge in order to produce new or substantially improved materials, devices, products, processes, systems or services prior to the commencement of commerical production."

The standard suggests that:

"expenditure incurred on pure and applied research can be regarded as part of a continuing operation required to maintain a company's business and its competitive position. In general, one particular period rather than another will not be expected to benefit and therefore it is appropriate that these costs should be written off as they are incurred. The development of new and improved products is, however, distinguishable from pure and applied research.

[17] The classic example of what can go wrong with research and development expenditure was illustrated by the collapse of the Rolls Royce Company in 1971. During the years leading up to the collapse Rolls had changed their accounting treatment of research and development several times. These changes did not affect the eventual outcome, but meant that people were not aware of the problems as soon as they might have been (see J. Argenti *Corporate Collapse; Causes and Symptoms*, which retells the story in some detail).

Expenditure on such development is normally undertaken with a reasonable expectation of specific commerical success and of future benefits arising from the work, either from increased revenue and related profits or from reduced costs. On those grounds it may be argued that such expenditure should be deferred to be matched against future revenue."

In accordance with this analysis the standard requires the following treatment:

"The cost of fixed assets acquired or constructed in order to provide facilities for research and development activities over a number of accounting periods should be capitalised and written off over their useful life.

Expenditure on pure and applied research (other than that referred to above) should be written off in the year of expenditure.

Development expenditure should be written off in the year of expenditure except in the following circumstances when it may be deferred to future periods:

(a) there is a clearly defined project, and
(b) the related expenditure is separately identifiable, and
(c) the outcome of such a project has been assessed with reasonable certainty as to
    (i) its technical feasibility, and
    (ii) its ultimate commerical viability considered in the light of factors such as likely market conditions (including competing products), public opinion, consumer and environmental legislation, and
(d) if further development costs are to be incurred on the same project the aggregate of such costs together with related production, selling and administration costs are reasonably expected to be more than covered by related future revenues, and
(e) adequate resources exist, or are reasonably expected to be available, to enable the project to be completed and to provide any consequential increases in working capital."

The Companies Act 1985 also deals with research and development expenditure but does not define these terms and must therefore be interpreted in the light of SSAP 13.

- The Act prohibits the inclusion of research expenditure in the balance sheet thereby confirming SSAP 13.
- It incorporates a heading of development costs in the balance sheet format, but lays down that expenditure may only be shown here where there are special reasons for capitialising the development costs in question. In such cases the following information must be given in a note to the accounts:

(a) the period over which the amount of those costs originally capitalised is being written off.
(b) the reasons for capitalising the development costs in question.[18]

The Act does not distinguish between pure and applied research.

[18] The Companies Act 1980 lays down that development costs must be treated as a realised loss unless there are special reasons for not doing so for the purpose of calculating distributable profits. (CA 1980, s. 42 as amended by CA 1981, s. 84). It is not stated whether the special reasons that justify capitalisation of development costs in the first place will justify not treating them as a realised loss for distribution purposes. In practice capitalisation in accordance with SSAP 13 is likely to be sufficient to comply with the 1980 Act.

FOREIGN CURRENCY TRANSLATION

Because of the considerable fluctuations in exchange rates that have arisen in recent years, it is not surprising that the topic of foreign currency translation has caused some difficulty to accountants and has necessitated a statement of standard practice. In the main SSAP 20 deals with translation of accounts prepared by subsidiary companies located overseas, which is dealt with in Chapter 6. However it also deals with translation at the individual company stage. The standard states that where a company enters into transactions which are denominated in a foreign currency the result of each transaction should be translated into the company's own currency using the rate in operation on the date on which the transaction occurred, but if the rates do not fluctuate significantly for a period an average rate for a period may be used as an approximation. Exceptions to this rule are allowed where the transaction is to be settled at a specified rate, or a forward contract exists covering the transaction, under which currencies are to be exchanged at a specified future date and at a specified rate.

As transactions are completed and when the balance sheet is prepared differences may arise between the rate used for the original entry and that used for settlement or translation in the accounts. In general such differences will result or already have resulted in cash flow profits or losses. It is therefore the general rule that such profits or losses should be reflected in the profit and loss account as part of the ordinary activities, unless by virtue of their nature they qualify as extraordinary.[19]

CONCLUSION: ACCOUNTING PRINCIPLES AND THE BANKER

This chapter has dealt with the Accounting Principles and Rules laid down in the Companies Act and the Fundamental Accounting Concepts referred to in Statement of Standard Accounting Practice No 2 dealing with the Disclosure of Accounting Policies. It also dealt with the Accounting Rules incorporated in the Act dealing with the treatment of stocks and work in progress and research and development, and explained their interrelationship with the Accounting Standards dealing with the same topics. In practical terms the detailed application of accounting standards is of little direct concern to the banker. However, it is important for him to appreciate the assumptions which underlie the accounts of which he makes use. In this respect two points of particular importance emerge from this chapter:

(1) Accounts are drawn up on the assumption that the business will continue in operational existence for the foreseeable future. However, this

[19] This requirement of SSAP 20, may give rise to credits to the profit and loss account which are unrealised at the balance sheet date in contravention of the rules of the Companies Act that the profit and loss account must only include realised profits. The ASC take the view that it is illogical to charge losses on translation to the profit and loss account but not to credit gains on translation. The standard therefore requires companies to depart from provisions of the Act in order to show a true and fair view.

assumption is often abandoned by bankers using accounts as the basis for estimating a break up value. When so doing it is important to be aware that the accounting figures are prepared on a vastly different assumption, and that if asked to prepare accounts on the basis that the company is not a going concern the figures prepared by most accountants would be entirely different.

(2) It is a point of cardinal importance that the accounting policies used by a company are applied consistently. If this principle is abandoned then comparisions become highly misleading. However, in times of trouble the temptation on the directors of a company to adjust their accounting policies to reflect "more realistically" the circumstances of the company are considerable. Regrettably examples of this happening are only too common.

Without giving the matter much thought bankers might be tempted to assume that the detailed aspects of accounting policies are of little concern to them. However, the contents of this chapter should have shown that accounting practice allows those responsible for preparing accounts some degree of latitude in the selection of accounting policies. In a complicated world this freedom is generally considered necessary if the worst features of a rigid code of rules are to be avoided. However this freedom carries with it certain dangers. In times of difficulty directors may be tempted to adapt their accounting policies in an attempt to improve upon the picture of events shown in the accounts. The message to bankers is clear; they must be especially cautious in circumstances where they discover that a company has changed its accounting policies in a critical area. In such circumstances the detailed information concerning the change will usually be found in a note to the accounts, and it is important for the banker to remember that the notes are an integral part of the accounts. In cases where it is necessary to place reliance on the accounts a study of the information given in the notes is just as important as a consideration of the information shown on the face of the profit and loss account and balance sheet. Bankers should be particularly careful where a company has not followed the rules described above in order to value stock but instead shows it at "directors valuation", which in the words of one leading member of the insolvency branch of the accountancy profession "could mean absolutely anything."

FURTHER READING

This chapter had dealt both with the Companies Act and with certain Accounting Standards. Accordingly reference should be made to the books listed at the end of Chapter 5, where relevant. With regard to the application of Accounting Standards the following publications are particularly useful.

Accounting Standards Committee, *Accounting Standards*, (ICAEW).
L. Skerrat, ed., *Financial Reporting*, (ICAEW, published annually to 1985).
J. Blake, *Accounting Standards* (Longmans, revised edition, 1984).
F. A. J. Couldery, *Accounting Standards Study Book* (Van Nostrand Rheinhold (UK), 3rd ed., 1982).

Table 2.2
A Summary of Accounting Rules and Accounting Standards

Historic cost accounting rules	*Alternative accounting rules*
Current assets (inc. stocks) To be shown at the lower of purchase price or production cost and net realisable value. *Purchase price:* actual price paid plus expenses incidental to the assets acquisition. *Production cost:* purchase price plus production costs directly attributable to the production of that asset. May also include: ● reasonable proportion of indirect costs; ● interest on capital borrowed to finance production (to be shown); each in respect of the period of production. *May not include* distribution costs.	Stocks may be shown at current cost (comparable historical cost amount need not be shown).
Stocks (and other fungible assets) To be shown on the basis of any one of following or similar methods; ● FIFO ● LIFO ● WAP Method chosen must be appropriate to circumstances of the company. Resulting amount materially different from replacement cost: difference to be disclosed in note to the accounts.	
Base stocks May be used for assets constantly being replaced where: ● value is not material ● quantity, value, and composition are not subject to material variation.	
Research and development costs Research may not be shown as an asset. Development costs may be shown as an asset in special circumstances.	
Fixed assets to be shown at purchase price or production cost, subject to systematic depreciation over the expected useful economic life, where this is limited.	May be shown at a market value or current cost.
Intangible fixed assets to be shown is in accordance with the rules for fixed assets.	May be shown at a market value or current cost.
Goodwill only to be shown as an asset if acquired for valuable consideration, subject to being written down over a period not exceeding the useful economic life.	Must be shown at historical cost.
Investments *Shown as current assets:* At the lower of purchase price or net realisable value. Unnecessary provisions to be written back.	May be shown at current cost.
Shown as fixed assets: Purchase price subject to depreciation where life is limited. Provision permissible against loss of value, and required if loss is expected to be permanent. Unnecessary provisions to be written back.	May be shown at a market value or a value determined by the directors.

Accounting standards

No standard for Current Assets

SSAP 9 Stocks to be shown at lower of cost and net realisable value. Cost defined as expenditure incurred in the normal course of business in bringing the product or service to its present location and condition including cost of purchase and cost of conversion (p. 35). The latter includes *all* production overheads in bringing the stock to its present location and condition (normally excluding interest).

Method chosen to give fairest approximation of actual cost LIFO normally considered unsuitable.

SSAP 1/SSAP 9 Base stocks permitted where necessary to show a true and fair view.

SSAP 13 Research (pure and applied) to be written off to profit and loss account as incurred. Development costs may be capitalised under certain circumstances (see p. 40).

SSAP 12 Depreciation to be charged on a fair basis in each accounting period during the expected life of all assets having a finite useful life. *SSAP 19 Investment properties* Special provisions apply.

SSAP 22 Goodwill to be shown at cost and written off immediately on acquisition against reserves or amortised against profits over its useful economic life

No equivalent standard.

No equivalent standard.

Chapter 3

Accounting Principles and Practice II

INTRODUCTION

The last chapter was devoted to the accounting principles underlying the preparation of all accounts and the rules to be followed in determining the amounts to be shown in respect of stocks and work-in-progress, long-term contracts, and expenditure on research and development. It was noted that whilst companies must comply with the basic rules laid down in the Companies Act, the requirement to show a true and fair view means that companies must also follow the detailed provisions of Accounting Standards, which overlap the statutory rules. In this chapter the rules relating to several other important items are considered:

(1) Fixed Assets: tangible and intangible;
(2) Investments: held as current and fixed assets;
(3) Liabilities: including capitalised government grants, contingent liabilities, leases, and pensions;
(4) Post Balance Sheet Events.

DEPRECIATION AND ACCOUNTING FOR FIXED TANGIBLE ASSETS

It was noted in the previous chapter that the treatment of stocks and work-in-progress highlights the conflict which often exists between the accruals principle and the principle of prudence. In dealing with fixed assets the same issue emerges once again. The fundamental feature of fixed assets is that their useful economic life extends over a period of more than a year, often over a period of several years. Accordingly the accruals principle requires the cost of using such assets to be matched against the revenue arising in several accounting periods. However, in order to do this an estimate must be made of the expected life of the asset concerned and of any disposal proceeds likely to arise at the end of the expected life. In making these estimates accountants tend to follow the prudence concept, and to take a very conservative view of the likely outcome. In practice it is extremely difficult to estimate the useful economic life of certain assets when, irrespective of previous expectations, technological and market changes may suddenly render them obsolete.

METHODS OF DEPRECIATION

In order to carry out the process of matching the cost of fixed assets to the periods benefitting from their use accountants apply the system of depreciation or amortisation.[1] Various methods exist for calculating depreciation, and that chosen by a company for its main assets must be disclosed in the accounts because of the impact it is likely to have on the results. The most common methods are as follows:

Straight line. Under this method the same amount is charged each year to the profit and loss account. The sum charged is found by dividing the cost of the asset, less any expected residual value, by its expected economic life.

Example

An item of plant costs £1,000 and has an expected life of six years. At the end of its life it is expected to have a disposal value of £100.

$$\text{Depreciation charge} = \frac{(\text{Cost} - \text{residual value})}{\text{expected life}}$$

$$= \frac{£1{,}000 - £100}{6 \text{ years}} = \frac{£900}{6} = £150$$

The rate of depreciation may be described as over a certain number of years or as an annual percentage charge. Thus in the example above the plant is being written off over a period of six years or at a rate of approximately 17%.

The straight line method of depreciation is usually described in accounts as being "by equal annual instalments on cost (less any expected residual value)" and in practice is both the most simple and most popular of the methods available.

Reducing balance. Under this, the second most popular method, the amount charged each year declines, with a higher charge being made in the early years of life of the asset. It is sometimes said that this method is useful where maintenance charges are low initially, and rise over the life of the asset in a mirror image to the depreciation charge.

As can be seen from the example the charge to the profit and loss account for depreciation declines gradually over the life of the asset. As a result profits are lower than would be the case using the straight line method in the early years

[1] Depreciation is an example of an accounting base which is designed to provide a consistent, accurate, and as nearly as possible objective solution to the problem of seeking to allocate the cost of using fixed assets over several accounting periods. The term amortisation is generally reserved for those assets which have a predetermined life such as leases.

Example

Details as above

	£
Cost	1000
1st year at 32%	320
Written down value	680
2nd year	216
Written down value	464
3rd year	148
Written down value	316
4th year	101
Written down value	215
5th year	68
Written down value	147
6th year	47
Balance/residual value	100

of life, but higher towards the end. In this case the balance of expenditure was written off in the final year of life. However, without such a decision the depreciation charge could carry on towards infinity becoming smaller and smaller year by year. The depreciation rate required to write down the asset to its realisable value on disposal is influenced by the proportion of value recoverable at the end of its useful life. For example, if in the example above the asset had cost £910 with a realisable value of only £10 the required rate would have been 53% giving a first year charge of £482. However if the cost had been £1,200, with a disposal value of £300 the rate would have been only 21%. In all three cases the sum of £900 is written off over six years, but the variation in the charge to profit and loss account is considerable.[2]

[2] The rate of depreciation required to write an asset down to its recoverable value can be found by applying the following formula:

$$r = \left(1 - \sqrt[n]{\frac{S}{C}}\right) \times 100\%$$

Where r = the rate of depreciation
n = the years over which depreciation is to be charged
S = the salvage of disposal value
C = cost

The rate of depreciation used in the example is found as follows:

$$r = \left(1 - \sqrt[6]{\frac{100}{1000}}\right) \times 100\% = 32\%$$

The impact of varying the disposal value can be demonstrated as shown below.

Continued on next page.

Sum of the digits method. Because of the erratic behaviour of the reducing balance method where there is a low residual value some businesses prefer to use the sum of the digits method. Under this method the depreciation charge declines over the life of the asset, but it does so in proportion to the expected years of life.

Example

Details as for previous example.

Year	*Calculation*	*Charge* £	*Net book amount* *Cost £1,000*
1	6/21 × 900	257	743
2	5/21 × 900	214	529
3	4/21 × 900	171	358
4	3/21 × 900	129	229
5	2/21 × 900	86	143
6	1/21 × 900	43	100
21			

The impact of the three methods of depreciation discussed is demonstrated in the Table 3.1 below.

Continued from previous page.

	£	£
Cost	910	1,200
Residual value	10	300
	900	900
Rate of depreciation	53%	21%
Book amount	910	1,200
1st year	482	252
	428	948
2nd year	227	199
	201	749
3rd year	106	157
	95	592
4th year	50	124
	45	468
5th year	24	98
	21	370
6th year	11	77
Disposal value	10	293

Table 3.1
Impact of differing methods of Depreciation on profits

Year	1	2	3	4	5	6
Depreciation						
● Straight line	150	150	150	150	150	150
● Reducing balance	320	216	148	101	68	47
● Sum of the digits	257	214	171	129	86	43
Variation in charge to profit and loss account						
Straight line v. Reducing balance	−170	−66	−2	−49	+82	+103
Straight line v. Sum of digits	−107	−64	−21	+21	+64	+107
Reducing balance v. Sum of the digits	+63	+2	−23	−28	−18	+4

Other methods. Apart from the methods outlined above several other methods are found in particular industries where they are more suitable.

Units of Extraction. Under this method the total available usage expected from a fixed asset is estimated in advance and the depreciation charge calculated on the basis of the use made of the asset during the financial period. For example, a machine costing £300,000 may be used for 100,000 hours before being scrapped. Thus if in a particular year the usage amounts to 17,685 hours the depreciation charge would be calculated as follows:

$$\text{Depreciation charge} = \frac{\text{Hours used}}{\text{Capacity usage}} \quad \frac{17{,}685}{100{,}000} \times £300{,}000 = £53{,}055$$

Alternatively, it can be shown that the cost of using the machine is £3 per hour, and that for 17,685 hours this amounts to a cost of £53,055. Thus the depreciation charge may be found by multiplying the units used or extracted by the cost per unit or period. This method may also be used to calculate the depreciation of mines, where the total capacity is known or can be estimated, and for any other wasting asset. In the case of machines it is useful where depreciation is largely based on usage, and this varies considerably from year to year.

Sinking fund method. In this case the life of the asset is estimated and a sum set aside in an investment to provide sufficient funds to allow for the replacement of the asset in question. The investment chosen may be in the form of an insurance policy, but any external investment will suffice. As sums are invested, a sinking fund investment account is debited, and a like sum is charged to the profit and loss account and credited to the depreciation provision. Ultimately the investment is realised and received as cash. At this point the sinking fund investment account and the depreciation provision are eliminated in the books of account. This method of depreciation ensures that the funds for asset replacement are kept separate from those generally used within the business, but it does so by denying the business the use of those funds in the meantime. It is to be hoped that the return which could be obtained by using the funds within the business would be greater than that obtained in a safe investment outside. Thus the sinking fund method does not commend itself to those seeking to maximise the profits of the business. A further objection to the sinking fund method is the implied assumption that the objective of depreciation is to provide funds for the replacement of specific assets. However as we shall see below, the main purpose of depreciation is to match the cost of using up the service potential of fixed assets with the related revenue. A byproduct is that the capital associated with the asset is retained in the business. However, the business may not wish to replace the asset with an identical item at the end of its life, and furthermore in a period of inflation it is likely that funds retained as a result of the depreciation charge will be inadequate to finance a replacement.

Valuation. In the case of small items such as tools, jigs and moulds having a life stretching over several accounting periods depending on use it is hardly worth keeping detailed records in order to calculate depreciation using any of the methods described above. Accordingly such items are often counted and valued at the year end. The depreciation charge can then be calculated on the basis of the opening balance, the expenditure during the year and the closing balance, in much the same way as the cost of sales calculation described in the previous chapter[3].

MISCONCEPTIONS CONCERNING DEPRECIATION

Depreciation and the Replacement of Assets

It is sometimes stated that the object of depreciation is to accumulate funds for the replacement of fixed assets at the end of their lives. However, the emphasis in the preceeding discussion has been on the way in which the cost of using a fixed asset should be spread over its expected useful life. There is a relationship between these two ideas, but it is not as direct as is sometimes supposed.

As a result of charging depreciation the profits of a company are reduced, thereby limiting the amount which a company may legally distribute as dividends and an unincorporated business may regard as a withdrawal of profit. Because profits are reduced the resources generated must stay within

[3] A further method of accounting for depreciation often advocated by academic writers on accounting is the annuity method. Under this method account is taken of the interest which is earned on the funds retained within the business by virtue of the depreciation charge. As a result the depreciation charge *increases* over the life of the asset. Whilst this method is consistent with the use of the return on capital return ratio, it requires a subjective estimate of the likely return on funds, and is not generally considered acceptable by financial accountants.

the company, although not necessarily in the form of cash for replacement. However, when an asset reaches the end of its life the amount which has been charged as depreciation will be represented by assets of some type, unless these have been lost through trading losses. Thus the capital of the company will have been maintained, and the company should be able to continue operating. In practice companies are replacing assets gradually over time, and also buying new assets to facilitate expansion. Were it not for the system of depreciation there would be no way of knowing whether the capital contributed by the shareholders was being maintained intact.

There is one further point regarding depreciation and the replacement of assets. Because of rising prices it is likely that when assets must be replaced the funds required will be greater than the assets maintained within the company. Thus not only does the depreciation system *not* ensure that there will be funds available for the replacement of assets, it also does not ensure that there would be enough. Furthermore, the charge made to the profit and loss account does not generally reflect the current cost of using up the life of the asset. This is a problem which will be considered in more depth in Chapter 7.

Depreciation and the Valuation of Assets

A second misconception regarding depreciation is that the objective of the system is to reduce the amount at which fixed assets are shown to their current valuation at the end of each period. However, as has been noted the approach adopted by the accountancy profession is to regard depreciation as a means of spreading the cost of using the assets over the years of life. Only incidentally will the resulting figure correspond to market value, but this discrepancy will not matter so long as there is no intention to sell the item in the meantime. The critical point is that it should be written down over a period close to its economic life and the accounts of each period reflect benefit which the company derives from using it.

For the users of accounts this is an important point to appreciate, especially if the accounts are being used as the basis for a valuation of the firm and its assets. Once again this is a point to which we shall return, in this case in Chapter 13, which deals with valuation.

ACCOUNTING REGULATIONS GOVERNING TANGIBLE FIXED ASSETS AND DEPRECIATION

The Companies Act

This defines fixed assets as those assets which are intended for use on a continuing basis in the company's activities. All such assets must be shown in the sections of the standard balance sheet formats designated "fixed assets" which in each case carries the letter B. They must be shown in the order and under the subheadings given, which means that intangible assets must be shown as the first item, and that all investments must be allocated to either the fixed or current asset sections of the balance sheet.[4]

The Historic Cost Rules

The Companies Act lays down that all fixed assets are to be shown at purchase price or production cost (which applies where assets are constructed by a firm for its own use). These terms have already been defined in the previous chapter.

Where a fixed asset has a limited useful economic life its book value must be systematically reduced by provisions for depreciation calculated to write it off over its useful economic life. The amount charged is to be based on the purchase price or production cost, except where it is estimated that the asset will have a residual value at the end of its useful economic life. In the latter case the amount to be written off is reduced by the expected residual value. These rules apply to tangible and intangible assets alike, with the exception of goodwill which is considered separately on p. 61.

Where any fixed asset is subject to a diminution in value, which is expected to be permanent, a provision shall be made to reduce the book value to the correct amount. However, if it is subsequently found that the reason for any provision ceases to apply, then the Companies Act requires the provision to be written back to the extent that it is no longer necessary. This rule also applies to investments held as fixed assets, which are considered below.

Where provisions made or written back in accordance with these rules are not shown in the profit and loss account details must be given in a note to the accounts.

The Alternative Accounting Rules

These rules state that tangible fixed assets may be shown at a market value determined at the date of their last valuation or at their current cost. This provision allows companies to revalue freehold and leasehold properties to reflect their current market value, which many companies have done for several years. In such cases depreciation is to be calculated on the revalued amount. However the Companies Act does not require the full amount of depreciation to be charged against profits, but permits companies to charge the amount based on the historical cost amount in their profit and loss account instead. The remainder of the depreciation charge is then set against the revaluation reserve. However this approach does not comply with SSAP 12, which is discussed below, and cannot be applied because of the true and fair view requirement. Where a company does revalue its fixed assets it must show, as notes to the accounts, the historical cost component of the balance and, with regard to the aggregate amount of the cumulative provision for depreciation, the amount attributable to the historical cost of the items

[4] The Companies Act 1981 abolished the power under the 1948 Companies Act 1948 to show a category of assets that were neither fixed nor current.

concerned. All intangible fixed assets, other than goodwill, may be shown at current cost under the alternative rules.

SSAP 12 Accounting for Depreciation

Although no accounting standard has been issued dealing with fixed assets in general, SSAP 12 deals with the treatment of depreciation. In large measure the Companies Act reinforces the provisions of the standard, and points of difference are only minor.

SSAP 12 defines depreciation as "a measure of the wearing out, consumption of other loss of value of a fixed asset whether arising from use, effluxion of time or obsolescence through technology or market changes". It states that depreciation should be:

> "allocated to accounting periods so as to charge a fair proportion to each accounting period during the expected useful life of the asset. Depreciation includes amortisation of fixed assets whose useful life is pre-determined (e.g. leases) and depletion of wasting assets (e.g. mines).
>
> Assessment of depreciation, and its allocation to accounting periods, involves in the first instance consideration of three factors:
>
> (a) cost (or valuation when an asset has been revalued in the financial statements);
> (b) the nature of the asset and the length of its expected useful life to the business having due regard to the incidence of obsolescence;
> (c) estimated residual value.
>
> An asset's useful life may be:
>
> (a) pre-determined, as in leaseholds;
> (b) directly governed by extraction or consumption;
> (c) dependent on the extent of use;
> (d) reduced by obsolescence or physical deterioration."

In the light of this analysis the SSAP 12 lays down the following detailed rules:

"● Provision for depreciation of fixed assets having a finite useful life should be made by allocating the cost (or revalued amount) less estimated residual values of the assets as fairly as possible to the periods expected to benefit from their use.
● Where there is a revision of the estimated useful life of an asset, the unamortised cost should be charged over the revised remaining useful life.
● However, if at any time the unamortised cost of an asset is seen to be irrecoverable in full it should be written down immediately to the estimated recoverable amount which should be charged over the remaining useful life.
● Where there is a change from one method of depreciation to another, the unamortised cost of the asset should be written off over the remaining useful life on the new basis commencing with the period in which the change is made. The effect should be disclosed in the year of change, if material.
● Where assets are revalued in the financial statements, the provision for depreciation should be based on the revalued amount and current estimate of remaining useful life, with disclosure in the year of change, of the effect of the revaluation, if material."

As can be seen the rules laid down by SSAP 12 are similar to those contained in the Companies Act 1981. In addition the former lays down similar disclosure requirements as set out below:

"(a) the depreciation methods used;
(b) the useful lives or the depreciation rates used;
(c) total depreciation allocated for the period;
(d) the gross amount of depreciable assets and the related accumulated depreciation."

The Standard does not specify which depreciation method should be used but in the explanatory notes states:

> "The management of a business has a duty to allocate depreciation as fairly as possible to the periods expected to benefit from the use of the asset and should select the method regarded as most appropriate to the type of asset and its use in the business."

Problems with the Standard

Prior to the introduction of SSAP 12 some companies did not provide depreciation on freehold buildings – arguing that it was unnecesary because of the tendency of property to appreciate. In the standard it is argued that two separate transactions are taking place.

(1) the buildings are increasing in value due to inflation – an unrealised profit;
(2) the buildings are wearing out due to use – a realised loss.

It therefore requires a split to be made between the value of land and buildings so that the latter may be depreciated. Nonetheless, opposition to SSAP No. 12 remains strong.

- Many buildings have extremely long lives (e.g. +200 years) which are impossible to estimate.
- It seems illogical to many people to charge depreciation on properties which are obviously increasing in value and which it is not intended to dispose of.
- Some properties are acquired for investment purposes and do not depreciate materially during ownership.

As a result of this criticism a change was made in the standard to exempt investment properties from its requirements.

In 1985 the ASC published ED 37 which proposed a number of minor changes to clarify the provisions of SSAP 12.

SSAP 19 Accounting for Investment Properties

Where a significant proportion of the fixed assets of an enterprise is held not for consumption in the business operations but as investments, the disposal of which would not materially affect any manufacturing or trading operations of the enterprise, a treatment different to that required by SSAP 12 is specified. In such a case the current value of these investments and changes in that current value, are of prime importance rather than calculation of systematic annual depreciation. Consequently, for the proper appreciation of the financial position, a different accounting treatment is considered appropriate for fixed assets held as investments.

The standard specifies that investment properties should be included in the balance sheet at their open market value, and should not be subject to periodic depreciation. Changes in value are to be credited or debited to an investment revaluation reserve, and various additional information must be given in the accounts. This treatment is restricted to investment properties which are defined as an interest in land and/or buildings:

"(a) in respect of which construction work and development have been completed: and
(b) which is held for its investment potential, any rental income being negotiated at arm's length."

The following are exceptions from the definition:

"(a) A property which is owned and occupied by a company for its own purposes is not an investment property.
(b) A property let to and occupied by another group company is not an investment property for the purpose of its own accounts or the group accounts."

SSAP 4 Accounting for Government Grants

It is convenient to discuss the treatment of government grants with the topic of fixed assets because most grants relate to the purchase of such assets. However, it is important to recognise that some grants are of a revenue nature and are designed to offset certain costs, such as interest, or to compensate for losses. Such items should simply be brought into the profit and loss account of the relevant period. Those grants relating to assets having a life spanning several accounting periods present a more complex problem. The accruals concept requires the benefit of the grant to be taken into account over the periods concerned. This may be achieved in two ways:

(1) The grant may be incorporated in the balance sheet as deferred income (item H9, E9, or item J in format 1 or item C9 or D of the liabilities in format 2.) and taken into the profit and loss account over the life of the asset concerned.
(2) The grant may be deducted from the cost of the asset concerned at the outset with the net amount being shown in respect of the cost of the asset. In this case the depreciation charge will be reduced proportionately.

Whichever method is chosen the impact on the profit and loss account is identical as shown by the following example.

Method	*Deferred income*	*Net cost*
Gross cost	£10,000	£10,000
Grant at 25%		2,500
Balance sheet amount	£10,000	£ 7,500
Depreciation at 20%	£ 2,000	£ 1,500
Investment grant credit	£ 500	—
Net impact on profit and loss account	£ 1,500	£ 1,500

SSAP 4 allows companies to use whichever of the two methods outlined above they wish. However, in doing so they must of course disclose the policy chosen and apply it consistently from year to year. It is perhaps worth noting that under the second method the figure for assets and capital employed will be lower, and that this is an important point to bear in mind when using the return on capital employed ratio as a criteria for assessing company performance, and especially so when making comparisons between firms. It is widely believed that the Companies Act now obliges companies to use only the first method, by virtue of its prohibition of the practice of setting assets against liabilities. However, there is no conclusive authoritative guidance on the point.

ACCOUNTING FOR LEASES AND HIRE PURCHASE CONTRACTS

Before leaving the topic of accounting for fixed assets it is necessary to consider the way in which assets purchased by instalments are shown in accounts. This is the subject of SSAP 21.

The subject of accounting for leases has grown in importance over the past five years as companies have financed the use of a greater proportion of their fixed assets through lease agreements.

Accounting standards are concerned with items which have a material impact on financial statements. So long as leasing remained a minor activity the need for an accounting standard did not arise. It was the growth in importance of leasing as a source of finance for industry and commerce that made it necessary to consider the implications for financial reporting.

There are many types of lease but in the accounting standard two broad categories are identified, namely finance leases and operating leases. The terms of a finance lease are intended to ensure to the lessor the repayment of all or almost all the purchase price of the asset and his financing and other costs – in substance it is very similar to hire purchase financing. All other leases are classified as operating leases.

In the past the majority of lessees treated both finance leases and operating leases in the same way: they merely wrote off the rentals payable against profits and did not show the asset or the obligation to pay future rentals in the balance sheet.

The methods of accounting put forward in the exposure draft are based on the consideration of substance over form whereby transactions or other events should be accounted for and presented in accordance with their financial reality rather than their legal form.

SSAP 22 Accounting Leases and Hire Purchase Contracts

A finance lease should be recorded in the balance sheet of a lessee as an asset and as an obligation to pay future rentals. At the start of the lease the sum to be recorded both as an asset and as a liability should normally be the amount for which the leased asset could be purchased at the start of the lease, adjusted for any grants receivable (i.e. the fair value).

Rentals payable should be apportioned between the finance charge and a reduction of the outstanding obligation for future amounts payable. The total finance charge under a finance lease should be allocated to accounting periods during the lease term normally so as to produce a constant periodic rate of return on the remaining balance of the liability for each accounting period.

An asset leased under a finance lease should be depreciated over the shorter of the lease term or its useful life.

The rental under an operating lease should be charged on a straight-line basis over the lease term, even it the payments are not made on such a basis, unless another systematic and rational basis is more appropriate.

An asset held under a hire purchase contract should be accounted for by the hirer on a basis similar to that adopted by the lessee under a finance lease.

(The standard also deals with accounting by lessors, which is not considered here).

ACCOUNTING FOR INTANGIBLE FIXED ASSETS

The standard formats for company accounts introduced in the Companies Act 1981 requires intangible fixed assets to be shown as item BI in the balance sheet. It also lays down certain rules governing the amount at which such items shall be shown in the accounts. We have already considered the treatment of expenditure on research and development,[5] and deal with the topic of goodwill below. The other items shown under this heading must comply with the general rules governing fixed assets and be shown at purchase price or production cost and be written off over their useful economic lives. Under the alternative accounting rules these items may be shown at their current cost.

GOODWILL

The treatment of "goodwill" has long posed a problem to accountants. It is given special treatment by the Companies Act and is the subject of an accounting standard — SSAP 22.

Goodwill has been defined as the difference between the value of the business as a whole and the fair value of its separable net assets. Its existence becomes apparent when a business is incorporated, when one business acquires another, or when profit sharing arrangements change in a partnership. However, although the existence of goodwill is most obvious at these times – when it needs to be recorded as part of business transactions – it may exist

[5] See p. 40.

continuously, being created and depreciating as the business continues to operate. However, because it is intangible by nature and may not be separated from the assets to which it relates the treatment of goodwill has caused considerable difficulty to accountants over the years.

According to ED 30 which preceeded SSAP 22 goodwill may be either positive or negative, and may be purchased or non-purchased. The proposed standard devoted some space to considering the nature and meaning of goodwill.

Positive goodwill arises from advantageous circumstances such as an effective management team, weakness of competitors, a prime location or established customers; *negative goodwill* arises from disadvantageous circumstances such as weak markets or marketing.

Goodwill is intangible, intrinsic to the business and incapable of realisation separate from the business. These characteristics of goodwill distinguish it from most other items in the accounts. Its other characteristics are that;

"(a) the value of goodwill has no reliable or predictable relationship to any costs which may have been incurred in its creation;
(b) individual intangible factors which may contribute to goodwill cannot be valued;
(c) the value of goodwill may fluctuate widely according to internal and external circumstances over relatively short periods of time; and
(d) the assessment of the value of goodwill is subjective, in the sense that not only its value but also the assessment of its actual existence varies according to the valuer."

Thus, any amount attributed to goodwill is unique to the valuer and to the specific point in time at which it is measured, and is only valid for that point in time, and in the circumstances then prevailing.

All businesses have an element of non-purchased goodwill, in that as going concerns they are worth more (positive goodwill), or less (negative goodwill), than the sum of the fair values of their separable net assets. However, except when goodwill is evidenced by a purchase transaction, it is not an accepted practice to recognise it in financial statements. This is partly because, under the existing accounting conventions (historical cost and current cost) it is not the function of the accounts of a business to show the market value of the business as a whole, and because non-purchased goodwill is not capable of the kind of objective and consistent appraisal applicable to most other kinds of assets. It is also worth noting that the Companies Act only allows goodwill to be shown as an asset if it was acquired for valuable consideration. However as ED 30 pointed out

> "There appears to be no difference in character between purchased goodwill and non-purchased goodwill. They are identical in principle: both actually exist or have existed: both may have cost money to produce. However, purchased goodwill, although arising from a subjective valuation of the business, is established as a fact at a particular point in time by a definitive market transaction; this is not true of non-purchased goodwill.
>
> The amount of non-purchased goodwill fluctuates, unrecognised in the accounts, increasing or decreasing depending on all the innumerable factors which go to build up its value."

Because purchased goodwill is held to decrease in value, it is considered necessary to write it off by matching it against profits. One approach is to write it off as soon as it is acquired against reserves, another is to amortise it over its useful economic life. However, whilst the latter alternative is simple in theory, there are considerable difficulties in measuring the value of life of goodwill. Accordingly, it was felt that there should be a maximum period over which the amortisation should be allowed. ED 20 stated:

> "A number of factors may affect the useful economic life over which goodwill is being amortised. However, to avoid improbably long write-off periods and on the grounds that there must be a length of time beyond which it is not possible to anticipate earnings, the standard provides that purchased goodwill should not be written off over a period longer than 20 years."

The choice of 20 years was inevitably arbitrary, a point highlighted by the fact that the European Community Rules suggest 5 years, and in the United States a period of 40 years is allowed. When the Exposure Draft was converted into a standard the 20-year maximum was abandoned.

The treatment of Goodwill under the Companies Act 1981

The Act lays down that goodwill which is acquired for valuable consideration may be shown at purchase price, subject to the following provisions;

- the amount acquired shall be written down over a period chosen by the directors of the company, which must not exceed its useful economic life;
- the accounts must show the period chosen, and the reasons for choosing it as a note.

These provisions do not apply to goodwill arising on consolidation in the accounts of groups of companies which will be dealt with by a later Companies Act to be passed when the European Community directives on Group Accounts is agreed. However they do prohibit the common practice of showing goodwill as a deduction from share capital and reserves, an approach sometimes referred to as the "dangling debit" method.

SSAP 22 Accounting for Goodwill

SSAP 22 lays down that purchased goodwill should be written off immediately upon acquisition directly against reserves representing realised profits, or alternatively should be amortised through the profit and loss account in arriving at profit or loss on ordinary acitvities on a systematic basis over its useful economic life.

It should be noted that this requirement differs slightly from the Companies Act in specifying a write off "over its useful economic life", whereas the Act requires a write off over "a period *not exceeding* its economic life". It would seem that in accordance with the standard a write off over a shorter period than the expected economic life, as permitted by the Act, will not be acceptable unless immediately charged directly to reserves.

The standard lays down a number of detailed rules governing the treatment of goodwill, and the following disclosure provisions.

> "The accounting policy followed in respect of goodwill should be explained in the notes to the accounts.
>
> The amount of goodwill recognised as a result of any acquisitions during the year should be shown separately for each acquisition where material.
>
> Where the amortisation treatment is selected, purchased goodwill should be shown as a separate item under intangible fixed assets in the balance sheet until fully written off. In addition, the following should be disclosed:
> a) the movement on the goodwill account during the year, showing the cost, accumulated amortisation and net book value of goodwill at the beginning and end of the year, and the amount of goodwill amortised through the profit and loss account during the year; and
> b) the period selected for amortising the goodwill relating to each major acquisition.
>
> If the acounting treatment of goodwill existing at the date of introduction of the standard is different from the policy followed in respect of all other goodwill, that treatment and the amounts involved should be disclosed."

ACCOUNTING FOR INVESTMENTS

Until the introduction of the Companies Act 1981 companies were able to show investments as current assets, fixed assets, or under a category of assets that were neither fixed nor current. The 1981 Act effectively abolished the last category, by requiring that all investments must be shown as either item B II or C III in the balance sheet. Furthermore the Act lays down basic rules for determining the amount at which investments are to be shown, one set for those held as fixed assets, and a different set for those included as current assets.

INVESTMENTS SHOWN AS CURRENT ASSETS

In common with all current assets investments are to be shown at the lower of purchase price, or production cost (which in this case is not appropriate), and net realisable value. The Act stipulates that where a provision made to reduce the amount to net realisable value is no longer required in part or in full it shall be written back to the extent that it is no longer necessary.

Under the alternative accounting rules investments shown as current assets may be shown at their current cost.

These rules largely confirm best accounting practice. Although not essentially so, investments held as current assets are usually marketable securities such as public stocks or listed securities, for which a current value is ascertainable. Difficulties can arise if the holding is a large one, so that the current or realisable value is not the quoted market price, or if an unquoted investment, for which no quoted price exists, is held as a current asset. There are no accounting standards dealing with the treatment of investments held as current assets.

INVESTMENTS HELD AS FIXED ASSETS

The Companies Act requires investments held as fixed assets to be shown on the same basis as other fixed assets. This will normally therefore be at purchase price, and in those cases where the assets have a limited economic life a depreciation provision must also be made. The Act also states that where a fixed asset investment has diminished in value a provision *may* be made, but that where the loss in value is expected to be permanent a provision *shall* be made. Where the reasons for the provisions cease to exist it must be written back to the extent that it is no longer necessary.

Under the alternative accounting rules fixed assets may be shown at either:

- a market value determined at the date of their last valuation;
- a value determined on any basis which appears to the directors of the company to be appropriate in the circumstances of the company.

In the latter case particulars of the method of valuation adopted and of the reasons for adopting it shall be disclosed in a note to the accounts. This provision might appear to permit considerable latitude to directors. However it must be remembered that they are obliged to show a true and fair view of the state of the company's affairs in the balance sheet, and must select a valuation basis with this in mind. These provisions are broadly in line with best accounting practice. There are no accounting standards dealing with such investments, apart from those in which the company is able to exercise a significant influence. These are considered in Chapter 6 which deals with the accounts of groups of companies.

ACCOUNTING FOR LIABILITIES

The Companies Act 1981 did not lay down any valuation rules governing liabilities, but the formats and the supplementary notes do require a mass of detail to be provided regarding liabilities.[6] Furthermore several Accounting Standards deal with the disclosure of certain liabilities; these are outlined below.

ACCOUNTING FOR CONTINGENCIES

The term contingency is applied to a condition which exists at the balance sheet date, where the outcome will be confirmed only on the occurrence or non-occurrence of one or more uncertain future events. Under SSAP 18 which deals with accounting for contingencies:

> "contingencies existing at the balance sheet date should be taken into consideration when preparing financial statements. Estimates of the outcome and of the financial effect of contingencies should be made by the board of directors of the company. These estimates will be based on consideration of information available up to the date on which the

[6] See Appendix 1 for details.

financial statements are approved by the board of directors and will include a review of events occurring after the balance sheet date. As an example, in the case of a substantial legal claim against a company, the factors to be considered would include the progress of the claim at the date on which the financial statements are approved, the opinion of legal experts or other advisers and the experience of the company in similar cases."

A contingency may result in a loss or a gain. Where a loss is *probable* a provision must be made to cover the expected amount, but where only *possible* disclosure by way of a note to the accounts is required. No mention need be made of losses which are only *remotely possible*, or of any contingent gains unless the probability of a gain is high.

In respect of each contingency which is required to be disclosed, the following information should be stated by way of notes in financial statements:

"(a) the nature of the contingency;
(b) the uncertainties which are expected to affect the ultimate outcome; and
(c) a prudent estimate of the financial effect, made at the date on which the financial statements are approved by the board of directors; or a statement that it is not practicable to make such an estimate."

The Companies Act requires the disclosure of the amount of any contingent liability, its legal nature, and what security (if any) has been provided by the company."

ACCOUNTING FOR POST BALANCE SHEET EVENTS

Often events occur, or information becomes available regarding the position of a company after the date of the balance sheet. Much of this information relates to events which occurred before the end of the year, and is taken into account in the normal way, in order to determine the amount of prepayments and accruals. However, it is clearly important that the readers of accounts know about important events which affect the position of the company, but properly fall to be treated in the following year. Equally it is necessary to determine at what point a company has determined the amounts to appear in the accounts. The Companies Act makes two references to post balance sheet events.

(1) Under the accounting principles contained in the Act companies must determine profits on a prudent basis and take into account items which only become apparent between the date of the accounts and the date on which the balance sheet is *signed* on behalf of the board of directors.
(2) The Director's report must contain particulars of any important events affecting the company or any of its subsidiaries which have occurred since the end of the year.

These provisions are slightly at variance with those laid down in SSAP 17. This defines post balance sheet events as those occuring up to the date on which the accounts *are approved* by, as opposed to being signed on behalf of, the directors. In practice this will often be a simultaneous event. Furthermore

SSAP 17 classifies post balance sheet events into two categories:

Adjusting events which are defined as providing evidence of conditions existing at the balance sheet date requiring revision of estimates used in the preparation of financial statements. Examples of such events include information about bad debt provisions, amounts received and receivable in insurance claims, and items such as dividends, transfers to reserves and tax provisions.

Such items correspond to those which the Companies Act requires to be taken into account under the prudence principle, and the standard also requires such items to be taken into account in the financial statements.

Non-adjusting events are defined as events which arise subsequent to the balance sheet date and which concern conditions which did not exist at the time. As examples the standard quotes new share issues, major changes in the composition of the company, and losses of assets due to catastrophies. The standard requires such events to be disclosed by way of a note where they represent abnormal charges, especially where their non-disclosure would affect the ability of users of the financial statements to make proper evaluations. In such cases no provision would be charged against the profits of the year completed, although one might be needed in the subsequent period. Instead the directors should take account of the event when deciding on any distributions and on transfers to reserves. It should be noted that whilst SSAP 17 requires such events to be disclosed to shareholders through a note to the accounts, the Companies Act requires a reference in the Directors' report. It will normally be possible to satisfy both sets of regulations by showing the details in the accounts and by making a suitable, but informative, reference to the note in the directors' report.

Other commitments and liabilities In addition to the items discussed above the Companies Act requires details to be disclosed in the notes to the accounts of pension commitments, contracts for capital expenditure entered into by the company, and amounts authorised by the directors, and of "any other financial commitment entered into by the company which has been provided for and is relevant to assessing the company's state of affairs."

CONCLUSION: SIGNIFICANCE FOR THE BANKER

This chapter has been devoted to the accounting rules laid down in company law and standard practice for dealing with fixed assets, investments and various liabilities. Much of the information concerning these items must be shown as notes to the accounts. However, the items discussed are of considerable importance to the readers of accounts, especially to lenders to the business. Accordingly this chapter closes, as did the last, with the comment that it is essential to read the small print in a set of accounts and to be alert to the significance of the accounting policies used. This is especially so whenever it is intended to rely on the accounts as an indication of the state of affairs of a business enterprise in a lending decision.

FURTHER READING

This chapter has dealt both with the Companies Act and with certain Accounting Standards. Accordingly reference should be made to the books listed at the end of the previous chapter, where relevant. With regard to the application of Accounting Standards the following publications are particularly useful.

Accounting Standards Committee, *Accounting Standards*, (ICAEW).
L. Skerrat, ed., *Financial Reporting*, (ICAEW, published annually to 1985).
J. Blake, *Accounting Standards* (Longmans, revised edition, 1984).
F. A. J. Couldery, *Accounting Standards Study Book* (Van Nostrand Reinhold (UK), 3rd ed., 1982)

Chapter 4
Taxation

INTRODUCTION

Taxation plays an important part in determining the cash flow and ultimate profitability of most businesses. Therefore it is essential to understand the accounting treatment of taxation in order fully to understand the position shown in a set of accounts or forecasts. A complete understanding is difficult to obtain without some knowledge of the taxation system and the way in which it affects business enterprises. This chapter therefore begins with a description of the basic system of taxation as it affects companies, and to a lesser extent, partnerships and sole traders. It continues with a consideration of the way in which taxation is shown in company accounts, including the important problem of taxation which is deferred as a result of differences in the treatment of items for taxation and accounting purposes. Finally consideration is given to the way in which other taxes affect company accounts including value added tax and tax deducted from employees emoluments.

The tax legislation of the UK remains extremely complex and the discussion which follows is only a general outline. Those seeking a complete understanding of the topic should refer to one of the texts mentioned at the end of the chapter.

CORPORATION TAX

Corporation tax is payable by all UK resident companies on income and capital gains wherever arising, and by all non-UK resident companies on profits from trade arising in the United Kingdom. Residence is based on the place where central management is exercised, normally determined by board meetings.[1]

[1] In January 1981 it was announced that consideration is to be given to possible new statutory rules defining the residence of companies.

The tax is charged on profits made during each financial year to 31 March, and where a company accounting period straddles two years the rate for each year is apportioned on a time basis. The corporation tax rate for each financial year is announced retrospectively for each year in the budget speech, thus companies must estimate the rate which will apply to their profits for at least part of the year. From 1 April 1973 the rate stood at 52%. However, in the 1984 budget the Chancellor announced that the rate for the year ending in March of that year would be reduced to 50%, and that progressive reductions would be made in future years in accordance with the following table.

Table 4.1
Corporation Tax Rates

Financial year commencing 1 April	*Corporation tax rates*	*Small companies' rate*
1982	52%	38%
1983	50%	30%
1984	45%	30%
1985	40%	30%
1986	35%	30%

After 1986 it is intended that the rates will remain at 35% and 30%. As shown in the table there is a special rate for small companies, which applies where taxable profits do not exceed £100,000. For the first four years of the small company relief the rate was set at 40%, and the limit was gradually increased from the original figure of £70,000. There is marginal relief for companies with profits up to £500,000.

Corporation tax is charged on the earliest of the following dates:

- a period of 12 months since the end of the last corporation tax accounting period;
- the normal accounting date;
- cessation of trade; or
- cessation of residence or other reason for falling within the scope of corporation tax.

Tax is levied in accordance with the provisions contained in a number of schedules of detailed rules. The most important of these for companies being:

Schedule A – governing income from UK real property;
Schedule D Case I – governing trading income;
Schedule D Case III – governing interest from UK sources.

For each corporation tax accounting period an assessment is raised by the Inspector of Taxes in accordance with the rules set out in the relevant schedule. If the company does not agree with the assessment it may appeal to the General or Special Commissioners of the Inland Revenue for the assessment to be changed. Appeal may be made to the courts on points of law.

Corporation tax is payable nine months after the end of the accounting period or 30 days from the date of assessment whichever is later. Where a company was trading prior to 1 April 1965, when corporation tax was introduced, it is allowed to maintain the gap between the end of its accounting period and the due date for payment under the old rules. For such companies there may be a gap of up to 22 months before payment is due.

ADVANCE CORPORATION TAX

The corporation tax payments referred to above are termed "mainstream corporation tax." In addition companies are obliged to make an advance payment of tax whenever they make a dividend payment to shareholders. Such payments, known as advance corporation tax (ACT), count as a payment of income tax at the basic rate, by the shareholders, and basic rate tax payers have no further obligation to pay tax.[2] When the company comes to pay its mainstream liability it may offset the advance corporation tax payment against its liability, subject to certain restrictions.

Example

		£	£
UK company – taxable income 31.12.81			200
Dividend paid 1.8.81 £70			
ACT payable 14.10.81 (3/7 of £70)		30	
	£		
C.T. at 52% of £200	104		
Less ACT set off	(30)		
Mainstream C.T.		74	
Total tax			104
After tax income			96

ACT on dividends must be paid to the Inland Revenue in respect of any payments made in the period ending on the preceeding quarter day on 14 January, April, July, and October.

Where a company receives a dividend on which ACT has been paid the income is termed "franked investment income" and no further taxation is payable. The extent to which ACT may be set against the mainstream corporation tax liability is restricted to the amount which would be payable if the whole taxable income had been distributed. Thus where a company pays dividends from past profits, it may not be able to set the full amount of ACT against its mainstream liability. ACT which is not relieved in the ordinary way may normally be treated in two ways:

[2] This system is known as the imputation system because tax is imputed to the shareholders.

(1) It may be carried back and set against the liability in the preceeding six years (two years for periods up to 31 March 1984); or
(2) It may be carried forward without limit, and set against future payments.

ACT cannot be carried forward where there is a change in the ownership of the company coupled with a major change in the nature or conduct of the trade or business, or where the activities of the trade or business become small or negligible. There are special provisions governing ACT for groups of companies.

ASCERTAINING TAXABLE INCOME

To arrive at the taxable trading income of a business certain adjustments must be made to accounting profits. These include the following:

(1) Items not taxable under Schedule D Case I must be excluded.
(2) Relief must be given for certain reliefs against income, including capital allowances.
(3) Relief must be given for trading losses where relevant.
(4) Items not acceptable as expenses under Schedule D, such as entertaining domestic customers must be excluded.
(5) Items which are allowed or taxed on an actual, rather than an accrued basis, must be adjusted.

These points are discussed in more detail below, and then illustrated by an example.

CAPITAL ALLOWANCES

Depreciation is not allowed as a charge for taxation purposes, and allowance is given for the cost of using capital equipment by a system of capital allowances. Expenditure on commerical buildings does not attract an allowance except in enterprise zones, or where they are part of an industrial building, and their cost does not exceed 25% of the whole.

Plant and Machinery

This term has been interpreted widely over the years and in addition to aircraft, ships and office equipment includes most moveable capital items. Prior to 14 March 1984 a 100% first year allowance was given for expenditure on plant and machinery other than private motor cars and certain leased assets, for which separate arrangements applied. The allowance was available whether the asset was new or secondhand, and whether or not it was in use at the end of the period, provided it was eventually used. A company was able to disclaim part or all of its first year allowances and the balance of expenditure was then subject to an annual writing down allowance of 25%.[3]

[3] It is proposed to introduce separate treatment for capital allowances in respect of short life items (less than 5 years) in the Finance Act 1985.

Table 4.2
Capital Allowances: Table of Main Allowances

Category	*Expenditure Prior to 14.3.84*			*Expenditure After 14.3.84 (+)*		
	First year	*Initial*	*Writing down*	*First year*	*Initial*	*Writing down*
Plant and machinery	100%	Nil	25% RB *	Nil	Nil	25% RB **
Motor cars	Nil	Nil	25% RB **	Nil	Nil	25% RB **
New industrial buildings	Nil	75%	4% SL	Nil	Nil	4% SL

Code
+ See p. 72 for details of transitional arrangements to 1.4.86
* From year 2
** From year 1
RB Reducing balance
SL Straight line

In the 1984 budget the Chancellor announced the intention of abolishing first year allowances over a transitional period as shown below.

Capital Allowances for Plant and Machinery

Expenditure incurred:	First year allowance
prior to 14.3.84	100%
14.3.84 to 31.3.85	75%
1.4.85 to 31.3.86	50%
after 1.4.86	Nil

In the period from 14 March 1984 to 31 March 1986 companies will be able to claim the writing down allowance of 25% in addition to the first year allowance on expenditure, thus increasing the aggregate allowances to 100% and 75% in the period concerned. After 1 April 1986 only the 25% writing down allowance will be available, which will apply each year on a reducing balance basis. When assets are disposed of the lower of the proceeds or the original cost is deducted from the pool of undepreciated expenditure, and a "balancing charge" is made where the proceeds exceed the value of the pool. In cases where the proceeds exceed the original cost the surplus is treated as a "chargeable gain" and taxed separately.[4]

Motor Cars

Private motor cars do not attract first year allowances unless they are used for hire, or are industrial vehicles. Instead a writing down allowance of 25% is given for each year in which the car is used for the purposes of trade.

The allowance is based in the balance outstanding and is adjusted where the vehicle is used for only part of a year. The writing down allowance on a car costing more than £8,000 is limited to £2,000 p.a., thus delaying the receipt of allowances. Each such car is treated as a separate pool of expenditure from which any proceeds on disposal are deducted, giving rise to a balancing charge for surpluses over written down amount, and balancing allowances for unrelieved expenditure.

Industrial Buildings

Where a building is in use as a mill or factory, or is used in a trade involving manufacturing or processing, it counts as an industrial building. Expenditure on the construction or improvement of such buildings is subject to an annual straight line allowance of 4% on any unrelieved expenditure. A system of initial allowances is being phased out as a result of the 1984 budget.

Industrial Buildings Initial Allowance

Expenditure incurred	
prior to 14.3.84	75%
14.3.84 to 31.3.85	50%
1.4.85 to 31.3.86	25%
after 1.4.86	Nil

[4] If the full allowance is claimed and a tax loss created it may only be relieved in accordance with the loss relief provisions discussed later in the chapter. It may sometimes be advantageous for a company to defer receipt of allowances.

The operation of capital allowances is illustrated by the following example.

Example

Polytechnic PLC is set up to print text books. It acquires the following assets in its first year.

(a) A factory costing £200,000 – which is entirely new, £18,000 of the cost being attributable to an office forming part of the building.
(b) Sundry plant and machinery costing £120,000.
(c) A Volvo Estate for the Managing Director costing £10,000 and a Ford Capri for the Sales Representative for £4,500.
(d) Two general purpose vans costing £6,000 and £4,000.

The company decides to use only £60,000 of the first year allowance on the plant and machinery in year 1. During the second year it acquires £80,000 of plant and machinery, which it does not use until after the year end, and constructs a store adjoining the factory for £20,000.

The capital allowances are calculated on the assumption that the company was established:
(1) On 1 April 1980
(2) On 1 April 1986

Solution Polytechnic PLC – Company Established 1.4.80

	Plant £	*Pool* £	*Motor cars* £	*Motor cars +£8,000* £	*Industrial buildings* £
Year 1					
Expenditure	120,000		4,500	10,000[c]	200,000[d]
	10,000[d]				
	130,000				
First year/initial allowance	60,000				150,000
	£70,000	70,000			50,000
Writing down allowance			1,125	2,000	8,000
Carried forward		£70,000	£3,375	£8,000	£42,000
Year 2					
Expenditure	80,000[a]				20,000
First year/initial allowance	80,000				15,000
					5,000
Brought forward		70,000	3,375	8,000	42,000
					47,000
Writing down allowance		17,500	844	2,000	1,880
Carried forward		£52,500	£2,531	£6,000	£45,120

Total allowances for each year are as follows:

	Year 1	Year 2
	£	£
Plant and motor cars		
First year allowance	60,000	80,000
Writing down allowance	3,125	17,500
		844
		2,000
	63,125	100,344
Industrial buildings		
Industrial buildings/initial allowance	150,000	15,000
Writing down allowance	8,000	1,880
Total allowances	£211,125	£117,224

Solution Polytechnic PLC – Company Established 1.4.86

	Plant	Motor cars	Motor cars +£8,000	Industrial buildings
	£	£	£	£
Year 1				
Expenditure	120,000	4,500	10,000[c]	200,000[b]
	10,000[d]			
	130,000			
Writing down allowance	32,500	1,125	2,000	8,000
Carried forward	97,500	3,375	8,000	192,000
Year 2				
Expenditure	80,000[a]			20,000
	177,000	3,375	8,000	212,000
Writing down allowance	44,375	844	2,000	8,800
Carried forward	133,125	2,531	6,000	203,200

	Year 1	Year 2
Total allowances	£43,625	£54,219

Notes

a Although the plant was not used until after the end of the year it attracts capital allowances for the year in which it was acquired provided it is eventually brought into use.

b The office attracts an industrial building allowance provided it forms part of the industrial building and its cost is not more than 25% of the total construction cost.

c The Volvo Estate must be treated as a separate pool of expenditure because it costs more than £8,000.

d The motor vans do not count as motor cars but may be treated as plant.

The allowances for 1986 are based on the assumptions that no further changes will be introduced in the system of capital allowances.

The Impact of the 1984 Tax changes

It can be seen that the changes in the capital allowances system have had a major impact on the size of the allowances available to the company. However, it should be noted that as the writing down allowances are claimed the full expenditure will eventually be relieved against the corporation tax liability. The effect of the changes is therefore to delay rather than to remove the reliefs. However, the impact of this delay may be to make certain projects less profitable, and to affect company cash flow adversely for a period. The impact will be mitigated by the reduction in the rate of corporation tax, and for each company will be affected by any tax losses brought forward. In order to assess the economic significance of the changes on each firm use may be made of the discounted cash flow techniques described in Chapter 11.

These techniques take account not only of the amount of the tax allowances concerned, but also of their value at the time received.

STOCK APPRECIATION RELIEF

Between 1974 and 1984 relief was given to companies to offset the additional cost of holding stocks in a period of rising prices. The system, which was revised in 1980, extended relief by reference to an all stocks index, to amounts in excess of £2,000. The relief, which was abolished in 1984, is illustrated by an example.

Example

A company holds stocks valued at £500,000 at the start of its financial year on 1 April 1982. The all stocks index shows the following values:

1.4.82	218.9
31.3.83	231.4

Relief is calculated as follows:

$$(\pounds500{,}000 - \pounds2{,}000) \times \frac{231.4 - 218.9}{218.9}$$

= £488,000 × 0.057
= £27,866.

The all stocks index was published monthly by the Business Statistics Office of the Department of Industry and Trade.

DISSALLOWED ITEMS

The following items are not generally allowed as trading expenses for tax purposes:

- Business entertaining and the provision of gifts and hospitality; exceptions include entertaining overseas customers on a reasonable scale, entertaining members of staff, and the provision of small gifts incorporating a conspicuous advertisement, or gifts which it is part of the companies trade to supply.
- Losses arising from foreign exchange transactions, which are treated as capital and losses.
- Pre-trading expenditure, except that incurred during the year immediately prior to the commencement of trading.
- Provisions of a general, as distinct from a specific, nature.
- Expenditure on improving a acquiring fixed assets including legal expenses, although capital allowances may be available.
- Charitable donations – which may be allowed as a charge on income, as opposed to a trading expense, where a deed of covenant capable of exceeding three years has been entered into.

The treatment of these aspects in computing the tax liability of a business is illustrated by the following example.

A BASIC TAXATION COMPUTATION

Example

Diploma Ltd has just completed its first year of trading and the accountant is preparing a taxation computation. The auditor, who acts as tax advisor, has informed him that the capital allowances to which the company is entitled amount to £199,000.

The accounts of Diploma Ltd show a profit of £460,000 including a depreciation charge of £60,000. Further examination of the accounts shows that the company had spent £4,000 on entertaining. Of this amount £1,500 related to overseas customers, £500 to overseas suppliers and the balance to UK suppliers. £750 had been spent on diaries valued at £1 each, which had been distributed to customers – showing the company's name and principal products.

During the year the company had purchased a freehold interest in some land and had incurred legal fees of £700. The profit figure included £5,000 of bank interest of which only £4,500 had been received during the year.

Calculate the profits chargeable to tax for Diploma Ltd, at a rate of 52% (Ignore the small company rate ot tax).

Diploma Ltd

	£	£	£
Profits per accounts			660,000
Add: depreciation		60,000	
entertaining UK	4,000		
Less: overseas buyers[a]	1,500		
		2,500	
Legal expenses[b]		700	
			63,200
			723,200
Bank interest per accounts[c]			(5,000)
			718,200
Capital allowances			199,000
			519,200
Add: bank interest paid (Taxed under Schedule D III)			4,500
Taxable profit under Schedule DI			£523,700
Corporation tax at 52%			£268,324

Notes

[a] Entertaining expenses are only allowable when incurred in relation to an overseas *buyer*. The expenditure on diaries may be treated as an allowable expense.
[b] Legal fees in relation to capital items do not count as an allowable expense.
[c] Bank interest receivable for the period is excluded and treated on an actual basis under Schedule D III.

CAPITAL GAINS

Companies do not have to pay capital gains tax, but are liable to pay corporation tax on chargeable gains. In order to achieve a comparable burden between the two taxes the gains of a company were reduced by 15/26ths of the total. The result is that at a Corporation tax rate of 52% the gain was taxed at an effective rate of 30%. Following the changes made in 1984, appropriate adjustments to the relief apply each year. Where a company makes losses on capital they may be set against capital gains of the accounting period and then carried forward without time limit and set against future gains. The payment of tax on chargeable gains may be deferred where the proceeds are reinvested in certain new trading assets.

Under the roll-over relief provisions the tax is not payable until assets are realised and not replaced. Then the full amount of any gain, including that part deferred, is taxed. All taxpayers are now able to deduct an "indexation allowance" from any gross gain provided the asset has been held for 12 months. The purpose of this allowance is to ensure that any real gains are taxed rather than nominal gains caused by inflation.

RELIEF FOR LOSSES

Relief for trading losses are given in a number of ways:

- Losses may be carried forward without limit, after taking account of capital allowances and charges on income such as interest, and then set against trading income from the same trade. However, relief is not given where there is a change in ownership and a major change in the nature or conduct of the trade.
- Losses may be set against any income and the total trading profits of the same accounting period, including those from other trades, or against those of the immediately preceeding accounting period.
- Losses on first year allowances on plant and machinery may be carried back three years and set against profits of the same trade. However charges on income may not be carried back.
- Losses on the cessation of business may be carried back for three years and set against profits.
- Non-trading losses may only be carried forward and set against income from the same source.
- Capital losses may only be set against current and future capital gains.

Special provisions operate for groups of companies which allow losses by one company to be set against profits of another within the group. Relief is also given where the profits of a company have already been subject to overseas taxation.

CLOSE COMPANIES

Where a company operates under the control of five or fewer participants, or of participants who are directors, provisions operate to ensure that the income of each participant is subject to income tax, notwithstanding that dividends have not been paid by the company. In such companies the Inland Revenue may treat the whole of the company's income as having been distributed for tax purposes and may apportion it amongst the participators, who will normally comprise the shareholders, loan creditors and their associates.

In recent years the regulations governing close companies have been amended considerably in order to assist the development of small businesses. Thus there are a number of significant exceptions to the apportionment provisions. These include:

- the trading income of a trading company;
- certain property income; and
- the investment or property income of a trading company if the apportionment would be prejudical to the company's business.

A trading company which discloses all relevant income to the Inland Revenue may request "clearance" that an apportionment will not be made in respect of any accounting period.

TAXATION OF PARTNERSHIPS AND SOLE TRADERS

In many respects the taxation of non-corporate firms is similar to that of companies, both are assessed under the same schedules of rules and both are able to claim capital allowances, and stock relief.

However, sole traders and partnerships are liable to income tax on their profits and to pay capital gains tax on their capital gains. Another important difference between the two systems is that unincorporated firms must pay tax on the basis of the taxable profits of the accounting period ending in the preceeding financial year. Thus it is important when starting such a business to select the commencement date carefully. For example if a business makes up accounts to 14 April 1984, these will form the basis of taxation in the tax year 1985/86, because they end in the preceeding tax year which runs from 6 April 1984 to 5 April 1985. The tax is payable in two instalments on 1 January and 1 July. Thus the firm in this example will pay tax for the year 1985/86 on 1 January and 1 July 1986. Where there is a delay in issuing an assessment the tax becomes payable in 30 days from the date of assessment.

There are special rules for the opening and closing years of a business. The basic system is illustrated below:

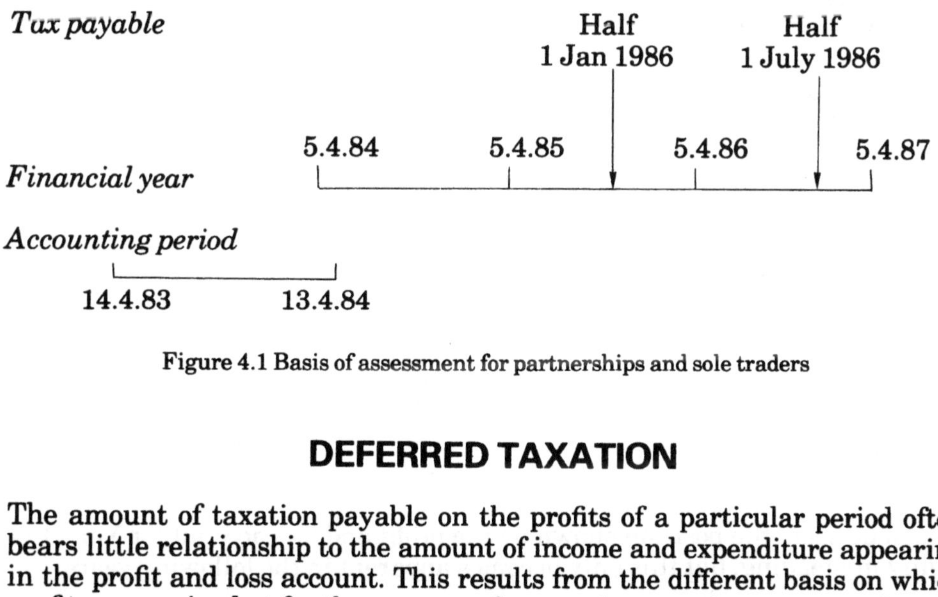

Figure 4.1 Basis of assessment for partnerships and sole traders

DEFERRED TAXATION

The amount of taxation payable on the profits of a particular period often bears little relationship to the amount of income and expenditure appearing in the profit and loss account. This results from the different basis on which profits are arrived at for the purpose of computing taxation as opposed to the basis on which profits are stated in financial statements.

This difference arises for two main reasons:

First, the fact that certain types of income may be tax-free or that certain expenditure is disallowable, giving rise to "permanent differences" between taxable and accounting profits. Secondly, the existence of items which are included in the financial statements of a period different from that in which they are dealt with for taxation, giving rise to "timing differences":

Timing differences arise under four main categories:

(1) short-term timing differences from the use of the receipts and payments basis for taxation purposes and the accruals basis in financial statements;
(2) availability of capital allowances in taxation computations which are in excess of the related depreciation charges in financial statements;
(3) revaluation surpluses on fixed assets for which a taxation charge does not arise until the gain is realised on disposal; and
(4) surpluses on disposals of fixed assets which are subject to rollover relief.

During the period of 100% first year allowances the amount of tax deferred was considerable as shown by the following example.

Example

A company makes a trading profit of £500 a year. It acquires new fixed assets in the first year and none for the next four years. Corporation tax is 50% and it pays dividends of £250.

	Year 1	*Years 2–5*
Profit per accounts	500	500
Depreciation added back (calculated on new assets £250 depreciated at 20%)	50	50
	550	550
Capital allowances 100% first year	250	
Taxable profit	300	550
Tax at 50%	150	275

Extract from accounts	*Year 1*	*Years 2–5*
Profit (Loss) before tax	500	500
Taxation	(150)	(275)
Profit (Loss) after tax	350	225
Dividends	250	250
Retained profit	100	(25)

As can be seen, the position shown by the profit and loss account for Year 1 is highly misleading, but this only becomes apparent in the following years.

In practice the destabilising effects of deferred taxation during the era of accelerated capital allowances were not as serious as the example might suggest. Most companies bought new fixed assets each year. Thus as timing differences were realised new balances emerged in their place turning the deferred tax balance into a more or less permanent item. This tendency was heightened by the fact that due to rising prices the capital allowances arising each year tended to increase. However where a company reduced its expenditure on items attracting capital allowances it incurred an increased tax charge.

This effect of increasing capital expenditure on the deferral of tax is illustrated by the following example.

Example

A company buys a new machine for £5,000 each year for five years. The machines have a life of five years and accordingly are written down at 20% per annum. They attract 100% first year allowances in the year of acquisition. After five years the company replaces the machine first acquired, and adds no further items. By employing each machine the company earns a trading profits of £2,000 before changing depreciation.

A. *Accounting profit*					
Year	1	2	3	4	5
Number of machines	1	2	3	4	5
	£	£	£	£	£
Trading profit	2,000	4,000	6,000	8,000	10,000
Less Depreciation	1,000	2,000	3,000	4,000	5,000
Profit	1,000	2,000	3,000	4,000	5,000
B. *Taxable profit (loss)*					
Trading profit	2,000	4,000	6,000	8,000	10,000
Less Capital allowances	5,000	5,000	5,000	5,000	5,000
Taxable profit (loss)	(3,000)	(1,000)	1,000	3,000	5,000
Tax loss B/F	—	(3,000)	(4,000)	(3,000)	—
Tax loss C/F	(3,000)	(4,000)	(3,000)	—	—
Taxable Profit	—	—	—	—	5,000
C. *Written down book value of machines*					
Machine 1	4,000	3,000	2,000	1,000	
2		4,000	3,000	2,000	1,000
3			4,000	3,000	2,000
4				4,000	3,000
5					4,000
Taxable profit deferred	4,000	7,000	9,000	10,000	10,000
D. *Analysis*					
Taxable profit (loss)	(3,000)	(1,000)	1,000	3,000	5,000
Acounting profit	1,000	2,000	3,000	4,000	5,000
Taxable profit deferred	4,000	3,000	2,000	1,000	—
Cumulative B/F		4,000	7,000	9,000	10,000
C/F	4,000	7,000	9,000	10,000	10,000

Note

The taxable profit deferred consists of the difference between accounting profits and taxable profits.

The example illustrates the way in which the use of 100% capital allowances defers the tax liability as investment increases within the business. From Year 5 investment is restricted to replacement and the company starts to pay tax. The tax deferred in Years 1 to 4 remains deferred so long as the company continues to replace plant. If a programme of increased expenditure is undertaken the tax charge will reduce. However were the company to reduce expenditure on machinery, the tax charge would rise because of the absence of capital allowances.

The impact of timing differences from an accounting point of view are serious because if the tax charge shown in the accounts based on the tax paid was the only information given, users of accounts would have no information concerning the possible impact of a decline in capital spending in the future. Such a change could produce a severe decline in post tax earnings and in the value of a company's shares. Whilst the problem of timing differences did not originate with the introduction of first year allowances in 1972, the problem did assume a new dimension. The response of the accountancy profession was to consider the use of deferred taxation or tax equalisation accounts.

Using the figures for the first example, such an account would operate as shown below.

Example

Profit and loss account	*Year 1*	*Year 2*	*Year 3*	*Year 4*	*Year 5*
	£	£	£	£	£
Profit before tax	500	500	500	500	500
Taxation					
Current tax	150	275	275	275	275
Deferred tax (credit)	100	(25)	(25)	(25)	(25)
Profit after tax	250	250	250	250	250
Deferred taxation					
Opening balance	—	100	75	50	25
Profit and Loss charge (credit)	100	(25)	(25)	(25)	(25)
Closing balance	100	75	50	25	—

In the first year the tax deferred is charged to the profit and loss account and transferred to a special provision for deferred taxation. In succeeding years withdrawals are made from the provision as the tax becomes payable. As a result the profit after tax is "equalised" and the destabilising effects of the timing differences are eliminated.

When 100% first year allowances were first introduced the problem of deferred taxation was given new impetus, especially as this coincided with a general increase in inflation. The response of the ASC was to issue an accounting standard (SSAP 11) which required a full provision to be made for deferred taxation. However before the standard came into force further events occurred which led to its withdrawal. The impact of inflation on company finance during 1974 was so severe as to persuade the government to introduce a special relief to offset the increased cost of holding stocks. This relief gave rise to further timing differences and to greater deferred tax balances. However in this case the balances would only to be withdrawn if a fall in stocks exceeded the rise in prices. The balance arising from stock relief seemed likely to become permanent unless the relief was withdrawn, which appeared unlikely because of the impact such a change would have had on industry.

As a result of these developments a lively debate ensued on the merits of providing for deferred tax. The main features of discussion are summarised below:

Against Deferred Tax Accounts	*For Deferred Tax Accounts*
(a) As fixed assets are constantly being added to at inflating prices the capital allowances almost always exceed the charge for depreciation. Thus the sum provided against deferred taxation is rarely reduced and in practice the annual additions tend to exceed the withdrawals and the balance is forever increasing.	If the company reduces its expenditure on fixed assets, as happens in severe recessions, there can be a significant rise in tax, hence the need to equalise by means of a deferred tax account.
(b) The effect of reducing capital allowances would be so deleterious to company cash flow that it could never happen. (In 1984 this was precisely what did happen, see p. 000 for a discussion of the consequences).	It is by no means certain that 100% capital allowances will continue indefinitely.
(c) Potential chargeable gains are not taxable until the assets are realised and no provision should be made until then. If gains are realised most companies will reinvest the proceeds and will claim "rollover relief". In practice serious problems can arise in a liquidation.	Notwithstanding that no liability exists it is wrong to credit the full gain to the shareholders when it could never be realised for their benefit. The effect is to overstate the net tangible assets of the company.
(d) The deferred taxation account becomes a hotchpotch which represents no real liability. The profit and loss account has been elevated at the expense of the balance sheet.	Prudence always predominates over the accurals concept.
(e) In time the deferred taxation account becomes enormous and misleading to lenders who regard it as a real liability.	It is unfortunate that readers of the accounts do not appreciate the significance of the items shown – but the solution must be a process of education rather than a change of policy.

In the light of the representations made to it the ASC produced a revised standard (SSAP 15) which only required a provision to be made for "probable" liabilities. (The actual words used required that a provision be made for all timing differences and other differences "except where it could be demonstrated with reasonable probability that the deferral would continue in the future").

In 1980 the system of stock relief changed, rendering the reliefs obtained permanent, and by 1983 the ASC decided to revise SSAP 15 in the light of the experience gained from using it.

Proposed Accounting Standard: Accounting for Deferred Taxation (ED 33)

ED 33 identified three possible approaches to the deferred tax problem.

(1) *A nil provision or flow through approach*
The tax charge shown in the accounts is that actually paid and the effect of timing differences is ignored.

(2) *A full provision*
A full tax charge is made, irrespective of the remoteness of eventual payment (the approach required by SSAP 11).

(3) *A partial provision*
The tax charge is based on the probable eventual tax liability. This is the approach adopted by SSAP 15 and ED 33.

The proposed standard (ED 33) states:

> "Partial provision recognises that, if an enterprise is not expected to reduce the scale of its operations significantly, it will normally have what amounts to a hard core of timing differences so that the payment of some tax will be permanently deferred. On this basis, deferred tax only has to be provided where it is probable that tax will become payable as a result of the reversal of timing differences. Because it is based on an assessment of what will actually be the position, partial provision is preferable to the other bases described above."

The main provisions of ED 33 are as follows:

Deferred tax should be provided in respect of the tax effects arising from all timing differences of material amount to the extent that it is probable that a liability will crystallise.

Reasonable assumptions need to be formulated in order to assess whether or not it is probable that tax liabilities will crystallise as a result of the reversal of timing differences and accordingly whether or not a deferred tax provision is necessary. These assumptions will be based upon information available up to the date on which the financial statements are approved by the board of directors and upon the intentions of management. This information will include financial plans or projections, where available, covering a period of years sufficient to enable an assessment to be made of the pattern of future tax liabilities. Further guidance is given in the appendix.

The provision for deferred tax liabilities should be reduced by any deferred tax debit balances arising from timing differences, trading losses or advance corporation tax which will be available for offset against those liabilities.

Deferred tax debit balances arising from timing differences, trading losses or advance corporation tax should not be carried forward so as to give rise to a deferred tax asset except to the extent that recovery without replacement by equivalent debit balances is assured beyond reasonable doubt.

CALCULATION OF DEFERRED TAX LIABILITY

There are two methods of calculating the liability for deferred tax – the liability method and the deferral method. SSAP 15 did not specify which should be used, but ED 33 clearly implies that the first method is preferred.

(1) *The liability method.* Under this method the taxation effects of timing differences are regarded as liabilities for taxes payable in the future or as

assets representing recoverable taxes. Thus the deferred taxation balances will be calculated on the basis of the current rate of tax on the grounds that the most recent rate of tax is the best available guide to the likely position when tax is actually paid or recovered. Whenever there is a change in the rate of taxation there will be a revision of the opening balance of deferred taxation; the effect of such a revision will normally be shown in the profit and loss account as a part of the taxation charge but may, if it arises from a radical change in the taxation system, be treated as an extraordinary item.

(2) *The deferral method.* This is a procedure whereby the taxation effects of timing differences are regarded as deferrals of taxation payable or recoverable to be allocated to future periods when the differences reverse. Balances on the deferred taxation account are regarded as deferred credits or deferred charges rather than as amounts payable or recoverable and are not revised on changes in the rate of taxation.

DEFERRED TAXATION AND THE 1984 TAX CHANGES

As a result of the changes introduced in 1984, deferred taxation will eventually cease to be a significant problem in accounts. As Table 4.3 shows, the differences between depreciation charges and capital allowances will often be insignificant, and where the tax allowances are greater, income will be stated more conservatively. This is demonstrated by Table 4.3, in which the depreciation charge for plant written down on a straight line basis at 15% is compared with the impact of a 25% writing down allowance for tax purposes. In the first two years the tax allowances exceed the depreciation provision, and tax is thereby deferred. From Years 3 to 5 the depreciation charge is

Table 4.3
Comparison of Tax Allowances and Depreciation Charges

Example: Plant costing £1,000 written off at 15% with a charge of £100 in the final year of life. Tax chargeable at the proposed rate of 35%.

Year	*Tax allowances*		*Depreciation*		*Differences*		
	Writing down allowance 25% R.B.	*Written down amount*	*Annual charge 15% S.L.*	*Written down amount*	*Annual*	*Cumulative*	*Tax deferred*
	£	£	£	£	£	£	£
0		1,000		1,000			
1	250	750	150	850	(100)	(100)	(35)
2	188	562	150	700	(38)	(138)	(48)
3	140	422	150	550	10	(128)	(45)
4	106	316	150	400	44	(84)	(29)
5	79	237	150	250	71	(13)	(5)
6	59	178	150	100	91	78	27
7	45	133	100	—	55	133	46

greater and the deferred tax becomes payable. Where a deferred tax account is maintained the amounts concerned would be charged to the account. After Year 5 the accumulated depreciation charge exceeds the accumulated tax allowances, and by the time the asset has been written off completely in the accounts, there are still unused tax allowances of £133. In the examples tax is charged at the standard corporation tax rates; the small company provisions being ignored.

Where a company undertakes a similar level of investment each year the timing differences will tend to cancel out. However, where investment is increased tax will be deferred, but the timing differences will reverse, and the tax charge will rise if the increase is not maintained. The reduction proposed in the rate of corporation tax has helped to reduce the impact of the timing differences. Nevertheless, although the impact of the changes will be fairly neutral in the long run, the immediate effect will be a significant rise in company tax bills. This effect is illustrated by the case of a company which owns five machines costing £5,000, each having a life of five years, and nil scrap value, with a new machine having been purchased each year. Under the old system the company would receive a first year allowance of £5,000 each year which would offset the depreciation charge in the accounts. Provided the company continued to replace a machine each year, the tax deferred would not have become payable. The total deferred liability at the end of the year in which the last machine was purchased, and for which no provision was required under either SSAP 15 or ED 31, would have been as shown below. The effect of the small companies' rate which reduces the impact is ignored in this and the following examples.

Example
Deferred tax liability under old rates of Corporation Tax

Machine purchased (years ago)	*Book written down amount*
	£
5	—
4	1,000
3	2,000
2	3,000
1	4,000
	10,000
Tax written down value	—
Excess of tax allowances over depreciation charges	10,000
Tax deferred at 52%	5,200

If the company did not replace any of its machines in the future, the tax charge would exceed that chargeable on the accounting profit by £5,200 over a period of five years.

As a result of the proposed change in rate of corporation tax, the amount of the potential deferred tax liability has been reduced. In order to calculate the amount deferred it is necessary to determine when the charge would become payable as a result of new allowances not arising. This can be found by ascertaining the amount by which the depreciation charge would exceed the tax allowance in each year. With no replacement of machinery the figures would be as shown below, where the first year commences on 1st April 1983, and a machine is purchased in that year.

Example
Deferred Tax Liability under new rates of Corporation Tax

Year	*Excess of depreciation over tax allowances*	*Tax rate*	*Tax*
	£		£
1	—	52%	—
2	4,000	50%	2,000
3	3,000	45%	1,350
4	2,000	40%	800
5	1,000	35%	350
	£10,000		£4,500

As a result of the change in the rate of tax, this company is able to reduce its potential tax liability by £700.

In practice few companies are likely to suspend all investment completely, but the impact of the change in the capital allowance system will be to increase the tax charge for several years. This may be illustrated using the example already considered, in which a machine costing £5,000 is acquired each year. The allowances and tax charges which will arise are shown in the example below.

Example
The impact of the altered system of Capital Allowances

Year commencing	1.4.83	1.4.84	1.4.85	1.4.86	1.4.87
	£	£	£	£	£
1st year allowance	5,000	3,750	2,500	—	—
W.D.A.	—	1,250	1,250	1,562	2,472
Total allowances	5,000	5,000	3,750	1,562	2,472
Increase in taxable profit	—	—	1,250	3,438	2,528
Corporation tax rate	50%	52%	45%	40%	35%
Increase in tax charge	—	—	562	1,375	885

As result of the abolition of first year allowances, the total tax deferred at £4,500 will gradually be reduced, except where increased capital expenditure creates new timing differences and defers it. In the case given the total annual allowances arising under the writing down allowance gradually increase, reaching £4,855 by the year commencing 1 April 1985. Because of the use of the reducing balance method, the effect of the change from accelerated allowances will never be entirely cleared from the system.

Under ED 33 and SSAP 15 companies must estimate the extent to which their future tax charges will rise as a result of the reversal of timing differences, and make a full provision for the amount concerned. Where a company undertakes increased capital expenditure it will attract fresh allowances which may offset the reversal of timing differences and reduce the size of the provision required.

DEFERRED TAXATION IN THE EVENT OF LIQUIDATION

If a company is liquidated and assets are sold it is possible that tax which has been deferred will become payable. Regrettably it is rarely if ever possible to predict the extent of the likely liability with any degree of accuracy. Much will depend upon the circumstances which prevail at the time, including the value at which assets are realised, and the extent of trading losses. The maximum liability must be shown as a note to the accounts, but it would be quite unrealistic to regard this as a genuine liability in a successful firm. The practical consequence of this dilemna seems to be that bankers must base their lending decision on a going concern evaluation in most cases rather than upon an estimate of available assets in a break up situation. This is a point which we shall consider in more detail in Chapters 8–13 of this book. As a result of the abolition of first year allowances, the significance of deferred tax balances will diminish gradually in the future, and by the early 1990s will be immaterial.

FRANKED AND UNFRANKED INVESTMENT INCOME

Investment income on which corporation tax has already been levied is not subject to further taxation when in the hands of an investing company. Such income is termed "franked investment income" and requires special treatment in the accounts of the receiving company. The amount received will have resulted in payment of advance corporation tax by the distribution company, and no further ACT is payable when the amount is passed on to shareholders. In the profit and loss account the investment income is "grossed-up" to include the ACT paid on the original distribution, and the ACT is included in the charge for taxation shown in the accounts. Thus where a company receives a dividend of £700 it will credit £1,000 to the profit and loss account as investment income, and will add £300 to the total for taxation. This transaction does not result in any further payments being made to the Inland Revenue.

Unfranked investment income consists of income such as interest on loan stock and royalties, which has not been subject to corporation tax. However, when payments are made from UK sources income tax is withheld and only the "net" amount is received. In the accounts the gross amount is credited to the profit and loss account and becomes subject to corporation tax. However the tax withheld may be credited against the corporation tax liability or recovered if none is due. Alternatively it may be set against the company's own liability to account for income tax on annual payments such as loan stock interest.

THE PRESENTATION OF TAXATION IN COMPANY ACCOUNTS

The presentation of tax liabilities in the balance sheet is complicated by the range of possible payment dates and the practice of setting the corporation tax rate retrospectively. This point is illustrated by Figure 4.3.

Tax due 9 months after year end

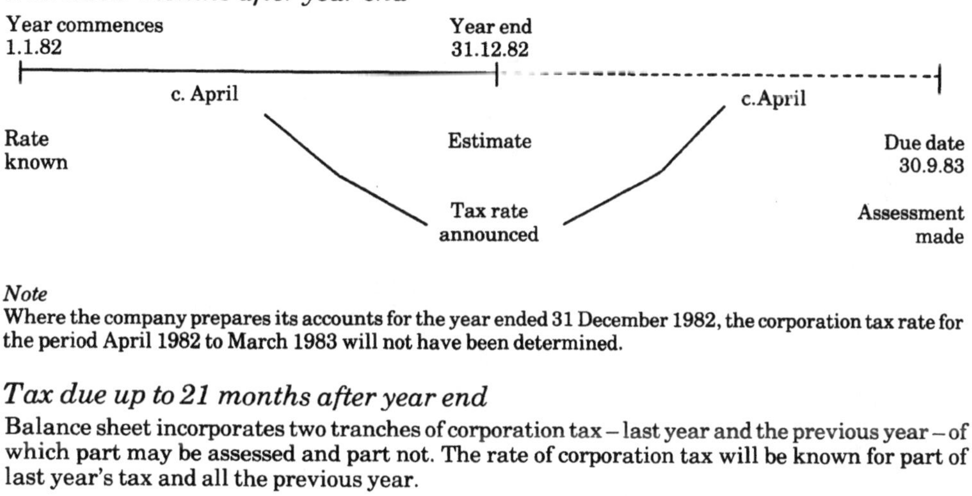

Note
Where the company prepares its accounts for the year ended 31 December 1982, the corporation tax rate for the period April 1982 to March 1983 will not have been determined.

Tax due up to 21 months after year end
Balance sheet incorporates two tranches of corporation tax – last year and the previous year – of which part may be assessed and part not. The rate of corporation tax will be known for part of last year's tax and all the previous year.

Figure 4.3 Corporation tax payment dates

In the case of a group of companies there may be a whole range of different payment dates and assessment situations.

In addition to corporation tax, a company may also have liabilities in respect of various other taxes for which it acts as a collection agent for the government. These include income tax deducted from employees emoluments, income tax deducted from interest payments on debentures and, value added tax. The presentation of these items in the balance sheet is summarised in Table 4.4 shown below, and illustrated by the example which follows.

Table 4.4
Balance Sheet Presentation of Taxation Items (References to Format 1)

Tax	*Frequency of payment*	*Balance sheet headings*	*Format reference* *I*	*II*	*Comment*
Income tax (PAYE)	Payable monthly	CREDITORS: Other creditors (inc. taxation and social security)	E8	C8	*(Company acts as "collecting agent" for income tax and value added tax and makes payment monthly and quarterly).*
Value added tax	Payable quarterly On 14 January, April, July or October following payment of a dividend in preceding quarter.	CREDITORS: Other creditors (inc. taxation and social security)	E8	C8	
Corporation tax	Payable annually – period depends on whether company traded prior to April 1965	*Amount estimated* – CREDITORS – Other creditors (inc. taxation and social security) Due – 12 mth.	E8	C8	*(Traditionally tax has been treated as a creditor notwithstanding that no assessment had been made and the rate was in part uncertain).*
		Other creditors (inc. taxation and social security) Due + 12 mth.	H8	C8 & note	
		Amounts disputed – PROVISIONS FOR LIABILITIES AND CHARGES: Taxation including deferred taxation.	I2	B2	
ACT and charges on income	Payable quarterly	CREDITORS: Other creditors (inc. taxation and social security).			
Tax deferred	Variable	*Probable liability* – PROVISIONS FOR LIABILITIES AND CHARGES: Taxation including deferred taxation.	E8	C8	
		Potential liability – Contingent Liability (note to accounts).	I2	B2	

Example

The accounts of Rimmer Ltd at 31 December 1982 included the following balances:

	Dr	Cr
	£	£
Interim dividend	14,000	
Advance corporation tax	6,000	
Corporation tax payable		
1 January 1981		43,000
Deferred taxation		2,630

The following additional information is available:

(i) Profits for the year amounted to £249,000 and include the following items:
  (a) Dividends received £11,410 (Franked investment income)
  (b) Royalty payments received £2,800 (unfranked investment income)
  (c) Loan stock interest amount paid £14,000 (Unfranked investment income) bank interest £7,800.

(ii) Corporation tax payable on the adjusted profits for the year is estimated at £58,000 and the liability for the previous year has now been agreed at £43,560.

(iii) The deferred taxation account is to be reduced to £1,850.

(iv) A final dividend totalling £21,000 is proposed.

(v) The ACT rate is 30% and the corporation tax rate is 50%.

Solution

Extracts from Profit and Loss Account

	£	£	£	£
Trading profit				200,900
Investment income				
Dividends			16,300	
Royalties			4,000	20,300
Operating profit				221,200
Interest				27,800
Profit before tax				249,000
Taxation – Mainstream		62,890		
Adjustment		560		
Deferred		(780)		62,670
Profit after tax				186,330
Dividends interim	14,000			
final	21,000			35,000
Retained profit				151,330

Balance Sheet Presentation

Creditors			
E8	*Taxation and other creditors*		
	Corporation tax	43,560	
	Advance corporation tax	9,000	
	Income tax	4,800	
—	*Dividends*	21,000	
Creditors			
H8	Taxation	58,000	(or I2)
Provisions			
I2	Deferred taxation	1,850	Notes to show details
Current assets			
—	Advance corporation tax recoverable	9,000	

Workings

Corp tax

ACT	6,000[f]	Bal	43,000
Bal	95,560	P & L	560
Divs. Rec.	4,890[a]	P & L	62,890
	106,450		106,450

Deferred tax

P & L	780[e]	Bal	2,630
Bal	1,850[e]		
	2,630		2,630

ACT Payable

		ACT Recoverable	9,000[g]

ACT

Bank	6,000	CT	6,000[f]
ACT payable	9,000[g]		

Dividends payable

Bank	14,000	P & L	14,000
		P & L	21,000

Royalties received

P & L	4,000	Bank	2,800[a]
		I Tax	1,200[b]
	4,000		4,000

Interest

Bank	7,800[d]	P & L	27,800
Bank (L Stock)	14,000[c]		
I Tax	6,000[c]		
	27,800		27,800

Income tax

Royalties	1,200(b)	Interest	6,000[c]
Bal	4,800		
	6,000		6,000

Dividends received

P & L	16,300	Bank	11,410
		Corp Tax	4,890
	16,300		16,300

Notes

[a] Franked Investment Income (dividends received) is grossed up for ACT and the tax taken to the corporation tax account.

[b] Unfranked Investment Income (royalties received) is grossed up and the income tax set against income tax deducted from annual charges n.c.

[c] Income tax in deducted from the annual charge, interest on loan stock is set against income tax on royalties, and the balance paid to the Inland Revenue on the due date.

[d] Bank interest is recorded without deduction of tax.

[e] Deferred tax is adjusted to the probable liability.

[f] ACT paid relating to the interim dividend is set against corporation tax.

[g] ACT on the final dividend is provided and carried forward to be set against corporation tax in the following year.

TAXATION AND THE BANKER

It has been the objective in this chapter to outline the basic features of the UK taxation system, and the way in which the tax affairs of a company are reported in the accounts. Because of the great complexity of the subject matter the result has been no more than a general outline. In practice most companies put their taxation affairs in the hands of an advisor, usually their accountant. By devising the appropriate strategy it is often possible to delay or avoid the payment of tax. Some of the reliefs available to companies have created a pool of finance which amounts to a semi-permanent government loan. However, its continuance is often dependent on continued activity and further expenditure. A serious and unforeseen cutback in expenditure on capital items can result in a steep rise in the tax charge at a time when a company can least afford it. In prior years, the accounts will have been drawn up on the basis of reasonable assumptions concerning future trading activity. Only when these are confounded by events will serious problems arise. Nevertheless the banker should always bear in mind that many companies have substantial contingent tax liabilities. In the event of serious difficulties these could materialise and trigger financial collapse. It is therefore unwise to place too much reliance on the value of assets upon realisation where there are significant deferred tax liabilities. In the short term such a company should be able to meet its liabilities provided it maintains adequate cash flow. Where there are any special difficulties it is often wise for the banker to ensure that the impact of tax on future cash flow is examined by the the company's tax advisors.

It is also essential that a company takes the effect of future tax payments into account in drawing up cash flow projections, and before taking on any major financial commitments. Unfortunately many companies fail to do so, with serious and often "fatal" results. Thus in cases where cash flow projections fail to show the effect of future tax payments the banker should refer the customer back to his accountant with the advice that he obtains a forecast of his tax payments over the next year, and an estimate of his likely payments in the two succeeding years. Such advice is more than ever needed in view of the changes in company taxation introduced in 1984.

FURTHER READING

The Allied Dunbar Tax Guide is an excellent introduction to the complexities of taxation for the layman. In addition most large accountancy firms prepare booklets which they make available to clients and to other interested parties on request.

W. I. Sinclair, *Tax Guide* (Allied Dunbar, published annually).

Chapter 5
The Accounting Requirements of the Companies Acts

INTRODUCTION

By law every company must lay accounts before its members for each accounting period. These accounts must be drawn up in accordance with the accounting rules described in Chapters 2 and 3. In addition they must show a mass of information set out in the Companies Act under the heading and subheadings of prescribed formats. These formats were introduced in 1981, and similar versions are in use throughout the European Community. This chapter deals with the formats and rules governing their use, which are illustrated by a number of examples drawn from the accounts of several public companies.

The provisions referred to above govern the accounts which all companies must lay before their shareholders. In addition all limited companies must deposit accounts with the Registrar of Companies. However, for this purpose small and medium-sized companies are allowed to modify their accounts to show less information.

This chapter deals with two further aspects of Company Law:

(1) the calculation of distributable profits; and
(2) the disclosure of transactions involving directors.

THE GENERAL REGULATIONS GOVERNING COMPANY ACCOUNTS

The Companies Act lays down the following basic requirements governing the accounts laid before the members:

- all accounts must comply with Schedule 4 of the Act with respect to their form and content; and

- all accounts must show a true and fair view of the state of affairs at the balance sheet date and of the results for the period.

The requirement to show a true and fair view overrides all other requirements of the Companies Act. The Act also states that companies may depart from its detailed requirements where to comply would prevent a true and fair view being shown by the accounts and also where additional information is required in order for the accounts to show a true and fair view. However in such cases the accounts must show particulars of the departure, the reasons for it, and its effect. The significance of these provisions is that accounts must comply with generally accepted accounting practice, often embodied in accounting standards, in order to show a true and fair view at all times. Where both the auditors and the directors agree on an alternative presentation in order to show a true and fair view this will be acceptable under the Companies Act. However, this provision does not enable companies to show less information than the Act requires because of the obligation to explain departures.

THE STANDARD FORMATS FOR ACCOUNTS

The Companies Act lays down a number of general rules governing the use of the standard formats. It stipulates that every balance sheet and profit and loss account prepared by a company shall show the items listed, in the order, and under the headings and sub-headings given in the format adopted. There are two alternative balance sheet formats and four profit and loss account formats.

The formats are reproduced on p. 100 to 103 and will be discussed in more detail below, but before doing so it is necessary to outline the general rules governing their use.

- The items shown in the formats are designated by letters, roman numbers and arabic numbers. For example the letter B represents Fixed Assets, BII refers to Tangible Assets, and BII 2 represents Plant and Machinery. The purpose of the letters and numbers is to denote the position of items; they do not form part of the formats as such, and are not to be reproduced as part of the accounts.
- Those items prefaced by arabic numbers may be combined if not material or if the combination facilitates assessment of the state of affairs of the company or of the profit or loss for the year. Those amounts combined to facilitate assessment must be shown in the notes to the accounts.
- The directors of a company are required to rearrange and to adapt the items designated by arabic numbers where the special nature of the company's business requires it.
- Companies are allowed to introduce additional items where necessary and to show items in greater detail.
- Companies may disregard any amounts which are immaterial in the

particular context of any provision of Schedule 4 to the Act which contains the formats and rules.

- Where there are no amounts for any particular heading then that item need not be shown, unless there was an amount in the preceeding year.
- Corresponding amounts must be shown for each item appearing in the accounts, and where these are not comparable to the amount appearing in the previous accounts the amount must be adjusted. In such cases particulars of the adjustment, and the reasons for it are to be disclosed in the notes to the accounts.
- Amounts in respect of items representing assets or income may not be set off against amounts in respect of liabilities or expenditure or vice versa. Thus a company may not set amounts due from group companies against amounts due to group companies except where there is a genuine legal right of set off.

Once a company has adopted one of the standard formats it must continue to use it in subsequent years, unless in the opinion of the directors there are special reasons for change. In such circumstances the notes to the accounts must disclose particulars of the change and the reasons for it. Under this provision a company would be entitled to adopt a new format where the basic nature of the business had changed, and the old format was not longer suitable.

The overall effect of these provisions is that many companies show most of the items appearing in the formats as notes to the accounts, and in the balance sheet generally show only the headings denoted by letters and roman numerals.

THE BALANCE SHEET

The Companies Act provides two alternative formats for the balance sheet. *Format 1* incorporates a division of creditors into those falling due within one year and those falling due within a longer period. This split permits the calculation of a figure for net current assets or liabilities, although it is worth noting that the figure produced includes debtors falling due after more than a year. The Act does not stipulate where the balance sheet total is to be taken. Under format 1 this may be, *inter alia*, after item J to balance with the capital and reserves, or at line G to balance with items H, I, J, and K.

Format 2 arranges items as assets and liabilities, but does not specify whether they must be listed vertically or horizontally, thus in the latter arrangement a traditional balance sheet is possible. It is interesting to note that in this case the historic arrangement of capital at the top left hand corner of the balance sheet will end with fixed assets usually taking its place. This change has the advantage of making balance sheets consistent with the precepts of double entry book-keeping where assets always appear on the left! It also seems likely that format 2 will appeal to those companies which suffer from perrenial liquidity problems, and which would rather not show the net current liabilities item required in format 1.

The Act stipulates that companies may not include certain items as assets in their balance sheet. These are:

- preliminary expenses;
- expenses of and commission on the issue of shares or debentures; and
- costs of research.

As a result, such items must be charged to the profit and loss account in the year in which they are incurred. The last named is, in any case, prohibited under Standard Accounting Practice, although development expenditure may be shown as an asset under certain restricted circumstances.

Although the first item in the balance sheet is Called Up Share Capital Not Paid few companies open their balance sheets with this item because, apart from being fairly rare in practice, it may also be shown in a less conspicuous position as Item CII 5, which most companies prefer. However it is worth noting that before the 1981 Act came into force this item was usually shown as a deduction from share capital. Most bankers would probably prefer not to regard unpaid calls as an asset. Similarly, many companies also adopted the practice of showing intangible assets as a deduction from share capital. However, since the 1981 Act this practice has also been prohibited. The general effect of the Companies Act rules is that most companies commence their balance sheets with fixed assets, and with any intangible assets as the first of these.

Fixed Assets. The Act defines fixed assets as "those assets acquired by the business and intended for use on a continuing basis." Because of the limited number of headings available it is necessary for each company to decide whether an item is a fixed or current asset and to present it accordingly. The heading of assets which are neither fixed nor current, allowed under the old regulations, was abolished by the Act.

The categories of fixed assets shown in the format is not exhaustive and needs to be adapted and augmented by most firms. For example there is no category for motor vehicles, which must either be shown within another heading such as plant and machinery, or brought in as an additional item.

Investments. The several headings shown for investments are designed for the accounts of individual companies, which may themselves be part of a group. The Companies Act 1981 was not framed to take account of group accounts because of the impending publication of the Seventh Directive on company law by the European Community Commission which deals with this topic. However, companies must adapt the formats when preparing group accounts. This topic, and the definitions of group companies and related companies is considered in more depth in Chapter 6.

The headings shown under investments for own shares (BIII 7 and CIII 3) will rarely be used as companies were barred under the Companies Act 1980 from acquiring their own shares. The 1981 Act revised the position so that, under certain circumstances, a company may purchase its own shares. However in this case the shares must be cancelled. As a result, the only occasions in which these headings are likely to be used are when the shares are acquired under the direction of the court, or when the shares are received as a gift, and are shown at a valuation. Neither circumstance is likely to be very common!

Current assets. The detailed provisions regarding current assets are fairly straightforward, although it is important to note that trade debtors, prepayments and other debtors must now be shown separately.

Creditors. Whichever format a company uses, the information to be disclosed in the accounts is identical. However, format 1 requires the split into items due within and after one year to be shown on the face of the balance sheet, whilst with format 2 it is shown as a note. Strangely, the formats include a heading for bills of exchange payable, although bills receivable is not shown. The formats require companies to show long term finance, including debentures as part of creditors, and not as an addition to share capital and reserves.

Share capital and reserves. Five main headings are laid down, each of which is designated by a roman number, and must therefore appear on the face of the balance sheet. The revaluation reserve must include all surpluses arising on the revaluation of fixed assets, including those arising before the new legislation came into force. However the Act permits companies to call this reserve by another name if they wish. Share premium accounts show the sum received when shares are issued at an amount above par value, so far as this has not been used for the limited purposes allowed by the Companies Act: issuing fully paid up bonus shares, writing off preliminary expenses or expenses on the issue of shares or debentures, or (subject to certain restrictions) paying a premium on the redemption of shares. A capital redemption reserve must often be created when shares are redeemed. These topics will be considered in more depth in Chapter 12.

THE PROFIT AND LOSS ACCOUNT

The Companies Act includes four alternative formats for the profit and loss account. However, the information shown in formats 1 and 2 differs from that shown in formats 3 and 4, respectively, only with regard to the arrangement of the figures. The latter alternatives offer horizontal arrangements of the items shown in the layouts reproduced on pp. 107 and 108.

Format 1. The distinguishing feature of format 1 is the analysis of costs under the headings cost of sales, distribution costs, and administrative costs, and disclosure of a figure for gross profit. In calculating the cost under each heading depreciation attributable to each category must be included, but the amount concerned does not have to be separately disclosed. The use of this format permits calculation of the relationship between turnover and gross profit.

Companies Act — Balance Sheet Format 1

	£	£	£
A CALLED UP SHARE CAPITAL NOT PAID			X
B FIXED ASSETS			
I INTANGIBLE ASSETS	X		
1 Development costs	X		
2 Concessions, patents, licences, trade marks and similar rights and assets	X		
3 Goodwill	X		
4 Payments on account	X		
	—	X	
II TANGIBLE ASSETS			
1 Land and buildings	X		
2 Plant and machinery	X		
3 Fixtures, fittings, tools and equipment	X		
4 Payments on account and assets in course of construction	X		
	—	X	
III INVESTMENTS			
1 Shares in group companies	X		
2 Loans to group companies	X		
3 Shares in related companies	X		
4 Loans to related companies	X		
5 Other investments other than loans	X		
6 Other loans	X		
7 Own shares	X		
	—	X	
C CURRENT ASSETS		—	
I STOCKS			X
1 Raw materials and consumables	X		
2 Work-in-progress	X		
3 Finished goods and goods for resale	X		
4 Payments on account	X		
	—	X	
II DEBTORS (Amounts due after more than one year to be shown separately)			
1 Trade debtors	X		
2 Amounts owed by group companies	X		
3 Amounts owed by related companies	X		
4 Other debtors	X		
5 Called up share capital not paid (or as Item A)	X		
6 Prepayments and accrued income (or as Item D)	X		
	—	X	
III INVESTMENTS			
1 Shares in group companies	X		
2 Own shares	X		
3 Other investments	X		
	—	X	
IV CASH AT BANK AND IN HAND		X	
		—	
D PREPAYMENTS AND ACCRUED INCOME		X	X
		X	X
		—	—
			XX

Note Totals and sub-totals are shown in order to assist presentation – they are not part of the standard formats of the Companies Act.

Companies Act – Balance Sheet Format 1 continued

		£	£	£
			X	X
E	CREDITORS: AMOUNTS FALLING DUE WITHIN ONE YEAR			
	1 Debenture loans	X		
	2 Bank loans and overdrafts	X		
	3 Payments received on account (in so far as not deducted from stocks)	X		
	4 Trade creditors	X		
	5 Bills of exchange payable	X		
	6 Amounts owed to group companies	X		
	7 Amounts owed to related companies	X		
	8 Other creditors including taxation and social security (taxation and social security to be shown separately)			
	9 Accruals and deferred income (or as Item J)	X	—	
		—	X	
F	NET CURRENT ASSETS (LIABILITIES)			X
				—
G	TOTAL ASSETS LESS CURRENT LIABILITIES			X
H	CREDITORS: AMOUNTS FALLING DUE AFTER MORE THAN ONE YEAR			
	1 Debenture loans (convertible loans to be shown separately)	X		
	2 Bank loans and overdrafts	X		
	3 Payments received on account (in so far as not deducted from stocks)	X		
	4 Trade creditors	X		
	5 Bills of exchange payable	X		
	6 Amounts owed to group companies	X		
	7 Amounts owed to related companies	X		
	8 Other creditors including taxation and social security (taxation and social security to be shown separately)	X		
	9 Accruals and deferred income (or as Item J)	X	X	
		—		
I	PROVISIONS FOR LIABILITIES AND CHARGES			
	1 Pensions and similar obligations	X		
	2 Taxation, including deferred taxation	X		
	3 Other provisions	X	X	
		—		
J	ACCRUALS AND DEFERRED INCOME		X	
			—	
				X
				—
				XX
				═
K	CAPITAL AND RESERVES			
	I CALLED UP SHARE CAPITAL			X
	II SHARE PREMIUM ACCOUNT			X
	III REVALUATION RESERVE			X
	IV OTHER RESERVES			X
	1 Capital redemption reserve		X	
	2 Reserve for own shares		X	
	3 Reserves provided for by the articles of association		X	
	4 Other reserves		X	
			—	X
	V PROFIT AND LOSS ACCOUNT			X
				—
				XX
				═

Companies Act – Balance Sheet Format 2

	£	£	£
ASSETS			
A CALLED UP SHARE CAPITAL NOT PAID			X
B FIXED ASSETS			
I INTANGIBLE ASSETS			
1 Development costs	X		
2 Concession, patents, licences, trade marks and similar rights and assets	X		
3 Goodwill	X		
4 Payments on account	X		
	—	X	
II TANGIBLE ASSETS			
1 Land and buildings	X		
2 Plant and machinery	X		
3 Fixtures, fittings, tools and equipment	X		
4 Assets under construction/payments on account	X		
	—	X	
III INVESTMENTS			
1 Shares in group companies	X		
2 Loans to group companies	X		
3 Shares in related companies	X		
4 Loans to related companies	X		
5 Other investments	X		
6 Other loans	X		
7 Own shares	X		
	—	X	
		—	X
C CURRENT ASSETS			
I STOCKS			
1 Raw materials and consumables	X		
2 Work-in-progress	X		
3 Finished goods and goods for resale	X		
4 Payments on account	X		
	—	X	
II DEBTORS (amounts due after more than one year to be shown separately)			
1 Trade debtors	X		
2 Amounts owed by group companies	X		
3 Amounts owed by related companies	X		
4 Other debtors	X		
5 Called up share capital not paid (or as item A)	X		
6 Prepayments and accrued income (or as item D)	X		
	—	X	
III INVESTMENTS			
1 Shares in group companies	X		
2 Own shares	X		
3 Other investments	X		
	—	X	
IV CASH AT BANK AND IN HAND			X
D PREPAYMENTS AND ACCRUED INCOME			X
			—
			£XX
			—

Companies Act – Balance Sheet Format 2 continued

	£	£	£
LIABILITIES			
A CAPITAL AND RESERVES			
I CALLED UP SHARE CAPITAL		X	
II SHARE PREMIUM ACCOUNT		X	
III REVALUATION RESERVE		X	
IV OTHER RESERVES			
1 Capital redemption reserve	X		
2 Reserve for own shares	X		
3 Reserves provided for by articles of association	X		
4 Other reserves	X	X	
V PROFIT AND LOSS ACCOUNT	—	X	
		—	
B PROVISIONS FOR LIABILITIES AND CHARGES			X
1 Pensions and similar obligations	X		
2 Taxation including deferred taxation		X	
3 Other provisions		X	
		—	X
C CREDITORS (amounts due after more than one year to be shown separately)			
1 Debenture loans (convertible loans to be shown separately)		X	
2 Bank loans and overdrafts		X	
3 Payments received on account (in so far as not deducted from stocks)		X	
4 Trade creditors		X	
5 Bills of exchange payable		X	
6 Amounts due to group companies		X	
7 Amounts due to related companies		X	
8 Other creditors including taxation and social security (taxation and social security to be shown separately)		X	
9 Accruals and deferred income (or as item D)		X	X
D ACCRUALS AND REFERRED INCOME		—	X
			£XX

Nevertheless it must be noted that most of the terms used in the Act are not defined and therefore it is likely that a wide disparity of practice will result. One term which is defined is Turnover, which is stated to be "the amount derived from the provision of goods and services falling within the companies ordinary activities, after deduction of trade discounts, value added tax, and other taxes based on the amounts so derived."

Format 2. This format allows companies to avoid disclosing gross profit to competitors and is best suited to use by manufacturing concerns. Items 6 and 7, must be disclosed as notes when format 1 is used. As with format 1, some terminology is confusing, with no definition provided of the terms "other external charges" and "other operating charges".

Apart from items 1 to 6 in format 1 and items 1 to 9 in format 2 the items in each format are identical. Of the items shown on p. 107 and 108, three do not have numbers. These items are not part of the standard formats laid down in the Act, but are required to be included under the general regulations governing their operation. As a result they do not have arabic numbers to denote their position, and must always be included on the face of the profit and loss account. By contrast the other items shown in the formats are designated by numbers, and therefore under the rule already noted may, in theory at least, all be shown as a note to the accounts. In practice few companies take advantage of this provision in its entirety, although many show some items as notes.

As with the balance sheet the directors are obliged to show items under the headings shown, and must thus use the terminology of the Act except where the special nature of the business requires an alteration. In practice this will often be the case, because many firms find that the formats do not suit their business completely. In addition it is necessary to interpret the provisions flexibly, for instance omitting words such as "other", "profit", and "loss" where they are clearly inappropriate or redundant. The formats incorporate the words, exceptional, ordinary, and extraordinary, without defining them. However such terminology is dealt with in Statement of Standard Accounting Practice No. 6, and it is convenient to deal with this subject here.

EXTRAORDINARY ITEMS, EXCEPTIONAL ITEMS AND PRIOR YEAR ADJUSTMENTS

For accounts to show a true and fair view it is essential, not only that the items are calculated accurately, but also that they are disclosed and described in a manner which properly reflects their importance to shareholders. In particular the profit or loss for the year should include only the normal recurring activities of the business. Thus SSAP 6 was introduced in order to lay down a standard treatment for "unusual" items. The standard was largely intended to stamp out the practice of showing embarrassing items as movements in reserves, hidden in the notes to the accounts, which are often not examined by shareholders – a process known as "reserve accounting". SSAP 6 introduced two terms to describe unusual items and these have been incorporated in the profit and loss account formats of the Companies Act. In addition the standard also dealt with the problem of items which affect the figures of prior years. By 1985 a number of problems had arisen with the application of SSAP 6 and the ASC decided to propose a revised standard, ED 36, with the same title: "Extraordinary items and prior year adjustments". The definitions and examples which follow are derived from ED 36, but are not significantly different from those contained in SSAP 6.

Extraordinary items are defined as:

> "Those items which derive from events or transactions that fall outside the ordinary activities of the company and which are both material and expected not to recur frequently or regularly. They do not include items which, though exceptional by virtue of size or incidence (and which therefore require separate disclosure), fall within the ordinary

activities of the company. Neither do they include prior year items merely because they relate to a prior year."

In ED 36 it is explained that examples of extraordinary items could be the profits or losses arising from the following:

"(a) the discontinuance of a significant business segment, either through termination or disposal;
(b) the sale of an investment not acquired with the intention of resale, such as investments in subsidiary and associated companies;
(c) provision made for the permanent diminution in value of a non-current asset because of unusual events or developments during the period; and
(d) the expropriation of assets."

In order to present fairly the results from the ordinary activities of the business ED 36 states that extraordinary items are required to be shown in the profit and loss account following the ordinary results. Companies should use the appropriate headings shown in the formats of the Companies Act. *Exceptional items* are defined as:

"Those items which, whilst deriving from events or transactions that fall within the ordinary activities of the company, need to be disclosed separately by virtue of their size or incidence if the financial statements are to give a true and fair view."

ED 36 lists the following examples of items which may be exceptional where they are material:

"(a) redundancy costs relating to continuing business segments;
(b) reorganisation costs unrelated to the discontinuance of a business segment;
(c) previously capitalised development expenditure written off other than as part of a process of amortisation;
(d) profits appropriated to employee share schemes;
(e) profits or losses on the disposal of fixed assets;
(f) abnormal charges for bad debts and write-offs of stocks and work in progress;
(g) abnormal provisions for losses on long-term contracts;
(h) surpluses arising on the settlement of insurance claims; and
(i) amounts received in settlement of insurance claims for consequential loss of profits."

In accordance with standard practice exceptional items should be reflected in the ascertainment of profit or loss on ordinary activities although, because of their exceptional size or incidence, they require separate disclosure for the financial statements to give a true and fair view. It will normally be sufficient to disclose exceptional items in a note to the financial statements although, if this treatment is adopted, exceptional items should be clearly identified as such, in order to avoid confusion with other statutory disclosure items. However, the standard requires that, where it is necessary to show separately the profit before exceptional items in order to give a true and fair view, exceptional items should be disclosed as a separate item in the profit and loss account.

Under the Companies Act exceptional items must be shown as supplementary information to format 1, but appear within the format as item 7(b) of format 2 if the amount written off relates to current assets. Under this format it appears that exceptional credits relating to current assets and all other exceptional items must also be shown as supplementary information, but it is left to individual companies to determine the heading under which to allocate the item concerned. Whichever format is chosen the inclusion of an exceptional item will affect the amount of the profit or loss on ordinary activities before tax which appears after line 12 in format 1 and line 14 in format 2.

The formats include four subheadings relating to extraordinary items, but in practice most companies combine these as one figure in the profit and loss account and show the individual amounts as a note. In each case the items are included after the calculation of profit or loss on ordinary activities before tax. When calculating the amount of an extraordinary item any tax liability or relief must be taken into account and excluded from the item for taxation on ordinary profits. The amount of tax on the extraordinary item must then be shown as item 18 or 20 depending on the format used. This contrasts with the case for exceptional items where the tax relating to the item must be shown as a note in accordance with SSAP 6, but the amount concerned is shown before deduction of tax, and the tax charge (or credit) is incorporated in the tax on ordinary activities.

Prior year adjustments are defined as:-

> "Those material adjustments applicable to prior years arising from changes in accounting policies and from corrections in fundamental errors. They do not include the normal recurring corrections and adjustments of accounting estimates made in prior years.

The standard requires prior year adjustments to be accounted for by restating prior years, with the result that the opening balance of retained profits will be adjusted accordingly. The effect of the change should be disclosed where practicable by showing separately in the restatement of the previous year the amount involved. Items which represent the normal recurring corrections and adjustments of accounting estimates made in prior years should be included in the profit and loss account for the year, and if material, their nature and size should be disclosed.

Example

A company to use a different method of valuing stocks with the result that £450,000 must be written off the reserves brought forward for 1974 of £48,890,000. Of the amount written off £275,000 relates to the years prior to 1973, and the balance to 1973 itself. The accounts must also include a full explanation of the reasons for the prior year adjustment.

Statement of retained profits/reserves

		£'000 1974		£'000 1973
Retained profit for the year		4,605		4,715
Retained profits/reserves at beginning of year				
As previously reported	48,890		44,000	
Prior year adjustment	450		275	
(Note)		48,440		43,725
Retained profits at end of year		53,045		48,440

A statement of retained profits and reserves showing any prior year adjustment should immediately follow the profit and loss account for the year, or else a reference to its disclosure should be given in the notes to the accounts.

Companies Act – Profit and Loss Account Format 1

		£	£
1	Turnover		X
2	Cost of sales *		(X)
3	Gross profit or loss		X
4	Distribution costs*		(X)
5	Administrative expenses *		(X)
6	Other operating income		X
7	Income from shares in group companies	X	
8	Income from shares in related companies	X	
			X
9	Income from other fixed asset investments	X	
10	Interest receivable and similar income †	X	
			X
11	Amounts written off investments		(X)
12	Interest payable and similar charges †		(X)
–	Profit or loss on ordinary activities before taxation		X
13	Tax on profit or loss on ordinary activities		(X)
14	Profit or loss on ordinary activities after taxation		X
15	Extraordinary income	X	
16	Extraordinary charges	(X)	
17	Extraordinary profit or loss	X	
18	Tax on extraordinary profit or loss	(X)	X
19	Other taxes not shown under the above items		(X)
20	Profit or loss for the financial year		X
–	Dividends		(X)
–	Transfer to (from) reserves		£XX

* including depreciation or diminution in value of assets (depreciation to be disclosed separately in a note to the accounts)

† income and interest from (to) group companies to be shown separately

Note
Format 3 shows identical information in a horizontal fashion.

Companies Act – Profit and Loss Account Format 2

	£	£	£
1 Turnover			X
2 Change in stocks of finished goods and in work-in-progress			X
3 Own work capitalised			X
4 Other operating income			X
5 (a) Raw materials and consumables	(X)		
(b) Other external charges	(X)	(X)	
	—		
6 Staff costs:			
(a) Wages and salaries	(X)		
(b) Social security costs	(X)		
(c) Other pension costs	(X)	(X)	
	—		
7 (a) Depreciation and other amounts written off tangible and intangible fixed assets	(X)		
(b) Exceptional amounts written off current assets	(X)	(X)	
	—		
8 Other operating charages		(X)	(X)
		—	—
			X
9 Income from shares in group companies		X	
10 Income from shares in related companies		X	
11 Income from other fixed asset investments		X	
12 Other interest receivable and similar income		X	X
			—
			X
13 Amounts written off investments			(X)
			—
			X
14 Interest payable and similar charges			(X)
			—
– Profit or loss on ordinary activities before taxation			X
15 Tax on profit or loss on ordinary activities			(X)
16 Profit or loss on ordinary activities after taxation			X
17 Extraordinary income		X	
18 Extraordinary charges		(X)	
19 Extraordinary profit or loss		X	
20 Tax on extraordinary profit or loss		(X)	
21 Other taxes not shown under the above items		—	X
			(X)
			—
22 Profit or loss for the financial year			X
– Dividends			(X)
– Transfer to (from) reserves			—
			£XX
			═

Note
Format 4 shows identical information arranged in a horizontal fashion.

THE SUPPLEMENTARY NOTES TO THE ACCOUNTS

Apart from the information which companies choose to show as notes to the accounts, rather than on the face of the profit and loss account or balance sheet, the Companies Act requires the disclosure of a mass of supplementary information. Much of this was already required under the 1948 Act, as amended in 1967, but several significant changes were made in 1981. A summary of the main provisions is shown as Appendix 1 but the key points are referred to below.

Accounting policies. Companies must disclose details of the accounting policies adopted in determining the amounts included in the accounts and in determining the profit or loss. (This information was already required by accounting standards but is now a legal requirement.)

Fixed assets. Details must be given of all movements in fixed assets, including investments held as fixed assets, and of movements in the cumulative depreciation provision.

Indebtedness. Details must be given of each item shown under creditors which falls due either in full or in part after five years unless the result would be a statement of excessive length. Furthermore companies must show the aggregate amount of items in respect of which security has been given, and since 1981 an indication of the nature of the security.

Guarantees and other financial commitments. Companies are required to give details of various other liabilities and potential liabilities, including contingent liabilities, contracts for capital expenditure, and pension commitments. In addition details must be given of any other financial commitment which has not been provided for and is relevant to assessing the company's state of affairs. This information is of particular use to bankers and other creditors, as well as to shareholders.

Turnover and results by class of business. Companies are required to give details of the turnover and profit or loss before tax attributable to each class where they are engaged in two or more substantially different classes of business. They must also show turnover, but need not show profit or loss, attributable to each geographical market where markets differ substantially from each other. However, the information need not be disclosed where, in the opinion of the directors, this would be seriously prejudicial to the interests of the company, but in this case the fact that such information has not been disclosed must be stated. Prior to the 1981 Act export turnover was disclosed in the directors report but this provision has been repealed.

Apart from the requirements of Schedule 4 companies are also required to show details of directors' emoluments, emoluments of highly paid employees, the identity of their ultimate holding company, and details of investments in subsidiaries, in each case if relevant. This information is required by other parts of the Companies Acts, and is described in more detail in Appendix 1.

THE DIRECTORS' REPORT

The Companies Act 1981 made significant changes in the information to be disclosed in the directors' report, but much of the information dates from earlier legslation. A summary of the items to be included is shown on p. 110–111, but a number of points are worth highlighting.

- For the first time the Companies Act 1981 brought the directors' report within the scope of the auditor's examination. (Many auditors had considered the report prior to 1981, but had done so unofficially.) The auditor need not make any reference to his examination of the directors' report when reporting on the accounts, but he must have considered whether the information given is consistent with the accounts. If there is any inconsistency then he must report the matter to the shareholders.
- Until the introduction of the Companies Act 1981 companies were able to include information required as part of the accounts within the directors' report, provided comparative figures were shown. This power was abolished in the 1981 Act.
- Under the 1948 Act directors were obliged to report to the members on the state of the company's affairs. This provision was extended in 1981 to require a fair review of the development of the business. In particular reference must be made to important post balance sheet events, likely future development, and an indication of activities in research and development, if any. In practice the information given under this provision has, in the past, been less helpful than it might have been.
- The remaining information to be given in the directors' report dates largely from 1967, but companies may now chose to show details of directors' interests in shares and debentures as a note to the accounts.
- Where a company continues to prepare accounts under the old provisions as shown in Schedule 9 to the Companies Act, it must show certain information concerning its classes of business, employees, and their remuneration within the directors' report.

The Companies Act – Information to be disclosed in the Directors' Report

1. Information to be given in Directors' Report
   - a fair review of the development of the business of the company and its subsidiaries;
   - particulars of important post-balance sheet events;
   - an indication of likely future developments;
   - an indication of activities in research and development (if any);
   - the amount of recommended dividends;
   - proposed transfers to reserves.
2. Directors' names.
3. Principal activities and significant changes.
4. Significant changes in fixed assets.
5. Market value of land – where substantially different from book value.

6. Interests of directors in contracts with the company.

7. Directors' interests in shares or debentures (May be given as note to accounts).

8. Arrangements for securing the health, safety and welfare at work of employees. (When and as prescribed by the Secretary of State).

9. Action taken to introduce, maintain, or develop arrangements concerned with employee involvement (if over 250 employees).

10. Statement of describing the company's policy in respect of the employment of disabled person. (if over 250 employees)

11. Political and charitable contributions.

12. Particulars of acquisition of company's own shares.

The auditors are to consider whether the information given in the directors' report is consistent with the accounts.

Where accounts are prepared under Schedule 9 (Special Category Accounts)
(e.g. Shipping, Banking and Insurance Companies)
Analysis of turnover and profit or loss before taxation
Average number of employees by category
Aggregate remuneration paid or payable to employees

Examples Drawn from the Accounts of Public Companies

Set out on p. 113 to 120 are extracts drawn from the accounts of several public companies which illustrate the way in which the provisions of the Companies Act may be employed.

Example 1 – Profit and Loss Account Format 1: Details shown on Face (Brooke Bond PLC)

Example 1 illustrates a profit and loss account where most of the items are shown on the face of the account. The company has introduced the additional heading "Operating Profit", and adapted the format to include the share of profits attributable to minority interests. Interest payments and receipts have been combined as one item and shown as a note to the accounts.

Example 2 – Profit and Loss Account Format 1: Details shown as Notes (Barratt Developments PLC)

This example illustrates how the profit and loss account will appear where most of the information is shown as a note to the accounts. Here the company discloses turnover as the first item, but the next 11 items are, where appropriate, shown as a note to the accounts. Thus the next figure appearing on the face of the profit and loss account is profit on ordinary activities before taxation.

Example 3 – Profit and Loss Account Format 2: Details on Face (Link House Publications PLC)

In this example (a Format 2 profit and loss account) the company shows the required headings on the face of the profit and loss account. It may be noted that it has adapted the heading "change in stocks" by omitting the words "in finished goods and in work in progress". It has classified the bulk of its expenses under the heading "other external charges" rather than "other operating charges", although there is no information in the accounts to indicate the distinction drawn between each.

Example 4 – Profit and Loss Account Format 2: Details as Notes (Glaxo Holdings PLC)

In this case the company has shown most of the profit and loss account items as a note to the main accounts. It has also rearranged the order of the items shown, apparently under the power conferred to rearrange items where the special nature of the business requires it. It may be noted that in this case the company has no amount shown under the heading "other external charges", but a considerable sum under that for " other operating charges". It has abbreviated the heading "taxation on ordinary activities" although the reasons for doing this is not obviously apparent.

Example 5 – Profit and Loss Account Format 1: Adapted (A and J Mucklow PLC)

This company derives its income from two different types of business: property rentals, and the sale of industrial buildings. Accordingly it has been necessary to adapt the profit and loss account which is designed for companies with only one form of income. It might be argued that both forms of income count as turnover in accordance with the definition shown on p. 103.

Example 6 – Profit and Loss Account Format 1: Adapted (Baillie Gifford Japan Trust PLC)

This example shows the extent to which specialised companies such as investment trusts need to adapt the formats of the Companies Acts. Here the company has shown income and interest from its investment portfolio as the first part of the profit and loss account, and has adapted the heading for profit to show revenue before and after taxation.

Example 7 – Balance Sheet Format 1 (Brooke Bond PLC)

The vast majority of companies use format 1 for their balance sheet. In this case the company has taken a total after line J, and included minority interest as an addition to share capital and reserves. All the subheadings from the format are shown as notes to the accounts.

Example 8 – Balance Sheet Format 1 (Mitchell Cotts)

As in the previous example this company has shown the subheadings as notes to the accounts. However it has added a new heading "Claims against governments". It has also added the headings "total net assets" and "total shareholders funds" against the appropriate totals. Once again the balance sheet has been totalled after line J, but in this case minority interests have been shown as a deduction from this figure.

These examples show that in practice the rules of the Companies Act allow wide diversity in the form and presentation of the statements prepared for shareholders.

EXAMPLE 1 – BROOKE BOND PLC

Group Profit and Loss Account – Format 1: Details on Face

for year ended 30 June 1983

Historical cost	*Notes*	*1983* *£m*	*1982* *£m*
Turnover	2(a)	913.7	953.7
Cost of sales		676.0	723.8
Gross profit		237.7	229.9
Distribution costs		120.4	118.4
Administrative expenses		59.1	62.0
Other operating income		2.1	2.9
Share of profits of related companies		3.3	4.4
Operating profit	2(b)	63.6	56.8
Interest	4	15.4	21.5
Profit on ordinary activities before tax	5	48.2	35.3
Tax on profit on ordinary activities	8	22.0	17.5
Profit on ordinary activities after tax		26.2	17.8
Minority interest		2.0	1.6
Earnings		24.2	16.2
Extraordinary items	9	(13.2)	(2.4)
Profit for the financial year	10	11.0	13.8
Dividends	11	12.8	12.2
Amount transferred from reserves	18(d)	(1.8)	1.6
Earnings per share on the net basis	11	7.77p	5.22p
Dividends per share		4.10p	3.905p

EXAMPLE 2 – BARRATT DEVELOPMENTS PLC

Group Profit and Loss Account – Format 1: Details as Notes

for year ended 30 June 1983

	Note	1983 £m	1982 £m
Turnover	1	512.9	385.8
Profit on ordinary activities before taxation	1	52.2	40.2
Tax on profit on ordinary activities	4	18.6	8.1
Profit on ordinary activities after taxation		33.6	32.1
Dividends	5	13.2	9.1
Profit retained		20.4	23.0
Dividend cover		2.5	3.5
Earnings per share	8		
Before taxation		31.1p	26.2p
After taxation		20.0p	20.9p

EXAMPLE 3 – LINK HOUSE PUBLICATIONS PLC & SUBSIDIARIES

Profit and Loss Account – Format 2: Details on Face

for year ended 30 June 1983

	Note	*1983*	*1982*
		£'000	£'000
Turnover	2	28,209	26,252
Change in stocks		77	(226)
Other operating income		20	44
		28,306	26,070
Less costs of operating:			
Raw materials and consumables		3,010	3,230
Other external charges		13,647	12,449
Staff costs	3	5,322	4,915
Depreciation	11	394	358
Other operating charges		219	136
Share of loss of related company		22	28
		22,614	21,116
Operating profit	4	5,692	4,954
Income from investments	5	708	697
Profit on ordinary activities before taxation	2	6,400	5,651
Tax on profit on ordinary activities	6	3,305	2,880
Profit on ordinary activities after taxation		3,095	2,771
Extraordinary item after taxation	7	39	—
Profit for the financial year		3,056	2,771
Dividends	8	1,668	1,476
Retained profit for the year	9	1,388	1,295
Earnings per share	10	25.79p	23.09p

The notes numbered 1 to 22 form part of these financial statements

EXAMPLE 4 – GLAXO HOLDINGS PLC

Consolidated Profit and Loss Account – Format 2: Details as Notes

for year ended 30 June 1983

	Note	1983 £m	1982 £m
Turnover	3	1,027.5	865.8
Operating costs	4	849.3	739.6
Trading profit		178.2	126.2
Share of profits of associated companies	3	9.8	6.4
Investment income less interest payable	6	4.4	1.0
Profit on ordinary activities before taxation		192.4	133.6
Taxation	7	75.2	52.2
Profit on ordinary activities after taxation		117.2	81.4
Minority interests		1.8	1.0
Profit for the financial year		115.4	80.4
Dividends	9	32.9	24.0
Retained profit transferred to reserves		82.5	56.4
Earnings per share	10	31.5 pence	23.4 pence

Note 4 shows the following information

4 Operating costs

The following are included in operating costs:	1983 £m	1982 £m
Raw materials, consumables and goods for resale	415.9	357.9
Staff costs	223.6	198.7
Depreciation	29.8	24.2
Other operating charges	214.8	183.7
	884.1	764.5
Deduct: Change in stocks of finished goods and work in progress	23.6	16.6
Own work capitalised	5.1	4.2
Other operating income	4.2	2.5
Investment and development grants	1.9	1.6
	34.8	24.9
	849.3	739.6

Other operating charges include:		
(i) Auditors' remuneration (Holding Company £68,000: 1982 – £60,000)	0.8	0.8
(ii) Hire of plant and machinery	5.9	4.8

EXAMPLE 5 – A AND J MUCKLOW GROUP PLC

Profit and Loss Account Adapted – Format 1

for year ended 30 June 1983

	Notes	*1983* *£000*	*1982* *£000*
Gross rentals	2	6,437	6,230
Property outgoings		(632)	(539)
Rental income		5,805	5,691
Turnover	3	3,262	6,080
Cost of sales		(2,745)	(4,861)
Trading profit		517	1,219
Investment income	4	457	298
		6,779	7,208
Distribution costs		—	(158)
Administration expenses		(1,189)	(1,562)
Interest payable	5	(752)	(774)
Profit on ordinary activities before taxation	6	4,838	4,714
Taxation	8	1,269	960
Profit on ordinary activities after taxation		3,569	3,754
Dividends	9	2,374	2,241
Retained profit		1,195	1,513
Earnings per share	10	6.80p	7.17p

The notes attached are an integral part of the accounts.

EXAMPLE 6 – THE BAILLIE GIFFORD JAPAN TRUST PLC

Profit and Loss Account Adapted – Format 1

for year ended 31 August 1983

		Notes	1983 £	1982 £
Income				
Income from investments		2	195,961	92,603
Interest receivable and other income		3	23,036	72,810
Gross income			218,997	165,413
Interest payable		4	*159*	*70*
			218,838	165,343
Administrative expenses		5	*175,070*	*92,062*
Revenue before taxation		-	43,768	73,281
Taxation		6	*29,660*	*29,312*
Revenue after taxation			14,108	43,969
Dividend proposed	0.10p 0.40p		*10,000*	*40,000*
Accumulated revenue				
Retained profit for the year			4,108	3,969
Brought forward			3,969	—
Carried forward			8,077	3,969
Earnings per ordinary share		7	0.14p	0.44p

EXAMPLE 7 – BROOKE BOND PLC

Group Balance Sheet Format 1: Minorities as Capital

at 30 June 1983

	Notes	1983		1982	
Historical cost		£m	£m	£m	£m
Fixed assets					
Tangible assets	12(a)		194.0		195.9
Investments	14(a)		14.2		14.6
			208.2		210.5
Current assets					
Stocks	13	195.3		181.0	
Debtors	15	148.2		142.5	
Cash at bank and in hand		16.1		24.7	
		359.6		348.2	
Creditors: amounts falling due within one year	16(a)	163.4		187.0	
Net current assets			196.2		161.2
Total assets less current liabilities			404.4		371.7
Creditors: amounts falling due after more than one year	16(b)		101.9		78.7
			302.5		293.0
Provisions for liabilities and charges	17		18.2		6.1
			284.3		286.9
Capital and reserves	18				
Called up share capital			77.9		77.9
Share premium account			31.0		31.0
Revaluation reserve			60.7		63.8
Other reserves			14.3		14.4
Profit and loss account			85.4		85.5
Shareholders' funds			269.3		272.6
Minority interest	19		15.0		14.3
			284.3		286.9

The accounts were approved by the board of directors on 18th October 1983 and are signed on its behalf by:

JOHN CUCKNEY

Directors

H.F. SOMERVILLE

EXAMPLE 8 – MITCHELL COTTS PLC

Consolidated Balance Sheet – Format 1: Minorities and Additional Headings

at 30 June 1983

	1983 £000s	*1982 £000s*	*Notes*
Fixed assets			
Intangible assets	5,424	*2,451*	9
Tangible assets	41,068	*39,148*	10
Investments	10,053	*10,883*	11
	56,545	*52,482*	
Current assets			
Stocks	35,139	*39,046*	12
Debtors			
Long term	3,242	*3,536*	13
Claims against governments	2,952	*2,952*	14
Other debtors	66,684	*66,416*	15
Cash at bank and in hand	6,833	*4,033*	
	114,850	*115,983*	
Creditors			
(amounts falling due within one year)			
Bank loans and overdrafts	26,009	*18,940*	16
Other creditors	62,636	*68,586*	17
	88,645	*87,526*	
Net current assets	26,205	*28,457*	
Total assets less current liabilities	82,750	*80,939*	
Creditors			
(amounts falling due after more than one year)			
Long and medium term loans	19,974	*21,805*	16
Provisions for liabilities and charges	1,032	*821*	18
Minority interests	283	*356*	
Total net assets	61,461	*57,957*	
Capital and reserves			
Called up share capital	19,046	*19,045*	19
Share premium account	5,787	*5,786*	20
Revaluation reserve	7,409	*7,675*	20
Other reserves	19,214	*15,076*	20
Profit and loss account	10,005	*10,375*	20
Total shareholders' funds	61,461	*57,957*	

Approved by the Board on 3rd November 1983

P.P. Dunkley Chairman
John R. Storar Deputy Chairman

THE ACCOUNTING EXEMPTIONS FOR SMALL AND MEDIUM-SIZED COMPANIES

The provisions described above govern the content of the accounts which all companies must lay before their shareholders. However, companies must also deposit a copy of their accounts with the Registrar of Companies for public inspection within their annual return. Whilst it was felt necessary for large companies to make available the same details as are submitted to their shareholders, it was considered that smaller companies deserved some privacy from the gaze of their creditors, competitors and the public generally. Accordingly the Companies Act 1981 provides for small and medium-sized companies to submit modified accounts to the Companies Registry. These exemptions are not available to public companies, banks, insurance and certain shipping companies, or to groups containing such companies. Thus a large public company cannot take advantage of these provisions to reduce the amount of information disclosed regarding its subsidiaries. However, a large private company could take advantage of the provisions for certain companies within the group. The exemptions are available for groups of companies which meet the criteria described below, with regard to the group accounts deposited at Companies House. The holding company's own accounts must follow the treatment related to the size of the group. Thus a holding company which files a modified set of accounts under the medium-sized exemptions for itself and its subsidiaries, cannot claim to be a small company on its own.

The criteria for distinguishing small and medium-sized companies is shown in Table 5.1 below. In applying these provisions account is taken of any two of the criteria shown, for the current and preceeding year. Thus a company may claim exemption as a small company if it has 50 employees, but no more, and its turnover did not exceed £1.4m provided it was entitled to exemption on the basis of the previous year's figures, but not necessarily on the same criteria. In this case the balance sheet total is of no relevance because two of the criteria have already been met, which is all that is required.

Table 5.1

Criteria for Small and Medium Sized Companies

Criteria	Balance sheet Total (Items A–D in Formats)	Net turnover	Average weekly no. of employees throughout year
Small	£0.7m	£1.4m	50
Medium	£2.8m	£5.75m	250

Note

The value of the criteria will be changed from time to time in line with price levels.

Once a company has obtained status as a small or medium-sized company it is allowed to retain its classification in the first year in which it is unable to meet the criteria. However, if in the succeeding year it again fails to do so it must change its status.

THE MODIFIED ACCOUNTS OF A SMALL COMPANY

A small company or group of companies, as defined by the Companies Act, is allowed to deposit a modified balance sheet. The provisions are as follows:

- Items preceded by arabic numerals may be grouped together, and need not be shown in the notes to the accounts.
- It is therefore only essential to show items covered by the letters and the roman numbers.
- Debts falling due and payable in greater than a year must be disclosed in total.
- Creditors falling due and payable in less than a year, and those falling due and payable in more than a year need only be shown in total.
- A small company is relieved of the requirements to deposit a profit and loss account and a directors' report.

NOTES TO THE ACCOUNTS

Information relating the the following must be given:

- accounting policies;
- share capital;
- particulars of allotments;
- particulars of debts;
- basis of translation of foreign currency;
- corresponding amounts for previous year.

Information on directors emoluments and higher paid employees need not be given.

Shown on page 123 and 124 is an example of a modified form of a balance sheet for a small company and the accompanying notes.

THE MODIFIED ACCOUNTS OF A MEDIUM-SIZED COMPANY

The exemptions granted to a medium-sized company are far less generous than those given to a small company. It may modify its profit and loss account so that turnover and certain cost items are not shown. In the case of format 1 a company may combine under one heading of gross profit the items shown as items 1, 2, 3, and 6. Those companies using format 2, are able to combine items

Companies Act – Modified form of Balance Sheet for Small Companies (Format 1)

		£	£
B	FIXED ASSETS		
	I Intangible assets		X
	II Tangible assets		X
	III Investments		X
			X
C	CURRENT ASSETS		
	I Stocks	X	
	II Debtors	X	
	III Investments	X	
	IV Cash at bank and in hand	X	
		X	
E	CREDITORS		
	Amounts falling due within one year	(X)	
F	NET CURRENT ASSETS (LIABILITIES)		X
G	TOTAL ASSETS LESS CURRENT LIABILITIES		X
H	CREDITORS		
	Amounts due after more than one year		(X)
I	PROVISIONS FOR LIABILITIES AND CHARGES		(X)
			£XX
K	CAPITAL AND RESERVES		
	I Called up capital		X
	II Share premium account		X
	III Revaluation reserve		X
	IV Other reserves		X
	V Profit and loss account		X
			£XX

1 to 5. Similar provisions operate for companies using formats 3 and 4. However a medium-sized company must show all of the remaining items in the standard format in the profit and loss account filed at Companies House, and it must also deposit a full balance sheet and a copy of the directors' report.

THE AUDITOR'S SPECIAL REPORT

The Accounts deposited at the Companies Registry must, where appropriate, include a statement by the directors that they have relied upon the exemptions for small and medium sized companies. In addition a special auditor's report is required stating that in his opinion the requirements for

Companies Act – Example of Modified Form of Notes

1. ACCOUNTING POLICIES
   ( ) . . . .
   ( ) Amounts in foreign currencies have been translated into sterling on the basis . . .

2. SHARE CAPITAL

	£
Authorised	XX
Allotted	XX

. . . shares were allotted during the year at an amount of . . . per share for the purpose of . . .

3. CREDITORS
   The analysis of borrowings by repayment date is as follows:

	£	£
Repayable otherwise than by instalments		
Due within five years	X	
Due after five years	X	X
Repayable by instalments		
Due within five years	X	
Due after five years	X	X
		£XX

The amount of £XX included above is secured by . . .

Note
Other disclosure requirements included elsewhere in the Companies Acts still apply. For example:

- Directors' loans (CA 1980, s. 54)
- Identity of ultimate parent (CA 1967, s. 5)

Specific exemption for disclosure of directors' remuneration under CA 1948, s. 196 and CA 1967, ss. 6–8 is given by CA 1981, s. 6(2).

exemption are satisfied, followed by the full text of the audit report made on the statutory accounts.

DISTRIBUTABLE PROFITS UNDER THE COMPANIES ACTS

Prior to the Companies Act of 1980 there were no statutory rules governing the profits which a company might distribute to its shareholders. Such rules as existed were derived from a body of case law much of it uncertain in significance, and some of it appearing to conflict. Accordingly it was felt necessary to regularise the position and this was done in the Companies Act 1980. This Act laid down that a company might only make a distribution of its assets to its shareholders out of profits available for the purpose. These are defined as its accumulated undistributed realised profits less its accumulated realised losses, so far as each has not been utilised or written off. There are further restrictions on public companies which must also consider their unrealised profits and losses. In the case of public companies, at the time of the distribution, the amount of net assets must not be less than the aggregate of called up share capital and undistributable reserves. Additionally the aggregate of the share capital and undistributable reserves must not be reduced as the result of a distribution. The undistributable reserves are defined as comprising the share premium account, the capital redemption reserve, accumulated unrealised profits (less unrealised losses), and any reserve which the company is prohibited from distributing by statute of by its memorandum or articles. This last category includes the capital redemption reserve, which must not be distributed by law. The effect of this complicated provision is that a public company must consider any unrealised losses. If these exceed the accumulated unrealised profits then the amount of the excess must be set against the surplus of realised profits less losses, and will reduce the distributable profits.

An important aspect in interpreting these provisions is the meaning to be put on the term "realised". This might be taken to mean realised in the form of cash, realised as an enforceable debt (the usual assumption in accounting), or realised in accordance with accounting practice, as is the case with profits or long-term contracts which are assumed to be realised during the progress of the contract. Unfortunately no definition of the term realised was provided in the 1980 Act, although a change was made in the 1981 Act to correct the position. "Realised profits" are to be calculated in accordance with the generally accepted accounting principles in force at the time when the accounts are prepared. Unfortunately this definition is not itself without problems, because it is not always clear just exactly what is an accepted accounting policy at a particular time. However, it is certainly likely to mean that the accounts must comply with the accounting principles and rules laid down by the Companies Act, and with Accounting Standards where these are relevant. However, there are a number of areas where accounting practice includes a variety of treatments, and where opinions differ on whether they are all generally acceptable.

The 1980 Act stipulates that the calculation of distributable profits must normally be made by reference to the most recently audited balance sheet. In cases where the audit report contains a qualification no dividend may legally be paid unless the auditor has stated in writing, either at the time of his report or subsequently, whether in his opinion the qualification is material for the purpose of determining whether the distribution would contravene the Act.[1]

[1] The calculation of distributable profits under the Companies Act 1980 is a complex matter and the discussion here only summarises the main provisions. Those wishing to consider the position in more depth will find two statements issued by the Consultative Committee of Accountancy Bodies, both published in *Accountancy* in October 1982, of particular value. These are

"The determination of realised profits and disclosure of distributable profits in the context of the Companies Acts 1948 to 1981" and
"The determination of distributable profits in the context of the Companies Acts 1948 to 1981."

The foregoing provisions may be illustrated by a simple example.

Example

Langrick Ltd has prepared its accounts for the year ended 31 March 1984. These show the following balances:

	£
Called up share capital	200,000
Share premium account	27,500
Revaluation reserve	(37,500)
Profit and loss account	94,000
	£284,000

The distributable profits would be calculated as follows:
(i) For a private company: all retained profits – £94,000
(ii) For a public limited company: realised profits less the excess of unrealised losses over unrealised profits – £84,000.

Where the revaluation deficit does not arise on a revaluation of all the fixed assets excluding goodwill, a private company must treat the deficit as a realised loss. Consideration by the directors of the value of all fixed assets counts as a revaluation for this purpose.

In addition to the basic provisions, the Companies Act 1980 laid down a number of detailed rules, some of which were amended by the 1981 Act:

- Realised losses must include provisions against current assets.
- Unrealised profits cannot be used:
  to write-off realised losses;
  in paying up debentures or any amounts unpaid on any of its issued shares.
- There may be more restrictive requirements regarding profits available for distribution in a company's memorandum.
- Capitalised development costs are a realised loss unless special circumstances justify otherwise.
- If a company has:
  revalued a fixed asset so that it gives rise to an unrealised profit, and
  charges depreciation on the revalued amounts against *distributable* profits, then the additional depreciation charged because the asset has been revalued *may* be added back to the realised profit for the purpose of calculating distributable profits and deducted from the revaluation surplus.
- Surpluses arising on the revaluation of assets over original cost are invariably recognised as unrealised in accordance with best accounting practice. However, in some cases part of the surplus may arise from the writing back of a realised loss frequently attributable to past depreciation. There is at present no unanimity of opinion as to whether such a surplus, to the extent that it represents the writing back of a realised loss, particularly when the realised loss arises from past depreciation, constitutes a realised profit. Where reliance is placed on such a profit being realised in order to

make a distribution, it may be appropriate for the directors of the company to seek legal advice.

- Revaluation deficits are to be treated as realised losses unless appearing on a revaluation of *all* the fixed assets of the company except goodwill. However, where the directors "consider" the value of any fixed asset this may count as a revaluation. Where assets are treated as revalued in this way the directors must be satisfied that their aggregate value at the time in question is not less than the aggregate amount at which they are being stated in the company's accounts.

THE DISCLOSURE OF TRANSACTIONS INVOLVING DIRECTORS

Transactions involving directors are of particular importance to many users of company accounts including bankers and other creditors. Whatever the law might say on the subject regarding the separate identity of a company and those who administer it, there is little doubt that many company directors regard the activities of "their" company as merely an extension of their own business activities and the company's assets as their own. Nevertheless it is important to third parties that assets do not leave companies except through the legally controlled distribution procedures described above. In order to achieve this objective the Companies Act 1948 laid down that loans to directors were illegal, except in certain specified circumstances. However it has proved particularly difficult to enforce this provision and accordingly in the Companies Act of 1980 the old regulations were repealed and replaced by an entirely new set of rules, which are intended to be more effective.

It is beyond the scope of the present text to describe the provisions governing loans to directors in the detail which the subject requires for a full understanding. Thus only the main essentials will be dealt with, and where necessary reference should be made to the relevant sections of the Companies Act.[2]

The Companies Act of 1980 lays down that with a few exceptions loans to directors are illegal. Furthermore it applies the prohibition to "persons on whose directions or instructions the directors of a company are accustomed to act" who are termed "*Shadow Directors*". Thus, those who are directors in all but name and control a company are covered by the legislation. Furthermore the Act prohibits most loans to persons closely related to or in partnership with the director; such persons being termed *connected persons*. In addition the provisions deal not only with simple loans, but also cover *quasi-loans*, where the director is the debtor of the company which is itself liable for the debt, as happens where a director uses a company credit card for a private transaction, and *credit transactions*, where goods are supplied to a director with the company acting as the immediate debtor in place of the director. The prohibition on loans also covers situations in which the company provides security, and assumes rights, obligations and liabilities under an arrangement which would have been illegal if actually undertaken by the company.

[2] The relevant sections of the Companies Act 1985 are 330 to 344.

The most important exemptions from prohibition are that loans not exceeding £2,500 are allowed, as are loans to meet expenses incurred or to be incurred on behalf on the company, subject to approval by general meeting or repayment within six months if approval is not given. In the case of a public company or a private company which is a member of a group including a public company, termed a relevant company, the latter exemption is limited to £10,000. There are special regulations governing loans by money-lending companies in the ordinary course of business, in connection with house purchase, and by group companies where the director is a nominee of the company concerned.

The Companies Act 1980 includes severe penalties for the breach of these regulations by a public company, but in the case of a private company seeks to regulate such loans by means of their disclosure in the accounts, whether legal or illegal.

Disclosure Provisions. The Companies Act requires disclosure of all loans and other transactions involving directors and connected persons. This provision applies to loans of less than £2,500, which are allowed under the Act, and to all other types of transaction similar in effect to the giving of a loan as outlined above. The Act stipulates that the accounts must show:

- a statement of the fact that the transaction subsisted;
- details of the principle terms;
- the names of the parties concerned and the nature of their interest;
- in the case of a loan:
  - the amount outstanding at the beginning and end of the period
  - the maximum liability during the period
  - the amount of any interest due but unpaid
  - the amount of any provision to cover default; and
- in the case of a guarantee or provision of security similar details.

There are a number of exemptions to these requirements covering recognised banks and small interests in transactions other than loans.

THE COMPANIES ACTS AND THE BANKER

The Companies Act 1981 produced some positive gains for the banker but also some adverse developments. The accounts of companies prepared under the Act are rather more informative than under the previous legislation. In particular the analysis of costs is more detailed, and the provisions governing the disclosure of indebtedness and other liabilities more comprehensive. However, this information has often been available to bankers on a confidential basis whilst not disclosed in the published accounts. The introduction of modified accounts for smaller companies is of little consequence, for lending bankers are well advised to insist on seeing the accounts which were submitted to the shareholders.

However, in cases where the banker needs to refer to accounts deposited at Companies House he will find them less informative than before. In this respect it must be observed that in the past many companies have been remiss in submitting accounts promptly or at all. For a bank's customers, the Act imposes a considerable burden, with shareholders compelled to receive more detailed, and probably more expensive, accounts whether they want to or not. The opportunity to submit less information to Companies House is also a dubious benefit requiring, as it does, the preparation of a separate set of figures, and a second audit report.

Before leaving the topic of the Companies Acts, and particularly that of the 1981 Act, two further points should be made. First, the Companies Act 1981 did not deal exclusively with company accounts; it also includes sections dealing with the purchase by a company of its own shares, the issue of redeemable shares, and loans to enable others to buy a company's own shares. All of these provisions are highly complex, and beyond the scope of the present work. However they are potentially of great value to companies, especially the small family concern. Thus every banker should become familiar with this legislation. Secondly, the Act of 1985 is unlikely to mark the end of changes in company law. The European Community has issued or plans to issue other directives on company law. Within the United Kingdom the topic of company insolvency has been the subject of a committee of inquiry, and major changes are taking place in the company law on the subject.

FURTHER READING

Many books have been published on the Companies Act 1981, several of them containing the full text of the Act. The complexities posed by the inter-relationships with other Companies Acts and Accounting Standards are well dealt with in books published by Butterworth's and Coopers and Lybrand, respectively. Most major firms of Accountants have prepared their own booklets on the 1981 Act and will often make these available to bankers on request. The book by Sutcliffe and Patient was prepared by Deloitte, Haskins and Sells, Chartered Accountants.

A. Hardcastle and M. Renshall (eds)., *The Companies Act 1981* (ICAEW, Butterworths 1981).

K. Walmsley (ed)., *Butterworth's Company Law Handbook* (3rd ed., 1982)

Coopers and Lybrand, *Form and Content of Company Accounts*, (Financial Training, 1982).

C. E. T. Sutcliffe and M. L. Patient, Tolley's Accounting Problems of the Companies Acts, (Tolley Publishing Company Ltd, 1984).

Chapter 6
Group Accounts

INTRODUCTION

As a business grows it may discover new opportunities for expansion, either by making investments in other companies on a long-term basis, or by establishing new ventures on its own account or jointly with others, the range of possibilities is shown in Figure 6.1 on p. 132. This chapter deals with the way in which accounts are prepared in order to deal with groups of companies. It begins by dealing with those companies in which the parent does not have a controlling interest. These fall into two categories: those in which the company has an interest on a long-term basis of less than 20%, which are generally referred to as trade investments, and those where the interest exceeds this level in which case the special provisions contained in the Companies Act and SSAP 1 come into force. Regrettably each set of regulations differs slightly, and adopts different terminology, the Act using the term "related companies", and the standard the title "associated companies", to refer to such interests. The bulk of the chapter deals with the accounting requirements which apply when a company holds a controlling interest in another company which is then termed a subsidiary. In such cases a company is required to submit accounts to its shareholders dealing not only with its own affairs, but also with those of its subsidiaries. Such group accounts generally take the form of consolidated accounts, in which the accounts of the parent and its subsidiaries are presented as if they were one entity.

The chapter concludes with a discussion of two aspects of group accounting which have engaged the activities of the standard setters in recent years. The first is the problem of accounting for an amalgamation effected by an exchange of shares, which may be treated as a merger or as an acquisition. The choice of method adopted has important implications for the distribution

Figure 6.1 *Expanded Forms of Business Organisation*

SOLE TRADER

An individual trading on his own account.

PARTNERSHIP

Several individuals trading in common with a view to profit.

COMPANY

A legal entity formed by several members in order to carry on trading.

INVESTMENTS

TRADE INVESTMENT	*JOINT VENTURE*	*RELATED COMPANY*	*SUBSIDIARY COMPANY*
Long-term interest of less than 20% in another firm – usually a customer, competitor or supplier. Shown as fixed asset investment in parents' accounts.	Long-term interest in separate firm established jointly with others. Shown as fixed asset investment in parents' accounts. Treated as Associate (Related Company) in group accounts.	Long-term interest in 20% or more of equity share capital of another firm. (Associated Company SSAP 1 almost identical) Shown as fixed asset investment in parents' accounts. Almost always treated as Associate shown under equity method of accounting (per SSAP 1) in group accounts.	Long-term interest of more than 50% of equity share capital or giving control of Board of Directors of another firm. Shown as fixed asset investment in parents' accounts. Group accounts (almost always consolidated) required.

of profits for the companies involved. The second issue is the treatment of foreign currency translation in group accounts. Two basic methods are now regarded as acceptable under specified conditions: the net investment method and the temporal method. Once again the method chosen makes a substantial difference to the results reported to shareholders.

Accounting for groups has been the subject of several accounting standards; SSAP 1 deals with associated companies; SSAP 14 deals with group accounts, and ED 3 and 31 and SSAP 23 have dealt with the topic of merger accounting. The Companies Act 1981 included temporary provisions dealing with groups pending the introduction of the Seventh Directive of the European Community which deals with group accounts. This directive was approved by the Community in May 1983, and must be in force in Member States by 1990. It will make little difference to practice in the United Kingdom, where group accounts have been required since 1948. However, considerable changes will occur in most other European states as a result of the introduction of the directive.

ACCOUNTING FOR TRADE INVESTMENTS

Although the term "trade investment" is not used in the Companies Act it is the most suitable one to use when referring to investments made for long-term trading reasons, as opposed to investments made in order to obtain a return on surplus funds. Under the Companies Act long-term investments are classed as fixed asset investments and must be shown under the heading BIII 5 "Other investments other than loans". In accordance with the historic cost accounting rules they must be shown at purchase cost and may be written down where there is a diminution in value. Where the diminution in value is expected to be permanent writing down is compulsory. Under the alternative accounting rules fixed asset investments may be shown at a market value or on any basis which appears to the directors of the company to be appropriate. In the profit and loss account a company will show the dividends received from its trade investments under subheading 9 (format 1) or 11 (format 2).

In practice most companies will show trade investments in the balance sheet at the original historical cost, unless there has been a fall in value, and the profit and loss account will only show dividends received irrespective of the overall profits made by the firm in which the investment is made. The same method is also used to show the investment in related and subsidiary companies in the parent company's own accounts, although under different headings in the standard formats. This approach is followed because it is not considered prudent for a company to take credit in its own accounts for its share of profits of other companies which have not been declared as dividends. The view is taken that the inclusion of undistributed profits would ignore the separate legal status of the entities concerned and, as regards the investing company, be contrary to the practice of not taking credit for investment until it is received or receivable. Whilst there is much to commend this reasoning it has the disadvantage that, as a result, the accounts will not reflect the success or failure of an investment as measured by the share in its profits and in the growth of its net assets.

Although this method is considered prudent for dealing with interests of modest size, it is generally regarded as unacceptable for dealing with larger interests for which alternative provisions exist.

ASSOCIATED AND RELATED COMPANIES

Where a company conducts an important part of its business through the medium of other companies, the mere disclosure of dividend income (or mere inclusion of dividend income alone) from these companies is unlikely to give sufficient information regarding the sources of its income and the manner in which its funds are being employed.

Accordingly it has been deemed necessary by both parliament and the ASC to define a separate class of investments for which special treatment is required. The former has defined such firms as related companies and the latter as associates; the definitions are set out below.

> *A related company.* Any body corporate (other than one which is a group company in relation to that company) in which that company holds on a long-term basis a qualifying capital interest for the purposes of securing a contribution to that company's own activities by the exercise of *any control or influence* arising from that interest. A qualifying capital interest arises when a company holds 20% or more of the equity share capital of another.
>
> *An associated company* is a company not being a subsidiary of the investing group or company in which:
> (a) the interest of the investing group or company is effectively that of a partner in a joint venture or consortium and the investing group or company is in a position to exercise a significant influence over the company in which the investment is made; or
> (b) the interest of the investing group or company is for the long-term and is substanial and, having regard to the disposition of the other share-holdings, the investing group or company is in a position to exercise *a significant influence* over the company in which the investment is made.[1]

The definition of a related company is wider than that of an associated company, which depends on the exercise of a "significant influence" rather than "any control or influence". Furthermore, under SSAP 1, where a company can demonstrate that is has a significant influence with less than a 20% holding in the equity share capital it may treat the interest as an associate. Thus it is possible for a company to be an associate but not a related company, and vice versa, depending on the particular circumstances. The department of Trade and Industry has indicated that the term "associated company" may be used in the accounts provided all related companies are associates, and a note is included in the accounts to this effect.

With regard to the exercise of signficant influence SSAP 2 states:

[1] Related company as defined in the Companies Act 1981, Sched. 1 para 91. Associated company as defined in SSAP 1.

"Significant influence over a company essentiallly involves participation in the financial and operating policy decisions of that company (including dividend policy) but not necessarily control of those policies. Representation on the board of directors is indicative of such participation, but will neither necessarily give conclusive evidence of it nor be the only method by which the investing company may participate in policy decisions."

Over the years some difficulties have arisen where companies adopted non-comparable policies in applying the concept of "active participation in commercial and policy decisions". Thus it became necessary to revise the standard on the following lines:

- Where the interest of the investing group or company amounts to 20% or more of the equity voting rights of a company, it should be presumed that the investing group or company has the ability to exercise significant influence over that company unless it can clearly be demonstrated otherwise. For example, there may exist one or more other large shareholdings which prevent the exercise of such influence.
- Where the interest of the investing group or company amounts to less than 20% of the equity voting rights of a company it should be presumed that the investing group or company does not have the ability to exercise significant influence unless it can clearly demonstrate otherwise. Unless there are exceptional circumstances, this demonstration should include a statement from the company in which the investment is made that it accepts that the investing group or company is in a position to exercise significant influence over it.

In each case an investing group or company may treat an interest in a joint venture or consortium as an associate notwithstanding the level of its shareholding.

THE ACCOUNTING TREATMENT OF ASSOCIATED COMPANIES (SSAP 1)

The Companies Act does not lay down any special rules for showing related companies in the accounts of the investing company. However, it allows such companies to be shown at a valuation where the company prepares group accounts. Under SSAP 2 associated companies are to be shown in the accounts of the investing company as a fixed asset investment. Where group accounts are prepared SSAP 2 requires the use of the equity method of accounting, and explains the requirements thus:

"The broad concept underlying the accounting treatment of the results of associated companies is the adoption in modified form of the consolidation procedures used for subsidiary companies. It follows from this that the investing company's share of associated companies' profits and losses are reflected in its consolidated profit and loss account, and its share of their post-acquisition retained profits or accumulated deficits are reflected in its consolidated balance sheet, though not in its own balance sheet as a legal entity.

The essential difference between a trade investment and an associated company is that in the latter the investing company actively participates in commerical and policy decisions, it thus has a measure of direct responsibility for the return on its investment, and should account for its stewardship accordingly."

SSAP 2 requires the following items to be shown in the group profit and loss account:

- share of pre-tax profits or losses of associated companies;

- taxation attributable to the share of profits of associated companies (within the taxation charge and disclosed separately in a note to the accounts);
- extraordinary items – the group's share to the extent to which they are material;
- net profit retained by associated companies.

If the results or the assets and liabilities of one or more associated companies are so material in the context of the financial statements of the investing group that more information is required in order to show a true and fair view, then this should be given.

In accordance with SSAP 2 associated companies must be shown in the group balance sheet on the following basis:

> "(a) the investing group's share of the net assets other than goodwill of the associated companies stated, where possible, after attributing fair values to the net assets at the time of acquisition of the interest in the associated companies; and
> (b) the investing group's share of any goodwill in the associated companies' own financial statements, together with
> (c) the premium paid (or discount) on the acquistion of the interests in the associated companies in so far as it has not already been written off or amortised.
>
> Item (a) should be disclosed separately but items (b) and (c) may be shown as one aggregate amount."

Where the company has made loans to associated companies or received loans from such companies, the total must be disclosed in the group balance sheet under the appropriate headings. Similarly trading balances should be included under current assets or current liabilities.

The investing group's share of the post-acquisition accumulated reserves of associated companies and any movements therein should be disclosed in the consolidated financial statements. In arriving at the amount to be disclosed, it will also be necessary to take account of and disclose movements in associated companies' reserves which have not arisen from amounts passing through the profit and loss account, for example surpluses on revaluation of fixed assets. If the accumulated reserves of associated companies overseas would be subject to further tax on distribution, this should be made clear.

The financial statements used for the purpose of including the results of associated companies should be either coterminous with those of the investing group or made up to a date which is either not more than six months before or shortly after, the date of the financial statements of the investing group.

The Accounting Treatment of an associated company is illustrated by the following example.

Example

On 1 July 1983 G Book Ltd acquires a 20% interest in equity share capital of J Boulton & Sons Ltd, at a cost of £30,000, and on the same day two of its directors are invited to join the board of the company. The balance sheets of G Book Ltd and its subsidiary company at 30 June 1984 are shown below.

G Book Ltd and its Subsidiary Company

	£
Fixed assets	
Tangible	180,000
Investment in associated company (at cost)	30,000
	210,000
Current assets	565,000
	775,000
Less creditors	200,000
	£575,000
Capital and reserves	
Called up share capital	275,000
Profit and loss account	300,000
	£575,000

J Bouton & Sons Ltd achieved a pre-tax profit of £20,000, after tax £10,000, during the year, and paid no dividends. Its balance sheet on 30 June 1984 is shown below.

J Boulton & Sons Ltd

	£
Fixed assets	
Intangible – goodwill	30,000
Tangible	60,000
Current assets	55,000
	145,000
Creditors	25,000
	£120,000
Capital and reserves	
Called up share capital	50,000
Profit and loss account	70,000
	£120,000

Solution

At the time of acquiring its 20% interest the net assets of J Boulton would have been represented by the following balances.

		£
Share capital		50,000
Profit and loss	70,000	
Less year 83/84	20,000	
		50,000
Net assets		100,000
Less goodwill		30,000
Net tangible assets		£ 70,000

G Book acquires a 20% interest represented by the following:

	£
Share of net tangible assets	14,000
Share of goodwill in associate	6,000
	20,000
Cost	30,000
Goodwill/premium on acquisition	£10,000

On the 1 July 1983 G Book will record its interest at cost of £30,000. At the end of the year it will include in its group profit and loss account, the following:

Share of profits of associate	4,000
Taxation	2,000
Profit after taxation	£2,000

The group balance sheet will appear as follows:

	Note	£
Fixed assets		
Tangible		180,000
Investment in associated company	1	32,000
		212,000
Current assets		565,000
		777,000
Less creditors		200,000
		£ 577,000
Capital and reserves		
Called up share capital		275,000
Profit and loss account	2	302,000
		£ 777,000

Note 1

Investment in associated company	£
Share of net assets	16,000
Goodwill in associated company	6,000
Premium on acquisition of interest	10,000
	£32,000

There are no related companies other than associated companies.

Note 2
The Profit and loss account is dealt with as follows:

Holding company	250,000
Subsidiary company	50,000
Associated company	2,000
	£302,000

ACCOUNTING FOR GROUPS OF COMPANIES

Where at the end of any financial year a company has subsidiaries, it is required by the Companies Act 1948, as amended in 1981, to prepare group accounts. Such accounts are not required of a wholly owned subsidiary of another company incorporated in Great Britain. The Companies Act lays down the following important definitions:

Subsidiary company. A company shall be deemed to be a subsidiary of another if, but only if,
(a) that other either:
(i) is a member of it and controls the composition of its board of directors; or
(ii) holds more than half in nominal value of its equity share capital; or
(b) the first mentioned company is a subsidiary of any company which is that other's subsidiary.

Holding company. A company is a holding company of another if but only if that other is its subsidiary as defined above.

Group. A holding company and its subsidiaries.

Except in certain specified circumstances group accounts will take the form of consolidated financial statements. These are defined in SSAP 14, which deals with group accounts, as "One form of group accounts which present the information contained in the separate financial statements of a holding company and its subsidiaries as if they were the financial entity". Such a set of accounts is achieved by a process known as consolidation in which the investment shown in the accounts of the holding company in respect of the subsidiary is replaced by the net assets and liabilities of the subsidiary.

The next section of this chapter is devoted to explaining the basic principles of consolidation. In practice there are a number of complications which require adjustments to be made; these are ignored for the time being but are dealt with later.

THE BASIC PRINCIPLES OF CONSOLIDATED ACCOUNTS

The basic principles of consolidation are as set out below:

(1) The Net assets of the subsidiary are substituted for the investment in the subsidiary in the accounts of the parent to produce group accounts. The Share capital of the subsidiary (from subsidiary accounts) and investment in subsidiary (from parent's accounts) are eliminated.
(2) Where the consideration paid for an interest in a subsidiary *exceeds* the amount of the net assets acquired, the difference is termed cost of control or goodwill arising on consolidation.
(3) Where the consideration paid for an interest in a subsidiary *is less than* the amount of the assets acquired the difference is termed capital reserve arising on consolidation (it is often due to negative goodwill which is discussed below).
(4) Where the subsidiary has been trading prior to the acquisition of shares by the parent the pre-acquisition reserves are eliminated in the consolidation procedure.
(5) Where the parent does not acquire a 100% interest the balance of share capital and a similar proportion of reserves are attributable to minority shareholders and are termed minority interests.
(6) In preparing a group profit and loss account intra-group transactions are eliminated.

These principles are demonstrated in the following examples:

Example 1 – Basic Principles

A Ltd. has owned 100% of B Ltd. since B Ltd. was corporated. The balance sheets for each company after several years trading are shown below. In order to prepare a consolidated balance sheet the share capital of B, which represents the net assets of the company at the time the shares were acquired by A, are eliminated against the item shown as "investment in B" which appears in the accounts of A Ltd. The remaining items are added together.

	A Ltd	*B Ltd*	*Consolidation adjustments*	*A Ltd and its Subsidiary B Ltd*
	£	£	£	£
Share capital	20,000	10,000	(10,000)	20,000
Reserves	9,000	4,000		13,000
Current liabilities	3,000	3,000		6,000
	£32,000	£17,000		£ 39,000
Fixed assets-tangible	17,000	12,000		29,000
Current assets	5,000	5,000		10,000
Investment in B	10,000		(10,000)	
	£32,000	£17,000		£39,000

Example 2 – Goodwill arising on Consolidation

A Ltd. owns 100% of B Ltd., but paid £20,000 to acquire the company when it had net assets of £10,000 and had made neither profits nor losses (The company might have made a new discovery which justified the premium.)
As can be seen below, A Ltd. shows the investment in B Ltd. at its cost of £20,000. When consolidated accounts are prepared a difference of £10,000 arises which is termed the cost of control, or goodwill arising on consolidation.

Cost	£20,000
Net assets of B	£10,000
Goodwill	£10,000

	A Ltd £	*B Ltd* £	*Consolidation adjustments*	*A Ltd and its subsidiary* £
Share capital	20,000	10,000	(10,000)	20,000
Reserves	19,000	4,000		23,000
Current liabilities	3,000	3,000		6,000
	£42,000	£17,000		£49,000
Fixed assets				
Intangible – goodwill arising on consolidation	—	—	10,000	10,000
tangible	17,000	12,000		29,000
Current assets	5,000	5,000		10,000
Investment in B	20,000		(20,000)	—
	£42,000	£17,000		£49,000

Example 3 – Capital Reserve arising on Consolidation

A acquires 100% of B Ltd. for £10,000 when the net assets of B Ltd. were £21,000. (The discount may have arisen because B was making losses.) Since the acquisition B has made further profits of £2,000. In this case when A sets its investment against the net assets a difference of £2,000 arises, which is termed "capital reserve arising on consolidation."

Cost	£10,000
Net assets	£12,000
Capital reserve	£2,000

	A Ltd £	*B Ltd* £	*Consolidation adjustments* £	*A Ltd and its subsidiary* £
Share capital	20,000	10,000	(10,000)	20,000
Reserves – profit and loss	9,000	4,000	(2,000)	11,000
– other – capital reserve on consolidation	—	—	2,000	2,000
Current liabilities	3,000	3,000		6,000
	£32,000	£17,000		£39,000
Fixed assets	17,000	12,000		29,000
Current assets	5,000	5,000		10,000
Investment in B	10,000	—	10,000	
	£32,000	£17,000		£39,000

The effect of the adjustment made is to change £2,000 of reserves from a distributable profit to a capital reserve which cannot be distributed. This point is considered in more depth below.

Example 4 – Pre and Post Acquisition Reserves

A acquires 100% of B Ltd. for £12,000 when B has net assets of £12,000. In this case the net assets of B at the time of the acquisition are equal to the cost, but comprise share capital and reserves.

Share capital	£10,000
Reserves	£ 2,000

The reserves which accumulated prior to the combination are referred to as pre-acquisition reserves, and when distributed to the parent company may not be distributed to their shareholders. Instead the sums received must be used to write down the amount at which the subsidiary is shown in the parent's accounts, being regarded as a recovery of the original cost of the investment, rather than a receipt of profit made by the subsidiary. Those profits made since the acquisition are termed post acquisition profits and are fully distributable when received as dividends by the holding company.

	A Ltd	*B Ltd*	*Consolidation adjustments*	*A Ltd and its subsidiary*
	£	£	£	£
Share capital	20,000	10,000	(10,000)	20,000
Reserves	11,000	4,000	(2,000)	13,000
Current liabilities	3,000	3,000		6,000
	£34,000	£17,000		£39,000
Fixed assets	17,000	12,000		29,000
Current assets	5,000	5,000		10,000
Investment in B	12,000	—	(12,000)	
	£34,000	£17,000		£39,000

In this example the investment in B disappears and the combined reserves fall by £2,000. Were B Ltd. to pay a dividend to A of £3,000 the amount would be split as follows:

Post acquisition – distributable	£2,000
Pre-acquisition – non-distributable	£1,000

The sum of £1,000 would be set against the cost of the investment in B Ltd. in the books of A reducing the balance of £11,000, the reserves of A and B would now consist of:

Held by A Ltd	£11,000 + £2,000	£13,000
Held by B Ltd	£ 4,000 – £3,000	£ 1,000

The balance of £1,000 held by B would be set against the cost of the investment upon consolidation and would be eliminated from the balance sheet thus:

Cost of investment (written down)		£11,000
Net assets Share capital	£10,000	
Reserves	£ 1,000	£11,000

The effect of these transactions makes no difference to the group balance sheet, other than to increase the amount of the reserves held by the parent, and to increase the cash balance by the amount of the dividend received.

Example 5 – Minority Interests

A owns 60% of B Ltd acquired for £10,000 at the time of B's incorporation. In this case the balance of the shares are owned by minority shareholders, who are also entitled to a share of the profits. As in previous examples the assets and liabilities are added together as if the group were one entity. However, the share capital and share of profits attributable to the minority shareholders are shown separately in the balance sheet, and in the profit and loss account. In this example the profits have all been achieved since the acquisition of shares by the parent company, and therefore no reserves are set against the cost of the acquisition. Where a minority interest exists the pre-acquisition profits attributable to the minority are treated in the same way as post-acquisition profits and are added to minority interests.

	A Ltd	*B Ltd*	*Consolidation adjustments*	*A Ltd and its subsidiary*
	£	£	£	£
Share capital	20,000	10,000	(6,000) (4,000)	20,000
Reserves	9,000	4,000	(1,600) (4,000)	11,400
Minority interests			5,600	5,600
Current liabilities	3,000	3,000		6,000
	£32,000	£17,000		£43,000
Fixed assets – intangible – goodwill on consolidation				4,000
–tangible	17,000	12,000		19,000
Current assets	5,000	5,000		10,000
Investment in B	10,000		(10,000)	
	£32,000	£17,000		£43,000

In consolidating the balance sheet the following adjustments are made regarding the parents interest:

Investment	£10,000	£10,000
Net assets – 60% of share capital		£ 6,000
Goodwill arising on consolidation		£ 4,000

The holding companies share of reserves, all post-acquisition, are added to group reserves.

The minority interest are treated as follows:

Share capital	40% of £10,000	£4,000
Reserves	40% of £4,000	£1,600
		£5,600

Example 6 – Consolidation of the Profit and Loss Account

In order to illustrate the effect of consolidating the profit and loss account use will be made of the figures set out below. In this case A owns 60% of the equity shares of B, and during the year has acquired goods from its subsidiary costing £10,000. The cost of these goods to B had been £5,000 and distribution costs of £1,000 had been incurred. During the year B had paid a management fee of £2,000 to its parent, and dividends totalling £1,500. The management fee is shown as other operating income.

		A Ltd		*B Ltd*		*Consolidation adjustments*	*A Ltd and its subsidiary*
	£	£	£	£	£	£	£
Turnover		80,000		40,000	(10,000)[a]		110,000
Cost of sales		40,000		20,000	(10,000)[a]		50,000
Gross profit		40,000		20,000			60,000
Distribution costs	10,000		5,000			15,000	
Administration expenses	10,000		5,000		(2,000)[b]	13,000	
		20,000		10,000			28,000
		20,000		10,000			32,000
Other operating income		2,000		—	(2,000)[b]		—
Income from shares							
– group companies		1,500		—	(1,500)[c]		—
		23,500		10,000			32,000
Profit on ordinary activities before tax							
Taxation		11,750		5,000			16,750
		11,750		5,000			15,250
Profit on ordinary activities before tax attributable to minority shareholders					(2,000)		2,000
							13,250
Dividends		5,000		2,500	(2,000)[c]		5,000
Retained profit		£6,750		£2,500			£8,250

The consolidation adjustments which have been made and the resulting figures can be explained as follows:

(a) The sales made by B to A must be excluded from turnover because no sales have been made outside the group. Similarly the cost of sales entry arising as a result of the sale to A does not represent a purchase from outside the group. These two amounts are therefore set off one against the other.[2]

[2] Where stock arising from the sale is still held at the end of the year the profit must be eliminated from the amount at which stock is valued.

(b) The management fee must similarly be excluded from group income and eliminated from the total for group administration expenses.
(c) The dividend received by A from B must be eliminated from the group profit and loss account, and the balance of the dividend, which amounts to £1,000 is debited to the account for minority interests.

The minority interests are credited with their share of profit for the year of £2,000 and when the dividend paid in is debited to the account the result will be a balance of £1,000 which is held by B Ltd. for reinvestment in the business.

The retained profit may thus be reconciled as follows:

Retained by A Ltd		£6,750
Retained by B Ltd	£2,500	
Attributable to minority	£1,000	
Attributable to parent		£1,500
Balance of group reserves		£8,250

BOOKKEEPING PROCEDURES FOR CONSOLIDATION

Although the transactions arising as a result of the need to consolidate a set of accounts are essentially simple, it is often the case that a large number of adjustments need to be made to the underlying figures. Furthermore it is often the case that a holding company will have several subsidiaries with a fragmented pattern of shareholdings. It is therefore essential in practice to keep clear and comprehensive records of the consolidation procedure. There are two main approaches:

1. The Schedular approach

Under this method all of the figures appearing in the financial statements of each subsidiary are tabulated on a schedule and common items are added together. The necessary consolidation adjustments are recorded as journal entries and the combined figures adjusted. In appearance this method produces working papers similar to those used in the examples dealt with above. This method is particularly suitable for use with computer based accounts.

2. The Ledger approach

In contrast to the schedular method this approach makes use of a notional set of group books, in which the balances of each group company are recorded, and full double entry bookkeeping is applied using the traditional T-shaped account. Theoretically there is no difference between this method and the schedular approach, although it is perhaps more easily followed by a newcomer to the subject, and for this reason will be used in this text. The key feature of this method is the use of an "adjustment account" in which the investment in the subsidiary is set against the net assets acquired, represented by share capital and pre-acquisition reserves. The procedure for consolidation using this approach is summarised in Table 6.1 and is illustrated in the example following.

Table 6.1
Procedure for Consolidation using Ledger Accounts

1. Open a separate set of (nominal) books for consolidation transactions.
2. Enter balances from parent and subsidiary(ies).
3. Open adjustment (or cost of control) account and minority interest account (if required).
4. Transfer to adjustment account:
   Investment in subsidiary (from parent)
   Share capital (from subsidary) } In proportion to
   Pre-acquisition reserves (from subsidary) – if any } parent's holding
   A debit balance on the adjustment account represents goodwill arising on consilidation or cost of control.
   A credit balance on the account is a capital reserve arising on consolidation.
5. If there are minority shareholders then transfer share of:
   Share capital } to minority interests
   Reserves (pre- and post-acquisition) }
6. Transfer balance on all other accounts to relevant account of parent – including residue of reserves.

Note – Further complications can arise through:
profits on stock arising from inter-company sales
inter-company dividends
revaluation of assets at the time of acquisition
other adjustments to ensure common accounting policies

If a company proposes to pay a dividend to its parent from reserves accumulated prior to acquisition the parent must use the proceeds to write down the value of the investment in its own books.

If the acquisition takes place part way through the year the profits must be apportioned prior to and post acquisition. Profits accumulated prior to the transaction will form part of the net assets at the time of acquisition and will be eliminated on consolidation through the adjustment account.

Example

	N Ltd £000	*O Ltd £000*		*N Ltd £000*	*O Ltd £000*
Fixed assets					
Tangible	40	30	Share capital	100	60
Investments in subsidiary			Reserves	40	20
at cost			Current Liabilities	20	15
45,000 ordinary shares in					
O Ltd	50				
Current assets	70	65			
	160	95		160	95

The shares in O Ltd were acquired when O Ltd.'s reserves amounted to £12,000.

Procedure:
N Ltd opens a set of accounts for consolidation purposes. (It is important to note that the entries in the books of account kept by N and O Ltd are not affected by this procedure, which is carried out entirely through the vehicle of notional books.) The balances from O are transferred into the accounts as shown. An adjustment account and a minority interests account are opened to deal with the consolidation adjustments. The relevant accounts are shown below and the transactions coded where relevant to the notes below.

N Ltd. Notional Consolidation Ledger

N Ltd – Share capital

		Balance	100

N Ltd – Current liabilities

		Balance	20
		O Ltd Current liabilities[7]	15
			35

N Ltd reserves

		Balance	40
		O Reserves[5]	6
			46

N Ltd – Fixed assets – tangible

Balance	40		
O Ltd Fixed assets[8]	30		
	70		

N Ltd – Investments

"O" Ltd – Bal.	50	Adjustment A/C[10]	50

N Ltd – Current assets

Balance	70		
O Ltd – Current assets[9]	65		
	135		

Adjustment A/c

Investments O Ltd[10]	50	O Ltd Share Capital[1]	45
Balance c/d.[11]	4	O Ltd Reserves[3]	9
	54		54
		Balance[11]	4

O Ltd Fixed assets – tangible

		O Ltd Share Capital[2]	15
		O Ltd Reserves[4 6]	5
			20

O Ltd Share Capital

Adjustment A/c[1]	45	Balance	60
Minority Interest[2]	15		
	60		60

O Ltd Fixed assets

Balance	30	N Ltd – Fixed Assets[8]	30

O Ltd Reserves

Adjustment A/c[3]	9	Balance	20
Minority Interests[4]	3		
N Reserves[5]	6		
Minority Interests[6]	2		
	20		20

O Ltd Current assets

Balance	65	N Ltd Current assets[9]	65

O Ltd Current liabilities

N Ltd liabilities[7]	15	Balance	15

As a result of the consolidation procedure all of the accounts for O Ltd in the notional ledger are closed and the investment in O Ltd. disappears from the account for investments. The other important point are as follows:

[1, 2]. The share capital of O Ltd is eliminated, 75% being attributable to minority interests.
[3]. The pre-acquisition reserves amount to £12 of which 75% is attributable to N and is entered in the adjustment account. Three quarters of the balance of reserves are added to N's reserves to give group reserves of £46.[5].
[4, 6]. The minority reserves are transferred to the minority interest account. Although there is no necessity to divide these into pre- and post-acquisition components it is often easier to do so.
[7, 8, 9]. Balances transferred to corresponding group accounts.
[10]. Investment in O Ltd taken to the adjustment account.
[11] When the adjustment account is balanced it reveals a credit balance of £4 which arises because the parent paid £50 for net assets amounting to £54. The balance is shown as a capital reserves in the balance sheet which appears below.

N Ltd and its Subsidiary

	£		£
Fixed assets	70	Capital and reserves	
Current assets	135	Share Capital	100
		Reserves – profit and loss	46
		Capital reserve on consolidation	4
			150
		Minority interests	20
		Current liabilities	35
	205		205

FURTHER CONSOLIDATION ADJUSTMENTS

In addition to the basic adjustments which have been considered a number of additional adjustments are also necessary in order for the accounts to show a true and fair view.

1. Inter-Company Balances must be cancelled on consolidation

This requirements has already been encountered in dealing with the group profit and loss account above. In addition balance sheet items must be eliminated where they correspond.

2. Inter-Company Profits

Where one group company sells goods to another company within the group which have not been sold at the end of the accounting period it is necessary to make a provision to eliminate the profit which has not been achieved outside the group. The amount at which stocks are shown in the group balance sheet is reduced by the amount of the unrealised profit included in the profit and loss account of the vendor company within the group.

Example

Company B sells goods amounting to £80,000 during the year to its parent company A, of which one quarter were unsold at the end of the year. The goods were sold at a profit margin of 25%.

	A Ltd	*B Ltd*	*A + B*	*Consolidation adjustments*	*A Ltd and its subsidiary*
	£	£	£	£	£
Sales	75,000	80,000	155,000	Dr 80,000[1]	75,000
Cost of sales	60,000	60,000	120,000	Cr 60,000[2]	45,000
				Cr 15,000[3]	
Profit	£15,000	£20,000			£30,000
Adjustment to balance sheet					
Stock of goods from B	20,000			Cr 5,000[4]	15,000

The adjustments may be explained as follows:

[1] Sales within the group eliminated.
[2] Cost of goods from B sold during the year eliminated, leaving a balance of £20,000 which had cost B £15,000.
[3] Goods sold to A by B unsold at the end of the year eliminated from cost of sales.
[4] Profit on goods sold by B to A unsold at the end of the year eliminated from the stock amount to adjust the balance to cost.

Of the goods sold by B three-quarters have been sold by the group for £75,000. The cost of these goods was £45,000 giving a group profit of £30,000. B has made a profit of £5,000 on goods sold to A which have not been sold outside the group, and is therefore eliminated from the group profit and loss account. (In examination questions adjustments are often required to the value of stocks as a result of inter-group profits, without a profit and loss account being prepared. In such cases an adjustment is made to the balance of reserves). In cases where a minority interest exists the question arises whether a provision is required in respect of the profit attributable to minority shareholders on inter-company sales. It is generally accepted that, because the group is regarded as one entity in group accounts, a full provision should be made. The further question then arises, whether the provision should be charged to the parent company or split according to the proportion of minorities. Where the profit and loss account is adjusted as described above the minority profits will be adjusted automatically. However, many accountants consider that in accordance with the prudence principle the parent company alone should bear the provision against inter-company stock profits. In this case the parent should be charged and the minority credited with the amount of the profit eliminated.

3. Revaluation of Assets

It is a fundamental principle of group accounts that the amount at which the assets of a subsidiary are included upon consolidation should reflect their fair value. If this is not the case then the consolidation adjustments will give rise to a balance which does not truly reflect the cost of control over the subsidiary. Accordingly it is usual practice to revalue the assets of a subsidiary at the time of acquisition. Often the revalued amounts will be incorporated in the accounts of the new subsidiary. However this is not always possible, for example, where the subsidiary operates in a country where revaluations are not allowed, or where there are substantial minority interests. Where no revaluation is made in the books of the subsidiary at the time of the combination, the parent should make such adjustments as are necessary upon consolidation. It will be necessary to determine these adjustments at the time of the combination and take account of them when consolidated accounts are prepared each year.

Example

A acquires 100% of the shares in B when B has net assets of £2,000. The fixed assets of B at the time of the acquisition are valued at £3,500. Balance sheets for the two companies are set out below.

	A Ltd	*B Ltd*	*Consolidation adjustments*	*A Ltd and its subsidiary*
	£	£	£	£
Fixed assets				
Intangible – goodwill	—	—	500	500
Tangible	10,000	3,000	500	13,500
Current assets	4,000	2,000	—	6,000
Due from B	700	—	(700)	—
Investment in B	3,000	—	(3,000)	—
	£17,700	£5,000		£20,000
Capital	5,000	1,000	(1,000)	5,000
Reserves	9,700	2,000	(1,000)	10,700
Current liabilities	3,000	1,300	—	4,300
Due to A	—	700	(700)	—
	£17,700	£5,000		£20,000

The consolidation adjustments are shown in the following journal entry:

Investment in B Ltd		£3,000
Share capital B Ltd	£1,000	
Reserves (pre acq.)	£1,000	
Fixed assets (revaluation)	£ 500	
Goodwill (balance)	£ 500	
	£3,000	£3,000

The sum due from B, £700, is also eliminated on consolidation. Where assets having a finite useful life are revalued the group depreciation charge, which should be based on adjusted book value, will need to be increased. This is achieved by debiting the group profit and loss account, and crediting the balance of accumulated depreciation in the group balance sheet.

4. Intra-Group Dividends

As was noted earlier in this chapter dividends paid by companies within the group must be eliminated when group accounts are prepared. In practice adjustment is made to the profit and loss account as shown above. Where a dividend is proposed and appears in the subsidiary's balance sheet as a creditor, it is necessary to eliminate the item from the group balance sheet, the amount of the parent's share of the dividend being added to group reserves, and the minorities share, if any, being added to other creditors in the balance sheet.

5. Apportionment of Trading Items and Profits

Where an acquisition takes place part way through the year, the group profit and loss account will only include those items which related to the period since acquisition. The profits achieved prior to the date of combination will form part of the pre-acquisition profits and will therefore be taken to the adjustment account.

6. Interests of Preference Shareholders of Subsidiaries

The preference shares held by a company with a subsidiary are treated as other share capital upon consolidation and are eliminated against the cost of those shares through the adjustment account. Where some, or all, of the shares are held by other shareholders, the amount of the share capital concerned is shown as a minority interest in the group balance sheet.

Dividends paid to the holding company must be eliminated from the group profit and loss account in much the same way as other group dividends. However, where a minority exists a charge must be made under minority interests in the profit and loss account in respect of the dividend which the company will have to pay as a result of making a profit, even if the dividend has not yet been declared. A corresponding credit must be made to minority interests in the balance sheet.

The points discussed above are illustrated in the example below.

Example

G. Lewis Holdings PLC acquires an 80% interest in both the ordinary and preference share capital of L. Rudge & Co. Ltd on 30 June 1983. A group balance sheet is prepared on 31 December, 1983 based on the company accounts and information shown below.

G. Lewis (Holdings) PLC Balance Sheet as at 30 December 1983

	£'000	£'000
Fixed assets		
Tangible assets		3,350
Investment – group company		2,112
Current assets	3,450	
Creditors – falling due within one year	2,140	
Net current assets		1,310
Total assets less current liabilities		6,772
Creditors falling due after more than one year		1,350
		5,422
Capital and reserves		
Called up share capital		1,450
Share premium account		1,862
Revaluation reserve		730
Profit and loss account		1,380
		5,422

L. Rudge & Co. Ltd. Balance Sheet as at 30 December 1983

	£'000	£'000
Fixed assets		
Intangible assets		5
Tangible assets		1,665
Current assets	1,710	
Creditors – falling due within one year	1,360	
Net current assets		350
Total assets less current liabilities		2,020
Creditors falling due after more than one year	305	
Provisions for liabilities and charges	205	
		510
		1,510
Capital and reserves		
Called up share capital		600
Share premium		270
Revaluation reserve		290
Profit and loss account		350
		1,510

The following information is also relevant.

(1) The called up share capital of L. Rudge & Co. consists of:

300,000 ordinary shares of £1 each;
200,000 10% preference shares of £1 each.

(2) On the date of the acquisition the assets of L. Rudge & Co. were revalued. The intangible asset consists of a patent which has an estimated market value of £250,000. The tangible assets include properties with a market value of £760,000 compared with a book value of £610,000. All of the other assets were shown at book values which reflected their fair value on 30th June, 1983.
(3) During the year L. Rudge has achieved a profit of £120,000, which accrued evenly throughout the year.
(4) Shown within the creditors for Rudge is a dividend of 5p per share which is due to be paid on 16 January. A preference dividend is to be paid on the same date, but no provision has yet been made in the accounts of Rudge.
(5) Included within the totals of net current assets of Rudge, and the creditors falling due within one year of Lewis, is an amount of £84,000 representing trading balances outstanding. Included within the stocks of Lewis are goods acquired from Rudge for £64,000 on which it is estimated that a profit of £8,000 has been earned.

(Corporation tax and advanced corporation tax is ignored in this question).

Solution

Consolidation adjustments – see explanations below

(1a)	Dr. Rudge share capital (Ordinary and preference)	600	
	Cr. Cost of control A/c		480
	Cr. Minority interests		120
		600	600
(1b)	Dr. Rudge share premium	270	
	Cr. Cost of control		216
	Cr. Minority interests		54
		270	270
(1c)	Dr. Rudge revaluation reserve	290	
	Cr. Cost of control		232
	Cr. Minority interest		58
		290	290

Net assets of Rudge represented by share capital, share premium and revaluation reserve apportioned to parent and minority interest.

(2a)	Dr. Fixed assets tangible	150	
	Dr. Fixed assets intangible	245	
	Cr. Revaluation reserve arising on consolidation		395
		395	395
(2b)	Dr. Revaluation reserve arising on consolidation	395	
	Cr. Cost of control		232
	Cr. Minority interest		58
		395	395

Fixed assets revalued and surplus apportioned.

(3a)	Dr. Creditors		30	
	Cr. Profit and loss A/c (Rudge)			30
			30	30
(3b)	Dr. Profit and loss A/c (Rudge)		320	
	Cr. Cost of control			256
	Cr. Minority interest			64
		c/f	320	320

Ordinary dividend re-credited to profit and loss account of Lewis.		
Pre-acquisition profit divided as follows:		*380*
Balance on profit and loss account		*60*
Post-acquisition profit		
Pre-acquisition profit divided:		
cost of control (80%)	*256*	
minorities (20%)	*64*	
		320

		b/f	320	320
(4)	Dr. Profit and loss A/c (Rudge)		12	
	Cr. Creditors (due – 1 year)			10
	Cr. Minority interest			2

Post acquisition profits (for six months) of minorities allocated as follows:		
balance (20% of £60,000)		*12*
creditors (due 1 year)		
preference dividend	*4*	
ordinary dividend	*6*	
		10
balance to minority interests (retained profit)		*2*

(5a)	Dr. Profit and loss A/c (Rudge)	48	
	Cr. Stock (current assets)		8
	Cr. Lewis (profit and loss A/c)		40
		380	380
(5b)	Dr. Creditors (Lewis)	84	
	Cr. Rudge (current assets)		84
		84	84

Post-acquisition profits of L. Rudge (80% of £60,000) credited to G. Lewis profit and loss account, less a provision for inter-group profit on stocks held by Lewis _ all charged to group reserve. (£8,000)
Elimination of intra-group balances.

The Consolidation Ledger would show the following transactions. All of the accounts are for group balances with the exception of account 4, dealing with the profit and loss account of Rudge.

1. Cost of Control

Inv.	2,112	S. cap[1a]	480
		S. prem.[1b]	216
		Reval.[2c7]	232
		P and l a/c[3b]	256
		Reval. reserve[2b]	316
		Bal. c/d	612
	2,112		2,112
Bal. b/d	612		

2. Revaluation Reserve Consolidation

C. of C.[2b]	316	Int. assets[2a]	245
M.I.[2b]	79	Tangible assets[2a]	150
	395		395

3. Minority Interests

		S. cap.[1a]	120
		S. prem.[1b]	54
		Reval. reserve[1c]	58
		P and l a/c[3b]	64
		P and l a/c[4]	2
		Reval. on cons[2b]	79
			377

4. Profit and Loss Account (Rudge)

CoC[3b]	256	Bal.	230
Min. int.[3b]	64	Creditors[3a]	30
Cr. × M.I.[4]	12		
P and l[5]			
Curr Ass.[5]	40		
	380		380

5. Profit and Loss Account (Lewis)

		Bal.	1,380
		P and l a/c[5] (Rudge)	40
			1.420

6. Fixed Assets – Tangible

Bal.	3,350		
Lewis	1,665		
Reval. res.[2a]	150		
	5,165		

7. Intangible assets

Rudge – bal	5		
Reval. res.[2a]	245		
	250		

8. Creditors – 1 Year

P and l a/c[3a]	30	Bal.	2,140
C assets[5b]	84	Rudge	1,360
Bal. c/d	3,396	P and l a/c[4]	10
	3,510		3,510
		Bal. b/d	3,396

9. Creditors due in more than 1 year

Bal.	1,665	Bal.	1,350
		Rudge	305
	1,655		1,655

10. Current Assets

Bal.	3,450	P and l (Rudge)[5a]	8
Rudge	1,710	Cred[5b]	84
		Bal. c/d	5,068
	5,160		5,160
Bal. b/f	5,068		

11. Investment in Rudge

Bal.	2,112	CoC	2,112

G. Lewis (Holdings) PLC and its Subsidiary – Balance Sheet as at 31 December 1983

	£'000	£'000
Fixed assets		
Intangible assets*		862
Tangible assets		5,165
		6,027
Current assets	5,068	
Creditors – Falling due within 1 year	3,396	1,672
		7,699
Creditors – Falling due after 1 year +	1,655	
Provisions for liabilities and *charges*	205	1,860
		5,839
Capital and *reserves*		
Share capital called up		1,450
Share premium account		1,862
Revaluation reserve		730
Profit and loss account		1,420
		5,462
Minority interest		377
		5,839

**Intangible assets*	
● patent	250
● goodwill on consolidation	612
	862

MORE COMPLICATED ASPECTS OF CONSOLIDATION

In addition to the principles outlined above a number of further complications arise in practice.

1. Vertical Groups

Often a company will hold an interest in several companies which themselves have subsidiaries and sub-subsidiaries. Such an organisation is illustrated in Figure 6.2 below.

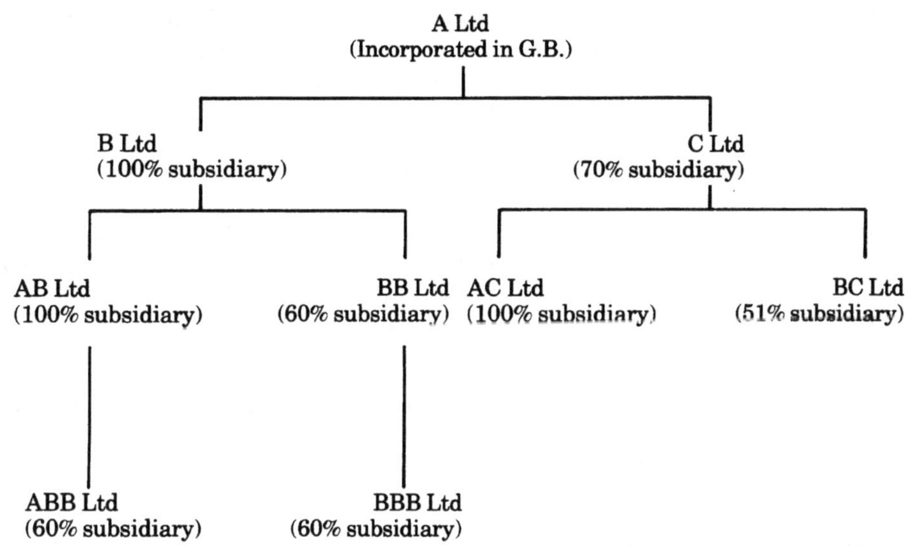

Figure 6.2

Interest of A Ltd in Group Companies

In B Ltd		100%
AB Ltd	(100% × 100%)	100%
ABB Ltd	(100% × 100% × 60%)	60%
BB Ltd	(100% × 60%)	60%
BBB Ltd	(100% × 60% × 60%)	36%
C Ltd		70%
AC Ltd	(70% × 100%)	70%
BC Ltd	(70% × 51%)	35.7%

In a vertical group the holding company is able to prepare consolidated accounts in one of two ways:

(i) The direct method under which each holding company within the group prepares consolidated accounts which are later used in the group consolidation. In the case of A Ltd shown in Figure 6.2 consolidation is required at two intermediate levels before the ultimate holding company

prepares group accounts. First, AB and BB must prepare consolidated accounts, and then B and C. Legally B and AB need not prepare group accounts as they are both 100% subsidiaries of a company incorporated in Great Britain.

(ii) The indirect method by which the holding company calculates its indirect interest in each company within the group as well as its direct interest in its immediate subsidiaries. Consolidated accounts are then prepared using the accounts of each group company with appropriate adjustments for minority interest. Where a group company is itself required to prepare consolidated accounts these are prepared as a separate exercise. As can be seen from Figure 6.2 these interests can be less than 50%. However where, as in the case of BBB Ltd., the parent holds a controlling interest in all of the intermediate companies the company is a subsidiary. A group with substantial "minority" holdings of this type is usually termed a mixed group.

2. Changes in the Degree of Control

In mixed groups a frequent complication is the acquisition or disposal of shares during the course of the year which alters the parent's degree of control and interest in the results and assets of the subsidiaries concerned. Such transactions do not pose new issues in consolidation, but are complicated to record.

Accounting treatment of the advanced aspects of consolidation discussed here is beyond the scope of this book and students who require a detailed analysis should refer to one of the texts listed on p. 70.

PROVISIONS OF THE COMPANIES ACT CONCERNING GROUP ACCOUNTS

The Companies Act stipulates that where, at the end of its financial year, a company has subsidiaries it must prepare and lay before its shareholders accounts dealing with the affairs of the company and its subsidiaries, referred to in the Act as group accounts. Such group accounts are not required where the company is, at the end of its financial year, the wholly owned subsidiary of another body incorporated in Great Britain, nor if the company's directors are of the opinion that:

(i) it is impracticable, or would be of no real value to members of the company, in view of the insignificant amounts involved, or would involve expense or delay out of proportion to the value of members of the company; or
(ii) the result would be misleading, or harmful to the business of the company or any of the subsidiaries; or
(iii) the business of the holding company and that of the subsidiary are so different that they cannot reasonably be treated as a single undertaking.

Apart from case (i) the approval of the Department of Trade and Industry is required if advantage is to be taken of this provision. The accounts which are prepared must combine the information contained in the separate accounts of the holding company and its subsidiaries but with such adjustments as the directors of the holding company consider necessary. As far as is practicable the accounts are required to comply with Schedule 4 to the Companies Act 1948, as amended in 1981. This means that the standard formats must be adjusted where necessary, but must otherwise be applied to show the group figures. PartIV of the revised Schedule 4 contains special provisions governing groups which are beyond the scope of this book.

STANDARD ACCOUNTING PRACTICE – GROUP ACCOUNTS (SSAP 14)

SSAP 14, lays down provisions for dealing with group accounts which are largely based on the requirements of the Companies Act, but provide more detailed treatment of certain aspects. The main provisions of the standard are summarised below:

Uniform group accounting policies should be followed by a holding company in preparing its consolidated financial statements. Where such group accounting policies are not adopted in the financial statements of a subsidiary, appropriate adjustments should be made in the consolidated financial statements. In exceptional cases where this is impracticable, different accounting policies may be used provided they are generally acceptable and there is disclosure of:

(a) the different accounting policies used;
(b) an indication of the amounts of the assets and liabilities involved, and where practicable, an indication of the effect on results and net assets of the adoption of policies different from those of the group;
(c) the reasons for the different treatment.

Group accounting periods and dates For the purposes of consolidated financial statements the financial statements of all subsidiaries should wherever practicable be prepared:

(a) to the same accounting date; and
(b) for identical accounting periods as the holding company.

If a subsidiary does not prepare its formal financial statements to the same date as the holding company and if it is not practicable to use for consolidated purposes special financial statements drawn up to the same date as those of the holding company (Department of Trade or other Government consent having been obtained as necessary), appropriate adjustments should be made to the consolidated financial statements for any abnormal transactions in the intervening period. The following additional information should be given for each principal subsidiary with a different accounting date:

(a) its name; and
(b) its accounting date; and
(c) the reason for using a different accounting date.

Where the accounting period of a principal subsidiary is of a different length from that of the holding company the accounting period involved should be stated.

Exclusion of subsidiaries from group accounts and consolidation. Group accounts need not be prepared, unless required by law, where the holding company itself is at the end of its financial year a wholly owned subsidiary.

When a company is not a wholly owned subsidiary and it does not prepare group accounts dealing with all its subsidiaries for one of the other reasons permitted under the Companies Act, the reason for the exclusion of any subsidiary must be stated. Consideration will need to be given as to whether the resulting financial statements give a true and fair view of the position of the group as a whole.

A subsidiary should be excluded from consolidation if:

(a) its activities are so dissimilar from those of other companies within the group that consolidated financial statements would be misleading and that information for the holding company's shareholders and other users of the statements would be better provided by presenting separate financial statements for such a subsidiary; or
(b) the holding company, although owning directly or through other subsidiaries more than half the equity share capital of the subsidiary, either:
  (i) does not own share capital carrying more than half the votes; or
  (ii) has contractual or other restrictions imposed on its ability to appoint the majority of the board of directors; or
(c) the subsidiary operates under severe restrictions which significantly impair control by the holding company over the subsidiary's assets and operations for the foreseeable future; or
(d) control is intended to be temporary.

The standard requires additional items to be disclosed in the accounts where subsidiaries are excluded from the consolidation.

Changes in composition of the group. When subsidiaries are purchased, the purchase consideration should be allocated between the underlying net tangible and intangible assets other than goodwill on the basis of the fair value to the acquiring company. If this is not done by means of adjusting the values in the books of the acquired company, it should be done on consolidation. Any differences between the purchase consideration and the value ascribed to net tangible assets and identifiable intangible asets such as trade marks, patents or development expenditure, will represent premium or discount on acquisition.

In the case of material additions to or disposals from the group, the consolidated financial statements should contain sufficient information about the results of the subsidiaries acquired or sold to enable shareholders to appreciate the effect on the consolidated results.

Where there is a material disposal, the consolidated profit and loss account should include:

(a) the subsidiary's results up to the date of disposal; and
(b) the gain or loss on the sale of the investment, being the difference at the time of the sale between:
  (i) proceeds of the sale and
  (ii) the holding company's share of its net assets together with any premium (less any amounts written off) or discount on acquisition.

Effective date of acquisition or disposal. The effective date for accounting for both acquisition and disposal of a subsidiary should be the earlier of:

(a) the date on which consideration passes; or
(b) the date on which an offer becomes or is declared unconditional.

This applies even if the acquiring company has the right under the agreement to share in the profits of the acquired business from an earlier date.

Outside or minority interest. Outside or minority interests in the share capital and reserves of companies consolidated should be disclosed as a separate amount in the consolidated balance sheet and should not be shown as part of the shareholder's funds;

debit balances should be recognised only if there is a binding obligation on minority shareholders to make good losses incurred which they are able to meet.

Similarly, the profits or losses of such companies attributable to outside interests should be shown separately in the consolidated profit and loss account after arriving at group profit or loss after tax but before extraordinary items. Minority interests in extraordinary items should be deducted from the related amounts in the consolidated profit and loss account.

Restrictions on distributions. If there are significant restrictions on the ability of the holding company to distribute the retained profits of the group (other than those shown as non-distributable) because of statutory, contractual or exchange control restrictions the extent of the restrictions should be indicated.

Before concluding this chapter it is necessary to refer briefly to two controversial aspects of group accounting which have recently been the subject of statements from the Accounting Standards Committee: accounting for acquisitions and mergers and accounting for foreign currency translation.

MERGER AND ACQUISITION METHODS OF ACCOUNTING FOR AMALGAMATIONS

The accounting treatment of acquisitions and mergers has been the subject of some controversy within the accountancy profession for many years. In the vast majority of cases an amalgamation takes place when one company acquires another, and in such cases the transaction is treated as a purchase by the acquiring company. The investment in the subsidiary is shown in the books of the parent at the amount of the consideration given in exchange for the shares acquired, whether this is in the form of cash or shares issued in the parent company. Upon consolidation the balance representing the investment is eliminated against the net assets of the subsidiary represented by share capital and pre-acquisition reserves. The effect of this procedure is to eliminate the pre-acquisition profits of the subsidiary from the pool of reserves available for distribution to shareholders. Whilst this approach is entirely sound it is argued that where two companies join together for the mutual benefit of their shareholders the distributable profit of the companies should not be reduced as a result of the transaction. The merger, or pooling of interest method, seeks to avert the "locking in" of reserves by recording the initial purchase at the nominal value of the shares issued rather than their fair value as required under normal consolidation principles. The contrast between the merger and acquisition methods is illustrated in the example below.

THE DEVELOPMENT OF STANDARD PRACTICE REGARDING MERGER ACCOUNTING

The first attempt within the UK to produce a standard dealing with merger accounting was ED 3, issued in 1971. This proposed standard sought to lay down criteria for determining whether an amalgamation should be treated as a merger or an acquisition. Strict criteria had to be met if an amalgamation was to qualify as a merger. However, the ED was never turned into a standard because the ASC received legal advice that the Companies Act 1948 required all companies to create a share premium account when shares were issued in exchange for a consideration which exceeded par value. The view expressed was that the merger method was illegal. Nevertheless, the position was not tested in the courts and a number of companies decided to use the merger method in appropriate cases.

Opponents of ED 3, and merger accounting in general argue that:

- the method allows unscrupulous companies to acquire others with distributable profits solely in order to bolster earnings and in order to mislead shareholders;
- any provisions introduced in order to prevent abuses will require the application of size criteria which will inevitably tend to be arbitrary;
- merger accounting, unlike acquisition accounting does not result in the revaluation of assets at the time of the combination, therefore the accounts are less likely to reflect true values.

In 1979 however, the position changed when, the courts held that share premium accounts were required whenever shares were issued in an amalgamation at a value exceeding par. This decision could have caused much difficulty to those companies which had adopted the merger method of accounting – and were now required retrospectively to adopt the acquisition approach. Therefore the government repealed the offending section of the 1948 Companies Act. In most cases of amalgamation it is not now necessary to create a share premium account.

This sequence of events thus left no guidance on when it is appropriate to use the merger method of accounting. As a result, the ASC has issued SSAP 23 to lay down standard practice in this area. The result is:

(1) Acquisitions for cash and amalgamations where substantial assets leave the group or a large minority holding exists (+ 10%).	Treat as acquisition (SSAP 14 applies)
(2) Amalgamations where consideration is by share exchange for 90% + of shares in acquired company and substantial assets do not leave the group.	Treat as merger (SSAP 23 applies)

ACCOUNTING FOR MERGER AND ACQUISITIONS (SSAP 23)

The conditions which must be met in order for a business combination to be accounted for as a merger are as follows:

- the business combination results from an offer to the holders of all equity shares and the holders of all voting shares which are not already held by the offeror; and
- the offeror has secured, as a result of the offer, a holding of (i) at least 90% of all equity shares (taking each class of equity separately) and (ii) the shares carrying at least 90% of the votes of the offeree; and
- immediately prior to the offer, the offeror does not hold (i) 20% or more of all equity shares of

the offeree (taking each class of equity separately), or (ii) shares carrying 20% or more of the votes of the offeree; and

- not less than 90% of the fair value of the total consideration given for the equity share capital (including that given for shares already held) is in the form of equity share capital; not less than 90% of the fair value of the total consideration given for voting non-equity share capital (including that given for shares already held) is in the form of equity and/or voting non-equity share capital.

Unless a business combination meets all of the foregoing criteria it must be accounted for as an acquisition in accordance with the provision of SSAP 14. In accordance with SSAP 23:

- In merger accounting, it is not necessary to adjust the carrying values of the assets and liabilities of the subsidiary to fair value either in its own books or on consolidation. However, appropriate adjustments should be made to achieve uniformity of accounting policies between the combining companies.
- In the group accounts for the period in which the merger takes place the profits or losses of subsidiaries brought in for the first time should be included for the entire period without any adjustment in respect of that poart of the period prior to the merger. Corresponding amounts should be presented as if the companies had been combined throughout the previous period and at the previous balance sheet date.
- A difference may arise on consolidation between the carrying value of the investment in the subsidiary (which will normally be the nominal value of the shares issued as consideration plus the fair value of any additional consideration) and the nominal value of the shares transferred to the issuing company. Where the carrying value of the investment is less than the nominal value of the shares transferred, the difference should be treated as a reserve arising on consolidation. Where the carrying value of the investment is greater than the nominal value of the shares transferred, the difference is the extent capitalised as a result of the merger and it should therefore be treated on consolidation as a reduction of reserves.

Example

On 31 December 1983, A. Eddison Holdings PLC (AEH) acquired all of the issued share capital of J. Oxley Ltd (JO). The terms were: 300,000 new AEH ordinary shares of 50p in exchange for the entire ordinary share capital of JO.

On the date of the acquisition the AEH shares had a market value of 160p each. It was agreed that the fixed assets of JO have a fair value of £300,000 and that all other items in the balance sheet are fairly valued at their book amounts. The summarised balance sheets of the two companies on 31 December, before recording the combination, were as set out below.

A. Eddison Holdings PLC

Liabilities	£
Capital and reserves	
Called up share capital	490,000
Profit and loss account	600,000
Creditors	400,000
	£1,490,000

Assets	£
Fixed assets – tangible	360,000
Current assets	1,130,000
	£1,490,000

The called up share capital of AEH consists of 980,000 shares of 50p.

J. Oxley Ltd

Capital and reserves	£
Called up share capital	100,000
Profit and loss account	140,000
Creditors	50,000
	£290,000

Assets	£
Fixed assets – tangible	180,000
Current assets	110,000
	£290,000

The called up share capital of JO consists of 100,000 ordinary shares of £1.

The acquisition method

Under the acquisition method AEH will incorporate the acquisition of JO at the market value of £480,000, giving rise to a share premium of 110p per share. The revised balance sheet will appear as set out below.

	£
Liabilities	
Capital and reserves	
Called up share capital	640,000
Share premium account	330,000
Profit and loss account	600,000
	1,570,000
Creditors	400,000
	£1,970,000

	£
Assets	
Fixed assets – tangible	360,000
Investments – shares in group companies	480,000
	840,000
Current assets	1,130,000
	£1,970,000

In consolidating the following adjustments are made in accordance with normal procedure and in order to recognise the fair value of the fixed assets.

	£	£
Dr share capital	100,000	
Dr profit and loss account	140,000	
Dr fixed assets	120,000	
Dr goodwill arising on consolidation	120,000	
Cr investments – shares in group co.		480,000
	480,000	480,000

The consolidated balance sheet of AEH appears as set out below.

A Eddison Holdings PLC and its subidiary

Liabilities	£
Capital and reserves	
Called up share capital	640,000
Share premium account	330,000
Profit and loss account	400,000
	1,570,000
Creditors	450,000
	£2,020,000

Assets	£
Fixed assets	
Intangible – goodwill arising on consolidation	120,000
Tangible	660,000
	780,000
Current assets	1,240,000
	£2,020,000

The merger method

Under the merger method AEH includes the acquisition of JO at the nominal value of the shares issued in exchange for the share capital of JO.

A . Eddison Holdings PLC

Liabilities	£
Capital and reserves	
Called up share capital	640,00
Profit and loss account	600,00
	1,240,000
Creditors	400,000
	£1,640,000

Assets	£
Fixed assets – tangible	300,000
Investments – share in group companies	150,000
	510,000
Current assets	1,130,000
	£1,640,000

When consolidating no account is taken of the fair value of the assets of JO which were incorporated at book value. The amount shown in respect of JO in the parent's accounts is set against the share capital of the subsidiary. In a few cases the amounts wil be equal, but in most cases they will differ and an adjustment will be necessary.

(1) Where the book value of the investment exceeds the share capital of the subsidiary the difference is written off against reserves.
(2) Where the book value of the investment is less than the share capital of subsidiary the difference is treated as an unrealised reserve arising on consolidation.

In the example the book value of JO amounts to £150,000 against share capital of £100,000. Accordingly the difference of £50,000 is written off against the profit and loss account balance to give the balance sheet shown below:

A. Eddison Holdings PLC and its subsidiary

	£
Liabilities	
Capital and reserves	640,000
Profit and loss account	690,000
	1,330,000
Creditors	450,000
	1,780,000
Assets	
Fixed assets – tangible	540,000
Current assets	1,240,000
	1,780,000

It is therefore possible to observe two differences resulting from the use of the merger rather than the acquisition approach. The merger method produces a figure for net assets which is £240,000 lower, of which goodwill arising on consolidation accounts for half. However, the merger approach gives a profit and loss account balance of £690,000 against £600,000. Furthermore if AEH receives a dividend from pre-acquisition profits it may credit it to profit and loss account and treat it as distributable up to an amount of £90,000. Any sums above this amount represent a reduction in capital and must be used to write down the cost of the investment in JO shown at £150,000 in the accounts of AEH.

Critics of the merger method argue that it is less valuable as an indication of fair value, and allows higher, and potentially imprudent, distributions. Advocates of the merger method do not deny these features but attach importance to offsetting their effect.

ACCOUNTING FOR FOREIGN CURRENCY TRANSLATIONS

With the advent of fluctuating exchange rates, companies have met great problems in accounting for the affairs of branches and subsidiaries located overseas. Several attempts have been made to develop an accounting standard to meet this problem. In the UK ED 16 and ED 21 were introduced and then subsequently withdrawn and in the USA FAS 8 is under review and will be replaced. The latest statement, SSAP 20, was issued by the ASC in April 1983 after ED 27 had been discussed for 2½ years. In order to understand the topic it is important to distinguish between two basic concepts:

Transactions In which one currency is converted into another possibly giving rise to a profit or loss if the sum realised is different from the figure at which the transaction was originally included in the books of accounts.

Translation where accounting balances are converted into another currency – but no actual transaction takes place giving rise to profit or loss. In such cases differences will arise if assets and liabilities have previously been recorded in the books at a different exchange rate – but no actual loss will occur until a conversion transaction takes place.

> "It is generally accepted that all transactions, profits or losses, should be reflected in the accounts of the period in which they arise – if appropriate as exceptional or extraordinary. However, considerable debate has surrounded the development of accounting practice for dealing with translations. Deficits or surpluses arising on translation which are passed through the profit or loss account, may substantially distort the results, notwithstanding that no loss has actually been incurred and that any notional loss may be reversed if exchange rates change in the future."

SSAP 20 makes a distinction between the accounting treatment for individual companies and groups and in the latter case permits two possible methods of accounting for translation – the net investment (closing rate) and temporal method.

Translation at the individual company stage is dealt with in Chapter 3.

THE CONSOLIDATED FINANCIAL STATEMENTS STAGE

The method used to translate financial statements for consolidation purposes should reflect the financial and other operational relationships which exist between an investing company and its foreign enterprises.

In most circumstances the closing rate/net investment method should be used and exchange differences accounted for on a net investment basis. However, in certain specified circumstances the temporal method should be used. SSAP 20 outlines the difference between the two methods in the following way.

THE CLOSING RATE/NET INVESTMENT METHOD

> This method recognises that the investment of a company is in the net worth of its foreign enterprise rather than a direct investment in the individual assets and liabilities of that enterprise. The foreign enterprise will normally have net current assets and fixed assets which may be financed partly by local currency borrowings. In its day-to-day operations the foreign enterprise is not normally dependent on the reporting currency of the investing company. The investing company may look forward to a stream of dividends but the net investment will remain until the business is liquidated or the investment disposed of.
>
> Under this method the amounts in the balance sheet of a foreign enterprise should be

translated into the reporting currency of the investing company using the rate of exchange ruling at the balance sheet date. Exchange differences will arise if this rate differs from that ruling at the previous balance sheet date or at the date of any subsequent capital injection (or reduction).

Amounts in the profit and loss account of a foreign enterprise should be translated at the closing rate or at an average rate for the accounting period.

THE TEMPORAL METHOD

For most investing companies in the UK and Ireland foreign operations are normally carried out through foreign enterprises which operate as separate or quasi-independent entities rather than as direct extensions of the trade of the investing company.

However, there are some cases in which the affairs of a foreign enterprise are so closely interlinked with those of the investing company that its results may be regarded as being more dependent on the economic environment of the investing company's currency than on that of its own reporting currency. In such a case the financial statements of the foreign enterprise should be included in the consolidated financial statements as if all its transactions had been entered into by the investing company itself in its own currency. For this purpose the temporal method of translation should be used.

The introduction to SSAP 20 lists the following examples of situations where the temporal method may be appropriate. Where the foreign enterprise:

(a) acts as a selling agency receiving stocks of goods from the investing company and remitting the proceeds back to the company;
(b) produces a raw material or manufactures parts or sub-assemblies which are then shipped to the investing company for inclusion in its own products;
(c) is located overseas for tax, exchange control or similar reasons to act as a means of raising finance for other companies in the group.

The mechanics of the temporal method are identical to those used in preparing the accounts of an individual company outlined on p. 42, with the result of each transaction being translated into the local company's currency using the exchange rate in operation on the date on which the transaction occurred or at an average rate for the period.

Under the temporal method the company may denominate its foreign equity investments in the appropriate foreign currencies and translate the carrying amounts at the end of each accounting period at the closing rates of exchange. Where investments are treated in this way, any resulting exchange gains or losses on the borrowings should then be offset, as a reserve movement, against these exchange differences.

In the consolidated financial statements, subject to certain conditions, the exchange gains or losses on such foreign currency borrowings, which would otherwise have been taken to the group profit and loss account, may be offset as reserve movements against exchange differences on the retranslation of the net investments.

The detailed accounting treatment of foreign exchange transactions is beyond the scope of this book, and is therefore not illustrated by an example.

CONCLUSION – GROUP ACCOUNTS AND THE BANKER

The general purpose of preparing group accounts is to show the affairs of a group of companies as if they were one entity. In practical terms this is often merely a recognition of commerical reality. Therefore whenever a banker wishes to review the performance and position of a group of companies he should examine the group accounts. Because of the use of the historic cost convention the accounts of the holding company will provide little useful information in this respect, the principle item appearing in such accounts being the interest in subsidiaries which will be shown at the original historic cost of the shares acquired. After several years trading this figure is unlikely to represent the worth of the underlying investment. However, bankers often make use of accounts in order to estimate the assets which might be available if a company were broken up. In this case it is important to recognise that the group accounts do not show the assets which might be directly realised for the benefit of the parent company's shareholders. Many of the assets of a group may be held by subsidiary companies in which the parent is only a shareholder. In the event of a liquidation the parent company would count as a shareholder, and would only share in the proceeds arising from the realisation of subsidiary company assets after many prior claims had been satisfied.

In practical terms the lending banker can greatly strengthen his position if he lends principally to those companies within a group which hold tangible assets, or alternatively lends to the parent company and obtains guarantees from its subsidiaries. However, when analysing accounts with such a course of action in mind it is important to bear two key points in mind:

(1) The accounts of any group of companies only show the position on the last day of each accounting period. At any other time it is probable that group assets will be located with other companies. For example accounts due may not be settled regularly but cleared only at the year end, and cash balances may be rapidly transferred to those companies which need them.
(2) The treatment of investments in group companies has caused much controversy over the years. Bankers should be especially careful in dealing with companies which change their accounting policies in relation to group affairs, sell or buy a few shares in an investment as a result of which its classification changes, or have significant exposure to foreign currency movements.

FURTHER READING

Of the books referred to at the end of Chapter 1, several include chapters on group accounts, including Wood (Vol. 2), Edwards and Mellett, Egginton, and Samuels, Rickwood and Pipes. Two of the best known specialist books on group accounts, more advanced than the level required for the Institute of Bankers examination are shown below:

M. H. Frankel, *The Preparation of Group Accounts* (Financial Training, 1982).
A. T. Roberston, W. J. Jarvis, *Group Accounts* (Gee & Co., 1980).

Chapter 7
Inflation and Accounting

INTRODUCTION

The fundamental approach to the preparation of accounts over many years has been to use the historical cost of each transaction as the monetary amount for recording it in the books and accounts. For many decades this approach worked perfectly well, and whilst it was not correct to say that the accounts gave the "value" of the items shown, the cost recorded for each item was rarely materially different from the contemporary cost at the time the accounts were prepared. Thus the accounts often gave some indication of the current cost of the items shown therein. However, with the development of rapid inflation, especially during the 1970s, this assumption was generally confounded. No longer did the accounts give a reasonable guide to the current *cost*, let alone the current *value* of the items shown. This deficiency presented severe problems to companies using accounts for decision making, and also to external users, including banks.

As a result of the deficiencies, the accountancy profession has attempted to develop ways of showing the effects of changing prices within accounts. The first proposal, to include a supplementary statement in the annual report showing accounts adjusted for the change in retail prices, was withdrawn in response to a report from the Sandilands Committee in 1975. This report advocated a system of accounting based on current costs, but the proposed standard developed in order to bring the system into effect was strongly attacked, and was withdrawn. In 1975 a compromise solution was introduced under which listed companies voluntarily included a supplementary current cost statement in the annual report. After a trial period a new standard was introduced which major companies were expected to follow.

SSAP 16 required all listed and larger unlisted companies to include a set of current cost accounts in their annual report in addition to, or in place of, the historic cost accounts. However, this system attracted a good deal of criticism, not least because it did not apply to all companies, yet all were required to show the same true and fair view in their accounts. Furthermore, it was felt that the accountancy profession brought itself discredit by preparing two sets of figures within the same report; it seemed impossible that each could show a true and fair view. Thus by 1984 it was felt that the time had arrived for fresh proposals to be introduced, and the Accounting Standards Committee published a statement of intent followed by an exposure draft, ED 35 showing details of a new system which would bring the adjustments to historic cost figures, required by the impact of changing prices, within the main set of accounts. However, this statement received little support and within a few months had been withdrawn.

This chapter includes a review of the impact of inflation on historic cost accounts, a description of the current cost accounts required by SSAP 16, with an example, and an outline of the revised system of current cost accounting proposed by the ASC in 1984. Table 7.1 shows the main events in the history of inflation accounting in the United Kingdom.

THE DEFICIENCIES OF HISTORIC COST ACCOUNTING IN A PERIOD OF INFLATION

The historic cost convention has a number of considerable advantages. The items shown in the accounts are based on factual transactions, and the amount of judgement used in preparing accounts is thus kept to a minimum. As a result the scope for bias and manipulation is minimised and the figures may be verified by external auditors against documentary and other evidence. However, where prices rise rapidly, the historic cost figure becomes of less and less significance, and the value of accounts for decision making is severely restricted. The particular deficiencies of historic cost figures are as follows:

(1) *There is no distinction in the accounts between real and fictitious growth.* Thus a rising figure for sales over a period of years might seem to indicate a growth in sales, but the truth may be very different. In order to determine the actual position it is necessary to know how individual product prices have changed over the period. The same problem arised in relation to the trend in profits, but in this case the position is further complicated by difficulties in measuring the profit figure itself.

(2) *Assets in the balance sheet tend to be undervalued.* Over a period of time the cost of non-monetary items in the balance sheet tends to move further and further from their current value due solely to changes in the value of money. This is particularly true of property and plant, and to a lesser extent of stocks. In practice many companies revalue land and buildings in order to show the current value.

(3) *The cost of consuming stocks and fixed assets is understated and profit thereby overstated.* This is a major problem and is best illustrated by two examples.

Table 7.1
A. Chronology: Accounting for Inflation in the United Kingdom

1960s –	*Historic Cost Accounting* – subject to periodic revaluation of certain items – i.e. property. ICAEW recommended special reserve to provide for increased cost of replacing assets.
	Philips Co NV using Replacement Cost Accounting in the Netherlands.
1973 –	*ED 8 Accounting for Changes in Purchasing Power of Money* – proposes CPP statement as supplement to accounts for listed companies only.
1974 – June	*PSSAP 7 Accounting for Changes in Purchasing Power of Money* – Implements ED 8.
1975 – Sept.	*Sandilands Report* – advocates Current Cost Accounting (CCA) ED 8 withdrawn.
– Nov.	*Inflation Accounting Steering Group (Morpeth Committee)* appointed to draw up detailed rules for implementing CCA.
1976 – October	*ED 18 The Morpeth Report.* Proposed to introduce Current Cost Accounting for main accounts in place of historic cost accounts – ultimately for all companies.
1977 – June	Morpeth proposals thrown out by Emergency General Meeting of the ICAEW.
– July	Accounting Standards Committee announces new review of Inflation Accounting.
– October	*Hyde Proposals* recommend supplementary statement of adjustments to historic cost profit or loss and summary current cost balance sheet. (Listed and other large companies only).
1979 – May	*ED 24 Current Cost Accounting* Proposed standard based on Hyde Guidelines.
1980 – March	*SSAP 16* – Current Cost Accounting – Implements ED 24 for all listed and larger unlisted companies. CCA Monitoring Working Party established.
1982 – July	*ICAEW General Meeting* – votes against motion to suspend 3 year trial period of SSAP 16.
– Sept.	Reconstituted ASC begins review of all standards including SSAP 16. Inflation Accounting Sub-Committee established.
1983 – April	*Interim Report of Neville Committee* (CCA Monitoring Working Party) published – recommends replacement of SSAP 16 supplementary statements.
– Sept.	Final report of Neville Committee – endorses interim proposals.
– Nov.	*Carsberg Report* – The Usefulness of Current Cost Accounting – a report on a research programme, recommends continuance of SSAP 16, subject to certain amendments.
1984 – Spring	*Statement of Intent – Accounting for the effects of changing prices* proposes CCA information shown as a note to the main accounts.
– July	*ED 35 – Accounting for the effects of changing prices* – proposes a statement of current cost information as a note to the accounts to be covered by the Auditor's Report.
1985 – April	*ED 35* withdrawn in response to widespread opposition.

Stock Replacement

Example

Each year a company buys 10,000 items on 1 January and sells them all by the end of the year. In 1983 the price was £5 each, but the supplier announces that on 1 January 1984 the price will rise to £6.

During 1983 the items were sold at £6 each and the company had other expenses of £5,000.

Under historic cost accounting the companies profit and loss account would appear as follows:

	£
Sales	60,000
Purchases	50,000
Gross profit	10,000
Expenses	5,000
Net profit	5,000

When the company attempts to buy new stock to replace that which it has sold it will need £60,000 (£6 × 10,000), but its cash resources amount to only £55,000 (sales proceeds £60,000 less expenses £5,000). Thus despite making a profit it is not in a position to maintain its operating capability without borrowing or raising further capital. In the real world it is unlikely that the situation will appear as starkly as this, but consist of a mass of small price increases which go unnoticed. The longer the delay between goods being acquired and their being sold, the more serious the position is likely to be.

Fixed Asset Replacement

Example

On 1 January 1984 a firm buys a machine for £10,000 which it expects to last for five years and have no scrap value. It has no other assets or liabilities and distributes all of its profits to its shareholders. Its profit – before taking account of depreciation – is expected to be £3,000 per annum. Ignore taxation.

The profit and loss account of the company for each year will be as follows:

	£
Trading profit	3,000
Depreciation	2,000
Net profit	1,000
Distributed	1,000
Retained	—

The cash generated by the business each year amounts to £3,000, represented by the trading profit; the depreciation charge merely amounting to an accounting charge in order to spread the cost of using the machine over its expected life. After five year's trading the firm will have generated £15,000, and distributed £5,000, leaving a balance of £10,000 representing the original capital, which may be returned to the owners, or reinvested. However, if there have

been significant price increases in the meantime, the firm will find that it has insufficient resources to replace the equipment, which has now reached the end of its economic life.
As with stock it is probable that a firm will replace fixed assets on a frequent basis, and that the funds retained by virtue of depreciation will not be used for direct replacement of the same machine. However the overall impact of the rise in prices will be the same. By charging depreciation on the historic cost, rather than upon the current cost of consuming the assets, the accounts will fail to show the true cost of maintaining the operating capacity of the business.

(4) *The amount of distributable profit shown by the accounts takes no account of the increased level of funds required to maintain the investment in working capital or of the extent to which the company's future investment in physical and monetary resources is likely to be met by borrowings.* In addition to requiring additional resources for investment in stocks and fixed assets, a firm needs to retain resources for working capital. The level of this investment is likely to increase as a result of rising prices, but this will not be measured by historic cost accounts. Thus traditional accounts do not measure the impact of changing price levels on the monetary assets and liabilities of the business.

In practice although it is likely that rising prices will increase the need for investment in the business, this will not be financed entirely by the shareholders. A large part of the increase will probably be met by borrowing and this fact should be taken into account in calculating what can be treated as distributable. In economic terms the lenders to the business bear part of the cost of changing prices, but are compensated by the interest received on the loans. These effects are not measured in traditional historical cost accounts.

(5) *As a result of the use of historical cost in calculating a company's taxation liability company liquidity is depleted.* During the period of rapid inflation substantial tax allowances were given to offset the effect of rising prices, but these have now been ended.[1]

(6) *Comparisions between the accounts of the same firm over a period, and between two firms in similar businesses are invalidated.* Because the accounts do not measure the profits in real terms, and the underlying assets are stated at price levels which vary, such comparisions are often misleading and unsafe. Only when all of the figures take full account of price changes since assets were acquired may valid comparisions be made.

SSAP 16 – CURRENT COST ACCOUNTING

The CCA system is based upon a concept of capital which is represented by the *net operating assets* of the business – i.e. the *operating capability*. A change in the input prices of goods and services used and financed by the business will affect the amount of funds required to *maintain the operating capability* of the net operating assets. In contrast to the HCA, CCA is designed to reflect this in the determination of profit and in the balance sheet.

[1] See Chapter 4 for details of accelerated capital allowances, and the stock relief provisions.

CURRENT COST PROFIT

This is determined in two stages:

(1) *Current cost operating profit* – the surplus arising from the ordinary activities of the business in the period after allowing for the impact of price changes on the funds needed to continue the existing business and maintain its operating capability.
(2) *Current cost profit attributable to shareholders* – is the surplus for the period after allowing for the impact of price changes on the funds needed to maintain the shareholders proportion of the operating capability.

In the balance sheet assets are stated at their *value to the business* based on current price levels. Surpluses arising from revaluations are credited to a *current cost reserve*.

SCOPE AND APPLICATION

SSAP 16 was published in March 1980, and applied to accounting periods starting on 1 January 1980, to annual financial statements intended to give a true and fair view of the financial position and profit or loss *other than* those of the following entities, which are exempt:

(a) "unlisted" entities which satisfy *two or more* of the following criteria:
  (i) *annual turnover* less than five million pounds;
  (ii) *historical* cost balance sheet value of fixed assets, investments and current assets, at the beginning of the accounting period is *less than* £2,500,000;
  (iii) average number of UK employees is *less than* 250.
(b) Wholly owned subsidiaries.
(c) (i) Authorised insurers;
  (ii) Property investment and dealing entities;
  (iii) Investment trusts, unit trusts and similar entities;
  (iv) Non-profit making entities.[2]

METHOD OF PRESENTATION

The entity may opt for any one of the three options in complying with the standard.

(a) *main* accounts – *historical cost* with *supplementary current cost accounts* which must be prominently displayed;
(b) *main* accounts – *current cost* with *supplementary historical cost accounts*;
(c) *only* accounts – *current cost accounts* with adequate disclosure of historical cost information in order to comply with the Companies Acts.

SSAP 16 requires publication of:

[2] The "size" criteria laid down are similar to those set out in the EEC Fourth Directive for defining a "large" company. The standard therefore requires current cost accounts for, amongst others, large unlisted companies. The standard uses the term "entities" and thus does not restrict the application to "companies".

(a) a *current cost* balance sheet;
(b) a *current cost* profit and loss account;
(c) *current cost* earnings per share *for listed companies.*

The (non-mandatory) explanatory note to SSAP 16 suggests that it "may assist users" to provide the following with the current cost accounts;

(a) an *explanation* of the current cost accounts and the adjustments made;
(b) a statement of change in the equity shareholder's interest;
(c) a current cost source and application of funds statement;
(d) an alternative gearing adjustment;
(e) selected current cost ratios.

In order to comply with the standard the following four adjustments are required:

(a) a cost of sales adjustment (COSA);
(b) a depreciation adjustment;
(c) a monetary working capital adjustment ((MWCA); and
(d) a gearing adjustment.

Each of the first two adjustments is designed to charge the cost of consuming the life of the assets based on their "value to the business".

SSAP 16 defines value to the business as:

(a) net current replacement cost;
or, if a permanent diminution to below net current replacement cost has been recognised;
(b) recoverable amount, (the greater of the net realisable value of an asset, and where applicable, the amount recoverable from its further use).

This point is illustrated in Figure 7.1.

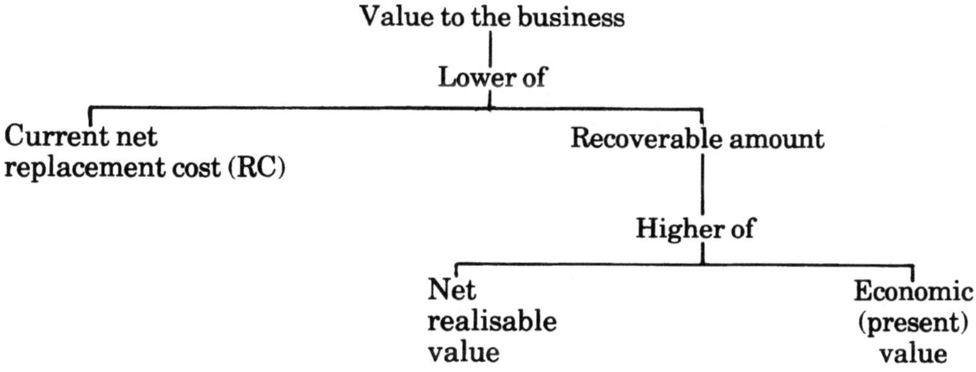

Figure 7.1 Value to the business

Where an asset will normally be replaced it is shown at the net current replacement cost, and charged on this basis in the profit and loss account. However where it is not to be replaced it is shown at its net realisable value, unless the value expected from using it is greater. In the latter case it is shown at its economic, or present value, which is calculated in the manner described in Chapter 12.

Plant and Machinery is normally valued on the basis of indices shown in the government publication *Price Index Numbers for Current Cost Accounting*. However, where the result is inappropriate the company may use its own index, quotations from suppliers, expert opinions, or market prices for equivalent second-hand equipment. Particular problems arise when an asset cannot be replaced because of changes in technology, especially where there are major gains in efficiency, as has been the case with computers. In such cases the assets must be revalued and the profit and loss account charged with the cost of consuming the modern equivalent.

Land and Buildings are normally valued on the basis of open market value. However, where the buildings are of a specialist nature they must be treated in the same way as plant and machinery.

Stocks and work-in-progress are usually valued by using an index. In practice, although the valuation of the majority of items is reasonably straightforward, particular problems do arise. It is beyond the scope of this book to discuss these, and the reader is therefore referred to the reading at the end of the chapter.

Example

The following are the final accounts of the Excelsior Company Ltd for the year ending 31 December 1981 together with balance sheets as at 31 December 1980 and 31 December 1981. The accounts have been prepared on an historical cost basis.

Notes

(1) The price indices for measuring the changes in the purchasing power of money were as follows:

	Beginning	*End*
1980	112	116
1981	116	120

(2) Fixed assets were acquired when the purchasing power index was 100.
(3) Assume that transactions, purchases and sales occurred evenly throughout the year.
(4) Stock at 1 January 1981 was acquired evenly during the last three months of 1980.
(5) Stock at 31 December 1981 was acquired evenly during the last three months of 1981.
(6) Depreciation of plant and machinery is at the rate of 14% on cost.
(7) The specific price indices relating to plant and machinery were as follows:

	Beginning	*End*
1980	120	140
1981	140	160

(8) The specific price index was 100 when the plant and machinery was purchased.
(9) The specific price indices for stock were as follows:

	Beginning	*End*
1980	115	131
1981	131	151

(10) The specific indices used for stock are to be used in computing the monetary working capital adjustment.
(11) The freehold premises were valued on an existing use basis, the value being £45,000 at 31 December 1980 and £75,000 at 31 December 1981.

(12) The debenture interest was paid on 31 December 1981.

(13) The aggregate monetary working capital adjustment to 31 December 1980 was £2,130 and the aggregate cost of sales adjustment £6,907. The accumulated depreciation adjustment to 31 December 1980 is to be charged equally between the profit and loss account and the current cost reserve.

Excelsior Company Ltd – Profit and Loss Account to 31.12.1980

	£	£	£
Sales			300,000
Opening stock		66,000	
Add purchases		180,000	
		246,000	
Less closing stock		72,000	
Cost of sales			174,000
			126,000
Less Expenses		73,500	
Debenture interest		1,500	
Depreciation		10,500	85,500
Net profit for year			£40,500

Balance sheets

31.12.80		31.12.81
£		£
	Fixed Assets: Tangible	
30,000	Freehold premises (at cost)	30,000
75,000	Plant and machinery (at cost)	75,000
(42,000)	Less depreciation	(52,500)
63,000		52,500
	Current assets	
66,000	Stock	72,000
43,500	Debtors	59,500
15,000	Cash	48,500
124,500		180,000
	Less current liabilities	
25,500	Creditors and Accruals	30,000
99,000		150,000
	Creditors due after more than 1 year	
15,000	10% Debentures	15,000
84,000		135,000
£147,000		£187,500
£	*Represented by:*	£
	Authoritised share capital:-	
	Allotted share capital:	
100,000	Ordinary shares of £1 each	100,000
47,000		87,500
£147,000		£187,500

Procedure
Adjustments to 1980 (opening) balance sheet

(1) *Revaluation of freehold property* From book value £30,000 to £45,000 (n. 11)		Dr freehold prop Cr current cost reserve (CRR)	£15,000 £15,000
(2) *Revaluation of plant and machinery* By index to 140 (n. 7)		Dr plant and m/c Cr current cost reserve	£30,000 £30,000
Cost $\frac{£75{,}000 \times 140}{100}$	105,000		
Cost	75,000		
Revaluation surplus	30,000		
(3) *Revalue accumulated depreciation* By index to 140 (n. 7), charging half to profit and loss account and balance to current cost reserve (n. 13).		Dr current cost reserve Dr profit and loss Cr depreciation	£8,400 £8,400 £16,800
H. C. depreciation $\frac{£42{,}000 \times 140}{100}$	£58,800		
Less H. C. balance	£42,000		
Depreciation revaluation	£16,800		
(4) *Revalue stock to replacement cost* Average index during last 3 months of 1980 $115 + \frac{(131 - 115) \times 21}{24}$	129	Dr stock Cr current cost reserve	£1,023 £1,023
Index 31.12.80	131		
Stock at historic cost	66,000		
Stock at replacement cost $\frac{66{,}000 \times 131}{129}$	67,023		
Adjustment (n. 9)	1,023		
(5) *Enter cost of sales adjustment in current reserve* (n. 13)		Dr profit and loss Cr current cost reserve	£6,907 £6,907
(6) *Enter monetary working capital adjustment in current cost reserve* (n. 13)		Dr profit and loss Cr CCR	£2,130 £2,130

Current Cost Reserve

	£		£
Depreciation (3)	8,400	Freehold property (1)	15,000
Balance carried down	46,660	Plant and machinery (2)	30,000
		Stock (4)	1,023
		Profit and loss (5)	6,907
		Profit and loss (6)	2,130
	£55,060		£55,060

Profit and Loss

	£		£
Depreciation (3)	8,400	Balance per historic cost accounts	47,000
Current cost reserve			
(5)	6,907		
(6)	2,130		
Balance C/D	29,563		
	£47,000		£47,000

The opening current cost balance sheet is shown below.

As a result of the foregoing transactions the current cost reserve and profit and loss account show the following transactions.

Excellsior Company Ltd – Current Cost Balance Sheet 31.12.80

	£	£
Fixed assets		
Freehold premises		45,000
Plant and machinery	105,000	
Less depreciation	58,800	46,200
		91,200
Current assets		
stock	67,023	
debtors	43,500	
cash	15,000	
	125,523	
Current liabilities		
Creditors and accruals	25,500	
Net current assets		100,023
		191,223
Creditors due after more than one year		
10% Debentures		15,000
		£176,223
Capital and reserves		£
Allotted share capital		100,000
Profit and loss account		29,563
Current cost reserve		46,660
		£176,223

After the opening current cost balance sheet has been prepared the four current cost adjustments are calculated.

Calculation of current cost adjustments

(7) *Current Cost Depreciation Adjustment*

The profit and loss charge for depreciation must be based on the cost of consuming the current value of the items concerned, and the historic cost charge increased by the difference. The charge is calculated on the average index for the year of 150.

HCA depreciation $10{,}500 \times \frac{150}{100} = 15{,}750$	
HCA depreciation charged	10,500
Current cost adjustment	5,250

Cr Depreciation	£6,300
Dr profit and loss	£5,250
Dr CCR	£1,050

In addition to this adjustment it is necessary to take account of the impact in the change in current costs between the average and the year end index used in calculating accumulated depreciation in the balance sheet.

Depreciation for year based on closing index	16,800
Historic cost depreciation	(10,500)
Current cost adjustment	(5,250)
Backlog to be charged to CCR	1,050

(8) *Cost of Sales Adjustment*

The cost of sales adjustment comprises the sum of the differences between the historic cost of each item sold, and its current cost at the time of sale. Fortunately it is not necessary to determine each difference individually. Instead the total difference for the year may be found by the use of "the average method".

Dr profit and loss	£9,778
Cr CCR.	£9,776

The average stock index for the year is 141 (n. 9), that for opening stock is 129 (see step 4. above), and that for closing stock 148.5 (see step 10. below)

Opening and closing stocks are adjusted to the average index rate for the year, and with purchases are used to find the current cost of sales figure. This is compared with the historic cost of sales to give the current cost adjustment.

Opening stock 66,000 × 141 =		72,140
	129	
Purchases		180,000
Closing stock 72,000 × 141 =		68,384
	148.5	
Current cost of sales		183,776
Historic cost of sales		174,000
Cost of Sales adjustment		9,776

(9) *Monetary working capital adjustment*
The purpose of the monetary working capital adjustment is to reflect the amount which should be retained from profits in order to maintain the monetary working capital intact for operations, subject to the gearing adjustment dealt with below.
The net monetary working capital consists of debtors and working cash balances, less creditors and any short term borrowings augmenting working capital. Any balances which are not considered part of working capital are reflected in the gearing adjustment analysed below.

The MWCA is found by converting the opening and closing net MWC to the average index rate for the year, using an index which reflects the nature of the working capital items. The resulting figures are used to find the change in monetary working capital due to volume changes, this amount is deducted from the total change in order to find the change attributable to changes in current costs.

	Opening	*Closing*
Debtors	43,500	59,500
Creditors	25,500	30,000
NMWC	18,000	29,500
	× 141	× 141
	131	151
Current cost NMWC	19,374	27,546
Change due to volume		8,172
Total change		11,500
Monetary working capital adjustment		3,328

Dr p and l.	£3,328
Dr CCR	£3,328

(10) *Gearing adjustment*

The object of the gearing adjustment is to take account of the capital structure of the company in determining the current cost profit attributable to shareholders. Where a company is partly financed by borrowings, the current cost adjustments are abated by the proportion of borrowings to net operating assets at current cost using the following formula:

$$\text{Abatement} = \frac{\text{NB}}{\text{NOA}}$$

where NB represents average net borrowings, and NOA represents average net operating assets shown on a current cost basis. (See current cost balance sheets for 1980 above and 1981 below.) Where a company has substantial cash resources which do not form part of working capital, and have not been taken into account in the MWCA, these are to be set against borrowings in calculating the gearing adjustment.

In the case of Excellsior the cash balances of £15,000 and £58,000 match or exceed the opening and closing borrowings of £15,000. Consequently there is no gearing adjustment in this case. Had there been no cash balances the adjustment would have been calculated as shown below.

$$\frac{\dfrac{15{,}000 + 15{,}000}{2}}{\dfrac{176{,}223 \times 247{,}213}{2}} = \frac{15{,}000}{211{,}718} = 7.1\%$$

In order to calculate the gearing adjustment it is necessary to determine the adjustments to the closing balance sheet, and to prepare the first part of the statement showing net operating assets at current cost.

Adjustments to 1981 (closing) balance sheet

(11) *Revaluation of freehold property*

From opening revalued amount £45,000 to £75,000 (n. 11)

Dr freehold prop.	£30,000
Cr CCR.	£30,000

(12) *Revaluation of plant and machinery*

By index from 140 to 160 (n. 7)

Dr p. and l.	£15,000
Cr CCR.	£15,000

Cost	$\pounds75{,}000 \times \frac{160}{100}$ =	120,000
Revalued 31.12.80		105,000
Revaluation surplus		15,000

(13) *Revalue accumulated depreciation*

By index from 140 to 160		Dr CCR.	£8,400
Balance	$£52{,}500 \times \frac{160}{100} = 84{,}000$	Cr depreciation	£8,400
Brought forward (n. 3)	58,800		
Shortfall	25,200		
p. and l. a/c charge (n. 11)	16,800		
Backlog	8,400		

The backlog depreciation arises from the revalution of costs incurred in prior years, and is charged to current cost reserve.

(14) *Revalue stock to replacement cost*

The closing stock adjustment from the preceeding year is reversed (n. 4). Revalue closing stock using average index for final three months

$$131 + (151 - 131) \times \frac{21}{24} = 148.5$$

Stock at historic cost	72,000	Dr p. and l.	£1,023
Stock at replacement cost		Cr CCR.	£1,023
$72{,}000 \times \frac{151}{148.5} =$	73,213	Dr stock	£1,213
Revaluation adjustment	1,213	Cr CCR.	£1,213

On the basis of the foregoing adjustments the part of the balance sheet showing the net operating assets can be prepared, and the gearing adjustment completed. The current cost profit and loss account and the current cost reserve may then be prepared, and the balance sheet finalised.

Excellsior Company Ltd Current Cost Profit and Loss Account for the period ending 31 December 1981

Extract		£
Profit before interest and taxation on a historical cost basis		42,000
Less Current cost operating adjustments		
Depreciation	5,250	
Cost of Sales	9,776	
Monetary Working Capital	3,328	18,354
Current cost operating profit		23,646
Gearing adjustment	—	
Debenture interest	1,500	1,500
Current cost profit attributable to shareholders for the year		22,146

Current Cost Reserve

			£
P. and l (5)	1,023	Balance b/d	46,660
Depreciation (7)	1,050	Freehold property (11)	30,000
Depreciation (13)	8,400	Plant and machinery (12)	15,000
Balance c/d	95,904	Stock (13)	1,213
		P. and L. (MWCA – 9)	3,328
		P. and L. (COSA – 8)	9,776
	£105,977		£105,977

Excellsior Company Ltd – Current Cost Balance Sheet 31.12.81

Fixed assets - tangible	£	£
Freehold premises		75,000
Plant and machinery	120,000	
Less depreciation	84,000	36,000
		111,000
Current assets		
Stock	73,213	
Debtors	59,500	
Cash	48,500	
	181,213	
Less current liabilities		
Creditors and accruals	30,000	
Net current assets		151,213
		262,213
Creditors due after more than 1 year		
10% Debentures		15,000
		£247,213
Capital and reserves		
Allotted share capital		100,000
Profit and loss account b/f	29,563	
for 1981	22,146	51,709
Current cost reserve		95,504
		£247,213

The Historical and Current Cost Accounts Compared

The current cost accounts produce a profit for the company of £22,146 compared with £40,000 on an historic cost basis. As a result, and because of adjustments relating to previous years, the retained profits available for distribution fall from £87,500 to £51,709. When the operating assets are shown at current cost the value rises by £59,713. If the current cost return on capital employed is found based on the average capital employed of £226,718 it falls to 10.4% compared with 33.7% on a comparable historical cost basis. Thus it can be seen that the current cost figures give more up to date information on the current cost of the assets employed, and on the returns achieved from their use. It is perhaps therefore surprising that current cost accounting has not attracted more support, particularly from the external users of accounts. It is the response to SSAP 16, and the proposals for a new accounting standard that we consider in the remainder of this chapter.

CRITICISMS OF SSAP 16 IN PRACTICE

When SSAP 16 was introduced in 1980 it was announced that no changes would be made in its content for a period of three years. A working party was set up to monitor its operation, and in due course to recommend any necessary changes. After a short while a number of difficult problems emerged, including the following:

(a) the selection of suitable indices for valuing specialist plant;
(b) obtaining suitable data for valuing plant located overseas particularly in countries where reliable and suitable indices are not produced;
(c) the valuation of specialist plant and buildings for which no obvious market exists and for which no suitable index is prepared;
(d) the calculation of a cost of consumption where an asset is not to be replaced because there is to be a change in the nature of a company's business;
(e) determining the cost of consuming the value of assets where there is no modern equivalent asset, possibly due to technological change;
(f) the definition of monetary working capital, and the components of the gearing ratio; and
(g) the application of current cost accounting to specialised industries such as commodity trading and shipping, where the concept of operating capital maintenance was not obviously relevant.

To each of these problems there was a theoretical answer based on the concept of maintaining operating capability. Sometimes a company would need to calculate its own index of prices.[3]

However, most of the solutions were somewhat subjective and therefore difficult to audit, and some tended to be expensive; accordingly there was considerable criticism of the standard. The monitoring working party found that current cost accounts were not widely used, and never in preference to the historical cost figures. Whilst it was generally agreed that historical cost accounts were misleading, there was little support for SSAP 16 and little agreement on the form which any successor should take.[4]

At about the same time as the working party prepared its report the results of a research study undertaken by the Research Directorate of the Institute of Chartered Accountants was published.[5]

This suggested that, given the relatively short time for which SSAP 16 had been in force, there was "surprisingly extensive use" made of current cost information in accounts. However, this conclusion was disputed by some. As the Accounting Standards Committee considered the problem of devising a successor to SSAP 16 three issues emerged as central to the debate.

(1) The need for accounting information relating to the impact of changing prices to be part of the companies statutory accounts, rather than a (confusing) supplement, not subject to audit, giving a separate and different set of results.

[3] For a full discussion of the problems and possible solutions see R. W. Scapens, A. J. Southworth, and G. Stacey, *Case Studies in Current Cost Accounting* (ICAEW).
[4] Report of the CCA Working Party (Chairman T. Neville) published by the Accounting Standards Committee.
[5] B. Carsberg, *The Usefulness of Current Cost Accounting: Conclusions from the Research Programme* (ICAEW).

(2) The need for all companies to follow the same basic set of rules in accordance with the requirement to show a true and fair view in the accounts – the issue of "universality".
(3) The consequence arising from the second issue that small companies and specialist companies should be able to follow different detailed requirements in order to show the impact of changing prices within their accounts – the issue of "flexibility".

The ASC spent many weeks attempting to resolve these issues. It became apparent that a uniform system would not command sufficient support to be effective, but that a flexible system would produce diversity in accounts rather than standard practice. Further, a supplementary statement was no longer considered acceptable, but exemption for small companies did not seem to be consistent with the requirements of the Companies Act which appeared to apply equally to all.

The issue was eventually resolved when the ASC received legal advice that the cost of preparing the information concerned might be taken into account in devising a system of inflation accounting for all companies. In other words, that small companies might be allowed to follow one system because it was not cost effective for them to follow that which applied to larger entities. As a result the ASC issued a Statement of Intent on Current Cost Accounting in March 1984 and four months later an Exposure Draft (ED 35).

THE STATEMENT OF INTENT AND ED 35

As a result of the evidence considered by it the ASC concluded that information about the effects of changing prices is valuable to the users of financial statements and should be provided where the effects are material, and the usefulness of the information justifies the cost of preparation. Because all businesses are affected by changing prices, all accounts should reflect this regardless of the size or activity of the entity concerned. However, the ASC believed that this could not be achieved at present for small companies and value based ones such as insurance companies, property companies, and investment based organisations such as unit trusts and investment trusts. Accordingly, the ASC announced its intention to issue a new proposed standard for non-value based public companies during 1984. All other companies and nationalised industries would be exempt from compliance with the new standard, although the government intended requiring public entities to comply on a voluntary basis. A standard for the excluded companies would not be introduced until a cost effective method of showing the effect of rising prices had been developed and a process of consultation and public comment had been undertaken. In July 1984 the ASC published ED 35, *Accounting for the effects of changing prices*.

In ED 35 the ASC proposed that most public limited companies should disclose current cost information either in the main accounts or as a note thereto. As a result the current cost information would form part of the statements on which the auditor reports, and which are required to show a true and fair view. The proposed standard would have required current cost adjustments for depreciation, cost of sales, monetary working capital and gearing, and the effect of these adjustments on the profit and loss for the year to be shown, as well as the current cost of stocks and fixed assets. Simplifications were proposed in the calculation of the current cost of certain items and in the calculation of the gearing adjustment.

Shortly after the commencement of the discussion period of the new exposure draft, two of the accountancy bodies forming the Accounting Standards Committee announced their opposition to ED 35. In April 1985 the ASC bowed to the opposition to the new standard; ED 35 was withdrawn. Shortly afterwards, the Stock Exchange announced that compliance with SSAP 16, which, technically, remained in force, was to become voluntary for all listed companies. The search for an acceptable solution to the problem of inflation accounting started again.

CURRENT COST ACCOUNTS AND THE BANKER

As major users of accounts it would be strange if banks alone did not find information about the effect of changing prices to be valuable. However, it would be wrong for the banks to want such information to be produced if the cost of so doing could not be justified by the company. Wherever the impact of changing prices on profitability is material, it is likely to play a crucial role in determining the viability of a lending proposal. Equally where an estimate of break up values is required it is likely to be more useful if it is based upon current values, rather than outdated ones. Thus bankers in general will benefit from the inclusion of current cost information in the main financial statements. It is to be hoped that in the near future a way can be found of reflecting the impact of changing prices in the accounts of all companies in a way which is both effective and economical.

FURTHER READING

Of the books listed below those by Farmer and Mallinson are practical introductions to the subject, whilst the text by Whittington covers the theoretical background.

E. R. Farmer, *Accounting for Inflation and Price Level Changes* (Gee, 2nd. ed., 1980).

D. Mallinson, *Understanding Current Cost Accounting* (Butterworths, 1980).

G. Whittington, *Inflation Accounting: An introduction to the Debate* (Cambridge University Press, 1983).

Chapter 8
Interpretation of Financial Accounts

INTRODUCTION

Bankers examine the financial accounts of companies for two main reasons: first, in order to determine whether the business is healthy and is likely to make repayment of any facilities in the ordinary course of business; and secondly in order to estimate the likely value of the company's assets if it proves necessary to liquidate the business and to realise the assets piecemeal. This chapter deals with the first objective, interpreting the accounts of a company as a going concern. The gone concern evaluation is dealt with in Chapter 13.

As anyone who has recently examined the annual report of a company will be aware, modern accounts contain a mass of detailed and daunting information. Reading a company report efficiently and effectively requires a good deal of skill, knowledge, and practice. As a result many organisations employ trained analysts in order to undertake the examination of company accounts. However, all businessmen require some skill in reading accounts, and those engaged in lending money especially. Fortunately, it is usually possible to obtain almost all of the important information shown in a set of financial statements by examining a few key aspects, and by monitoring the relationship between a number of major items within the accounts. The principal technique employed in order to undertake such an examination is that of ratio analysis. In many ways this term is a misleading one. Not all of the figures which are usually calculated are ratios, some are multiples, other percentages, but all deal with relationships between key figures. The basic approach is to identify changes in key relationships through comparisons with past periods, similar companies, and targets or yardsticks. The purpose of employing the technique is to simplify the information contained in the accounts so that the important features may be properly comprehended. If, in calculating the ratios, aspects are discovered which require investigation, then further probing must take place until a satisfactory explanation is obtained. The methodology of ratio analysis is summarised in Table 8.1. It will be seen that some of the approaches shown there relate to the internal figures produced by a company, and are not dealt with in this chapter. However, the basic approach and philosophy remains the same. This chapter concludes with a consideration of the academic work which has been carried out in order to determine which ratios and combinations of ratios provide the best means of predicting company failure. However, before dealing with ratio analysis as such, it is worth considering the items in the annual report which should be examined as a prelude to calculating ratios.

Table 8.1
The Methodology of Ratio Analysis

A. *COMPARISONS WITH PREVIOUS FIGURES*	
Funds statements	Analysis of changes in balance sheet/financial condition.
Common form statements	All figures expressed as proportion with balance sheet total as 100.
Ratios change	Each figure expressed as a ratio or percentage of the corresponding figure for the previous year. (e.g. Sales this year as ratio of last year).
B. *COMPARISONS WITH OTHER FIGURES IN ACCOUNTS*	
Ratio analysis relationships found by calculating ratio or percentages	Examples Profit to sales Profit to capital Current assets/current liabilities

Although called ratio analysis, the figures may be calculated as percentages or expressed in periods of days, weeks and months.

The ratios may themselves be compared with:

(a) Previous figures – trend analysis;
(b) Similar firms – interfirm comparisons;
(c) Targets (e.g. objective set for current ratios of 2:1).

C. *COMPARISONS WITH BUDGET*
Variance Analysis – expressed in monetary terms.

PRELIMINARY EXAMINATION OF THE ANNUAL REPORT

In Chapter 1 the major components of an annual report were outlined and it was observed that it is often useful to spend some time examining the Chairman's statement and the Directors' Report. Neither of these documents are technically part of the financial statements but the latter contains statutory information and must now be examined by the auditors in order to ensure that the information shown therein is consistent with that given in the accounts. The *Directors' Report* should be examined for the following reasons:

(1) In order to determine the principal activities of the company and whether there have been any significant changes during the year.
(2) In order to obtain information concerning the progress of the business including future developments, important post-balance sheet events, significant changes in fixed assets, and activities in research and development.
(3) In order to discover the identity of the directors and the nature and extent of their interest in the company.
(4) In order to discover whether there are any substantial minority shareholdings in the share capital (public companies only). In the case of larger companies the annual report will generally contain a *Chairman's Statement* which will be a useful source of information on:

- recent trading experience and future prospects; and
- the performance of the various parts of a divisionalised or multi-product company.

In general the Chairman's Statement will provide a useful interpretation of the figures appearing in the accounts. However, it is important to remember that in order to obtain an impartial or critical view of events, it may be helpful to refer to press comment as well. Although much briefer than the two statements referred to, the *Auditor's Report* is essential reading for all those wishing to place reliance on the information shown in a company's accounts. The auditor is appointed annually to report to the shareholders on the accounts laid before them. He is required by the Companies Act to form an opinion on whether proper books of account have been kept, and whether the accounts agree therewith. Provided he is satisfied on these points and obtains all the information and explanations he requires then no reference need be made to these points in his report. A typical auditor's report is shown below.

> "AUDITORS REPORT TO THE MEMBERS OF. . .
>
> We have audited the financial statements on pages . . . to . . . in accordance with approved Auditing Standards.
>
> In our opinion the financial statements (which have been prepared under the historical cost convention as modified by the revaluation of land and buildings) give a true and fair view of the state of the company's affairs at 31 December 19... and of its profit and source and application of funds for the year then ended and comply with the Companies Act 1985
>
> C . . . . . . Accountants
>
> Date . . . . . . Place . . . . . . "

This report is unqualified and indicates that the auditor was able to obtain all the evidence he required in order to express an opinion on the accounts.

Evidence is usually obtained by a process of sampling based on the auditor's judgement of what is required in order to formulate an opinion. If he is unable to obtain all of the evidence he requires, or otherwise disagrees with the view or figures shown in the accounts, then he will qualify his report. His qualification will fall into one of two categories:

(i) *Uncertainty* – where there is an uncertainty which prevents the auditor from forming an opinion on a matter.

(ii) *Disagreement* – where the auditor is able to form an opinion on a matter but this conflicts with the view given by the financial statements.

A further division arises from the seriousness of the circumstances giving rise to the qualification, thus four main types of qualification are possible as shown in Table 8.2

Table 8.2
Audit Report Qualifications

Nature of circumstances	*Material but not fundamental* (Knowledge of the matter would be likely to influence the user of financial statements)	*Fundamental* (so as to undermine the view given by the financial statements taken as a whole)
Uncertainty	"Subject to" opinion	Disclaimer of opinion
Disagreement	"Except" opinion	Adverse opinion

The significance of the four types of qualification is as follows:

Disclaimer – unable to form an opinion as to whether the financial statements give a true and fair view;

Adverse – auditor states that in his opinion the financial statements do not give a true and fair view;

Subject to – auditor effectively disclaims opinion on a particular matter which is not considered fundamental;

Except – auditor expresses an adverse opinion on a particular matter which is not considered fundamental.

In the case of a small company the auditor will often provide an accountancy service in addition to performing an audit and will prepare accounts on the basis of the explanations given to him by the directors. In such circumstances it is standard practice to include a qualification in the audit report along the following lines:

> "In common with many businesses of similar size and organisation the company's system of control is dependent upon the close involvement of the directors/managing director (who are major shareholders). Where independent confirmation of the completeness of the accounting records was not available we have accepted the assurances from the directors/managing director that all of the company's transactions have been reflected in the accounts."

Where for any reason the auditor is not satisfied with the view shown by the accounts he must qualify his opinion in the ordinary way, disclaiming an opinion altogether if necessary.[1]

RATIO ANALYSIS

The purpose of ratio analysis is to help the reader of a set of accounts understand the information shown by highlighting a number of key relationships. It is perfectly possible to calculate ratios involving every separate figure in the accounts. However, such a procedure would be meaningless as many of the figures are unrelated. Furthermore, many of the ratios tend to deal with aspects of the same relationship, and there is little point in calculating several ratios in order to investigate the same point. Thus in the analysis which follows only 14 ratios are used, although in some cases reference is made to further ratios which may be calculated if required. This should not be taken to suggest that there are no other valid ratios, merely that the ratios shown are those considered most useful to a banker in normal circumstances. Above all it should be emphasised that in undertaking ratio analysis it is important to keep an open mind and to be prepared to adapt the procedure to suit the particular circumstances of the case.

The ratios to be calculated are summarised in Table 8.4. The ratios shown are based on the formats required by the Companies Act, which presents a number of problems to analysts:

(1) The terminology used by the Act is not necessarily that which is appropriate for ratio analysis, for example, the heading "current assets" includes items which are not realisable within a year, and should therefore be excluded from the current ratio.
(2) Companies are able to adapt the formats to suit their special circumstances, thus any reference to the headings used in the Act may not be strictly applicable to every company. In each case the analyst must be flexible and apply the principle on which the ratio is based in order to produce a satisfactory result.
(3) The accounts need not show the reference, for the heading used in the Companies Act formats. Whilst this improves their presentation it tends to make the analyst's job more difficult.
(4) Companies are able to make use of any of the four profit and loss account formats, and the two formats for the balance sheet. It is, therefore, impossible to produce a comprehensive guide without making it unreasonably lengthy. In this case, reference is made only to the first two formats in each case, and the table must be adapted for use with the horizontal profit and loss account formats.

[1] Audit procedures and audit reports are now governed by Auditing Standards and Guidelines issued by the Auditing Practices Committee, a joint committee representing all of the professional bodies dealing with auditing. For further details see the authors' own articles on the subject "In our opinion" in *The Bankers Magazine* (April, 1980) and "Audit Reports: The new regulations and their significance to bankers" in *The Journal of the Insitute of Bankers* (February, 1981).

In order to resolve the problem of unsatisfactory terminology in the formats the items to be used in calculating ratios are redefined and shown in Table 8.3. Although this is an unsatisfactory device it is preferable to the alternative of calculating the ratios in accordance with the terms of the Act, even if the result is theoretically incorrect. In discussing the ratios in detail the reason for calculating such ratio in the manner suggested will be explained. The ratios are arranged under the following headings:

Activity;
Profitability;
Liquidity;
Control of Working Capital;
Solvency.

In order to demonstrate the calculation and interpretation of the ratios use will be made of the accounts of AC Ltd, which are based on the accounts of a real company. The figures used in calculating the ratios are shown on p. 199 and the ratios for the company are themselves shown on p. 213.

Example

AC Ltd Profit and Loss Account

		Year 1		*Year 2*		*Year 3*
		£000		£000		£000
Turnover		4,186		5,601		7,991
Cost of sales		2,830		4,071		6,327
Gross profit		1,314		1,530		1,664
Distribution costs	217		251		312	
Administrative expenses	718	935	832	1,083	912	1,224
Trading profit		379		447		440
Income from fixed asset investment		21		—		—
Operating profit		400		447		440
Interest payable		96		154		278
Profit before tax on ordinary activities		304		293		162
Tax on profit on ordinary activities		112		46		140
Profit on ordinary activities after taxation		192		247		20
Extraordinary items		—		71		241
Profit/loss for the financial year		192		176		(221)
Dividends paid		80		120		—
Profit retained		112		56		(221)

AC Ltd Balance Sheet

		Year 1		Year 2		Year 3
ASSETS		£000		£000		£000
Fixed assets						
Intangible assets						
Goodwill		80		70		60
Tangible assets (n. 1)		1,350		1,662		2,081
Investments		241		241		—
Current assets						
Stocks (n. 2)	830		1,446		2,390	
Debtors (n. 3)	1,357		1,450		1,872	
Cash	33	2,220	36	2,932	—	4,262
		3,891		4,905		6,403
LIABILITIES						
Capital and reserves						
Called up share capital		400		400		400
Share premium account		432		432		432
Revaluation reserve		112		193		750
Profit and loss account		720		776		555
		1,664		1,801		2,137
Provisions for liabilities and charges						
Deferred taxation	190		160		147	
Pension provision	48		80		110	
		238		240		257
Creditors						
Hire purchase loans			117		133	
Bank loans and overdrafts	706		1,159		1,853	
Other creditors (n. 4)	1,283	1,989	1,588	2,864	2,023	4,009
		3,891		4,905		6,403

Notes

	Year 1	Year 2	Year 3
(1) *Tangible assets* (at NBV)			
Land and buildings	671	752	1,309
Plant and machinery	488	703	583
Fixtures, fittings, tools and Equipment	191	207	189
	1,350	1,662	2,081

(NB: The published accounts contain full details of cost and depreciation. Land and buildings are shown at valuation and the other tangible fixed assets at cost less depreciation).

Depreciation for the year amounted to:

Land and buildings	4	5	7
Plant and machinery	121	175	170
Fixtures, fittings, tools and Equipment	38	41	38
	163	231	215

(2) *Stocks*	Year 1	Year 2	Year 3
Raw materials and consumables	271	617	820
Work-in-progress	190	189	176
Finished goods	369	640	1,394
	830	1,446	2,390

(3 *Debtors* All due within one year apart from an amount of £400 shown within other debtors representing a loan to a supplier of which £200 is repayable within 1 year.

Trade debtors	1,106	1,168	1,131
Other debtors	62	89	504
Prepayments	189	193	237
	1,357	1,450	1,872

(4 *Other creditors* All repayable within one year.

Trade creditors	958	1,287	1,494
Other creditors including taxation and social security	190	156	357
Accruals and deferred income	135	145	172
	1,283	1,588	2,023

Of the hire purchase loan the following amounts were due to be paid more than 12 months after the balance sheet date.

1974	*1975*
70	80

All of the bank borrowing was on overdraft and is repayable on demand.

ACTIVITY

The activity ratio is a measure of the relationship between sales and the total assets employed by the company. A sharp rise in this ratio may indicate that the company is expanding too quickly, and is allowing sales to increase more rapidly than the underlying asset base, a situation often referred to as "overtrading". Conversely a reduction in the ratio can indicate a decline in efficiency or a fall in demand for the company's products. It is not possible to specify the multiple which should be found when calculating this ratio, the interpretation of which must be made in the light of any trend which is observable in the figures, and in the other ratios calculated.

AC Ltd activity ratio

	Year 1	*Year 2*	*Year 3*
$\frac{\text{Turnover}}{\text{Total assets}}$	$\frac{4186}{3891} = 1.07$	$\frac{5601}{4905} = 1.14$	$\frac{7991}{6403} = 1.25$

In the case of AC Ltd there has been a 16% increase in the activity ratios over the period, however little can be determined from the trend, at this stage of the analysis.

PROFITABILITY

It is often said that profit is the criteria by which success or failure in a business should be judged. However, whilst a profit is obviously better than a loss, the degree of success cannot be judged until the profit is compared with some other feature such as the capital used to achieve it or the turnover from which it has been generated.

The profit margin ratio The profit margin ratio monitors the profit made in relation to sales. Where detailed company accounts are available it is usual to calculate the gross profit margin and the net profit margin separately, the former showing the profit made on sales before taking account of overheads. However, when ratios are calculated from published accounts it is only possible to calculate a gross profit margin when format 1 is used. In order to enable comparisions to be made between those companies which use formats 1 and 2 it is therefore best to base the ratio on the profit achieved before taking investment income, which does not influence turnover, into account. This line does not have a name in the standard formats but most companies regard this as trading profit. In interpreting the profit margin ratio it is again important to observe any trend, but in making comparisons between companies it is vital to appreciate that profit margins vary considerably from industry to industry. Companies engaged in retailing are likely to have quite rapid turnover and to operate on low margins allied to high volume, whilst those firms engaged in selling a few large items must make a high profit in relation to the sales value of each one. In interpreting this ratio it is important to bear in mind that the gross profit is only affected by a fall in prices or a rise in costs, whilst the net profit is determined by a combination of gross profit and overhead expenses.

AC Ltd **Figures used in Ratio Analysis**

	Year 1	*Year 2*	*Year 3*
1. Turnover	4,186	5,601	7,991
2. Trading profit	379	447	440
3. Operating profit	400	447	440
4. Profit before tax	304	293	162
5. Interest payable	96	154	278
6. Operating cash flow			
Profit after tax	192	247	20
Depreciation	163	231	215
	355	478	235
7. Total assets	3,891	4,905	6,403
8. Total capital employed			
Capital and reserves	1,664	1,801	2,137
Provision for liabilities and charges	238	240	257
Hire purchase loans	—	117	133
Bank loans and overdrafts	706	1,159	1,853
	2,608	3,317	4,380
9. Shareholders funds			
Capital and reserves	1,664	1,801	2,137
Goodwill	(80)	(70)	(60)
	1,584	1,731	2,077
10. Working capital			
Current assets	2,220	2,932	4,262
Current liabilities	(1,989)	(2,794)	(3,929)
	231	138	333

11. Current assets	2,220	2,932	4,262
Less long-term debtor			(200)
	2,220	2,932	4,062
12. Current liabilities	1,989	2,864	4,009
Less long-term hire purchase		70	80
	1,989	2,794	3,929
13. Liquid CA			
Debtors	1,357	1,450	1,872
Cash	33	36	
Long-term debtor			(200)
	1,390	1,486	1,672
14. Average sales per month (one twelfth of turnover)	349	467	666
	12	12	
15. Stocks	830	1,446	2,390
16. Trade debtors	1,106	1,168	1,331
17. Trade creditors	958	1,287	1,494
18. Total borrowings	706	1,276	1,986
19. Total external liabilities	2,227	3,164	4,266

AC Ltd profit margin ratio

	Year 1	*Year 2*	*Year 3*
$\frac{\text{Trading Profit}}{\text{Turnover}}$	$\frac{379}{4186} = 9.05\%$	$\frac{447}{5601} = 7.98\%$	$\frac{440}{7991} = 5.51\%$

An examination of the profit margin ratio of the company reveals an adverse trend suggesting difficult market conditions, and possibly rising costs. The company is engaged in manufacturing and selling earthenware products, and would be expected to earn a good deal more than 5% on sales. Although the turnover figure has grown impressively, these figures were recorded during a period of rapid inflation, and the growth in volume amounts to about 50% of the increase. An examination of the accounts shows that distribution costs and administrative expenses have increased more slowly than sales, confirming that the problem lies with selling prices and basic costs rather than with overhead costs or lack of volume. The gross profit shown by the accounts gives a ratio of 31.4%, 27.3%, and 20.8% over the three year period.

Return on capital. This ratio is central to any examination of the performance of a business. It measures the return achieved by the company on the capital employed by it during the period. Thus it enables comparisons to be drawn not only with other companies, but also with other forms of investment. In reaching any conclusions on the result obtained it is important to bear in mind the following points:

(1) The profit figure used in the calculation is subject to all of the vagaries of accounting discussed in Chapter 1–7 of this book, including the impact of changing prices, and of variations in calculating depreciation and stock values.

(2) The capital figure is based on the book values shown in the records of the company, it does not represent the figure which could be realised by investors and redeployed in alternative forms of investment.

Table 8.3
Companies Act 1981 – Definition of terms used in Ratio Analysis

Reference	*Name*	*Method of Calculation (References to Co. Act format headings)*			
		P and L Format 1	*P and L Format 2*	*B/Sheet Format 1*	*B/Sheet Format 2*
1.	Turnover	Item 1	Item 1		
2.	Trading profit	Total 1–6	Total 1–8		
3.	Operating profit	Total 1–11	Total 1–13		
4.	Profit before tax	As shown (no reference)	As shown (no reference)		
5.	Interest payable	Item 12	Item 14		
6.	Operating cash flow	Profit after tax plus Depreciation and any other charges not involving the use of funds (see Funds Statement)			
7.	Total assets			Items A–D	Assets A–D
8.	Total capital employed			Items H, I, J, K and E1, E2 and E5 *plus* any other borrowings	Liabilities A, B and C1, C2 and C5 *plus* any items shown under C repayable after more than a year *plus* any other borrowings
9.	Shareholders' funds less intangible assets (plus minority interests – group accounts only)			Items K less A or CII 5 and BI plus MI	Liability A less Assets A or CII and BI plus MI
10.	Working capital			Current assets *less* Current liabilities (as defined below)	
11.	Current assets			Items C and D *less* amounts due after more than 1 year	Assets C and D *less* amounts due after more than 1 year
12.	Current liabilities			Item E and J (if due within 1 year)	Liabilities C and D *less* amounts due after more than 1 year
13.	Liquid current assets			Current assets (see above) *less* CI, CII6 and D	Current assets (see above) *less* assets CI, CII6, and D
14.	Average sales per month	Item 1 divided by 12	Item 1 divided by 12		
15.	Stocks			Items CI 1–3	Asset CI 1–3
16.	Trade debtors			Item CII 1	Asset CII 1
17.	Trade creditors			Item E4 and H4	Liability C4
18.	Total borrowings			Items E1, 2, 5 and H1, 2 and 5	Liabilities C1, 2 and 5
19.	Total external liabilities			Items E, H, I and J	Liabilities B, C and D

Note
These definitions should not be applied rigidly. Some adaptation may be necessary where companies adapt the formats.

Table 8.4
Key Financial Ratios

Name	*Components*		*Interpretation*
Activity Asset turnover ratio	Turnover / Total assets	1 ÷ 7 × 100	Indicates the rate at which assets are turned over. Adequate sales are necessary to generate profit, but too a high level may indicate over-trading.
Profitability Profit margin ratio	Trading profit / Turnover	2÷1 × 100	The percentage of profit derived from sales before crediting other income and taking account of tax and interest. Where format 1 is used gross profit margin may also be calculated (format item 3 ÷ Item 1)
Return on capital employed ratio	Operating profit / Total capital employed	3 ÷ 8 × 100	The rate of profit achieved before financing borrowings, divided by the total capital resources utilised by the business.
Return on shareholders' funds ratio	Profit before tax / Capital and Reserves *plus* Minority interests (group accounts only). *Less* called up share capital not paid and intangible assets	4 ÷ 9 × 100	The rate of profit before tax achieved by the company (group) on its shareholders funds. Capital not paid is deducted and intangible assets are excluded in order to ensure comparability between companies.
Liquidity Working capital ratio	Working capital / Total assets	10 ÷ 7 × 100	Indicates the adequacy of working capital in relation to total resources. Empirical evidence suggests this ratio to be a good indicator of approaching problems.
Current ratio	Current assets / Current liabilities	11 ÷ 12 :1	Traditional ratio for measuring the ability of a company to meet to meet its debts as they fall due.

Table 8.4
Key Financial Ratios

Liquid (or quick) ratio	Liquid current assets (excluding stock and similar items) / Current liabilities	13 ÷ 12 :1	A narrower version of the current ratio.
Control of working capital			
Stock ratio	Stocks / Average sales per month	15 ÷ 14 months	Identifies changes in stock levels in relation to changes in the size of the business. (Where P and L A/c format 1 is used the ratio may (more correctly) be based on the cost of sales.)
Debtors' ratio	Trade debtors / Average sales per month	16 ÷ 14 months	Relates changes in the level of debtors to changes in the size of the business.
Creditors' ratio	Trade creditors / Average sales per month	17 ÷ 14 months	Relates changes in the level of creditors to changes in the size of the business. (Where purchases figure is known ratio should be calculated thereupon).
Solvency			
Gearing ratio	Total borrowings / Total capital employed	18 ÷ 8 × 100	Measures the company's dependance upon borrowed funds.
Liabilities ratio	Total external liabilities / Shareholders' Funds	19 ÷ 9	Indicates the total dependance of the business on external finance compared with shareholders funds.
Interest cover ratio	Operating profit / Interest payable	3 ÷ 5 times	Indicates the ability of the company to meet its external financing costs.
Borrowings/cash flow ratio	Total borrowings / Operating cash flow	18 ÷ 6 times	Indicates the ability of the company to repay its borrowings from the cash flow which it generates.

(3) Although the return on capital ratio permits comparisons to be made between alternative investments it must be borne in mind that investors will take into account the risk and uncertainty associated with each. Not all businesses should achieve the same return on capital, those in high risk industries must earn a premium to offset the additional risks run by investors.
(4) Any return achieved by a firm in an inflationary environment should provide a sufficient margin to compensate for the impact of inflation.

A number of alternative methods exist for calculating capital employed for use in this ratio. Theoretically the ratio should be based on the capital employed by the company during the year, but excluding any short-term items. In practice it is not possible to discover the capital employed on a day-to-day basis from the annual accounts, and for this reason some authorities advocate using an average of the opening and closing figures. There are two problems with this approach:

(1) The opening and closing figures may not reflect the typical position throughout the year.
(2) The annual report will only show the relevant figures for the current and preceeding year, thus if the averaging method is used it is not possible to obtain a comparable figure, unless the previous annual report is also obtained.

In practice it is often convenient to base the return on capital ratio on the closing figures. It is of course essential to calculate the ratio in an identical fashion for each of the years concerned, and in examinations to follow the instructions given in the question. The definition of the term capital for use in calculating the ratio is a complex matter. The total should clearly include shareholders' funds, and long-term borrowings, as well as any long-term liabilities. These figures were often added together in accounts prepared under previous Companies Acts. However it is now necessary to extract some of the relevant figures from the heading "creditors" in the balance sheet. In practice many companies use overdrafts as a source of long-term finance, and it is therefore sound practice to include all borrowings in the figure for total capital employed. A second reason for adopting this approach is to enable a comparison to be made with the profit earned before meeting finance costs.

The relationship between the return on capital ratio and the return on shareholders' funds ratio, discussed below, is shown in the following table:

Table 8.5
Definition of Profit and Capital

Operating profit	Total capital employed
Less Interest	*Less* Borrowing and non-current liabilities
Profit before tax	Shareholders' funds

The table demonstrates that whilst it is conceptually correct to compare operating profit with total capital employed. The correct figure for comparsion with shareholders' funds is the profit before tax, which is attributable to shareholders.[2]

It is therefore suggested that the total capital employed figure is calculated as follows:

Format 1	Capital and reserves	Item K
	Accruals and deferred income	J
	Provisions for liabilities and charges	I
	Creditors: amounts falling due after more than one year	H
	Creditors: amounts falling due within one year	
	Debenture loans	E 1
	Bank loans and overdrafts	E 2
	Bills of Exchange payable	E 5
	Plus any other borrowings	
Format 2	Capital and reserves	Liability A
	Provisions for liabilities and charges	B
	Accruals and deferred income	C
	Creditors:	
	Due within one year	D 1, 2 and 5
	Due after more than a year	D all

Strictly speaking accruals and deferred income should only be included if due after more than one year. Regrettably the Companies Act does not require companies to show the maturity of such items unless shown in the alternative format headings E9 and H9 (format 1) and C9 (format 2). It may not therefore be possible to determine the correct treatment of these items in every case.

AC Ltd – Return on capital ratio

	Year 1	*Year 2*	*Year 3*
$\frac{\text{Operating profit}}{\text{Total capital employed}}$	$\frac{400}{2608} = 15.33\%$	$\frac{447}{3317} = 13.48\%$	$\frac{440}{4380} = 10.04\%$

The return on capital employed figure for AC has fallen over the period. It is already known that profit margins have fallen, which provides part of the explanation, but it can also be seen that the capital employed figure has increased over the period whilst profit has remained virtually static. This is clearly an unsatisfactory trend.

Return on shareholders' funds ratio. The return on shareholders' funds ratio also deals with the return that the business achieves on the capital employed by it, but in this case the ratio deals only with the capital provided by the shareholders. Thus comparison is made between the profit attributable to the shareholders and the capital and reserves of the company, which are the "property" of these investors.

Several points should be noted:

- If the balance sheet includes called up share capital not paid (shown as item/asset A or CII 5) this should be deducted from capital and reserves in order to calculate the ratio.

[2] Where trading profit is given this should be compared with capital/assets employed in trading operations. Where the company has income from investments the profit from all operations may be used to compare with capital invested in trading assets and other investments.

- It is normal to calculate this ratio using the profit before tax figure because, as was noted in Chapter 5, the impact of the tax charge can distort profits after tax from year to year in a way quite unrelated to the efficiency with which the shareholders funds have been employed.
- Where the company has no preference shareholders it is acceptable to refer to the ratio as the *return on equity* capital. However, where shareholders with preferential rights exist, their dividends and capital must be excluded from the calculation of the ratio, if the return on equity capital is to be found.
- In the case of group accounts it is necessary to take account of the position of minority interests. The share of profits attributable to minority shareholders is included in profit before tax and therefore it is necessary to include the interest of minority shareholders in the total of shareholders funds.

In general the return achieved for shareholders should always exceed the return on total capital employed. As will be shown in Chapter 12, which deals with financing decisions, the purpose of borrowing should be to obtain capital at lower cost than it could be provided by shareholders, thereby enhancing their earnings. If the return achieved for shareholders is less than that obtained on total capital employed this objective is not being achieved.[3]

AC Ltd – Return on shareholders' funds

	Year 1	*Year 2*	*Year 3*
$\frac{\text{Profit before tax}}{\text{Capital and reserves}}$	$\frac{304}{1584} = 19.19\%$	$\frac{293}{1731} = 16.92\%$	$\frac{162}{2077} = 7.80\%$

AC Ltd has suffered a serious decline in the return achieved for its shareholders. In Year 1 the return obtained exceeded the return on total capital employed. However by Year 3 the return on shareholders funds was lower. This trend represents a serious erosion of profitability, and the return of 7.8% achieved in Year 3 cannot be regarded as satisfactory.

LIQUIDITY

The liquidity ratios deal with the ability of a company to meet its liabilities as they fall due. If a company has insufficient short-term assets in relation to its short-term liabilities it might be unable to meet its commitments, and be forced into liquidation. Thus ratios which compare the relationship between various groups of current assets and current liabilities are calculated. In general, companies encounter difficulties in this area when, unwisely, they use liquid funds in order to aquire fixed assets leaving themselves short of liquid resources, or when short-term funds are used to make long-term investments, or to finance losses.

[3] It should be remembered that accounts do not deal with capital gains within the profit and loss account, until they are realised. In some cases a company may show a poor return on capital but achieve substantial capital gains which will be realised by sale in a later period. This point should always be borne in mind when assessing the return on capital calculated from the accounts.

The working capital ratio. Although less widely used than the current ratio, considered below, there is some evidence to suggest that the working capital ratio is a better indication of liquidity problems. The ratio is found by comparing the surplus of current assets over current liabilities, termed net current assets or net working capital, with the total assets employed in the business.

Although it is not possible to specify a target level for this ratio, it seems probable that a decline in the level of net current assets relative to the overall assets total is a good measure of declining liquidity.

Some problems arise in calculating the ratio from the figures shown in the formats, as both formats include items due after more than one year within current assets (Item/asset C and prepayments and accrued income item/ asset D). These items should be excluded from current assets in calculating working capital. In the case of current liabilities the position varies according to the format used. Under format 1 it is necessary to add item E and those within J due within one year (if known) in order to find current liabilities. However, in the case of format 2, all of the items shown within liability C due after more than one year as well as similar items within liability D, if known, must be excluded.

AC Ltd – working capital ratio

	Year 1	*Year 2*	*Year 3*
$\frac{\text{Working capital}}{\text{Total assets}}$	$\frac{231}{3891} = 5.94\%$	$\frac{138}{4905} = 2.81\%$	$\frac{333}{6403} = 5.20\%$

AC Ltd has enjoyed a very low level of liquidity during the period. Although the total of net current assets in Year 3 exceeds that for Year 1, when working capital is matched against the increase in the level of total assets, a decline in the liquidity of the buisness is revealed.

The current ratio. The current ratio compares the total current assets with the total current liabilities, and is the oldest of the traditional ratios. It is sometimes stated that current assets should exceed current liabilities by 2:1. However, there seems to be very little justification for such a yardstick, and many sound companies have much lower figures, often as low as 1.3:1 amongst manufacturing concerns. The logic on which the ratio is based is that sufficient current assets must be available in order to meet current liabilities as they fall due, and that a margin must be available to cover unforeseen contingencies. Certainly if the company if forced to collect debtors and to sell stock quickly, the margin must allow for discounts. In the case of retail companies, with no investment in trade debtors it is common for current liabilities to exceed current assets. Provided such companies generate adequate profits and cash flow, and operate effective control over the level and composition of stocks, a current ratio below 1:1 is not a sign of weakness.

For the purposes of calculating this ratio current assets and current liabilities are calculated as described in the previous section dealing with the working capital ratio.

AC Ltd current ratio

	Year 1	Year 2	Year 3
$\frac{\text{Current assets}}{\text{Current liabilities}}$	$\frac{2220}{1989}$ = 1.12:1	$\frac{2932}{2794}$ = 1.06:1	$\frac{4062}{3929}$ = 1.03:1

The downward trend in the current ratio of AC Ltd is unmistakable, and has now reached an exceedingly low level, having been relatively low in Year 1.

The Liquid (or Quick) Ratio. The liquid ratio is found by comparing those current assets in liquid form with the current liabilities. Thus stocks and similar items are excluded from current assets, leaving items such as debtors and cash, which are already in liquid form, or may easily be converted into cash by discounting or factoring. This ratio, which is often referred to as the *quick ratio*, is based on the same logic as that used by the current ratio. It is sometimes said that the liquid ratio should be no lower than 1:1, but figures of 0.7:1 are common amongst sound manufacturing concerns. Once again any yardstick must be applied cautiously, and the ratio has little relevance to retailers with substantial stock levels, and few liquid assets.

AC Ltd – liquid ratio

	Year 1	Year 2	Year 3
$\frac{\text{Liquid assets}}{\text{Current liabilities}}$	$\frac{1390}{1989}$ = 0.70:1	$\frac{1486}{2794}$ = 0.54:1	$\frac{1672}{3929}$ = 0.42:1

The liquid ratio for the company shows a steep decline from an almost adequate level in Year 1. It now has only £42 available in the form of liquid assets in order to meet each £100 of current liabilities, and appears to be approaching a liquidity crises. At this stage it is not possible to determine the cause of the deterioration, but this will emerge from subsequent analysis.

In addition to the current and liquid ratios some writers on ratio analysis suggest the use of a *cash*, or *acid test, ratio* to compare cash and near cash resources with current liabilities. In practice such a ratio is of limited value, unless account is also taken of unutilised overdraft facilities. Furthermore, a profitable company with adequate capital and low borrowings can almost always borrow in order to replenish liquid resources. It is not necessarily a sign of either efficiency or strength to carry a substantial investment in low yielding liquid assets.

CONTROL OF WORKING CAPITAL

One possible explanation of an unsatisfactory trend in the liquidity position might be inadequate control over the investment in stocks, debtors and similar items and inefficient utilisation of trade credit. This area can be monitored by the working capital ratios.

The stock ratio seeks to monitor the level of stocks held by a business in relation to its size. It can be found by comparing the end of period stock figure with the average monthly or weekly figure for cost of sales. When using published accounts this figure is only available for companies using profit and loss account format 1. Accordingly, it is necessary to find a substitute figure which provides a measure of the activity level of the business. In practice the most convenient figure for this purpose is turnover, which is not directly related to stock and is therefore theoretically unsound. In calculating the stock ratio and the other working capital ratios a number of points should be borne in mind:

(1) The average figure for sales (or, where used cost of sales or purchases) will only be valid if sales occur evenly throughout the year. If there is a seasonal trend in the industry comparison of stock ratios may be highly misleading.
(2) The Companies Act requires disclosure of the composition of the balance shown for stock. It is important to note any trends in the amounts shown, for example a build up of finished goods, and in some cases it may be useful to calculate a stock control ratio for each major subheading.
(3) By delaying orders for goods near the year end it is possible to reduce the level of stocks shown in the balance sheet. Such a practice is a form of window dressing, and all users of accounts should bear in mind that a company may have put a good deal of effort into ensuring the levels of stocks and debtors at the year end are cosmetically attractive.

As with most other ratios it is not possible to lay down an ideal level for this ratio, which is of most use in identifying a trend such as a steady rise in the level of stock unrelated to the level of sales.

AC Ltd stock ratio

	Year 1	*Year 2*	*Year 3*
$\frac{\text{Stocks and work-in-progress}}{\text{Average monthly sales}}$	$\frac{830}{349} =$ 2.38 m	$\frac{1446}{467} =$ 3.09 m	$\frac{2390}{666} =$ 3.59 m

The stock ratio of AC reveals a steady increase in the level of stocks held. A close examination of the accounts shows a threefold increase in the level of raw materials over the period, and an increase of 3.8 times in the level of finished goods. Work-in-progress has declined marginally during the period, in which turnover rose by 90%. Without further investigation it is not possible to state why the increase has taken place. Generally such increases are due to one or more of the following factors:

- lax control over the levels of stocks in general;
- a build up of goods for resale which may eventually need to be sold below book value due to deterioration and obsolence; and
- a build up of raw materials and components, many of which may not now be of use, and some of which may have deteriorated and need to be written off.

Whatever the reason for the deterioration in the stock position of AC the trend is most unsatisfactory and has contributed to the deterioration in the return on capital and in the liquidity ratios.

The Debtors' Ratio is found by dividing the total for trade debtors by the average monthly sales figures. In this case the sales figure is directly related to trade debtors, but once again care must be exercised regarding seasonal trends and window dressing. The level of debtors will vary from industry to industry, and will in part reflect the terms of trade operating in the industry concerned. However, another key factor will be the effectiveness of the credit control system operated by the firm.

AC Ltd Debtor's ratio

	Year 1	Year 2	Year 3
$\frac{\text{Trade debtors}}{\text{Average monthly sales}}$	$\frac{1106}{349} = 3.17$ m	$\frac{1168}{467} = 2.50$ m	$\frac{1111}{666} = 1.67$ m

The figures for AC show a dramatic fall in the level of trade credit provided in relation to sales. It is possible that the company has been severly restricting trade credit, and has cut profit margins in order to counteract the damaging effect on sales of its credit policy or has allowed substantial and expensive settlement discounts.

Alternatively a major window-dressing exercise may have been carried out in order to reduce debtors at the year end.

The Creditor's Ratio matches the level of trade creditors with the total for purchases, or some proxy such as sales. It seeks to monitor the extent to which the company is relying on trade credit to finance its purchases. Leaving aside the question of lost settlement discounts, trade credit is an especially cheap source of finance, having no accounting cost, and therefore firms should take maximum advantage of this source of finance. However, excessive dependence on trade credit may eventually harm supplier relationships, and even disrupt production.[4]

AC Ltd – creditors' ratio

	Year 1	Year 2	Year 3
$\frac{\text{Trade creditors}}{\text{Average monthly sales}}$	$\frac{958}{349} = 2.74$ m	$\frac{1287}{467} = 2.75$ m	$\frac{1494}{666} = 2.24$ m

The creditors ratio for AC shows an increasing dependence on trade credit in Year 2, but this trend has been significantly reversed in Year 3. There is not obvious reason for this trend although a possible explanation might be that suppliers are becoming more restrictive.

SOLVENCY

The solvency ratios deal with the balance between a company's liabilities and the resources provided by the proprietors. As with the liquidity ratios they monitor the ability of a company to meet its financial obligations. However, this group of ratios deals with the long term situation rather than the immediate liquidity position. It is perfectly possible for a firm to be solvent, whilst temporarily illiquid. Whilst such a situation is undesireable, and at times dangerous, it is usually possible for a solvent firm to obtain additional short term funds in order to meet a temporary liquidity crisis. However, a firm which is close to being insolvent will find it extremely difficult to obtain liquid funds in an emergency.

The gearing ratio measures the extent to which a firm is financed by external as opposed to shareholders funds. In Chapter 12 the advantages of gearing to the shareholder will be considered in some depth. However, to the

[4] See Chapter 12 where this topic is considered in greater depth.

banker analysing a set of financial accounts the chief interest lies in identifying cases in which companies are overdependent on external finance and are thereby endangering their long-term viability. The chief difference from this point of view between borrowed and internal finance is that interest must be paid to lenders whether the company makes profits or not; failure to pay interest as it falls due could result in the failure of the business.

There are several alternative ways to calculate and express gearing ratios. In the analysis of AC Ltd the borrowed funds are expressed as a percentage of total capital employed. However, the ratio is often shown with borrowed funds as a proportion of shareholders funds. As gearing tends to vary from period to period and from industry to industry, it is impossible to lay down hard and fast rules on the level of gearing which might be expected in a particular firm. However, in determining the level of gearing a company must take account of a number of factors including:

- the relative stability of conditions within the industry including sales volume and prices;
- the proportion of borrowings which are of a short-term nature;
- any exposure to currency fluctuations;
- the level of annual cash flow in relation to borrowings;
- whether borrowings are financed by fixed or fluctuating interest rates.

AC Ltd gearing ratio

	Year 1	*Year 2*	*Year 3*
$\frac{\text{Total borrowings}}{\text{Total capital employed}}$	$\frac{706}{2608} = 27.1\%$	$\frac{1276}{3317} = 38.5\%$	$\frac{1986}{4380} = 45.3\%$

In view of the general deterioration in the condition of AC already identified it is hardly surprising that the company has sustained a considerable rise in the level of gearing. Over the period borrowings have risen by 180%. Closer examination of the accounts reveals that the company has revalued its properties with a consequent adjustment of reserves. This has had the effect of disguising the rise in gearing.

The liabilities ratio is another variant of the gearing ratio which takes account of the general dependence of the firm on external funding whether in the form of formal borrowings, as covered by the gearing ratio, or of sundry liabilities. This ratio provides a useful check on companies which reduce borrowings by delaying payment of trade creditors at the end of the year. The ratio may be calculated by dividing total liabilities by shareholders funds, and expressing the result as a proportion.

AC Ltd liabilities ratio

	Year 1	*Year 2*	*Year 3*
$\frac{\text{Total liabilities}}{\text{Shareholders' funds}}$	$\frac{2227}{1584} = 1.41{:}1$	$\frac{3164}{1731} = 1.83{:}1$	$\frac{4266}{2077} = 2.05{:}1$

The trend of the liabilities ratio highlights AC's growing dependence on borrowed funds and other liabilities. As with the gearing ratio the figures have been improved by the revaluation of the properties. If the revaluation surplus is removed for Year 3 the ratio shows a figure of 2.96. In essence this means that at the start of the period the company employed £141 of external finance for every £100 of shareholders funds; by the end of year three, ignoring revaluation surpluses, it used £296 of external finance for each £100 provided by shareholders.

The interest cover ratio relates the cost of interest with the profits available to meet it. It is found by dividing the profits before paying interest and tax (operating profit) by the cost of interest. It is often stated that in order to ensure an adequate margin of safety this ratio should be no less than 3 times.

AC Ltd interest cover

	Year 1	*Year 2*	*Year 3*
Operating profit / Interest	400 / 96 = 4.17	447 / 154 = 2.90	440 / 278 = 1.58

The trend in AC's interest cover ratio shows an obvious weakening in the company's position. From an adequate level of 4.17 the ratio has fallen by approximately one third. It can be seen that the reason for the decline is the increased level of interest charges in the face of static profits.

The borrowings/cash flow ratio. This ratio relates the level of borrowings to the operating cash flow generated by the firm. It is found by dividing total borrowings by the total of profit after tax plus any provisions not involving the use of funds, of which depreciation is the most significant. In essence this ratio compares the amount borrowed by the company with, the amount notionally available to repay it. There is some evidence that this ratio gives the most reliable indication of impending problems.[5]

AC Ltd borrowings/cash flow ratio

	Year 1	*Year 2*	*Year 3*
Borrowings / Operating cash flow	708 / 355 = 1.99	1276 / 478 = 2.67	1986 / 235 = 8.45

In Year 1 AC generates sufficient cash flow to have repaid borrowings in a couple of years. However, by Year 3, due to the combined effects of a drop in operating cash flow and a rise in borrowings, the ratio had risen to 8.45 times. This indicates a considerable loss of flexibility by the company.

AC Ltd Conclusion

As a result of calculating the foregoing ratios which are tabulated in Table 8.6 has been possible to identify that the company has a number of significant problems, and that its position has deteriorated considerably over the period covered by the accounts. Although not yet making losses the company has suffered a serious decline in profitability, due partly to declining sales margins, but also to a rise in capital employed. Over the period there has been a distinct deterioration in the liquidity position of the firm, largely as the result of an increase in stock levels, and in short term borrowings. An examination of the accounts reveals that all of the borrowings are short term, which increased the vulnerability of the firm. As a result of the additional borrowings gearing has arisen and interest cover has fallen. The level of cash flow has fallen considerably in relation to borrowings. Other points emerging from the accounts:

[5] See for example Beaver, *Journal of Accounting Research*, Vol. 4 (1966). Financial Ratios as predictors of failure.

- no dividend was paid in Year 3;
- the investment in plant and machinery is static; and
- an investment in a customer has been written off as an extraordinary item in Year 3.

Table 8.6
AC Ltd Ratios

	Year 1		*Year 2*		*Year 3*	
Activity	4,186	1.07 times	5,601	1.14	7,991	1.25
	3,891		4,905		6,403	
Profit margin	379	9.05%	447	7.98%	440	5.51%
	4,186		5,601		7,991	
Return on capital	400	15.33%	447	13.48%	440	10.04%
	2,608		3,317		4,380	
Return on shareholders' funds	304	19.19%	293	16.92%	162	7.80%
	1,584		1,731		2,077	
Working capital ratio	231	5.94%	138	2.81%	333	5.20%
	3,891		4,905		6,403	
Current ratio	2,220	1.12:1	2,932	1.06:1	4,062	1.03:1
	1,989		2,794		3,929	
Liquid ratio	1,390	0.70:1	1,486	0.54:1	1,672	0.42:1
	1,989		2,794		3,929	
Stocks/sales ratio	830	2.38 months	1,446	3.09	2,390	3.59
	349		467		666	
Debtors/sales ratio	1,106	3.17	1,168	2.50	1,111	1.67
	349		407		666	
Creditors/sales ratio	958	2.74	1,287	2.75	1,494	2.24
	349		467		666	
Gearing	706	27.1%	1,276	38.5%	1,986	45.3%
	2,608		3,317		4,380	
Liabilities	2,227	1.41:1	3,164	1.83:1	4,266	2.05:1
	1,584		1,731		2,077	
Interest cover	400	4.17	447	2.90	440	1.58
	96		154		278	
Borrowings/cash flow	706	1.99	1,276	2.67	1,986	8.45
	355		478		235	

Before taking any action regarding his findings a prudent banker should always confirm his suspicions with the firm's management. However, the calculations of ratios has identified a number of areas of concern, which warrant further investigation.

CONCLUDING COMMENTS ON RATIO ANALYSIS

Having calculated the ratios suggested for each company the analyst is in a position to draw conclusions about the state of the company. Before doing so he should undertake a brief review of the accounts in order to ensure that no major points have been overlooked. In preparing the ratios he will have become familiar with the composition of the annual report, and will now find it a much easier task to review the contents as a whole. He should consider the following points:

(1) Did the examination of the Chairman's Statement, the Director's Report and the Auditor's Report reveal any information having a bearing on the opinion?
(2) Is there a trend in profits and sales and what impact have changing price levels had on the figures? If the company has produced a five or ten year record, does this reveal any significant information?
(3) In the light of information obtained concerning the liquidity position and solvency of the company, does the funds statement provide any useful insights into the changes in the company's condition?[6]
(4) Have there been any changes in the material accounting policies of the company, are these explained in a satisfactory manner and are there any suspicious or undisclosed reasons for the changes which have taken place?
(5) Are there any changes in the corresponding figures appearing in the accounts which have not been adequately accounted for by other aspects of the examination?
(6) Are there any extraordinary and exceptional items shown in the accounts, what is the impact of treating them in this way, and is the treatment acceptable?
(7) What is the position regarding future commitments and authorised capital expenditure? In the light of the company's ability to generate funds, what impact will these commitments have on the financial structure of the business?

Having completed the review outlined above it is now possible to formulate an opinion on the position of the company. In doing so it is important to bear in mind that any interpretation will be undermined by:

[6] See Chap. 10 where funds statements are discussed.

- changes in the way in which either the figures in the accounts or the ratios are calculated;
- the impact of inflation on the figures;
- any comparisons made between companies that are fundamentally dissimilar, or between companies that prepare their accounts in a different way; and
- attaching too much importance to one or more figures in isolation.

In interpreting accounts all of the figures must be taken together. Some will indicate weakness, others strength. It is the job of the analyst to draw an overall conclusion, weighing strengths against weaknesses and taking account of all of the available facts. Some writers have suggested that this approach places too must importance on human skills, and that it should be possible to determine empirically which ratios give the most reliable indication of approaching business failure; their work is considered below.

EMPIRICAL RESEARCH ON THE PREDICTABILITY OF COMPANY ACCOUNTS

Although widely used, the technique of ratio analysis has developed pragmatically over many years to a stage where many different ratios are employed by analysts. In recent times academics have posed two major questions.

(1) To what extent are the ratios used good indicators of company progress and prospects – and in particular – to what extent are the ratios good predictors of company failure?
(2) Which ratios are the most effective and where several ratios are used, how should the information conveyed by each of them be interpreted to give an overall picture?

Ratio analysis was first used towards the end of the nineteenth century for examining the accounts of railway companies in the United States. The first ratio developed was the current ratio, which it was suggested show not be less that 2 to 1.[7] According to Professor Susan Dev.

> "In the 1960s interest grew amongst American academics, notably from Chicago, in the use of accounting data for predicting various events of concern to decision makers. Arising out of his particular interest in the predictive ability of ratios, Beaver carried out a study of failed companies. He compared the ratios of 79 companies that failed between 1954 and 1964 with those of the same number of similar, but non-failed, companies using univariate analysis (taking one ratio of variables at a time). On the lines of earlier studies, he initially compared mean values of ratios and found that the means of all six ratios that he selected for detailed study were less satisfactory for the failed companies for five years before failure than for the non-failed companies. His study differed from the earlier ones in that he tested cash flow ratios and, in the later part, he used more sophisticated statistical techniques. Eventually, he found that the apparently previously untested cash flow/total debt ratio was the best predictor of failure.[8]"

[7] See S. Dev, "Ratio Analysis and the Prediction of Company Failure" in *Debits, Credits, Finance and Profits*, ed. Edey and Yamey.
[8] See Beaver op.cit.

Altman was the first to make use of a technique which took into account all the ratio characteristics at one time – multiple discriminant analysis. He used this technique on data relating to 33 companies that failed between 1946 and 1965 and an equal number of non-failed concerns. It is interesting to note that Altman's function did not include the ratios that he found to be the best predictors when considering the ratios individually.

Altman found that by combining five ratios, appropriately weighted, he could obtain good predictions of which companies were failures rather than non-failures. The ratios identified by Altman were combined in the following formula.

$$Z = 0.012X_1 + 0.014X_2 + 0.033X_3 + 0.006X_4 + 0.010X_5$$

The ratios were:

X_1 Working capital/total assets
X_2 Retained earnings/total assets
X_3 Earnings before interest and taxes/total assets
X_4 Market value of equity/book value of total debt
X_5 Sales/total assets

Altman found that where a company had a Z-score of less than 1 it was highly probable that the company was a failure, whilst a score than 3 indicated safety.[9]

The major work in this area in the UK has been by a lecturer at the City University Business School, Richard Taffler. He has used multiple discriminant analysis on UK data to produce a similar function to Altman – but has not published the co-efficients discovered. Taffler claims that his model is able to predict failure up to four years ahead.[10]

The banks in the UK have received these techniques with varying degress of enthusiasm, but none have been prepared to abandon traditional techniques in their favour. Apart from traditional conservatism there are a number of reasons why discriminant analysis has not been widely adopted:

(1) The Z-score is found by comparing the accounts of failed and non-failed companies over a period in order to determine the variables and the weight which should be attached to each. In order for the score to be a good predictor in the future, conditions must be similar to those pertaining when the sample on which the score is based was calculated. In other words, the score is out of date as soon as it is calculated; the faster conditions change the less reliable it will become.
(2) In order to calculate a Z-score a study must be made of a substantial number of companies, including an equal number of failing and succeeding companies. In certain industries there are too few companies of either type to allow a score to be calculated.

[9] See E. I. Altman "Financial Ratios, Discriminant Analysis, and the Prediction of Corporate Bankruptcy" in *Journal of Finance* (Autumn, 1968).

[10] See R. Taffler and H. Tisshaw, "Going, going gone – five factors which predict" *Accountance*, (March 1977).

(3) Although the Z-score technique can state which companies have a high probability of failing under certain conditions, it cannot indicate what may be done in order to avert such a failure. In order to avert a collapse bankers must resort to traditional techniques of interpretation and investigation.
(4) It has not been demonstrated to the satisfaction of bankers and other users that the technique is superior to traditional analytical techniques, and that it cannot be defeated by window dressing the accounts.

In the light of these responses the Z-score technique has mainly been used as a screening device in order to identify those companies with a high risk of failure.

Whilst the work undertaken on the predictive ability of accounts has had only a limited impact on banking practice, a more favourable reception was given to the ideas proposed by John Argenti on the causes and symptoms of corporate collapse. This analysis is considered in Chapter 14 which deals with reorganisations and reconstructions.

CONCLUSION

Despite their undoubted deficiencies financial accounts play a vital role in lending decisions by bankers. There is no better way of obtaining an impartially examined statement of the position of a company, based on the view shown in its books, and of its results over a period. The problems in using accounts arise from the following factors:

- Accounts are drawn up under the historical cost convention in order to ensure that they are reliable and can be verified. Often this means that the resulting figures are less useful than they might be. For example accounts are not a statement of current values, and exclude most intangible assets possessed by the company even thought these may have considerable value.
- The annual report is produced only once a year and is subject to some delay before it is available. The information shown in the balance sheet reflects the position on only one day of the year and will be considerably out of date when it becomes available to bankers. The profit and loss account may deal with a period which began up to two years before it becomes available to lenders.
- Due to the variety of possible accounting practices there is some scope for window dressing the figures shown in the accounts. Although it is not possible to determine how widespread this practice is, the banker ought always to bear in mind the possibility that the company has engaged in "creative accounting". In his book *Corporate Collapse: Causes and Symptoms*, John Argenti writes:

"I have come to believe that (the phenomenon of creative accounting) is invariably associated with failure. I suspect that it is one of the most reliable of all symptoms. I am equally sure that nearly all non-failing firms do their best to present honest accounts (not forgetting the huge latitude that even the best accounting conventions allow, especially in times of inflation) and that nearly all proprietors and managers of failing companies who adopt creative techniques do so from the best of motives. To keep the company afloat until the clouds roll away."[11]

The banker can minimise the effect of these deficiencies in the following ways:

- He must bear in mind that accounts will not always show that a company is encountering problems. The accounts must be examined not because they will always show impending difficulties, but because it would be foolhardy to ignore the fact that they might, and often do.
- He must remember that examining the accounts is only one aspect of the lending decision, and that there are other important sources of information and other factors to be taken into account. The existence of a sound balance sheet, is not a substitute for the need to reach on opinion on the competence and trustworthiness of the customer's management. Even if the company appears sound, the banker should consider how he might recover any facilities were he to have misjudged the situation.
- Finally, if the company prepares management accounts these will provide information which is much more up-to-date than that appearing in the annual accounts. Wherever practicable the banker should also examine the management accounts, in conjunction with, but not as a substitute for, the annual report.

FURTHER READING

There are many texts on the interpretation of accounts, and it is only possible to list a handful here. Those by Farmer and Sugden and Holmes are amongst the very best. The text by Lee provides a highly readable guide to modern auditing.

E. R. Farmer, *Understanding and Interpreting Company Reports and Accounts* (Van Nostrand Reinhold, UK. 1983).
A. Sugden and G. Holmes, *Interpreting Company Reports and Accounts* (2nd ed., Woodhead Faulkner, 1982).
T. A. Lee, *Company Auditing – Concepts and Precepts* (2nd ed., Gee, 1979).

[11] See J. Argenti, *Corporate Failure: Causes and Symptoms* (Mc Graw Hill).

Chapter 9
Management Accounting and the Analysis of Profit Performance

INTRODUCTION

In recent years many speakers and writers have urged bankers to make greater use of management accounts. Speaking to the Cambridge Conference of the Institute of Bankers in 1975 D. V. Weyer commented:

> "The arm's length attitude of a clearing bank to lending an overdraft on a fully liquidating basis is not sufficiently sophisticated for dealing with long-term loans to industrial customers. So clearing banks are having to retrain their senior and middle management always with a greater emphasis on cash flow, liquidity and profits. A period of inflation has greatly damaged the credibility of the balance sheet as a safe banking aid."

In this chapter it is intended to highlight the features of management accounting which are of most use to bankers in taking lending decisions. The chapter begins with a comparison of the key features of financial and management accounts.

MANAGEMENT ACCOUNTS AND FINANCIAL ACCOUNTS

As its name suggests, management accounting has to do with management and specifically to do with the provision of information regarding the financial transactions of a business. It is generally agreed that management consists of several elements including, *inter alia*, exercising control over the activities of the business. Furthermore, it is widely agreed that in order to exercise control it is necessary to start with a plan and to monitor departures therefrom. In addition, from time to time businesses encounter unforeseen problems for which accounting information has to be specially assembled on an ad hoc basis. In order to be of maximum use in these three areas of planning, control and problem solving, accounting information must be relevant, reasonably reliable, and up-to-date. In other words the information produced should relate comprehensively to the problems and issues on hand – but should not include items which are of no relevance to these issues. To be of any use, the data must be reasonably reliable – but this reliability must not be achieved at the cost of a lengthy delay in preparation in order to ensure a high degree of accuracy. Often a trade off must be made, so that whilst they may be subject to some inaccuracy, the accounts are available when they are required and are of most use. For a variety of reasons financial accounts are unlikely to meet these criteria. The contrast between management and financial accounts is summarised in Table 9.1 below.

Table 9.1
Management Accounts and Financial Accounts Compared

Management Accounts and Financial Accounts Compared

	Financial accounts	*Management accounts*
Purpose	Stewardship	Internal decision making
Recipients	Shareholders	Management
Content determined by	Law and Accounting standards	Management
Degree of accuracy	True and Fair	Important but traded off against timeliness
Importance of timeliness	Not of great significance	Essential
Frequency	At least annually	As required

Whilst a good case can be made out for the use of some form of management accounts by most businesses, the cost of operating a full management accounting system is substantial and should not be incurred unless the benefits expected to be gained by having more information on costs and performance are greater than the cost of the service. Conversely, the costs of not having adequate information for decision making are potentially immense. It is extremely difficult to ensure that as a firm grows its management information system grows smoothly to meet its needs.

In general, every business should produce comprehensive information regarding its cash position on a regular basis, as well as selective data on key variables such as sales, prices and future orders. Only larger businesses will benefit from a full scale cost accounting system.

However, where a firm does produce some sort of accounting information for its own internal use, bankers will find that it can assist in three main areas:

(1) in assessing what the business *plans* to do;
(2) in reviewing how the business is *progressing*;
(3) in helping to resolve *problems* as they arise.

In assessing future plans considerable use can be made of company budgets. The chapter therefore continues with a discussion on the main features of budgeting and budgetary control. In larger companies for control to be truly possible, detailed analysis is necessary of cost behaviour. Some attention is therefore given to the topic of costing and cost behaviour. On the basis of this review it will become apparent that cost behaviour can have a very significant impact on profit which is in part determined by the volume of business activity. We shall, therefore, consider the important topic of cost-volume-profit analysis which is sometimes referred to as breakeven analysis. An examination of the budget in association with any cost-volume-profit analysis undertaken by the company will provide a useful insight into the future plans of the business.

In order to monitor its progress a company is likely to make use of one or both of the techniques of ratio analysis and variance analysis or standard costing. Bankers are likely to find that management accounts obtained from companies will show key ratios and will frequently take the form of a comparison between what the firm expected to happen (standard) and what has actually happened. The difference between actual and standard is termed a variance. In attempting to assess the progress being made by the firm, the banker will find it particularly useful to study the analysis prepared by the company's management accountant.

From time to time companies run into problems which are not foreseen or planned for. As a result it is unlikely that the management accounts will be prepared in such a way as to provide information to deal with such special situations. Consequently the accountant will need to prepare information on an ad hoc basis for decision making. In this respect one technique widely used by accountants is that of direct or marginal costing which endeavours to distinguish between those costs which vary with output and those which are fixed during the period concerned. Bankers will find that an appreciation of the principles of marginal costing is of considerable use when examining the position of a company in financial difficulties. They will find it especially important to be aware of the contrasts between this approach and that of full absorption costing, which is often found in practice, and can give quite misleading results if significant changes are made in the activities of a business.

All the terms and techniques referred to above are described and discussed in the remainder of this chapter.

BUDGETING AND BUDGETARY CONTROL

Budgetary control lies at the heart of management accounting – it is based on the simple idea that a business should plan its activities, compare the actual out-turn with the plan and investigate significant departures. Such a procedure is quite possible with fairly rudimentary monthly accounts and does not require a full scale costing system. However, every control system requires the preparation of a budget of some sort. Generally the budget is prepared by updating the previous year's figures in the light of some forward projections. Most businesses operate a budget cycle which involves all key managers, under the direction of a budget officer – usually the financial controller or management accountant.

The budget is built up from a number of subsidiary budgets covering:

Sales, Production, Administration, R and D, Capital expenditure.

These are eventually consolidated in a master budget comprising Profit and loss account, Balance sheet and Cash flow budget.

The budget must be worked and reworked until it is internally consistent. After formal approval it becomes a plan of action.

In practice the preparation of budgets is subject to a considerable degree of organisational politics – with a resulting compromise that may not be entirely realistic. Often budgets are used for motivational purposes and represent targets rather than plans of action. It is important that a banker appreciates these problems and by a few well aimed questions, ascertains to what extent the budget represents a realistic view of future prospects.

DEALING WITH RISK AND UNCERTAINTY IN BUDGETING

In order to draw up a budget, forecasts must be made of the expected level of all of the major variables. The most critical of these is termed the key factor. It is generally the level of sales, but may be production capacity, the availability of skilled labour or the supply of a key component.

There are a number of approaches to the problem of handling, as opposed to resolving, the problem of uncertainty. One method it to prepare a flexible budget in which a range of possible outcomes is shown. Control is exercised by comparing the result for each period with the budget alternative which most nearly corresponds with the outcome for the key factor.

Other common approaches to the problem are:

Best guess. The simplest approach is to base the figures used in the budget on the most likely outcome for each figure concerned. In practice this approach amounts to ignoring risk in preparing the figures, but (hopefully) taking account of the inherent uncertainty in utilising them.

Optimistic/best guess/pessimistic. A common approach to the problem of uncertainty is to prepare the budget using three possible levels of outcome for each variable. The result of this approach is to indicate the most likely result as well as the best and worst possible outcome. From a financial viewpoint, the company should ensure that finance is available to support each of the possible outcomes. On occasions a successful result may produce a need for substantial extra finance to support additional working capital and investment in fixed assets.

Sensitivity analysis. The object of sensitivity analysis is to discover how sensitive the outcome is to changes in key variables. After preparing a basic budget model, using the most likely assumptions, each key variable is manipulated to determine the impact on the profit and loss account, the balance sheet, and the financial situation of the business. As a result of this analysis the company may be able to determine that (say) a 5% fall in prices of output will result in a 50% drop in profits, and a funding deficit of £20,000. It will be possible to state which variables will have the greatest impact on the overall result, and by using optimistic and pessimistic inputs, to determine the best and worst outcomes. As a result of such analysis a firm may decide to alter its strategy in order to eliminate the most adverse outcomes. However, it can pursue the remaining course of action with some apppreciation of the range of possible outcomes and their effect. Thus sensitivity analysis may be viewed as a technique for exploring the uncertainty involved in commercial activity, it does not eliminate risk, but provides an insight into the extent to which it affects the business.

On a practical note, the value of the analysis will depend upon the rigour with which it is conducted. If the least desirable outcomes are regarded as unthinkable and are excluded from the analysis, then the result with not be valid. With the wide use of microcomputers the effort involved in undertaking sensitivity analysis has been considerably reduced. Even quite small firms can use computers to carry out budgeting, and may subject the results to sensitivity analysis with little extra expense.

However, for the results to be valid it is essential that the model of the firm used in the process is reliable. Firms should be careful to obtain good advice on the application of packaged programs to their own circumstances. If economies must be made in adapting the program to accommodate the unique features of a firm, it is usually better to dispense with the application altogether and to stick to manual methods.

Each of the three methods outlined so far recognises the existence of uncertainty and seeks to measure its effect. However, none of the methods described attempts to measure the degree of uncertainty in any systematic way. For example, sensitivity analysis can reveal the worst and best possible outcomes, but cannot say how likely each is to occur. In order to make effective use of the information that is available regarding the probability of the possible outcomes it is necessary to make use of formal techniques of risk analysis and decision theory.[1]

[1] Readers who wish to study the subject of decision theory in greater depth will find *The Anatomy of Decisions* by P. G. Moore and H. Thomas (Penguin) a useful introduction.

Decision theory. In order to appreciate the contribution of decision theory it is necessary to be aware of the distinction that is sometimes made between risk and uncertainty.

Risk – all of the outcomes are known and can be predicted or estimated.
Uncertainty – all of the outcomes are known but it is not possible to estimate their outcomes.

In practice most firms operate under neither risk nor uncertainty but within a situation sometimes described as "partial ignorance", where not all of the possible outcomes are known, and no prediction can be made of the possible outcome. However, in order to make sensible use of what is known about the likely outcomes affecting a budget, companies may assume that all of the outcomes are known and may place probability estimates on the range of possible outcomes relating to each variable. The result of this process is to produce a probability distribution. An example is shown below, in which the probability of 0.2 indicates that in 2 cases out of 10 the projected sales are expected to be £25,000.

Project sales	*Probability*
£25,000	0.2
£50,000	0.3
£75,000	0.4
£100,000	0.1
	1.0

It can be seen that the most likely result is a sales level of £75,000. However, if the probabilities are used to calculate an expected level of sales a different result is obtained.

Sales	*Weight*	*Expected value*
£25,000	0.2	£5,000
£50,000	0.3	£15,000
£75,000	0.4	£30,000
£100,000	0.1	£10,000
		£50,000

The significance of the result is that if the same conditions were repeated time after time the firm would average sales of £50,000, even though the most frequent result would be a total of £75,000. In most cases, therefore, a firm would be best advised to use the expected value for budgeting because it would produce the most reliable result in the long run. However, as this case shows, it is important to study the figures fully. In some cases the worst result might ruin the firm and in such cases it might be necessary to cater for the worst outcome, even if it is not the expected or most likely result. In other cases it might be worthwhile utilising some resources in order to achieve flexibility, for example in ensuring that the sales level of £75,000 can be met if it should occur. Inevitabily the result of this analysis will only be as good as the data which is used. In some cases it will be necessary to use subjective projections, albeit provided by expert managers. However, in other cases there will be sound statistical data covering past events which may be used. For example, oil companies will be aware of the likelihood of an exploration well finding oil from past results. This information may be used in evaluating the probable commercial success of drilling a new well.

Although decision theory is of obvious value in major projects, such as exploring for and exploiting oil deposits, it can also be used effectively by small companies. The chief feature of the technique is that it forces managers to consider the likely outcomes and the associated probabilities, and then to analyse the results systematically. The approach may be used to deal with all manner of uncertain variables including the level of sales, retail prices, debtors settlement periods and so forth. Its limitation is that it cannot deal with the combined impact of the various figures. If a firm wishes to use decision theory to analyse the impact of risk from a number of variables it must use more advanced simulation techniques. Monte Carlo simulation will enable a company to calculate the range of possible profit figures from a large number of variables and associated probabilities and will give an expected profit based on a random association between the factors concerned. More sophisticated models can incorporate known and measurable relationships between the variables, for example, between rates of price changes, the exchange rate for currency and interest rates.

EXAMINING A BUDGET

By the time it reaches the banker, the budget should be correct from an arithmetical viewpoint – and there is little point in devoting much time to checking arithmetic. However, if the banker wishes to rely upon the budget as an indication of what is likely to happen to the company, he is well advised to examine it critically from a number of other view points.

1 Overall Appraisal

(a) Do the budget statements make sense and appear to be internally consistent?
(b) Are all significant factors included? (e.g. interest, depreciation, tax)
(c) Is the budget consistent with recent performance? Here ratios are of great value including:
Return on capital employed;
Profit margins;
Debtors/stock/creditors v. turnover or cost of sales;
Current ratio;
Gearing.
(d) Is the closing balance sheet viable?
(e) Is the budget based upon meaningful forecasts – or upon targets?

2 Examination of Key Variables

(a) Are the assumptions used reasonable in the light of:
  (i) Past performance
  (ii) Future intentions
  (iii) External developments (e.g. market strength)

(b) The main key variables are usually:
Sales – volume;
price;
Overheads;
Labour – wage rates;
Purchases – prices;
Interest rates.

(c) Have the key relationships remained consistent, or are changes reasonable?
e.g. Stock levels;
Debtors collection period;
Credit taken from suppliers;
Manufacturing efficiency – labour output
wastage rates.

Clearly the banker cannot (or at least should not) know as much about the business as those running it – so his approach will be to identify points of interest and concern. He can then ask the company to elucidate or explain. The way in which the answers emerge usually gives a revealing insight into the knowledge and skill (or lack of it) of the managers of a business.

COSTS AND COSTING

All but the most rudimentary procedures demand an effective system for allocating costs to the relevant budgetary headings or responsibility centres. The extent to which costs are analysed depends upon the nature of the business and the sophistication of the system, but may be based upon:

- Function – e.g. production, administration, etc.;
- Cost Centres – e.g. departments;
- Cost Units – e.g. product or job.

Some costs may be clearly identified with a cost centre or unit – these are termed *direct costs* and may be *allocated*. Other costs including rates and other overheads, relate to a variety of centres and units and are termed *indirect costs*. Such costs therefore must be *apportioned* on a suitable basis to the relevant centres. Under the traditional absorption costing approach all costs are ultimately absorbed in a cost centre or cost unit.

A further important distinction must be made between:

- fixed costs – which do not vary with the level of output, e.g. management costs, rates, rents;

- variable costs – which vary with volume, e.g. raw materials;
- semi-variable costs – which are partly fixed and partly variable with output, e.g. telephone, heat.

In order to absorb all fixed costs it is necessary to make certain assumptions about the level of activity. However, if the outcome is different from that forecast, unit costs will change.

PROFIT VOLUME ANALYSIS

In addition to examining a company's budget a lender wishing to assess future plans will sometimes find it useful to investigate the impact of various sales levels on the profitability of the business. Where volume changes present an important challenge to profitability the management will often have undertaken such an analysis and presented the results in the form of a profit/volume or, as it is more commonly known, a break-even chart.

Break-even charts may be used to determine expected results at various levels of output and to determine the break-even point and the margin of safety. They may be adapted:

(a) to establish the cash break-even point; and
(b) to determine the impact of changing sales prices.

In practice it is often quite difficult to prepare break-even charts. However, if the company is able to provide one, the information is of some interest to the banker. The higher the customer's break-even point – especially the cash break-even point – the more vulnerable he is to fluctuations in sales volume and value.

In order to prepare a break-even chart data must be assembled on the level of costs at various levels of output or activity. This data may be based on past experience or be derived from management estimates. It is then plotted on a scatter-graph in order to enable the cost behaviour of the business to be analysed and the point at which revenue equals profit to be found. The technique is best illustrated by an example.

Example

Model Makers Ltd are able to manufacture 20,000 models per year which sell at £10 each. It is currently selling 8,000 units per year. From past experience the firm has found that sales and costs are as follows:

Sales	16,000 units*	Total costs £120,000
	12,000	100,000
Current output	8,000	80,000

The following steps must be followed in order to prepare a chart.

(1) The total costs at each level of activity are plotted and a line of best fit is drawn between them. The line will not necessarily pass through all of the points plotted although it does so in the example. This line shows the total level of costs at each level of output.

(2) One point is plotted for the revenue derived from any specific level of sales, say at 50% activity. A line is then drawn linking this point to the axis. This line shows the sales revenue which is achieved at each level of output, and it follows that when output is nil there will be no revenue. Because the line always passes through the axis only one point need be plotted.
(3) A horizontal line may be drawn at the point at which the total cost line intersects the vertical axis. At this intersection point the costs shown will be incurred without any sales being achieved, hence this line shows the total costs which are fixed whatever the level of output. The gap between the total cost line and the fixed cost line shows the variable costs of the business at each level of activity. The value of the graphical method is that it avoids the need to apportion semi-variable costs; this is achieved automatically within the graph.
(4) The gap between the break-even point and the present level of output is termed the margin of safety.

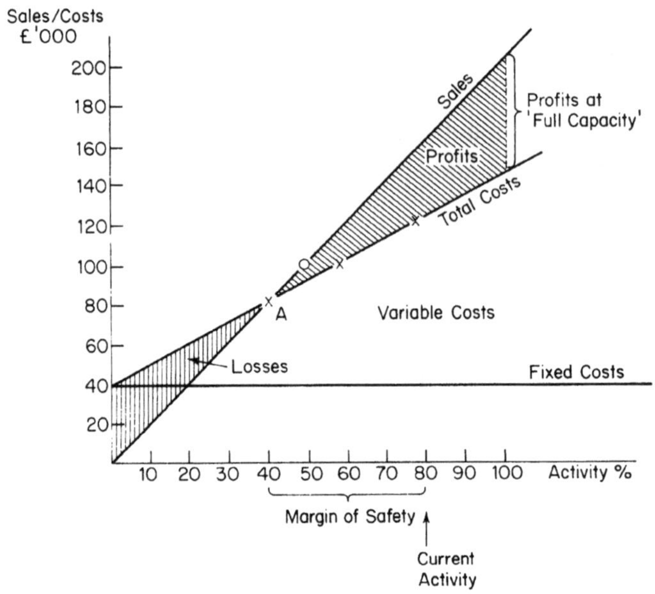

Figure 9.1

Interpretation

(1) The sales and total cost lines intersect at point A which is the break-even point; model makers will break even so long as they sell 8,000 units and operate at 40% capacity.
(2) Fixed costs are £40,000 and are incurred whatever the level of output.
(3) At full capacity the profit, which can be found from the difference between the sales and total costs is £60,000. Full capacity represents normal activity and output may often be increased beyond 100% by, for instance, working extra shifts.
(4) In the case of model makers the margin of safety is large, which will give some reassurance to the company's bankers. The company could halve its turnover and still break even.[2]

BREAK-EVEN CHARTS IN PRACTICE

The example used above to illustrate the value of a break-even chart was highly simplified and it is important to appreciate that in the real world it is much more difficult to prepare and interpret such charts. Several problems are worthly of mention:

(1) In practice it is difficult to ascertain costs over the full range of activity. If a company operates at a low level of output extra costs are often incurred. Accordingly, it is unwise to use such charts for making decisions about activity at levels outside the general range for which reliable recent figures are available.
(2) In the example output and sales were assumed to be equal. In reality it is likely that a company will add to and withdraw items from stock. If products are not sold promptly extra costs will be incurred.
(3) It was also assumed that fixed costs were the same whatever the level of output. In practice this is unlikely to be the case and the costs will increase by discrete steps as, for example, extra staff are employed and additional costs are incurred not directly related to the level of output.

---

[2] Break-even analysis may also be dealt with mathematically, as is illustrated below. In the case of model makers the information concerning cost may be expressed in the form of simultaneous equations which may be solved to give variable costs.

$$120{,}000 = F + 16{,}000\,V$$
$$100{,}000 = F + 12{,}000\,V$$

where F = fixed costs and V = variable costs.

Subtracting

$$20{,}000 = 4000\,V$$
$$V = \frac{20{,}000}{4{,}000} = £5$$

The information found may be manipulated to discover (i) contribution, (ii) fixed costs, (iii) the break even point.

(i) When variable costs are known the contribution may be found

Sale price £10	£10
Variable cost	£ 5
Contribution	£ 5

(ii) As total costs consist of fixed costs and variable costs, fixed costs may be found by deducting variable costs from total costs at a known level of output, e.g. at a production level of 8,000

$$\begin{aligned}\text{Fixed costs} &= \text{Total costs} - \text{variable costs}\\ &= £80{,}000 - £5 \times 8{,}000\\ &= £80{,}000 - £40{,}000\\ &= £40{,}000\end{aligned}$$

(iii) At breakeven point total contribution is sufficient to cover fixed costs, but does not yield a profit. Break even point is thus found by dividing the fixed costs by the contribution per unit.

$$\text{Breakeven point} = \frac{\text{Fixed costs}}{\text{Contribution per unit}} = \frac{£40{,}000}{£5} = 8{,}000 \text{ units}$$

(4) In the chart it was assumed that the price of goods was the same at all levels of output, and accordingly sales revenue was shown by a linear curve. In many cases prices change with output in order to influence the volume of goods sold. More complex charts make use of non linear curves.
(5) As soon as a chart is prepared changes will almost certainly render it inaccurate. In part these changes will be due to deliberate management action, but in part will simply reflect the uncertainties associated with all management accounting projections.
(6) Break-even charts are best able to deal with single products but many companies sell or manufacture a range of items. In order to cope with such situations individual charts can be prepared for each product. This necessitates dividing joint costs between products. As will be shown later in this chapter, this can be an arbitrary and dangerously misleading practice. If, instead, a chart is prepared for the company as a whole, it will be rendered inaccurate by any differences between the actual composition of sales (product mix) and that envisaged when the chart was prepared.

BREAK-EVEN CHARTS AND THE BANKERS

Despite their limitations break-even charts are of considerable value to a banker because they reveal whether a company is operating close to the point at which it will break even or has a considerable margin of safety. If a customer makes use of break-even charts then they will prove to be a useful lending aid. However, two important points should be made concerning their use:

(1) Not every company will find it useful to prepare break-even charts and there is little point in a banker insisting that one is prepared if it will prove unreliable or misleading. It is important to realise that the purpose of the chart is to measure the extent to which a company's profits are sensitive to changes in volume. A banker should always endeavour to discover whether and to what extent volume changes are an important factor in the success of a business. In order to answer such a question a customer may very well produce a break even chart. The banker should certainly beware of the customer who is unable to answer the question or has never considered the point.
(2) Although in the long run every business will only survive if it makes profits, in the short run it is quite possible to survive without doing so. This is due to the fact that companies fail when they run out of money, rather than cease making profits. This is a point which a banker must bear in mind when examining a break-even chart. Not all of the costs which a firm shows on the chart will result in an outflow of funds. The amount shown for total costs will include charges for the depreciation of fixed assets which were purchased in prior periods. Thus if cash costs are excluded from other costs it is possible to prepare a *cash break-even chart* which will show the point at which sales revenue covers cash outgoings;

such a chart is of particular use to bankers. It must be borne in mind, however, that irregular cash outgoings must also be taken into account in interpreting the figures shown, including loan repayments, tax, and vital expenditure on fixed assets. However, it is generally true to say that, subject to such items, a company with a high level of investment in fixed assets will have a high break-even point but a much lower cash break-even position.

CONTROL

In order to exercise control over their activities, companies adopt a number of techniques of which four are of particular importance.

BUDGETARY CONTROL

The main reason for undertaking the budgetary process already described is the opportunity which it provides for control to be exercised by making comparison between planned and actual outcomes. In general only significant departures from plan are investigated and reported to management – under the principle of management by exception. In practice it is difficult to ensure that the control procedures are valid and meaningful rather than tedious and repetitious.

RESPONSIBILITY ACCOUNTING

Each business may be divided into profit, investment, or cost centres so that an official can be made responsible for every item of income and expenditure. The management accountant then becomes responsible for identifying and classifying transactions, making comparisons with the budget, seeking explanations for departures, and reporting his findings to the management. In principle, officials should only be asked to account for those items over which they have control.

RATIO ANALYSIS

One common technique for controlling the business is through the use of ratios. Because management accounts include more information than statutory accounts it is possible to carry out a comprehensive analysis of operating efficiency based on the return on capital employed.

A set of typical ratios is shown in the diagram on p. 232.

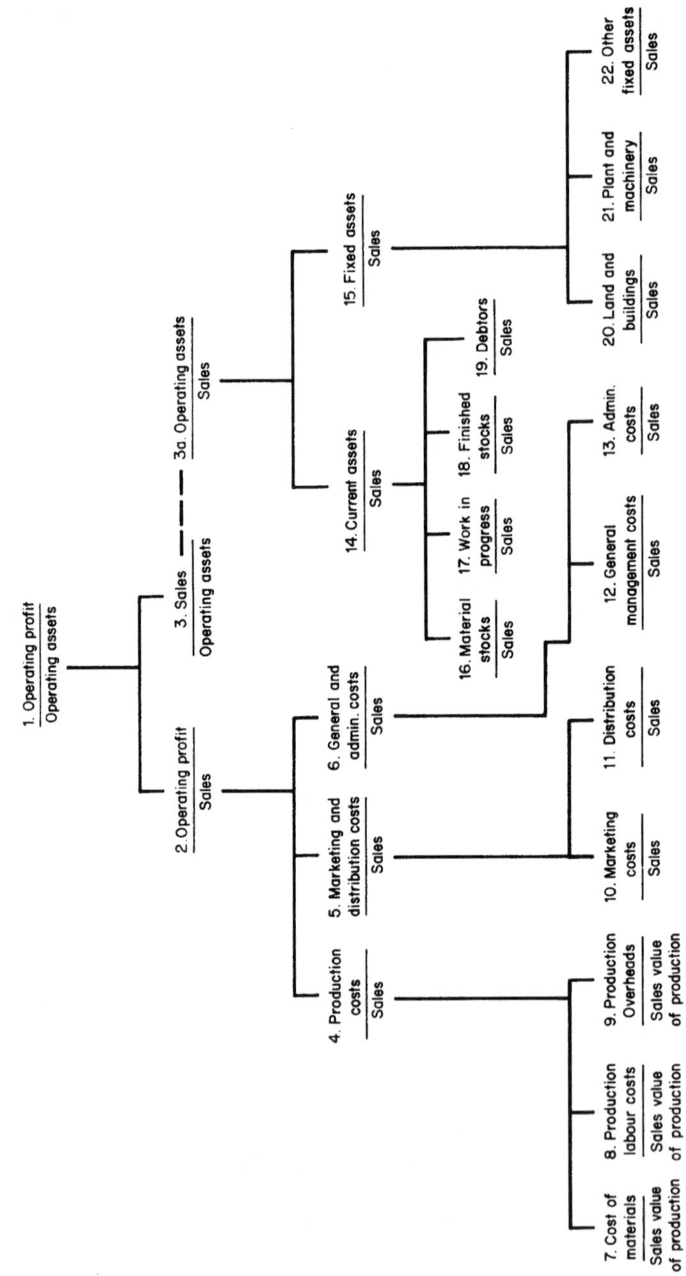

1. Operating profit / Operating assets
2. Operating profit / Sales
3. Sales / Operating assets
3a. Operating assets / Sales
4. Production costs / Sales
5. Marketing and distribution costs / Sales
6. General and admin. costs / Sales
7. Cost of materials / Sales value of production
8. Production labour costs / Sales value of production
9. Production Overheads / Sales value of production
10. Marketing costs / Sales
11. Distribution costs / Sales
12. General management costs / Sales
13. Admin. costs / Sales
14. Current assets / Sales
15. Fixed assets / Sales
16. Material stocks / Sales
17. Work in progress / Sales
18. Finished stocks / Sales
19. Debtors / Sales
20. Land and buildings / Sales
21. Plant and machinery / Sales
22. Other fixed assets / Sales

Figure 9.2

The ratios are shown as a "tree" of ratios which through two main branches explain the return achieved from the operating assets employed. One branch of the tree deals with the composition of costs incurred in relation to sales, and the other with the assets used in order to achieve those sales. The ratios shown are not exclusive and each company should devise an arrangement to suit its own cost and asset structure.

The ratios shown are those used by the Centre for Interfirm Comparisons (IFC), a non-profit organisation established by the British Institute of Management in association with the British Productivity Council specifically to meet the need for a neutral expert body to conduct interfirm comparisons on a confidential basis as a service to management. The comparisons aim to give a comprehensive review of overall company performance and the factors affecting it. They start by showing how overall success compares, and then go on to search out systematically the reasons for differences between companies in overall success. The pyramid of ratios provides the framework for the comparison, but is by no means the end of the story. Ratios at the base of the pyramid are in turn explored further so as to track down the specific areas of the company's operations which are responsible for the differences in overall success.

Membership of a scheme such as IFC enable companies to benefit from comparisons with similar companies which cannot be achieved by using published accounts, show far less detail than that made available on a confidential basis to IFC, and incorporated in the analysis.

Because of the considerable differences between industries no comment will be made here on how particular ratios should be interpreted. The general topic of interpretation through ratios was dealt with in Chapter 8. However, whether looking at internal ratios, or those derived from published accounts the approach is the same.

The objective of ratio analysis is to achieve an understanding of developments in the business by accounting for differences between:

target;
earlier periods;
similar firms.

The calculation of ratios should lead to enquiry, interpretation and ultimately action, if required. Ratio analysis is complicated by a number of factors including the effects of inconsistency between periods and firms, and the effects of changing price levels. All of these factors must be borne in mind when interpreting the results obtained.

The use of ratio analysis to interpret internal figures using industry norms is illustrated by the following example.

Example – Management Ratios

Extract from P & L A/C – Schools Hill Manufacturing

	£	£
SALES		725,250
Less Production Costs		
Materials	401,060	
Works Labour	89,200	
Production Overheads	120,390	
	610,650	
Distribution & Marketing	21,030	
Administration	49,320	
		681,000
Operating Profit		44,250

(Note – Sales value of production equals Sales – i.e. Stocks unchanged)

Extract from Balance Sheet – Schools Hills Manufacturing

	£	£
FIXED ASSETS		
Land and buildings		63,840
Plant and machinery		191,520
Vehicles		10,640
		266,000
CURRENT ASSETS		
Raw materials	47,000	
Work-in-progress	82,300	
Finished stocks	55,800	
	185,100	
Debtors	108,900	
		294,000
OPERATING ASSETS		£560,000

The figures for Schools Hill Manufacturing may be analysed by means of the following ratios for which the industry average (median) is also shown.

	Industry average	*Schools Hill manufacturing*
Operating profit/Operating Assets	11.3%	7.9%
Operating profit/Sales	10.9%	6.1%
Sales/Operating Assets	1.09 times	1.29 times
Department costs (as % of Sales)		
Production costs	79.6%	84.2%
Distribution & Marketing	3.6%	2.9%
Administrative costs	5.7%	6.8%
Production costs (as % of Sales Value of Production)		
Materials cost	53.0%	55.3%
Works labour cost	10.1%	12.3%
Production overheads	16.9%	16.6%

Asset utilisation (as £'s per £1000 of sales)	£	£
Total operating assets	918	772
Current assets	400	405
Fixed assets	518	367
Current asset utilisation (as £'s per £1000 of sales)	£	£
Material stocks	68	65
Work-in-progress	104	113
Finished stocks	84	77
Debtors	148	150
Fixed asset utilisation (as £'s per £1000 of sales)	£	£
Land and buildings	102	88
Plant and machinery	363	264
Vehicles	13	15

Interpretation

SHM (Schools Hill Manufacturing) is achieving a lower return on operating assets than its competitors, due largely to lower operating margins. This may be due to a higher cost structure, or to the company charging lower prices than its competitors. The company appears to be achieving a higher rate of turnover on assets employed which compensates for the lower margins. However, closer examination of the figures reveals a low level of fixed asset utilisation compared with the industry average. This factor probably explains both the higher cost structure of the company, and lower margins, and the better figure for asset utilisation. In order to improve its performance it is likely that the company will need to invest in better productive equipment, and this possibility should be investigated by the management.

The internal ratios have not explained the firm's poor performance but have given an indication of the probable weakness.

STANDARD COSTING

Another major technique for operating control through management accounts is standard costing. Under this procedure standard price and performance is determined in advance and later compared with the actual outcome. Variances are identified, reported to responsible officials and explanations obtained. The management accountant collates the figures and responses and reports them to management and responsible officials.

Variances tend to highlight two facets:

(1) price;
(2) usage.

The calculation of some variances is complicated by the assumptions made regarding the absorption of overheads. As with management ratios variances may be shown in the form of a tree, such as that on page 236.

The ratios shown deal only with the main account headings, in practice variances may be calculated for any account classification provided a standard is set. The classification will vary according to the nature of the business as will variances.[3]

[3] For a description of conventional variance analysis see W. M. Harper, *Cost Accounting* Chap. 19.

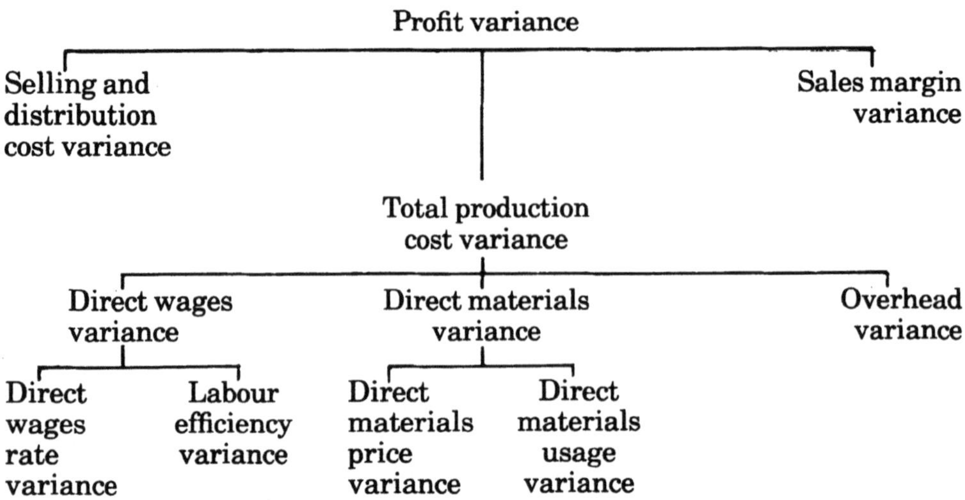

Figure 9.3 – Tree of Variances

A simple example will be used in order to illustrate the principles of variance analysis.

Example

A woodworker manufacturing chairs has found that a standard chair requires 6 feet of wood, costing 50p. per foot. He completes a chair and finds that he has used 8 feet of wood at a cost of 40p. per foot.

Materials variance:	*Standard*	*Actual*	*Variance*	
	£3.00	£3.20	£ .20 (A)	
Price Variance	(Actual Price − Standard Price) × Actual usuage.			
		(0.40 − 0.50) × 8		£0.80 (F)
Usage Variance	(Actual Usage − Standard Usage) × Standard Cost			
		(8–6) × 0.50		£1.00 (A)

Although there has been an adverse variance of 20p. on materials as a result of making the chair, this is composed of two separate aspects — a favourable variance in the price and an adverse variance in cost.

For a small business there will be little necessity to analyse cost behaviour in this way, although in a large manufacturing concern, assembling products using many components, it will be impossible to control production costs without such a system.

In the analysis of variances, emphasis should be placed upon the cost of variances rather than upon their relative size (%). Variances should be tailored to the business and their analysis should be of value to all levels of management. In practice much of their value is lost because reports are prepared as a matter of rigid routine and explaining variances becomes a burden rather than an opportunity for action. Many officials are asked to explain variances over which they have no control and many price variances are attributed to inflation with little effort being put into ascertaining whether this is the true cause, as opposed to inefficient purchasing. It is the role of the management accountant to design a system which analyses the performance of the business in an effective way, to calculate standards and variances, to obtain explanations for variances from supervisory management, and finally to collate the responses and prepare a report for management summarising his findings. It is the end product of the accountants endeavours that a banker is likely to encounter in practice rather than the detailed computations on which it is based.

MONTHLY MANAGEMENT ACCOUNTS AND THE BANKER

With any set of management accounts the banker is likely to find either or both ratios and variances.

Both methods provide a techniques for identifying and highlighting trends and departures from plan.

The valuc of both approaches lies in the extent to which their calculation leads to a meaningful analysis of what is happening to the business and to appropriate action being taken. By asking pertinent questions about trends and variances a banker should be able to find out a great deal about what is happening to a company and how the management is responding.

ABSORPTION COSTING AND MARGINAL COSTING

In addition to its role in planning and control, management accounting is of major use in solving problems. It is particularly useful in decisions concerning pricing and produce mix. In making such decisions it is important to be aware of which costs are relevant in a particular situation. In many cases absorption costing does not meet the requirement of relevance, and accountants make use of the technique of marginal costing.

Example

An absorption costing approach would result in the cost of a chair being shown as set out below.

		Cost Per Chair
		£
Direct materials:	Wood, Paint	0.50
Direct labour:	2 Chairs per worker per day	
	Wage £40 p.w. ÷ 10	4.00
Variable overheads:	Power, Light, Heat, etc.	
	Cost £100 per 100 Chairs	1.00
Fixed overheads:	Management, Office and	
	supervisory salaries, rates, rents	
	£10,000 p.a. – output 5,000 chairs	2.00
		£7.50

In the above example, the costs associated with manufacturing a chair have been analysed in a conventional absorption costing format. This approach apportions overhead costs at an assumed level of activity. In this case overheads are estimated at £10,000 – but this will only work out at £2 per chair if 5,000 chairs are manufactured. The rate of £2 per chair is referred to as an *overhead absorption rate*. In this case it is based on each unit produced, but a variety of bases can be used. In some cases it is based on the machine hours used, on others it is based on labour hours. Whichever method is used, and the choice is often made for convenience rather than precision, if output is different from budget the result will be misleading, with overheads being "over-recovered" or "under-recovered" by the costing system.[4]

Under a marginal costing approach the costs would be analysed as shown in the example.

Example

		Budget
Production level		5,000
		£
Price per chair		10.00
Variable costs:	£	
Materials	0.50	
Labour	4.00	
Overheads	1.00	5.50
Contribution		4.50
Budgeted contribution		22,500
Fixed costs		10,000
Profit		12,500

The value of marginal costing can be seen by considering the position when an order is received for 500 chairs at only £7 each. Under an absorption costing approach it would appear sensible to reject the order in order to avoid making a loss of £0.50 per chair. However, the marginal costing approach shows that at £7 per chair a contribution of £1.50 would be obtained towards the fixed costs of £10,000. The position can be appreciated by examining the impact of the various alternatives on the overall profitability of the business as shown in Table 9.2 below.

As can be seen, rejecting the new order results in a profit of only £1,250, whereas acceptance would increase profit to £2,000. With output of only 2,500 chairs and overheads recovered at £2 per chair the total recovered within the cost of £7.50 amounts to only £5,000 compared with the budgeted recovery of £10,000. Thus £5,000 of overheads are unrecovered. This example highlights the value of marginal costing information in a number of key areas.

[4] For a description of overhead recovery techniques see Harper op.cit., Chap. 19.

Table 9.2

	Budget	*Rejecting new order*	*Accepting new order*	
Production	5,000	2,500	3,000	
Prices	£10	£10	2,500	£10
			500	£7
	£	£	£	
Revenue	50,000	25,000	28,500	
Variable costs				
£5.50 per chair	27,5000	13,750	16,500	
Contribution	22,500	11,250	12,000	
Fixed costs	10,000	10,000	10,000	
Profit	£12,500	£1,250	£2,000	

(1) short-term pricing decisions;
(2) product mix decisions;
(3) decisions where the availability of key factor (e.g. labour) is limited.

In each of these cases the decision should be taken so as to maximise the contribution which is achieved towards fixed costs and profits. Despite its manifest value, the Marginal Costing approach is subject to a number of important limitations:

- All costs must be absorbed in the long run.
- If conditions improve after a "loss making" order is accepted, some opportunities may be lost.

Furthermore, costing information should only be used to determine the minimum price which a company should accept. The optimal price should be based upon an assessment by the marketing executives of "what the market will bear".

In order to demonstrate the significance of marginal costing in bank lending decisions use will be made of the following example, which deals with a typical situation in which the banker must form an opinion on a course of action proposed by the managing director of a company.

Example

Futura Furniture (Lombard St.) Ltd

Shortly after the end of its financial year Oscar Rivera, the Managing Director of Futura Furniture (Lombard St.) Ltd., calls to see his bank manager. He brings with him the company's management accounts, which show a small loss for the year. He reveals that the outlook is bleak, and although the company is taking action to improve matters, it will be unable to make the agreed reductions in its overdraft.

During the conversation he confesses that "things haven't been the same" since Bill Naylor, the Finance Director, had to retire following a heart attack and was replaced by Peter Wilkinson, a newly qualified management accountant. "This new chap works hard enough – but I don't understand half of the things he's on about. Why only the other day he was suggesting that we sell some of our products at a loss."

The company manufactures and sells Italian-style easy chairs, and in recent years has concentrated on two basic versions upholstered in synthetic cloth material, and a deluxe version in hide. The product range is:

	Price	*Units sold*
	£	
Turino	55.00	8,000
Milano	85.00	4,000
Roma	225.00	1,200

It emerges that the company has recently been approached by a major chain store and asked to produce an extra 4,000 chairs for sale through out the country under its own label. The chairs would be fundamentally the same as the Turino, but would not be recognisable as such to the average shopper. Consequently, they would not provide direct competition to the firm's existing range. It has been established that the additional output could be manufactured within the existing capacity of the business and that the extra labour required can be recruited. However, the store concerned is only prepared to pay £50 per chair and as a result the order will be rejected.

It is also learned that competition has been especially fierce in the luxury market and that a price increase is out of the question. However, the accountant has suggest cutting the price of the Roma to £215 which, it was estimated, would increase sales by 600 units.

Rivera tells the bank that he has discussed matters with his colleagues and decided on the following course of action.

(1) As it is unprofitable, manufacture of the Turino will cease forthwith.
(2) All of the company's efforts will be directed towards selling the Milano. By expanding the number of outlets it is expect that sales will increase to 7,000 units.
(3) No changes will be made with regard to the Roma, although when conditions permit the price will be increased.

No changes are expected in the price or usage of materials, in wages or in variable overheads. Fixed overheads will remain at the same level despite the changes proposed.

The following information is shown in the accounts.

	£	£
Sales		1,050,000
Direct materials	345,600	
Direct wages	324,800	
Variable overheads	136,400	
Fixed overheads	243,600	
		1,050,400
Loss for the year		£400

A schedule to the accounts shows the following detailed information

	Turino	*Milano*	*Roma*
	£	£	£
Unit costs			
Direct materials	14.00	20.00	128.00
Direct wages			
Fabrication	8.00	12.00	14.00
Upholstering	10.00	12.00	24.00
Finishing and inspection	2.00	4.00	6.00
	20.00	28.00	44.00
Prime cost	34.00	48.00	172.00
Variable overheads			
Fabrication	4.00	5.00	8.00
Upholstering	4.00	4.00	7.00
Finishing and inspection	1.00	2.00	2.00
	9.00	11.00	17.00
Fixed overheads	15.00	21.00	33.00
Total cost	58.00	80.00	222.00
Selling price	55.00	85.00	225.00
Unit profit (loss)	(3.00)	5.00	3.00
Unit sales	8,000	4,000	1,200
Product profit (loss)	(24,000)	20,000	3,600
Overall loss		£400	

Further notes reveal that wages are variable with output. Fixed costs are calculated on the assumption that the sales levels shown above are achieved, and on this assumption amount to 75% of the cost of direct wages for each product.

Interpretation

The case of Futura Furniture highlights the potentially misleading nature of detailed accounting information if the assumptions made in preparing it are not well understood. In particular, it demonstates the shortcomings of the traditional technique known as "absorption costing" in relation to decisions involving product pricing and product mix decisions. In many cases such niceties are of no concern to the banker. However, in many others, such as that of Futura, a customer's cash flow projections and banking arrangements are based directly on such information. If the banker is being asked to back the customer's judgement, it is often useful to be able to examine the commerical assumptions in some detail.

The Shortcomings of Futura's Figures

The detailed schedule provided by Futura incorporates an analysis of the costs associated with each of the models made by the company. Within this analysis fixed overheads which amount to £243,000 have been apportioned across the three product ranges in direct proportion to the cost of direct wages incurred on each model. It can be seen that, in aggregate, fixed overheads represent 75% of the total of direct wages.

$$\frac{\text{Fixed overheads}}{\text{Direct wages}} \quad \frac{£243{,}600}{£324{,}800} = 0.75$$

Thus, for each product fixed overheads are absorbed at this rate on the cost of direct wages.

	Turino	*Milano*	*Roma*
Direct wages	£20.00	£28.00	£44.00
Fixed overheads 75%	£15.00	£1 00	£33.00

This method of apportionment, which is very widely used, will only produce an accurate estimate for decision making provided the output in future periods corresponds to that used in the analysis. For whilst the variable costs change in proportion to the level of output, fixed costs do not.

Futura will only exactly recover its overheads if its output is as follows:

	Volume	*Fixed overhead*	*£*
Turino	8,000	£15	120,000
Milano	4,000	£21	84,000
Roma	1,200	£33	39,600
			£243,600

Unfortunately, Oscar Rivera does not appreciate this point and proposes making major changes in the volume of the products manufactured and sold without considering the impact on overhead recovery. (At this stage it should be noted that in practice the distinction between fixed and variable costs, although important, is difficult to make. Very often wages, although treated as variable, are to a great extent fixed, at least in the short term. In the long run almost all cost are to some extent variable.)

The Marginal Costing Approach

The true significance of the costing information available can better be appreciated by using a "marginal costing" approach. This has been done in the table below. The first line – total variable costs – has been calculated by adding all of the costs shown in the original cost analysis prior to the inclusion of fixed overheads. By comparing the total variable costs with the selling price the "contribution" obtained from each model is found. No attempt is made to apportion fixed overheads, but these are set against the total contribution to reach the overall trading result.

	Turino	*Milano*	*Roma*
	£	*£*	*£*
Total variable costs	43.00	59.00	189.00
Selling price	55.00	85.00	225.00
Contribution	12.00	26.00	36.00
Unit sales	8,000	4,000	1,200
Production contribution	£96,000	£104,000	£43,200
Total contribution		£243,200	
Fixed overheads		£243,600	
Loss		£400	

Rivera's Plan

One advantage of the marginal costing approach is the ease with which figures may be manipulated in order to test alternative assumptions. When Rivera's figures are tested in this way it can be seen that the effect of his plan would be to increase the company's loss. This position arises because the contibution lost as result of discontinuing the Turino is greater than the increased contribution from the Milano. Based on Rivera's plan the following result would be achieved.

	Milano £		Roma £
Total variable cost	59.00		189.00
Selling price	85.00		225.00
Contribution	26.00		36.00
Unit sales	7,000		1,200
Product contribution	£182,000		£43,200
Total contribution		£225,200	
Fixed overheads		£243,600	
Loss		£18,400	

(It may be noted that, if the Milano sales can be increased by 708 units to generate an additional contribution of £26 each, the resulting net revenue £18,408 will enable the company to break even.)

Wilkinson's Plan

When a similar approach is applied to Wilkinson's plan it can be seen that the result is a considerable improvement. If it is assumed that the company continues to manufacture both the Turino and Milano and accepts the own label order it will gain an additional contribution of £28,000. Furthermore, by cutting the price of the Roma it generates an additional contribution of £26 on 600 new sales – which at £15,600 exceeds the drop in contribution of £10 per item on its existing sales and increases company profits by £3,600.

	Turino £	Milano £		Roma £	Own label £
Total variable cost	43.00	59.00		189.00	43.00
Selling price	55.00	85.00		215.00	50.00
Contribution	12.00	26.00		26.00	7.00
Unit sales	8,000	4,000		1,800	4,000
Product contribution	96,000	104,000		46,800	28,000
Total contribution			274,800		
Fixed overheads			243,600		
Profit			£31,200		

Conclusion

The analysis of Futura's plans using a marginal costing approach has shown the original analysis based on full absorption costing to be dangerously misleading. In the real world it is often difficult to determine cost behaviour with the precision assumed here. Furthermore, it should be emphasised that a solution to the company's problems might lie in the marketing sphere and that all of the alternatives have not been exhausted. The marginal costing approach does not reveal what price should be charged – although it provides a useful contribution to pricing and volume decisions. Nevertheless, were the banker to have carried out the analysis used here he would certainly not have gone along with Rivera's plan for reducing his overdraft!

MARGINAL COSTING AND THE BANKER

From the bankers viewpoint, there is little doubt that marginal costing information can be enormously useful when a business is in trouble. If the correct decisions are to be taken companies must use a relevant costs approach and not rely upon conventional absorption costing. Whilst the banker can hardly expect to calculate the relevant costs himself, he should certainly be able to identify situations in which a company is failing to do so – and it is clearly in his interest to ensure that the most advantageous short term decisions are taken in emergencies.

CONCLUSION

Despite its complexity management accounting offers bankers a great opportunity for taking decisions which are based on information which is relevant, reliable and up-to-date. In particular, it can be of use in examining plans, monitoring progress and in helping to resolve problems. Rarely will the information produced in a set of management accounts include all of the information which a banker needs – but it should lead him to ask more of the right questions. Finally, a few words should be added regarding inflation. If a company is to recover its costs and maintain an adequate cashflow, it is essential that it takes account of current prices. For a business to stay viable it must maintain adequate finance in order to replace assets which it uses up including stocks and fixed assets.

Bankers should be alert to any situation in which companies are using historic costs for decision making – as these are unlikely to reflect the real costs of operating the business.

FURTHER READING

There are many texts on Management Accounting – most going into considerably more detail that is useful for the lending banker. Possibly the best general introduction is that by Sizer.On points of details the M & E Handbooks by Harper are useful. Sizer contributed a series entitled "Management Accounting and the Banker" to the *Bankers Magazine* between February 1976 and December 1977. A simpler series by Michael Pitcher appeared in the Journal of the Institute of Bankers between February 1976 and June 1978 – and has now been published under the title "Management Accounting for the Lending Banker". (Institute of Bankers.)

In recent years, some writers have begun to question some of the conventional approaches to Management Accounting. A useful collection of essays dealing with some of these issues is edited by Carsberg, Arnold and Scapens. Drury's book is a comprehensive review of the topic which will be useful for those who wish to pursue the subject at a more advanced level.

J. D. Arnold and T. Hope, *Accounting for Management Decisions* (Prentice Hall, 1983).

J. Sizer, *An Insight into Management Accounting* (Penguin 2nd ed., 1979).

W. M. Harper, *Cost Accounting* (M & E Handbooks).

W. M. Harper, *Management Accounting* (M & E Handbooks).

M. Pitcher, *Management Accounting for the Lending Banker* (Institute of Bankers).

B. Carsberg, J. Arnold, R. Scapens *Current Issues in Management Accounting* (P. Allen, 2nd ed).

J. C. Drury, *Management and Cost Accounting* (Van Nostrand Rheinhold, 1985).

Chapter 10
Planning and Controlling Working Capital and the Flow of Funds

INTRODUCTION

Whilst the criteria for business success, and some would say, its principle objective, is to make a profit, profits alone will not ensure that a firm stays in business, indeed some firms have stayed in business for many years without making profits, whilst others have gone out of business still claiming to be profitable. The reason for this apparent anomaly is that businesses fail when they run out of money, rather than when they stop making profits. Therefore an important facet of financial management is to ensure that the firm has the finance available in the short term in order to ensure that it stays in business. In order to achieve this objective it must control its investment in working capital, and the flow of funds within the business. This chapter commences with a brief review of the way in which funds flow around a business. It continues with a review of the methods employed in order to plan the cash requirements of a business including the preparation of cash budgets and projected funds' statements. The chapter concludes with a consideration of the techniques available for exercising control over working capital including the use of ratios, the preparation of statements showing changes in the working capital cycle, and the way in which this may be analysed and reported upon to shareholders through the preparation of source and application of funds statements.

THE FLOW OF FUNDS WITHIN A BUSINESS: THE WORKING CAPITAL CYCLE

Figure 10.1 below shows the flow of funds within a typical manufacturing business. In order to operate the firm must acquire raw materials which it manufactures into finished goods for sale to debtors.

The investment in goods and services through this cycle must be financed until payment is made by debtors for the goods received. Often suppliers do not require immediate payment and it is therefore only necessary to finance part of the investment in working capital; the total net of trade and other creditors. Periodically payment must be made to those who have provided goods and services from the sums received from debtors. As long as the firm is operating profitably the amounts received will generally exceed the amounts to be paid out, and this surplus is often referred to as cash flow. From the amount generated, funds must be applied in paying taxation, and rewarding the providers of capital both lenders and shareholders. What is left over will be available for reinvestment in the business, either in the form of new or replacement fixed assets or of additional investment in working capital. If the business expands it will need to invest more in these areas, and often these funds are generated internally. In other cases additional finance must be obtained by borrowing or by raising more share capital.

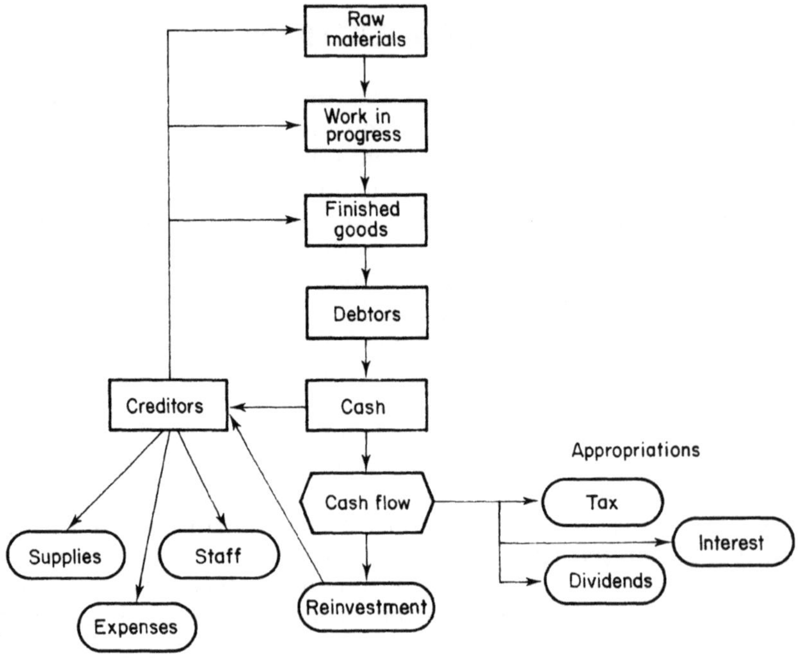

Figure 10.1 The Working Capital Cycle

PLANNING THE FLOW OF FUNDS

There are two main methods of planning the flow of funds within a business:

(1) Projected funds' flow statements
(2) Cash flow budgets

A projected funds' statement shows the envisaged changes in the financial condition of the business and the resulting effect on working capital and liquid resources. The closing figure of the statement shows the change in liquid resources, and thus the additional funds required by the firm in order to finance its activities. A cash flow budget is a statement showing the projected payments and receipts of the firm on a periodic, often month by month basis. The difference between the inflows and outflows of cash will give the net surplus or deficit for the month, and thus the change in liquid resources, usually shown in the form of the firm's cash balance. The latter feature makes a cash flow budget potentially a very useful document to a banker seeking to control the level of an overdraft on the company's current account. Each of these two statements will be illustrated by an example.

A useful by product of the preparation of a funds' statement is the possibility of preparing a *projected balance sheet*, an examination of which will show the gearing and liquidity position resulting from the flow of funds occuring during the period.

PROJECTED FUNDS' FLOW STATEMENTS

The procedure for preparing a projected funds' flow statement is illustrated by the example shown below.

Example

The Chief Accountant of Parkin Ltd, a fast growing manufacturer of sports equipment, is preparing a paper for the directors showing the company's anticipated financial requirements for the financial year ending March 1982. The accounts for 1981 have just been completed and relevant details are shown below.

The Marketing Director has provided the following forecast of sales for 1981/82. In view of the current uncertainty in the economy he has provided three probable outcomes and estimated their probability.

Sales forecast	*Probability*	*Sales* £'000
Poor	0.4	2,460
Average	0.5	2,700
Good	0.1	2,900

Gross profit is normally 30% of sale value and it is expected that overhead costs (excluding depreciation and interest charges) will amount to £421,000 whatever the level of sales.

Because of a high level of investment in plant and stocks in recent years the company has substantial unutilised tax losses brought forward. As a result, the company will pay no mainstream corporation tax even if it achieves the most optimistic level of sales forecast by the Marketing Director.

Capital expenditure during 1982 will include the acquisition of an advanced machine costing £220,000 and sundry plant and machinery amounting to £30,000. Because of fierce competition and the danger of obsolescence it is company policy to depreciate all equipment at 20% per annum on a straight line basis – with a full charge in the year of acquisition.

In recent years the company has increased dividends by 10% per annum irrespective of the level of earnings a policy which the directors believe meets with the approval of the shareholders.

Creditors and stock levels are expected to reflect the growth in sales, but in order to boost sales it has been decided to extend the credit period allowed to customers by 25% with effect from 1 April 1981. All customers are expected to take advantage of the new settlement terms and this, together with sales growth, will be reflected in future debtors' figures. Taxation is payable at 50%.

Extracts from the Accounts of Parkin Ltd.

Profit and Loss Account for 1981

	£000	£'000
Sales		2,100
Profit before depreciation, interest and tax		296
Depreciation	70	
Interest charges	41	111
Profit before tax		185
Tax		24
Profit after tax		161
Proposed dividend		56
Retained		105

Balance Sheet as at 31 March 1981

	£,000	£,000
Assets employed		
Land and buildings at valuation		750
Plant and machinery at cost	350	
Less depreciation	170	
		180
		930
Stocks	410	
Debtors	190	
Cash	12	
	612	
Creditors	272	
Tax	24	
Dividends	56	
Overdraft	147	
	499	113
		1,043
Financed by		
Share capital (Ordinary £1 shares)		400
Reserves		493
10% Loan stock 1985/90		150
		1,043

Solution

The first stage in drawing up a projected funds statement is to calculate the funds which the firm expects to generate from its own activities. This requires a calculation of the probable sales and the profit arising thereform. In the case of Parkin we are given a range of possible sales levels and may calculate the expected level of sales from the probabilities given. Expecting sales are as follows:

Sales	*Probability*	*£'000*
2,460	0.4	984
2,700	0.5	1,350
2,900	0.1	290
	Expected Sales	2,624

Expected sales represent an increase of 25% over the previous year.

$$\text{Percentage increase} = \frac{2,624 - 2,100}{2,100} \times 100 = 25\%$$

The next stage is the preparation of a projected profit and loss account.

		£'000
Gross profit (30% of Sales)		787
Overheads		421
Net profit		366
Depreciation (350 + 250 = 600 × 20%)		120
		246
Interest		
overdraft	25	
loan stock	15	40
Profit before tax		206
Tax (at 50%)		103
Profit after tax		103
Dividends (56 × 110%)		62
Retained profit		41

Gross profit is stated to be 30% of the increased sales of £2,624,000. Depreciation is charged at 20% on the existing plant and machinery, and on the new items totalling £250,000 giving a total charge for depreciation of £120,000. Interest must often be estimated on an approximate basis, and in this case it is assumed that £25,000 will be payable on an overdraft, in addition to loan stock interest. Future taxation and dividends may be disregarded for the purposes of the funds statement, and will remain as unpaid items in the closing balance sheet. The balances outstanding at the previous year end are shown as applications for the period. From this information it is possible to prepare a funds' statement showing projected financial requirements.

Parkin Ltd – Projected Cash Requirement

	£'000	£'000
Profit before tax		206
Depreciation		120
		326
Uses of funds		
Fixed assets acquired	250	
Dividends	56	
Tax	24	
		330
		(4)
Changes in working capital		
Increase in debtors		
Sales growth (190 × 0.25)	48	
Extended credit (238 × 0.25)	54	
	107	
Stocks (410 × 0.25)	102	
	209	
Less creditors (272 × 0.25)	68	
		(141)
Total financing required		145

The projected funds' statement for Parkin Ltd shows that the company will generate £326,000 in the coming year from its operations, but slightly more than this will be used in paying dividends and tax, and in acquiring fixed assets. As a result of this experience the company will need additional funds of £145,000 in order to finance its additional working capital requirements. From the balance sheet it can be seen that at the end of 1981 the net current assets amounted to only £113,000. The effect of the projected flow of funds during 1982 will be to reduce this amount to a bare surplus. Therefore the company should consider raising long-term finance in order to meet its additional requirements.

PROJECTING THE BALANCE SHEET

In order to project the balance sheet it is simply necessary to adjust the opening balance sheet to take account of the flow of funds which are projected for the year. Two items require different treatment:

(1) The figures for dividends and taxation shown in the funds statement are those derived from the profit and loss account which will not be paid until the following year.
(2) The profit and loss account balance is found by adding the retained profit to the balance brought forward. The result for Parkin Ltd is shown below.

Parkin Ltd. – Projected Balance Sheet

		£,000	£,000
Land and buildings			750
Plant and machinery	(350 + 250)	600	
Depreciation	(170 + 120)	290	
			310
			1,060
Stocks	(410 + 102)	512	
Debtors	(190 + 107)	297	
Cash		12	
		821	
Creditors	(272 + 68)	340	
Tax		103	
Dividends		62	
Overdraft	(147 + 145)	292	
		797	
			24
			1,084
Financed by:			
Share capital			400
Reserves (493 + 31)			534
10% loan stock 1985/90			150
			1,084

An examination of the projected balance sheet of Parkin Ltd. reveals gearing rising from 24% to 32%, and the current ratio declining from 1.2:1 to 1.03 by the end of the year.

CASH FLOW BUDGETS

Cash flow budgets may deal with periods of any length for which reasonably reliable data is available, and may show the cash requirements for each quarter, month or week during the period. In practice the most difficult aspect of cash budgeting is obtaining adequate data on key variables such as sales, purchases, and expenses for inclusion in the budget. Advice must be obtained from the relevant operational managers on these aspects. After the basic trading information is established details must be obtained of all non-routine payments and receipts arising during the period. The information is then laid out in a tabular fashion as shown in the example below.

Example

Tompset and Watkins Ltd manufacture chocolate sweets for sale through a variety of outlets. 15% of sales are for cash and are paid for during the month of sale. The remainder of customers do not pay for goods until two months after sale. The company takes one month's credit on goods and services supplied. The following projections are made of transactions during the remainder of the year.

	Sales £,000	*Purchases* £,000	*Expenses* £,000	*Salaries and Wages* £,000
July	400	175	70	50
August	400	200	60	60
September	450	125	75	80
October	500	125	80	70
November	350	150	85	70
December	300	150	75	60

Sales during May amount to £250,000 and during June to £300,000. Trade creditors outstanding at the end of June totalled £130,000 and expenses £65,000. On average, PAYE amounts to 30% of salaries and wages and is paid in the following month – that outstanding for June amounted to £16,000. In addition to the items shown above the company expects the following transactions to take place.

1 July – corporation tax due £79,000.
1 August – payment for new motor vehicles £47,000.
5 September – payment for new machinery £140,000.
22 October – payment due for sale of surplus plant £17,000.
31 October – interim dividend payable £21,000.
15 November – advance corporation tax payable £9,000.
24 November – payment due for new plant £10,000.
27 December – receipts from sale of surplus land £23,000.
31 December – loan stock £200,000 to be repaid.

At the end of June the company has a balance of £37,300 at the bank.

Tompset and Watkins Ltd – Cash Flow Budget

	July	*August*	*September*	*October*	*November*	*December*
Receipts	£	£	£	£	£	£
Sales Revenue						
Cash	60,000	60,000	67,500	75,000	52,500	45,000
Credit	212,500	255,000	340,000	340,000	382,500	425,000
Sales of fixed assets				17,000		23,000
Total receipts	272,500	315,000	407,500	432,000	435,000	493,000
Payments						
Suppliers	135,000	175,000	200,000	125,000	125,000	150,000
Expenses	65,000	70,000	60,000	75,000	80,000	85,000
Salaries and wages	50,000	60,000	80,000	70,000	70,000	60,000
PAYE	16,000	15,000	18,000	24,000	21,000	21,000
Corporation tax	79,000				9,000	
Fixed assets purchased		47,000	140,000		10,000	
Loan repayment						200,000
Dividends				21,000		
Total payments	345,000	367,000	498,000	315,000	315,000	516,000
Net change	(72,500)	(57,000)	(90,500)	117,000	170,000	(23,000)
Opening cash balance	37,300	(35,200)	(87,200)	(177,700)	(60,700)	59,300
Closing cash balance	(35,200)	(87,200)	(177,700)	(60,700)	59,300	36,300

Interpretation

The cash flow budget for Tompset and Watkins shows a need for finance of up to £177,500 during the period, even though at the end the bank balance has returned to approximately the same level as at the outset. In interpreting such statements it is important to note that the balances shown at the end of the month may be exceeded during the period and that in some cases the peak financing requirement may be considerably more than that shown. For example in the case of Tompset and Watkins the payment for new machinery of £140,000 due in September arises on the 5th of the month. It is unlikely that all of the sales revenue for the month will have been received by this date and therefore it may be necessary for the company to arrange finance of up to £250,000 to cover this peak. In order to meet the financing requirement shown by a cash budget a company may attempt to delay or accelerate payments and receipts, as an alternative to raising additional short and long-term resources.

CONTROLLING THE FLOW OF FUNDS

There are four main techniques available for controlling the flow of funds:

(1) Use of ratios;
(2) Comparisons with budget;
(3) Analysis of funds flow statements;
(4) Calculation of the working capital cycle.

The use of ratios in order to interpret financial statements has been discussed in Chapter 8, and the use of liquidity ratios for internal control purposes presents no new issues. Comparisons with the cash budget, although possible, are rarely used for control purposes as much more can be learnt from examining operating budgets. In practice so many variables operate to affect the closing cash balance that little can be achieved by seeking to account for departures within the cash budget itself. However, it is important to up date the cash budget regularly in order to determine the effect of trading developments on cash needs and resources. Funds' statements provide a very useful analysis of the reasons for a change in the financial condition as has already been seen in this chapter. The calculation of the working capital cycle is illustrated by the following example, for which liquidity ratios are also calculated.

CALCULATING THE WORKING CAPITAL CYCLE

The concept of the working capital cycle has already been introduced at the start of this chapter. By calculating the duration for which items are held under each balance sheet heading it is possible to monitor the time which is taken for capital to pass through the cycle. The composition of the cycle for each period may be calculated, changes in the cycle identified, and explanations sought.

Example

Jackson & Feeney Ltd have just received the accounts of their subsidiary company J & F (Barnsley) Ltd, which fabricates sub-assemblies from components supplied by its parent. It is some time since the parent received any payment for goods supplied, as a result of which the current account balance has risen considerably. In the past subsidiaries have been allowed to operate with substantial independence in order to encourage enterprise and initiative.

Profit and Loss Account

		1981/82		*1982/83*
	£'000	£'000	£'000	£'000
Turnover (all sold on credit)		800		1,100
Opening Stock – raw materials	20		25	
Purchases	350		570	
	370		595	
Less closing stock of raw materials	25		65	
Cost of materials consumed	345		530	
Opening stock – work-in-progress	40		35	
	385		565	
Other costs of production	150		230	
	535		795	
Less closing work-in-progress	35		45	
Cost of production	500		750	
Opening stock: finished goods	50		70	
	550		820	
Closing stock: finished goods	70		160	
Cost of goods sold		480		660
Gross profit		320		450
Other costs (including depreciation)		260		362
Net profit		60		88

Balance Sheet

		1981/82		*1982/83*
	£,000s	£,000s	£,000s	£,000s
Fixed assets (at net book value)				
Freehold property		100		100
Plant and machinery		70		138
		170		238

Current assets				
Stocks – raw materials	25		65	
work-in-progress	35		45	
finished goods	70		160	
	130		270	
Debtors	105		190	
Bank	45		–	
		280		460
		450		698
Financed by:				
Ordinary share capital		200		200
Retained profit (after dividends)		85		138
Loan stock		100		100
		385		438
Creditors		60		110
Current account with parent		5		110
Bank overdraft (official limit £30,000)		–		40
		450		698

The figures may be analysed as follows:

Raw Materials. The figure for raw materials shown in the balance sheet is compared with the average daily cost of materials consumed.

	1981/82 £'000	*1982/83* £'000
Daily cost of materials	$\frac{345}{365} = 0.945$	$\frac{530}{365} = 1.452$
Raw materials at year end / Daily cost of raw materials	$\frac{25}{0.945} = 26$ days	$\frac{65}{1.452} = 45$ days

For convenience the two calculations may be combined as shown below:

$$\text{Raw materials at year end} \times \frac{\text{Days in year}}{\text{annual cost of raw materials}}$$

In order to calculate the figures for the remaining items in the cycle the following comparisons are made:

Work-in-progress – Cost of production
Finished goods – Cost of goods sold
Credit received – Purchases
Credit given – Sales

The full working capital cycle is calculated as shown below:

	1981/82	*Days*	*1981/82*	*Days*	*Change*
Raw materials	$\frac{25}{345} \times 365$	26	$\frac{65}{530} \times 365$	45	+ 19
Work-in-progress	$\frac{35}{500} \times 365$	26	$\frac{45}{750} \times 365$	22	− 4
Finished goods	$\frac{70}{480} \times 365$	53	$\frac{100}{660} \times 365$	88	+ 35
Credit received	$\frac{60}{350} \times 365$	(62)	$\frac{110}{570} \times 365$	(70)	(+ 8)
Credit given	$\frac{105}{800} \times 365$	48	$\frac{190}{1100} \times 365$	63	+ 15
		91		148	57 days

The working capital cycle of J and F (Barnsley) shows a considerable increase over the two years. The main change affects the level of finished goods, but substantial increases have also taken place in the level of raw materials and trade debtors. An examination of the liquidity and gearing ratios of the company also reveals that there has been a deterioration in liquidity and an increase in gearing.

Ratios

Current ratio	$\frac{280}{65} = 4.3{:}1$	$\frac{460}{260} = 1.8{:}1$
Liquid ratio	$\frac{150}{65} = 2.3{:}1$	$\frac{190}{260} = 0.7{:}1$
Gearing ratio	$\frac{100}{450} = 22\%$	$\frac{250}{558} = 44\%$

In calculating the gearing ratio the current account with the parent company has been treated as borrowing. Inspection of the balance sheet suggests that the subsidiary has utilised the current account with its parent in order to finance investment in fixed assets. The strong working capital position has deteriorated, and steps should clearly be taken to rectify the position. In practice the parent might require the subsidiary to pay the current account balance by realising surplus current assets.

STATEMENTS OF SOURCE AND APPLICATION OF FUNDS

The profit and loss account and the balance sheet of a company show, inter alia, the amount of profit made during the year and the disposition of the company's resources at the beginning and the end of that year. However, according to SSAP 10, for a fuller understanding of a company's affairs it is necessary also to identify the movements in assets, liabilities and capital which have taken place during the year and the resultant effect on net liquid funds. This information is not specifically disclosed by a profit and loss account and balance sheet but can be made available in the form of a statement of source and application of funds (a "funds statement"). It is stated:

> "The objective of such a statement is to show the manner in which the operations of a company have been financed and in which its financial resources have been used and the format selected should be designed to achieve this objective.
>
> A funds statement should show the sources from which funds have flowed into the company and the way in which they have been used. It should show clearly the funds generated or absorbed by the operations of the business and the manner in which any resulting surplus of liquid assets has been applied or any deficiency of such assets has been financed, distinguishing the long term from the short term. The statement should distinguish the use of funds for the purchase of new fixed assets from funds used in increasing the working capital of the company.
>
> The funds statement will provide a link between the balance sheet at the beginning of the period, the profit and loss account for the period and the balance sheet at the end of the period. A minimum of "netting off" should take place as this may tend to mask the significance of individually important figures; for example, the sale of one building and the purchase of another should generally be kept separate in a funds statement. The figures from which a funds statement is constructed should generally be identifiable in the profit and loss account, balance sheet and related notes. If adjustments to those published figures are necessary, details should be given to enable the related figures to be rapidly located."

Since 1976 all companies with a turnover greater than £25,000 have been required to include a funds statement within their annual report in accordance with SSAP 10. The standard states:

> "The statement should show the profit or loss for the period together with the adjustments required for items which did not use (or provide) funds in the period. The following other sources and applications of funds should, where material, also be shown:
>
> (a) dividends paid;
> (b) acquisitions and disposals of fixed and other non-current assets;
> (c) funds raised by increasing, or expended in repaying or redeeming, medium or long-term loans or the issued capital of the company;
> (d) increase or decrease in working capital sub-divided into its components, and movements in net liquid funds."

Although no standard layout is prescribed, the statement includes examples of possible approaches in an appendix; that for a company without subsidiaries is shown below. In the introductory comments to the standard it is stated:

> "Funds statements should, in the case of companies with subsidiaries, be based on the group accounts. They should reflect any purchases or disposals of subsidiary companies. In the interests of clarity, it will generally also be necessary to summarise the effects of the acquisition or disposal by way of a footnote indicating, in the case of an acquisition, how much of the purchase price has been discharged in cash and how much by the issue of shares."

Example

Company without subsidiaries Ltd – Statement of source and application of funds

	This Year			*Last Year*		
	£'000	£'000	£'000	£'000	£'000	£'000
Source of funds						
Profit before tax						
Adjustments for items not involving the movement of funds:						
Depreciation						
Total generated from operations						
Funds from other sources						
Issue of shares for cash						
Application of funds						
Dividends paid						
Tax paid						
Purchase of fixed assets						
Increase/decrease in working capital						
Increase in stocks						
Increase in debtors						
(Increase) decrease in creditors – excluding taxation and proposed dividends						
Movement in net liquid funds:						
Increase (decrease) in:						
Cash balances						
Short-term investments						

The procedure for preparing funds' statements is illustrated by the following example:

Example

Jaguar Ltd has just prepared its accounts for the year ended 31 March 1983 which are set out below with corresponding figures for the previous year.

Profit and Loss Accounts for the Years ended 31 March

		1983		*1982*
		£		£
Sales		23,500		20,500
Cost of goods sold		16,000		14,000
Gross profit		7,500		6,500
	£		£'000	
Selling expenses . . .	2,000		1,900	
Administration expenses	3,000		2,600	
		5,000		4,500
Net operating profit		2,500		2,000
Interest		500		300
Ordinary profit before taxation		2,000		1,700
Taxation		1,200		1,020
Ordinary profit after taxation		800		680
Undistributed profits b/fwd.		4,090		3,690
		4,890		4,370
Dividends paid – proposed		525		280
Undistributed profits c/fwd.		4,365		4,090

Procedure

(1) In accordance with SSAP 10 the first item to be shown in the funds' statement is the *profit before tax* figure of £2,000. This figure is extracted from the profit and loss account. The remaining items from the account including dividends and taxation represent uses of funds and are shown as such later in the funds statement. If there are no other sources or applications of funds the profit achieved will result in an increase in liquid resources subject to any payments of tax and dividends.

(2) An adjustment must be made for any items which have been charged against profits but have not resulted in a reduction in liquid resources or in applications of funds during the period. Chief of these is *depreciation*, which merely represents an attempt to spread the cost of using fixed assets over their expected working lives. The flow of funds associated with fixed assets arises when the assets are acquired, an application of funds shown later in the statement. The total for depreciation is extracted from the profit and loss account or from the notes to the accounts. In the case of Jaguar it amounts to £1,450.

(3) Where a company disposes of assets during the year it must match the cost or gross book value of the asset, less any accumulated depreciation, against the proceeds received. If the net value is less than the proceeds the deficit must be charged to profit and loss account. However, this item represents an under-provision for depreciation over the life of the asset

Balance Sheets at 31 March

		1983		1982
		£		£
Fixed assets:				
Tangible assets[1] ...		6,315		5,600
Investments ...		800		750
		7,115		6,350
	£'000		£'000	
Current assets:				
Stock	5,100		3,200	
Debtors	4,000		3,500	
Cash and bank	600		90	
	9,700		6,790	
Current liabilities:				
Trade creditors	3,163		1,870	
Dividend	367		280	
Taxation	1,070		1,020	
Bank overdraft	–		230	
	4,600		3,400	
		5,100		3,390
		12,215		9,740
Financed by:		£'000		£'000
Ordinary 50p shares authorised and issued fully paid		2,850		2,350
Share premium		500		–
Undistributed profits		4,365		4,090
		7,715		6,440
8% Unsecured convertible loan stock		4,500		3,300
		12,215		9,740

Note 1

At Cost	*Land and buildings*	*Plant and machinery*	*Total*
	£	£	£
As at 1 April 1982	3,860	4,140	8,000
Additions	160	2,195	2,355
Disposals	–	(610)	(610)
As at 31 March 1983	4,020	5,725	9,745
Depreciation			
As at 1 April 1982	540	1,860	2,400
Charge for year	80	1,370	1,450
Disposals	–	(420)	(420)
As at 31 March 1983	620	2,810	3,430
Net book amount	3,400	2,915	6,315

No payment was received in respect of the assets disposed of during the year.

and involves no outlay of funds during the period. Accordingly it is treated in the same way as depreciation and is added back to profit as an *item not involving the movement of funds*. Profits on sale which do not increase cash resources are treated as a deduction from profits. In the case of Jaguar it can be seen that plant and machinery having a gross value of £610 and accumulated depreciation of £420 was disposed of during the year without payment, giving rise to a loss of £190. This amount is added to depreciation within the heading "Items not involving the use of funds." In practice where these items are immaterial the amount is often shown within the accounts as part of the depreciation charge. Where cash proceeds are received on disposal these are shown as "other sources of funds" lower in the statement.

(4) The ordinary profit before taxation and adjustments for items not involving the use of funds are totalled to give a subheading "Total generated from operations".

(5) The next items to be taken into account are those not arising from operations. In the case of Jaguar the company has raised £1,000 of new share capital, including £500 of share premium, and £1,200 of unsecured convertible loan stock. These items are detected by comparing the figures shown in the balance sheet for the current year with those shown for the last. This section of the funds statement is used for any non-operational sources of funds including receipts from the sale of fixed assets and investments. The total of this section is added to give "Total sources of funds."

(6) The next section of the statement is used to show *applications of funds*. In the case of Jaguar this includes purchase of fixed assets, purchases of investments, the payment of dividends, and the payment of taxation. The information concerning fixed assets including investments is extracted from the relevant note to the balance sheet; that for current asset investments is obtained by comparing the two balance sheet figures and is shown under changes in working capital. In the case of tax and dividends it is necessary to deduce the amount paid by taking into account the amounts shown in the opening and closing balance sheets and the profit and loss account as shown below:

	Taxation	*Dividends*
Opening balance	1,020	280
Add Profit and loss account	1,200	525
	2,220	805
Less Closing balance	(1,070)	(367)
Amount paid	1,150	438

(7) The applications of funds are totalled and deducted from total sources. It can be seen that the only items of which no account has yet been taken are current assets and current liabilities, and it follows that the changes analysed up to this stage will result in a change in working capital. The

sub-total found at this stage is therefore termed "Increase or decrease in working capital", and the remainder of the statement analyses the changes in this area. If sources of funds exceed uses then the result will be an increase in working capital, but if the reverse is true the result will be to reduce net working capital.

(8) The working capital section of the funds statement is found by comparing the balance sheet figures for each of the items shown. This section is divided into two halves so that the change in liquid resources can be highlighted.

(9) The basic approach employed in preparing a funds' statement is to analyse the changes which have occurred in successive balance sheets. However, certain aspects require more investigation, most notably the change in retained profits, which should be explained by reference to the profit and loss account. This shows the use made of ordinary profits including the payment of taxation and dividends. The change in the figure for fixed assets appearing in the balance sheet provides insufficient information, and reference must therefore be made to the notes in order to identify the application of funds to acquire fixed assets and the charge for depreciation. It is sometimes necessary to adjust the figures shown to take account of additions and disposals of fixed assets.

Jaguar Ltd. – Funds Statement

	£	£	£
Sources of funds			
Ordinary profit before taxation			2,000
Adjustments for items not involving the movement of funds:			
Depreciation			1,450
Loss on disposal of fixed assets			190
Total generated from operations			3,640
Funds from other sources			
Ordinary shares issued at a premium			1,000
Unsecured convertible loan stock			1,200
			5,840
Applications of funds			
Purchase of tangible fixed assets		2,355	
Purchase of fixed asset investments		50	
Payment of dividends		438	
Payment of taxation		1,150	
			3,993
Increase/decrease in Working capital			£1,847
Increase in stock		1,900	
Increase in debtors		500	
Increase in creditors		(1,293)	
		1,107	
Increase in cash at bank	510		
Overdraft	230		
		740	
			£1,847

Interpretation

During the period Jaguar has generated £3,640, of which £2,000, was ordinary profit, and the balance depreciation and a loss on the disposal of fixed assets. To this sum was added £2,000 raised from the issue of shares and loan stock, giving total funds of £5,840. These funds were applied in paying tax and dividends amounting to £1,150 and £438 respectively, and in acquiring fixed assets of £2,355 and fixed asset investments; the remaining funds are used to augment working capital. However, the increase in stock and debtors was offset by an increase in trade credit, and funds were available to repay the overdraft and to establish a cash balance of £510.

Although funds' statements play an important role in explaining the changes which have taken place in the financial condition of a company, they cannot show whether the result has been to produce a satisfactory liquidity position, an optimal investment in working capital or to enhance the firms solvency. In order to understand a firm's financial position, it is also necessary to make use of other techniques including ratio analysis. A funds' statement gives an insight into the direction in which a firm is heading, but it cannot show where it started from, or where it has arrived.

CONCLUSION

Although largely ignored by academic writers on finance, the management of working capital is of major importance in the day-to-day responsibilities of financial managers. Many small companies have collapsed because of an inability to control the flow of funds within the business. For this reason bankers have increasingly tended to request cash flow budgets from even the smallest business customers. In many cases the exercise of completing a cash budget serves to highlight the likelihood of disaster if unrealistic plans are pursued while in other cases it reveals that additional funds are essential if a project is to be seen through to a successful conclusion.

FURTHER READING

For further discussion of the management of working capital, reference should be made to the texts listed at the end of Chapters 9 and 11. The books by Sizer, Van Horne and Brearley and Myers, and Harper and Drury all contain sections dealing with this topic.

Chapter 11
Investment Decisions

INTRODUCTION

Investment decisions pose an important problem to businessmen for two reasons. They involve the commitment of substantial sums of money, at least in relation to the firm's resources, and they offer recovery of the funds over a lengthy period of time. If an error is made in allocating funds to a significant investment project the managers of the business will find it very difficult and often very expensive to reverse the mistake. On a simple level it might seem sensible to allocate funds to any project which can be financed and which yields a "reasonable" reward on the capital invested. However, apart from the problem of determining what counts as a "reasonable" return in each particular case, this approach fails to recognise the time value of money. Funds which are received today are worth more than those which will be received in the future by virtue of the fact that they may be invested in the meantime. Any valid method of investment appraisal must take this factor into account, and be capable of distinguishing between funds which are recovered rapidly, and those which flow back more slowly. In order to deal with this problem a variety of investment appraisal techniques have been developed which, in various ways, try to provide guidance on whether or not to invest in a particular project and in choosing between alternative projects. Amongst these methods are a group of techniques which make use of discounting procedures. The chapter begins, therefore, with a discussion of the time value of money and an outline of the methods available for taking it into account. This provides a basis for the consideration of discounted cash flow methods of investment appraisal which follows. Despite the substantial theoretical support for discounting methods it has been found that more traditional non-discounting techniques are still widely used. Some attention is therefore given to the pay-back method and the return on capital approach, contrasting the results with those achieved by discounting. Finally, consideration is given to the important questions of taking account of inflation and of risk and uncertainty in investment decisions and of the procedures which should be followed in order to ensure that decisions are properly controlled and effectvely monitored.

THE TIME VALUE OF MONEY

An important consideration in all decisions involving the outlay and receipt of money over significant periods of time is the fact that money which is not required for immediate consumption may be gainfully employed by lending it to those who have a present use for it. In order to encourage individuals to forego immediate consumption borrowers are prepared to pay a rate of interest which in general reflects the demand for, and supply of, money. The role of interest is therefore to reflect the time value of money, and to create a balance between those who are prepared to meet the cost of interest in order to spend now, and those willing to forego present consumption in return for greater spending power at a later date.

In order to illustrate the significance of the time value of money, use will be made of two contrasting investments; one is an annuity, which offers a level return over a period of five years, and the other is a royalty on an invention which offers a greater sum over the same period but in rising amounts. For the time being it will be assumed that price levels are static, and that no need be taken of inflation. In each case the income is receivable at the end of the year.

Annuity	*Royalty*	
Income for 5 years	Year 1	£ 700
£1,200	Year 2	£ 800
	Year 3	£1,200
	Year 4	£1,600
	Year 5	£2,000
Total: £6,000	Total:	£6,300

In order to evaluate the two investments use will be made of two techniques:

Compounding under which sums received are invested to earn compound interest, and a terminal value is found.

Discounting under which the "present value" of the sum which will be received at the end of each year is found. The present value is the amount which, if invested at the specified discount rate would accumulate to the sum to be received by the due date. Thus in the abscence of any other factors there is no significant difference between an amount of £100 now on which interest at 10% per annum can be earned and £110 in one years time.

The results of applying these two techniques in shown in Table 11.1 below, with interest at 10%.

Table 11.1

Royalty Yearly income £		Compound interest $P(l+r)^N$	£	Present value $\frac{l}{(l+r)^n}$	£
1 – 700		1.464	1,025	0.909	636
2 – 800		1.331	1,064	0.826	660
3 – 1200		1.210	1452	0.751	901
4 – 1600		1.100	1,760	0.683	1,093
5 – 2000		1.000	2,000	0.621	1,242
6300		Terminal value	£7,301	Present value	£4,532
Annuity					
1		1.464			
2	£1,200 p.a.	1.331			
3	× 5	1.210			
4	= £6,000	1.100			
5		1.000			
		6.105	£7,326	3.790	£4,547
		Terminal value		Present value	

The present values and terminal values at compound interest are found by applying the factors shown for the future and present value of £1 at 10% for the period concerned. Tables showing these factors are to be found in Appendix 2. The factors are derived from the formulae shown at the top of the relevant column.[1] In calculating the compound interest factor and the present

[1] The compound value of a sum invested for n years can be found by applying the following formula:

$$\text{Compound sum} = P(1+r)n$$

Where P is the principle and r the rate of interest. The formula may be used to give the value of £1 invested at any specified rate of interest over a period. Tables showing this information may be found in most texts on accounting. By multiplying the factor shown for the value of £1 by any principal amount the compound sum may be found. For example the compound value of £1 invested for 5 years at 10% gives the following factor.

$$= (1+0.1)^5 \quad = 1.1^5 \quad = 1.6105.$$

The value of £456 after 5 years at 10% can be found by multiplying £456 by the factor 1.6105 to give £734.39. The discounted value of a sum may be found as follows:

$$\text{Present value} = \frac{1}{P(1+r)n}$$

As can be seen this formula is the reciprocal of the formula for compound interest. Tables are also widely available for the present value of £1 and may be used to obtain the value of any sum. Thus the present value of £1 at 10% over five years may be found as shown below:

$$\text{Present Value of £1} = \frac{1}{1(1+0.1)n} = \frac{1}{1(1.6105)} = 0.6209$$

The present value of £734.39 at 5% for 10 years can be found as follows:

Present Value = £734.39 × 0.6209 = £456.

value interest factor for the annuity the factor for each year has been added to give a factor for the whole period of six years. This is only possible in the case of an annuity, which consists of a level sum for a period. Where the amounts for each year are different the sums concerned must be multiplied by the factor before being added.

It can be seen that the royalty produces a terminal value of £7,301 whilst the annuity produces £7,326. Thus although the annuity has a lower flat value at £6,000, it is more valuable when the time value of money is taken into account. In present value terms the same result is found, with the annuity having a value of £4,547, against £4,532 for the royalty. If the present value of the annuity were invested at 10% it would amount to £7,326 by the end of the period, likewise if the present value of the royalty £4,532 were invested at 10% for 5 years it would produce a terminal value of £7,301.

A number of conclusions may be drawn on the basis of the foregoing analysis:

- The annuity is a preferable investment to the royalty at a 10% rate of interest, because it has a higher present (and terminal) value.
- A sum of £4,600 to be received immediately would be preferable to either alternative, both of which offer lower present values.
- If the two investments were offered for sale at a price of £4,500 a small profit could be obtained provided the investment were financed at 10%. The investment would produce a surplus under these conditions with a present value of £47 in the case of annuity and £32 in the case of the royalty. These sums may be described as the *net present value* of the investments and this approach forms the basis of the discounted cash flow methods of investment appraisal described below.

Although both present and terminal values take account of all of the income produced by the investments and of the timing of its receipt, the present value approach makes it possible to compare the value of projects with different terminal dates, with greater ease. The significance of the level of interest rates is best demonstrated by considering the situation if the two alternatives are discounted at 8% rather than 10%. The results are then:

Present values	*8%*	*10%*
Annuity	£4,791	£4,547
Royalty	£4,832	£4,532

It can be seen that the fall in interest rates has increased the present value of both projects. (Their terminal values have fallen because of the drop in interest rates.) It would not now be preferable to receive a sum of £4,600 because due to the lower interest rates this sum would not accumulate to give as high a terminal value as the royalty or the annuity. However, the most significant development is that at a discount rate of 8% the royalty has a higher present value than the annuity and is the better investment. The change has occurred because the earlier annuity receipts, which exceed the royalty payments, are of less value at 8%. Because the investments now have a higher present value their net present value as investments costing £4,500 increases to £291 and £332.[2] In considering investment opportunities within firms this approach may be employed in order to determine the present value of benefits to be received in the future from investing in capital projects.

DCF METHODS OF INVESTMENT APPRAISAL

NET PRESENT VALUE

In order to calculate the net present value of a project all of the resulting cash flows must be discounted at an appropriate rate of interest, representing the cost of capital.[3]

If the inflows exceed the outflows the result is termed positive and when the outflows are greater than the inflows the result is negative. A simple net present value calculation is shown below.

Example

Year	*Receipts*	*PVIF @ 10%*	*P.V.*
1	400	0.909	363.6
2	600	0.826	495.6
3	500	0.751	375.5
	1,500		1,234.7
Outlay	(1,000)		(1,000.0)
		Net Present Value	£234.7

The project yields a surplus of £234.70; the significance of this result is as follows:

- A firm which under takes this project will be able to repay the original capital of £1,000 and pay interest at 10% on the amounts outstanding. At the end of the period it will have a sum left which has a present value of £234.
- Such a sum of money will clearly benefit the owner of the business and therefore the project should be undertaken. In order to produce a decision rule for dealing with similar situations certain assumptions must be made about the firm and the environment in which it operates. The chief assumptions on which capital budgeting theory is based are:
  (1) The objective of the owners of the firm is to maximise the value of their interest in the firm.
  (2) The capital market is efficient and there is a free and immediate flow of information around the market.

[2] This feature provides an explanation of the tendency of stock exchange prices to rise when interest rates fall; future dividends have a higher present value when discounted at lower rates.

[3] The cost of capital is a technical term used by writers on business finance to refer to the rate which a firm must earn on its investments. Various models have been suggested as means of calculating the cost, and some of these are referred to in Chapter 12.

(3) There is no risk and therefore one rate of interest throughout the market for all investors and borrowers.
(4) There are no taxes or transactions costs.[4]

Based on the foregoing assumptions the net present value method provides a techniques for determining whether to accept or reject a project:

- *Those projects yielding a positive net present value should be undertaken because they will increase the value of the firm.*
- *Where a choice must be made between two mutually exclusive projects* (each of which automatically excludes the selection of the other if chosen) *the project which gives the highest NPV should be selected.*

In cases where the firm does not have access to unlimited funds, a situation known as *capital rationing*, these rules must be adapted. In such circumstances the projects which should be selected are those which together give the highest NPV. Where projects are divisible and may be undertaken in part the *profitability index* may be used in order to rank projects. This index is found by dividing the present value of the positive flows from a project by the sum of the outflows, in order to discover the present value produced in relation to the capital invested.[5]

Example

Using the information shown in the previous example.

$$\text{Profitability index} = \frac{1234.7}{1000.0} = 1.234.$$

Those projects are selected which have the highest profitability index. In cases where the projects are not divisible, recourse must be made to more advanced techniques for determining the optimum combination of projects, including linear programming.

[4] It will be immediately apparent that these assumptions are not entirely representative of the real world, and much academic work has been carried out in order to investigate how the imperfections which exist in the real world alter the conclusions which may be drawn about investment decisions on the basis of net present value analysis. Nevertheless, if the assumptions were valid a number of interesting results would follow from a decision to undertake the investment in the example above.

- If the company undertook the investment the perfect flow of information would result in investors seeking to buy the company at a price close to £234.
- The company could immediately borrow the necessary funds and pay a dividend of £234, and still generate sufficient cash flow to pay interest and repay the £1,000 or the original investment and the £234 used to pay the dividend.

In a perfect market it is unnecessary for firms to ration their investment in projects; supply and demand will alter the interest rate, so that any project which produces a positive NPV at the prevailing rate of interest should be accepted, and those which do not should be rejected. Because funds are unlimited, except to the extent that the cost of interest rises, all projects should be accepted if they yield a positive return, unless mutually exclusive with another project, as happens where for example both are ways of doing the same thing. In such cases the project yielding the highest NPV should be accepted. Readers wishing to follow this topic in more depth will find a discussion in all of the texts referred to under Further Reading. Bromwich provides a useful introduction.

[5] In this case capital acts as a key or limiting factor. The significance of key factors was outlined in Chapter 9.

THE INTERNAL RATE OF RETURN

The second discounted cash flow technique of investment appraisal is the internal rate of return method, which is based on a calculation of the return generated by a project. In order to be selected a project must achieve a target rate of return and, when a choice must be made between projects that achieving the highest IRR will be chosen. In order to calculate the internal rate of return the same basic data as that used in order to discover the NPV must be used. The cash flows must be discounted to find the rate at which the inflows and outflows are equal.

Example

Using the information from the previous example. The cash flows are discounted by trial and error.

	PVIF – 15%	PV	PVIF – 20%	PV	PVIF – 23%	PV
400	.870	348	.833	333	.813	325
600	.756	453	.694	416	.661	397
500	.658	329	.579	289	.537	268
		1130		1038		990
		1000		1000		1000
	NPV	130		38		(10)

The result obtained shows that the project has a net present value between 20% and 23%. The actual internal rate of return is 22.4% but for practical purposes it is often sufficient to be able to state that the result is approximately 23%.

The significance of this result is that the project produces a return equivalent to investing £1,000 at around 23%. If the company has a cost of capital of less than 23% then the project will yield a positive net present value and should therefore be accepted. A lower IRR will produce a negative impact on the wealth of the firm.

The decision rule emerging from the internal rate of return method is that a project should be selected if it produces an IRR greater than the cost of capital and should normally be rejected in other cases. Where the method is used to choose between mutually exclusive projects that which produces the higher rate of return should be selected.

THE NPV AND IRR METHODS COMPARED

The two methods discussed above both make use of discounted cash flow techniques and both fully take into account the amount and the timing of the cash flows arising from a project. The results obtained may be illustrated graphically by plotting the net present value at various selected discount rates.

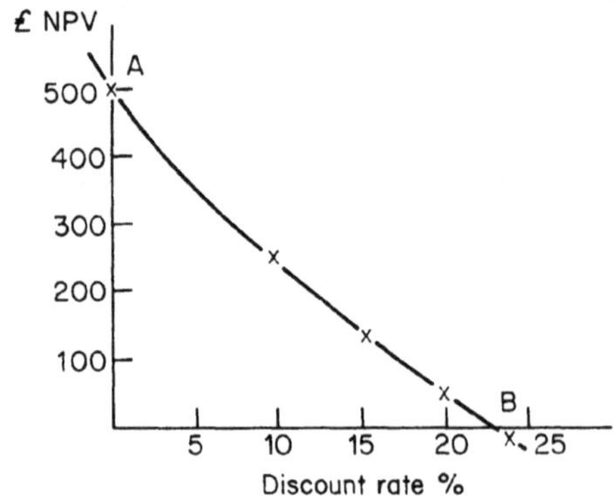

Discount rate %	Net present value £
0	500
10	234
15	130
20	38
23	(10)

Figure 11.1

NPV AND IRR — METHODS COMPARED

At point A the present value curve cuts the vertical axis at £500, the undiscounted surplus from the project. This happens because the vertical axis represents a discount rate of 0%. At point B the NPV is nil and the curve cuts the horizontal axis at the point which corresponds to the IRR of the project, 22.4%. At all discount rates below point B the net present value is positive indicating that the project should be accepted, whilst above this point the curve drops below the horizontal axis indicating negative returns and rejection.

Figure 11.1 reveals that in all cases where the methods are used for accept or reject decisions they will give an identical result. However the situation is more complicated if the methods are used for *project ranking* when conflicting results can be obtained. This point is best illustrated by an example.

Example

Project	*Outlay*	*Inflow Year 1*	*NPV 10%*	*IRR*
A	£10,000	12,000	908	20%
B	£15,000	17,700	1089	18%

This data is illustrated in Figure 11.2

The DCF analysis of the projects shows that project A has the greater internal rate of return but that project B produces the higher net present value at 10%. Figure 11.1 shows the NPV of each project at various discount rates from which it can be seen that the curves intersect at point C corresponding to a discount rate of 14%. At this point both projects have the same NPV and are equally attractive, below this point project B has the higher NPV although project A produces the higher IRR at 20%. Only at discount rates greater than

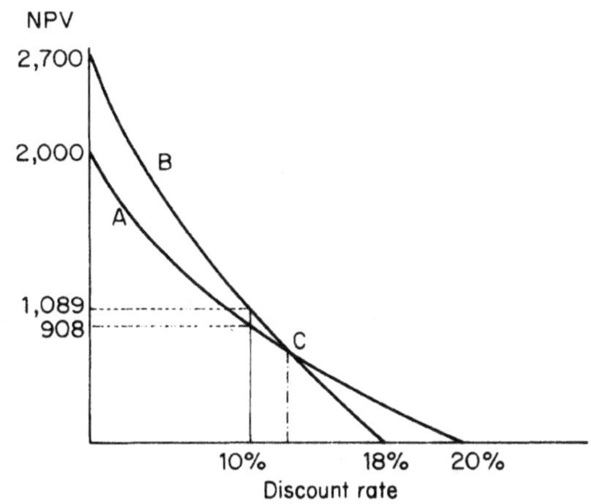

Figure 11.2

NPV AND IRR — IN PROJECT RANKING

14% will project A provide a higher net present value. The significance of this result is that the NPV method will give the correct solution in every case, selecting B at rates below 14% and A at rates above. However the IRR method will always select project A.

The reason for this divergence between the two methods is that the IRR method assumes that as funds are received they are reinvested at the internal rate of return, whilst the NPV method assumes reinvestment at the discount rate utilised. In practice there is no logical justification for assuming that a firm will be able to reinvest funds at the IRR especially in the case of unusually high yielding ventures. Therefore the NPV method which is usually closer to reality is preferred by most theorists. However, the IRR method is widely used by managers in industry often in preference to the NPV method. There are several reasons:

- Managers seem to prefer a result expressed in rate of return terms rather than as a net present value, the significance of which is more difficult to comprehend.
- The NPV method requires the specification at the outset of a required rate of return, cost of capital, or target rate. Under the IRR method the required rate need not be specified initially, although some criteria must be laid down for determining whether to accept a project on the basis of the IRR found.

Apart from the problems arising from the reinvestment assumptions of the IRR method, difficulties are encountered in dealing with non-conventional projects. This name is applied to projects in which negative cash flows occur in particular years during the life of the project, as may be the case when major renovation is required. In such cases the IRR method will produce a number of possible solutions. The problem of multiple rates of return can be resolved by the use of a "roll-back" technique in which the deficits in particular years are rediscounted and set against surplus years. However the result is not very satisfactory from a theoretical point of view.[6]

CONVENTIONAL METHODS OF INVESTMENT APPRAISAL

Apart from the discounted cash flow techniques outlined above, wide use is made of two conventional techniques; the payback method and the return on capital employed.

THE PAYBACK METHOD

Under the payback method projects are assessed on the time required to recover the initial investment. They may be ranked on the basis of the payback period, or matched against a predetermined criterion.

Example

Project		*A*		*B*	
Outlay		£120,000		£120,000	
Income	*Year*	*Cash flow*	*Cumulative cash flow*	*Cash flow*	*Cumulative cash flow*
		£	£	£	£
	1	20,000	20,000	40,000	40,000
	2	25,000	45,000	60,000	100,000
	3	35,000	80,000	30,000	130,000*
	4	40,000	120,000*	30,000	100,000
	5	80,000	200,000	10,000	170,000
	6	100,000	300,000	10,000	180,000
Payback		4 years		$2^2/3$ years	
NPV – 10%		£78,155		£15,000	

In the example project B has a payback period of 2⅔ years compared with 4 years for project A. However, the latter has an NPV of £78,155 against only £15,020 for B. Thus the payback method has, in this instance, selected a project which makes a lesser contribution to the value of the firm. The reason for this occurence is the inability of the payback method to take account of the funds received after payback has taken place. In this case project A produces major sums in years 5 and 6. Thus the payback method may be criticised on the grounds that it fails to take account of all of the inflows from the project. A second deficiency of the method is the failure to take account of differences within the payback period. However this weakness may be avoided by the use of the *discounted payback method* under which the income is discounted before being matched against the outlay. Despite these criticisms the payback method in each of its forms is widely used, often in conjunction with the DCF methods. There are several reasons for the popularity of the payback method:

[6] See A. J. Merrett and A. Sykes, *The Finance and Analysis of Capital Projects* (Longmans 1973), p. 158.

- It is simple and easy to understand.
- Although not taking account of the time value of money in a comprehensive and systematic way, it does recognise that money has a value and the method is based upon the rapidity of recovering the initial outlay.
- Because the method emphasises the rapid recovery of investment funds it is said to maximise liquidity. However, this depends upon the way in which the recovered funds are redeployed, and upon the inherent flexibility of the initial investment.
- The method is said to minimise risk, but once again much will depend upon the nature of the project. Some projects are exceedingly risky at the outset, but once established offer the prospect of good returns over a long period at low risk.

THE RETURN ON CAPITAL

The basis of this method, sometimes known as the accounting rate of return, is that the accounting returns achieved from a project are compared with capital outlay required.

Example

Details as previous case

Project			*A*	*B*
Outlay			120,000	120,000
Average			60,000	60,000
Income			300,000	180,000
Average	(over 6 years)		50,000	30,000
Depreciation	(over 6 years)	$\frac{120,000}{6}$	20,000	20,000
Profit			30,000	10,000
Return on capital (ARR)			$\frac{30,000}{60,000} = 50\%$	$\frac{10,000}{60,000} = 16.7\%$

The result produced by the accounting rate of return method conflicts with that found by the use of the payback technique. In this case it produces a result consistent with the NPV method but it cannot be relied upon to do so. The method has several deficiencies:

- The method takes no account of the timing of the cash flows received. By using an average income figure it is possible that large receipts late in the life of a project may boost its profitability, despite being of less value than earlier flows.

- The method takes no account of the availability of funds for reinvestment, which is the hallmark of the DCF methods.
- A wide variety of practice is possible regarding the definition of capital, the treatment of depreciation and the cost of finance.

INVESTMENT APPRAISAL METHODS – AN EXAMPLE

A company is considering an investment in a number of projects designed to increase the efficiency of its production process and to reduce costs. The details of each project are shown below:

Project	*A*	*B*	*C*
Outlay	£100,000	£60,000	£40,000
Cost savings anticipated after charging depreciation over	*5 Years*	*6 Years*	*4 Years*
1	30,000	12,000	8,000
2	25,000	12,000	9,000
3	20,000	12,000	10,000
4	15,000	12,000	12,000
5	10,000	12,000	
6		12,000	
	100,000	72,000	39,000

The company estimates its cost of capital at 12% for projects of this type which are normally required to "pay back" in no more than 3 years. Depreciation is charged on a straight line basis and there are no disposal values.

The alternative investments may be evaluated using each of the methods discussed above. In dealing with a question of this type only the relevant benefits and costs need be taken into account, all other profits and losses of the firm are unaffected by the decision and may thus be ignored. Consideration of the result obtained is postponed until all of the results have been calculated.

Net Present Value Method

In order to calculate the net present value of each project it is first necessary to ascertain the cash flow arising from each. This is found by adding the anticipated cost savings to the depreciation charge made in finding this sum; as shown below.

Project A

Year	*Cost saving*	*Depreciation*	*Cash flow*	*PVIF at 12%*	*£*
1	30,000	20,000	50,000	0.893	44,650
2	25,000	20,000	45,000	0.797	35,865
3	20,000	20,000	40,000	0.712	28,480
4	15,000	20,000	30,000	0.636	22,260
5	10,000	20,000	30,000	0.567	17,010
6	—	—	—	0.507	—
				4.912	148,265
				Outlay	100,000
				NPV	£ 48,265

Project B
This is a level sum of money for 6 years and may be solved using an annuity factor, found by adding the present value interest factor for each of the years 1 to 6, which amounts to 4.912.

Project B

Years	*Cost saving*	*Depreciation*	*Cash flow*	*PVIF at 12%*	£
1–6	12,000	10,000	22,000 ×	4.912=	90,464
				Outlay	60,000
				NPV	£30,464

Project C

Year	*Cost saving*	*Depreciation*	*Cash flow*	*PVIF at 12%*	£
1	8,000	10,000	18,000	.893	16,074
2	9,000	10,000	19,000	0.797	15,143
3	10,000	10,000	20,000	0.712	14,240
4	12,000	10,000	22,000	0.636	13,992
					59,449
				Outlay	40,000
				NPV	£19,449

The Internal Rate of Return Method

Each of the projects is discounted at various discount rates until the inflows and outflows are approximately equal. By interpolations the internal rate of return is found.

Project A

Year	*Cash flow*	*PVIF at 32%*	£	*PVIF at 33%*	£
1	50,000	0.758	37,900	0.752	37,600
2	45,000	0.574	25,830	0.565	24,425
3	40,000	0.435	17,400	0.425	17,000
4	35,000	0.329	11,515	0.319	11,165
5	30,000	0.250	7,500	0.241	7,230
			100,145		97,420
		Outlay	100,000		100,000
		NPV	145		(2,580)

$$\text{IRR} = 32 + \left(1 \times \frac{145}{145 + 2{,}580}\right)\% = 32.05\%$$

Project B
Because B is an annuity it is possible to reduce the work to be carried out by calculating the annuity factor and finding the rate to which this relates in the PV Annuity Tables.

$$\text{Annuity factor} = \frac{\text{Total outlay}}{\text{Annual cash flow}} = \frac{60{,}000}{22{,}000} = 2.727$$

Reference to the PV Annuity Tables shows the factor for 28% to be 2.759 and that for 32% to be 2.534. By interpolation the IRR for project B can be found. In this case it is necessary to interpolate over 4%, because the annuity tables do not show the intervening figures.

$$\text{IPR} = 28 + 4 \times \frac{(2.759 - 2.727)\%}{2.759 + 2.534}$$

$$= 28 + 4 \times \frac{(0.032)}{0.225}$$

$$= 28 + 4 \times 0.142$$
$$= 28.57\%$$

Project C

Year	*Cash flow*	*PVIF at 31%*	£	*PVIF at 32%*	£
1	18,000	0.764	13,734	0.758	13,644
2	19,000	0.774	10,906	0.540	10,260
3	20,000	0.431	8,621	0.435	8,700
4	22,000	0.324	7,128	0.329	7,238
			40,388		39,842
		Outlay	40,000		40,000
		NPV	388		(158)

$$\text{IRR} = 31\% + 1 \times \frac{388}{546}$$
$$= 31.71\%$$

PAY BACK METHOD

Project	*A*		*B*		*C*	
Outlay	£100,000		£60,000		£40,000	
Year	*Annual*	*Cumulative*	*Annual*	*Cumulative*	*Annual*	*Cumulative*
1	50,000	50,000	22,000	22,000	18,000	18,000
2	45,000	95,000	22,000	44,000	19,000	37,000
3	40,000	135,000	22,000	66,000	20,000	57,000
4	35,000	170,000	22,000	88,000	22,000	79,000
5	30,000	200,000	22,000	110,000		
6			22,000	132,000		
Pay back	2.12 Years		2.73 Years		2.15 Years	

ACCOUNTING RATE OF RETURN METHOD

Project	*A*	*B*	*C*
Total contribution to profits	100,000	72,000	39,000
Project duration	5 Years	6 Years	4 Years
Average "contribution"	20,000	12,000	9,750
Gross capital employed	100,000	60,000	40,000
Accounting rate of return	20%	20%	24%

PROFITABILITY INDEX

The profitability index for each project may be found by dividing the aggregate present value of the inflows by the aggregate present value of the outlays.

	Project A	*Project B*	*Project C*
Inflows	£148,265	£90,464	£59,449
Outlays	£100,000	£60,000	£40,000
P.I.	1.48	1.51	1.49

CONCLUSIONS

The appraisal techniques produce the following results:

	A	*B*	*C*
NPV	£48,265	£39,464	£19,449
IRR	32.05%	28.57%	31.71%
Pay back	2.12 Years	2.73 Years	2.15 Years
ARR	20%	20%	24.4%
PI	1.48	1.51	1.49

It has been emphasised that the decisions obtained from applying the investment appraisal techniques will depend upon nature of the decision to be made.

(i) *Where the projects may each be undertaken without affecting the others (Independent Projects).* In this case all of the projects should be undertaken because each produces a positive result, at the criterion rate, and an IRR exceeding it. All payback within the set period of three years.

(ii) *Where the selection of one of the projects automatically rules out adoption of the others (Mutually Exclusive Independent Projects).* In accordance with the NPV rules project A should be selected because it yields the highest NPV and the greatest IRR. It also pays back marginally quicker than project C, but the ARR achieved is lower.

(iii) *Where all the projects are independent, but only £100,00 is available for investment (Capital Rationing).* In this case projects B and C should be undertaken instead of A because their combined NPV amounts to £49,913 compared with £48,265 for A, thus making a greater contribution to the value of the firm. Projects B and C produce a better return in relation to the capital utilised for investment, as shown by their profitability indices.

DCF AND CONVENTIONAL METHODS OF INVESTMENT APPRAISAL COMPOUND

Despite their shortcomings the conventional methods are still widely used in investment appraisal, although recent evidence suggests that DCF techniques are now widely used as well.[7] In part, the reluctance to use DCF methods is due to traditional conservatism, although this is not the only factor. In the examples used above the figures shown have been chosen so as to highlight the divergencies between the various methods. In practice the results are often less marked.[8] Both NPV and IRR methods require predictions to be made of both future cash flows and the cost of capital. In the turbulent environment of recent years businesses have found it almost impossible to produce reliable forecasts and have tended to prefer projects which involve rapid repayment and therefore ensure maximum flexibilty. However, for some companies, especially those in capital intensive industries, long-term investment is essential and use must be made of the best available techniques for dealing with risk and uncertainty in appraising investment projects.

RISK AND UNCERTAINTY IN CAPITAL INVESTMENT

In Chapter 9 various techniques were described for dealing with risk and uncertainty in management accounting. Several of these techniques may be employed in analysing capital investment projects. In particular use may be made of sensitivity analysis in order to determine the impact of possible changes in key variables on the level and timing of cash flow. In addition use may be made of probability theory in order to produce expected values for use in investment appraisal. An important feature of the results produced will be the extent to which the range of results lie close to or depart from the expected value. This is best illustrated by an example.

Figure 11.3 shows two projects each having the same expected outcome based on a distribution of probable results. However, it can be seen that project B has a much wider range of possible outcomes than project A.

On the assumption that investors are normally risk averse, it is to be expected that they would require a premium for investing in a project where the potential gains and losses are more widely distributed. This feature can be incorporated in the DCF methods as a *risk premium* within the discount rate. Various models have been developed in order to explain the size of the

[7] In 1976, the ICAEW published two surveys dealing with investment appraisal methods: C. Westwick and P. Shohet, *Investment Appraisal and Inflation* and B. Carsberg and A. J. Hope, *Business Investment Decisions Under Inflation*.

Both surveys found that few companies dealt correctly with the impact of inflation in investment appraisal. Companies tended to prefer the IRR method to the NPV approach, and variations of the payback method were more popular than either, with many companies. This picture was confirmed by R. H. Pike in a survey conducted for the Institute of Cost and Management Accountants, *Capital Budgeting in the 1980s: A major survey of investment practices in large companies* (published in 1982).

[8] See H. Levy and M. Sarnet *Capital Investment and Financial Decisions* Chap. 8.

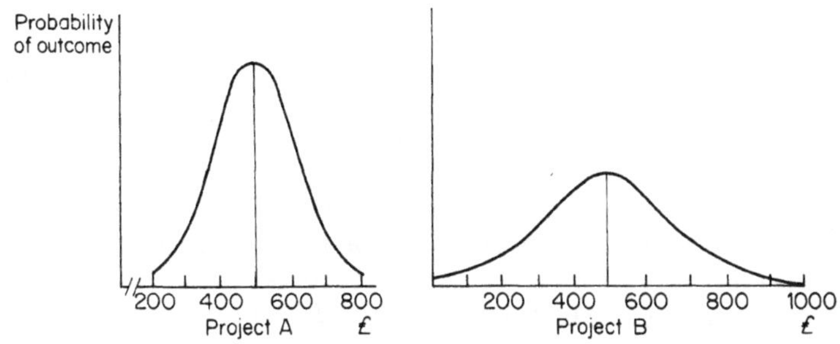

Figure 11.3

premium which investors will require on particular investment projects in order to obtain a satisfactory return.[9]

The nature of the risk which a firm undertakes within investment projects plays an important part in determining the discount rate which should be used in investment appraisal. Another important aspect is the way in which the firm is financed and the valuation which investors place on the securities that a firm can issue in order to finance new investment. Consequently, it is necessary to defer further discussion of the discount factor to be used in investment decisions until Chapter 12 which deals with financing decisions. Before doing so it is necessary to consider the impact of inflation on the conduct of investment appraisal.

INFLATION AND INVESTMENT APPRAISAL

It was stated above that interest rates compensate savers for losing the benefit of spending power, and thus operate as the price for money over a period of time. It was assumed for convenience that money had the same value thoughout the period concerned. However, in reality this has been far from the case in recent years. Consequently, it is to be expected that the return offered to investors will contain elements both to compensate for the loss of the use of the funds for the period and to compensate for the loss of the purchasing power of the sum lent due to changing price levels over the period. In addition, as stated above, investors are likely to require a premium to reflect the risk of investing in a particular firm and in its portfolio of investments. Thus the return required will consist of three main elements:

- the riskless real rate of interest;
- the expected annual rate of inflation over the period;
- a premium to reflect risk.

[9] The most popular of these models is the Capital Asset Pricing Model which attempts to base the premium on the systematic risk between the returns achieved by an investment and the return offered by investing in the market portfolio. For a full discussion of the model and its significance see R. Brearley and S. Myers, Chap. 9.

The first two elements together form the nominal riskless rate of interest

On the basis of this assumption firms have a choice of methods for taking account of inflation in carrying out investment appraisal:

(1) Projections may be based on current prices and discounted at a rate which excludes any premium to compensate for expected inflation, i.e. the riskless *real* rate of interest plus the risk premium; or
(2) Projections may be based on prices incorporating future predicted levels of inflation, and discounted at *nominal* interest rates and an appropriate risk premium.

As each firm must ensure that it has access to adequate funds, in order to finance operations at inflated prices, it makes more sense to incorporate rising prices within the projections and to discount them at nominal rather than real rates.

THE ADMINISTRATIVE FRAMEWORK FOR INVESTMENT DECISIONS

Because of the major and long-term consequences of capital investment decisions, and because of their contribution to corporate development, companies should employ thorough and systematic procedures for evaluating capital projects.

These should include:

(a) a systematic search for investment opportunities (corporate strategy) leading to:
(b) a long-range plan of capital investment;
(c) a thorough evaluation of returns and expenditure associated with each project;
(d) a systematic comparison of projects, taking account of the timing of payments and receipts, against:
  (i) alternatives
  (ii) a yardstick based on the cost of capital
(e) a suitable form for use throughout the firm showing:
  Date/No.
  Details
  Costs/income
  Reasons/benefits
  Date required/payment arrangements
  Calculations of pay back, NPV, IRR, return on capital;
(f) a thorough examination of proposals by an expert committee based on suitable documentation;
(g) a post investment review to ensure that projections are realised – or alternatively lessons are learnt for the future.

Where appropriate examination will take place as part of the annual budgeting programme.

CONCLUSION: INVESTMENT DECISIONS AND THE BANKER

In the past it has not been general practice for bankers to become deeply involved in the investment appraisal undertaken by customers. This partly reflects the traditional practice of lending through overdrafts, repayable on demand. Furthermore, although bankers would obviously prefer to see customers undertaking projects which offer a reasonable return to their shareholders, their chief concern must lie with the payment of interest and repayment of capital, which can be achieved without a proper return being obtained for shareholders.

However, one of the consistent criticisms made of both British businessmen and British bankers is their preoccupation with short-term profitability at the expense of long-term projects. In part this reflects the state of the UK economy in recent years. However, there is little doubt that the priority attached to a rapid payback from projects is unlikely to lead to the sort of market penetration which the Japanese have achieved in recent years. The case is increasingly being made for banks to provide funds on a longer time scale than in the past. As a result it is likely that bankers will become more involved in examing appraisals of investment projects prepared by customers. In doing so a number of important points should be borne in mind:

- Whichever techniques a company uses is less important than the thorough and systematic way in which the appraisal is undertaken. For good results to be achieved the programme must be comprehensive, and the analysis thorough. No analysis will be reliable unless it is based on sound estimates of future cash flows, and no analysis will be sound unless all of the key factors are taken into account, and the decision makers are aware of the inherent uncertainties.
- In interpreting the analyses produced the overall strategic situation must always be borne in mind. Sometimes a company must undertake projects which cannot be justified on normal investment criteria because it is the only way to enter or to maintain a position in a particular market. In such cases there is nothing wrong in deciding to depart from the analysis undertaken, provided it is done with a full understanding of the reasons and a recognition of the consequences.

As is the case in examining company management accounts, the chief value of examining an investment appraisal undertaken by a customer is the insight which it gives into the way in which the business is being managed.

FURTHER READING

Investment decisions lie at the heart of financial management and are therefore dealt with in all books on the subject as well as those dealing with management accounting. Bromwich's book provides an excellent introduction to the theoretical aspects of the subject as does his article. The works by Levy and Sarnet, Lumby and Van Horne provide similar approaches and are, in the author's opinion, amongst the best for those seeking to explore the more difficult aspects of the subject. Van Horne's book is one of the most widely used texts on financial management courses throughout the world. The text by Merret and Sykes was regarded as the bible on the subject in the UK for many years, although it was written some time ago. Sizer provides a clear introduction to the subject.

M. Bromwich, *The Economics of Capital Budgeting* (Harmondsworth: Penguin, 1976).
H. Levy and M. Sarnet, *Capital Investment and Financial Decisions* (2nd ed., Prentice Hall, 1982).
S. Lumby, *Capital Investment and Related Decisions* (Nelson, 1981).
A. J. Merrett and A. Skyes, *The Finance and Analysis of Capital Projects* (Longmans, 2nd ed., 1973).
J. Sizer, *An Insight into Management Accounting* (Harmondsworth: Penguin 2nd ed., 1979).
J. Van Horne, *Financial Management and Policy* (Prentice Hall 5th ed., 1980).
R. Brearley and S. Myers, *Principles of Corporate Finance* (McGraw Hill, 1981).

Article

M. Bromwich, "Capital Budgeting: a survey" in *Journal of Business Finance* 2 (Autumn 1970), pp. 3–26.

Chapter 12
Financing Decisions

INTRODUCTION

Successful financial management requires companies to deal effectively with two major types of decisions: investment decisions, which were dealt with in the previous chapter, and financing decisions, which are discussed in this chapter. If a company selects those projects for investment which make the greatest contribution to the value of the firm, it follows that it should endeavour to raise finance which will cost the least.

In addition the firm must ensure that it has adequate resources at all times, and does not fail through running out of funds. The principal source of finance for any firm is likely to be its proprietors. Within the profit and loss account there is no obvious cost to the business from raising finance from this source. However, it is important to remember that if funds are not remitted to shareholders they lose the opportunity to invest elsewhere. There is thus a cost to the owners of a business when funds are retained, because they lose the opportunity to invest elsewhere. It is a cardinal principle of financial management that decisions are taken in order to maximise the benefits to the owners, which will not always be achieved by maximising the profit shown in the accounts. As an alternative to raising equity finance companies may decide to increase the level of gearing; their dependence on borrowed funds. For a variety of reasons borrowed money is generally cheaper from the shareholders' viewpoint than equity, and its use will usually increase the benefits he receives. However, two qualifications must be made: the use of debt will not be beneficial if the increased risks associated with using borrowed money outweigh the benefits derived from its use; furthermore, short-term funds are likely to be the least expensive, but their use may not be beneficial if liquidity is impaired. Where a company makes excessive use of short-term borrowed funds, current profits will rise, but the resulting fall in the share price caused by investor anxiety, may cancel out any gains for shareholders.[1]

This chapter commences with an examination of the criteria which should be employed by management in selecting an appropriate mix of finance for a firm, then the principal types of finance in use will be described and evaluated. The chapter concludes with an explanation of the way in which the cost of finance to the firm may be found, taking account of each of the component parts.

THE CRITERIA FOR SELECTING FINANCE

The most important concept in understanding the management of financial resources is that of *gearing*. This idea has already been noted in Chapter 8, although, then attention was directed to the dangers inherent in excessive use of borrowed funds. It is important not to lose sight of the positive benefits of borrowed funds, whilst remembering the undoubted dangers.

Borrowed money is generally thought to cost less than equity finance for the following reasons:

- Lenders to the company stand ahead of shareholders both in terms of receiving interest from profit, and in the distribution of assets in the event of a liquidation. Thus, there is less risk associated with being a lender than with being a shareholder. It follows that shareholders will require additional reward for being at greater risk, and that lenders will receive a lower reward. Were the two to receive the same reward, rational shareholders would sell their shares in order to become lenders thereby achieving the same reward at less risk. The result of this would be to reduce demand for a company's shares and to bring down the price. Provided there was no change in the reward offered to shareholders, the yield would improve resulting in a higher return being offered to shareholders than to lenders.[2]
- Interest payments to lenders are an allowable charge against taxation and as a result borrowed finance has the effect of reducing the tax charge. The

[1] This criteria is of most relevance in the case of quoted companies on which most of the theory of finance is based. In the case of an unquoted company it may be assumed that in the long run the company might also be sold, but it should be remembered that in the case of private company the owners may have personal motives other that those assumed by theory.

[2] For example, where a company's shares sell for £2 and pay a dividend of 40p the return is 20%. If investors regard this return as inadequate and sell the shares the price will fall. When the price reaches £1.60 the dividends produce a return of 25%, which investors may consider adequate to cover the increased level of risk associated with holding the company's shares. In this case the sales will cease, and the price will fall no further. In practice the return obtained by shareholders is not restricted to the level of the present dividend but also includes prospective growth in the future, and possible gains on sale.

cost of borrowed money is therefore lower because the cost of interest can be set against the tax saving.[3]

It is not always easy to observe these effects because, whilst the reward offered to lenders is an observable rate of interest, that offered to shareholders consists of a combination of present and uncertain future dividends and the prospect of capital gains from appreciation in the share price. Nevertheless, it is generally accepted that debt is cheaper than equity, and suggested that by substituting the former for the latter it may be possible to reduce the cost of capital to the firm, thereby increasing the returns to shareholders.[4] The impact of gearing is illustrated in Figure 12.1 below.

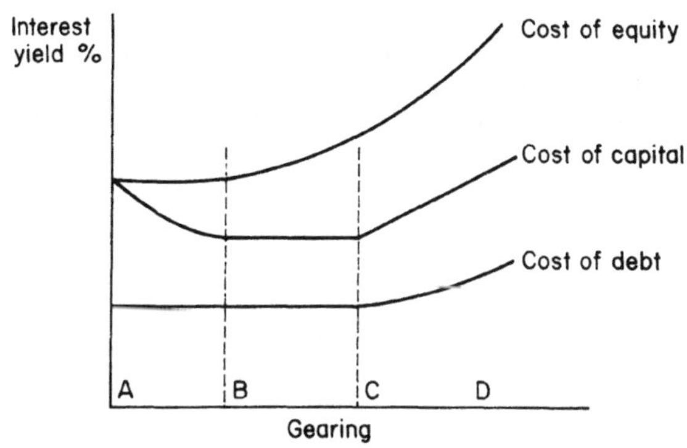

Figure 12.1 The Impact of Gearing in the Cost of Capital.

Figure 12.1 shows that the cost of capital falling over the range of gearing AB, as more low cost debt is used by the firm. Between points B and C the cost of equity capital begins to rise in order to offset the greater risks associated with gearing. This trend eliminates the benefits derived from the increased use of debt, to give a static cost of capital over the range BC. Beyond point C the cost of debt begins to rise as lenders seek to offset the risks of gearing, as a result the aggregate cost of capital begins to rise as well.

This view of gearing, generally referred to as the traditional approach,

[3] The benefit of taxation on the cost of debt may be illustrated by the following example.

	Company A	*Company B*
Profit	£1,000	£1,000
Interest	——	£ 200
	£1,000	£ 800
Tax at 50%	£ 500	£ 400
Profit after tax	£ 500	£ 400

Although the cost of interest on borrowings is £200, the drop in after-tax profits is only £100. This is due to the impact on gross interest charges on taxable profits as a result of which tax also falls by £100, thereby reducing the cost of borrowing.

[4] The theory of capital structure is one of the more controversial topics in finance. The discussion here is based on the "traditional theory", but it has been suggested that, but for corporate taxes, there would be no benefit from gearing because investors would adjust prices to compensate for risk in such a way that no benefit might be derived from gearing. For a full discussion of the theory including recent developments see R. Brearly and S. Myers, *Principles of Corporate Finance* Chaps. 17 and 18.

suggests that the substitution of debt for equity has the effect of reducing the cost of capital. However, beyond a certain point the gains are eliminated as the shareholders seek additional rewards to offset the greater risks inherent in gearing. The effect is to produce an optimal range of gearing with a stable cost of capital. Eventually lenders to the company begin to increase interest rates to offset the risks which then arise from the level of debt, thereby increasing the cost of capital beyond the optimal rate. It follows that companies should select a level of gearing within the range BC. The impact of gearing on earnings may also be demonstrated by an example.

Example

A company expects to earn a return of 10% on an investment of £1,000 before meeting the cost of finance. It considers two alternative methods of financing the investment, full use of equity provided by shareholders, and half equity and half debt at 5%. The impact on earnings per share is shown below:

	A	*B*
Capital structure		
Equity (£1 shares)	1,000	500
Debt 5%	—	500
	1,000	1,000
Net operating income	100	100
Interest	—	25
Net income	100	75
Earnings per share	10p	15p

Despite an identical trading position the earnings per share in case B are 50% higher than in A. This result is solely attributable to the use of debt gearing.

This example can be used to demonstrate the opportunities presented by gearing, and its inherent risks. Shown below is the position arising from a 100% increase in profits, and from a 50% decline in profits.

	100% increase		50% decrease	
	A	*B*	*A*	*B*
Net operating income	200	200	50	50
Interest	—	25	—	25
Net income	200	175	50	25
Earnings per share	20p	35p	5p	5p
Change in EPS	+ 100%	+ 133%	− 50%	− 67%

The geared position produces greater volatility in the earnings per share of the company, offering the prospect of a greater rise in earnings when trading profits grow, but the probability of greater loss if they decline. Were the trading profits to fall to £10, the geared company would make a loss of £15, whilst the ungeared company would still make a profit, albeit small. The impact of gearing is demonstrated graphically below.

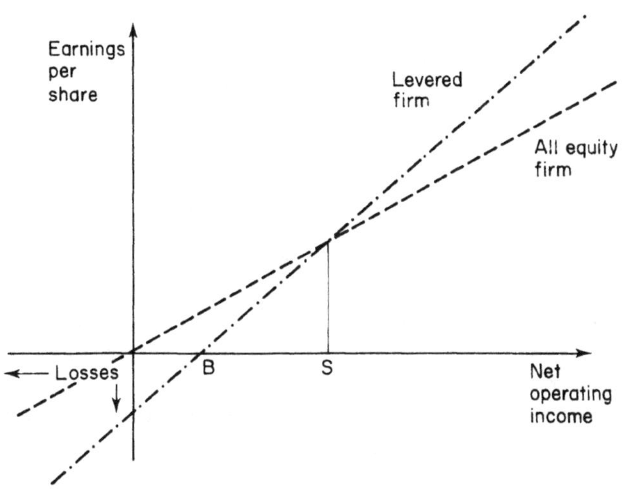

Figure 12.2 The Impact of Variations in Operating Income

At levels of net operating, or trading income greater than indicated by point S, the geared firm achieves superior earnings. However, below point S the earnings are lower because the return achieved on borrowed funds is lower than the cost of finance, thereby reducing the returns for shareholders. At point B operating income is just sufficient to meet the interest burden of the geared firm, and below this point the firm shows a loss.

The other criteria to be taken into account in determining capital structure include:

Maturity. Borrowed funds may be obtained on a short- or long-term basis. In general the cost of funds rises as the maturity increases. However, whilst the cost of finance may be reduced by selecting short-term alternatives, liquidity, the ability to meet immediate obligations will decline as a result. A serious decline in liquidity might affect the value of equity, and defeat the objectives of minimising the cost of finance.

Security. In general funds obtained on a long-term basis are more secure than short-term funds, and cannot be withdrawn merely because a company is currently unprofitable, unless a convenant entered into when the loan was agreed is broken. If use is made of short-term funds, it may be found that certain lenders are more reliable than others. The cheapest funds may not be the most dependable in times of difficulty. It may be worthwhile meeting a higher interest burden in order to obtain funds from a source which has proved reliable and sympathetic to the interests of the business in the past.

Interest Rate Exposure. Although short-term finance generally brings with it exposure to fluctuating interest rates, it also brings the prospect of benefitting from a reduction in interest rates immediately. In contrast long-term loans are usually made at a fixed rate of interest. Where funds are raised at times of low interest rates the benefits will be enjoyed into the future, whilst loans obtained when rates are high will seem expensive if rates fall. Generally a premium must be paid for a fixed rate of interest above prevailing rates. Thus yields on debentures are higher than the corresponding rates for medium-term loans and overdrafts. However, the use of a fixed rate debenture eliminates the risks associated with an adverse trend in rates. In deciding whether to opt for fixed or variable rate finance, it is necessary to take a view on likely trends in interest rates over the duration of the loan.

Exchange Rate Exposure. Where companies are active internationally, or are large enough to enter the international capital markets, it may prove beneficial to negotiate loans in foreign currencies. Although this may provide interest rate advantages, and a measure of flexibility, there are added dangers arising from the exposure to exchange rate changes. In the short term these may be minimised by entering into forward foreign exchange contracts, and in the longer term it may be possible to lessen exposure by holding assets in the same currency as that in which the loan is taken.

OPTIONS AND ALTERNATIVES

The financial markets offer companies a wide range of possible types of finance, and owing to the ingenuity of the financial community, these are being added to all of the time. In a book of this type it is not possible to discuss every type of financial instrument but the principal features of the most common will be discussed below. The key features of each is shown in Table 12.1 below.

Table 12.1
Sources of Company Finance: Features
Provided by Equity Shareholders

	Reward	*Fixed*	*Fixed rate*	*Other features*
Share capital Retained profits	Dividends (+ Growth ?)	X	X	Most risk to holders Least risk to firm
Non-Equity Sources				
Preference shares	Dividends	X	√	Variations
Long-term debt (+ 10y)				
Debentures or loan stocks	Interest	√	√	Tax deduction
Mortgages		√	√/X	
Medium-term debt (1 – 10y)				
Loans	Interest	√	X	Tax deduction
Leasing or hire purchase	Rentals	√	√ /X	Tax deduction + capital allowances
Short-term finance (– 1y)				Tax deduction
Overdrafts	Interest	√	X	Fluctuate with needs
Trade credit	Lost discount	–	–	
Commerical bills	Varies	–	–	
Factoring	Interest + service charge	√	X	

ORDINARY SHARE CAPITAL

The basic form of capital held in limited liability companies takes the form of share capital. Such shares may be denominated in amounts of any size but 25p and £1 shares are the most common. There is no minimum amount of share capital for a private company, but no company may issue more share capital than that which it is authorised to issue by its Memorandum of Association. Capital must be contributed in money or monies' worth, but not all the capital which members have agreed to subscribe need be called up at any time. Shareholders have a liability to meet uncalled capital should the company encounter difficulties.

A public company must register as such and must have a minimum share capital of £50,000. Only public companies may offer their shares for sale to the public. Where this is done a prospectus must be issued, the details of which comply with the requirements of the Companies Act. Often companies wishing to issue shares to the public apply for a listing on the Stock Exchange or on the Unlisted Securities Market.[5] A new issue of shares is generally made as an offer for sale by a merchant bank acting as an issuing house. Where an established company wishes to raise additional share capital this will generally be done in the form of a rights issue, in which the shares are offered to the existing members. The Companies Act 1981 introduced two important changes with regard to share capital: Companies may now issue redeemable shares of an equity type, and may purchase their own shares, subject to meeting a set of complex requirements designed to protect minority shareholders and creditors. These two changes offer the possiblity of reducing share capital where it is no longer required, and of the company buying shares from members who wish to end their association with the firm.

Another important scheme introduced to assist small companies in raising equity finance is the Business Expansion Scheme, formerly called the Business Start-up Scheme. Under these provisions investors receive special tax reliefs for money invested in small businesses, which have the effect of providing much better potential returns than could be earned elsewhere.[6]

As was noted above, because the shareholders bear the residual risk associated with the business, it is assumed that they will receive the greatest reward. This takes the form of dividends paid periodically from profits, which may rise or fall according to the fortunes of the enterprise. In addition, shareholders may benefit from growth in the share price as earnings and assets increase. The reward to shareholders takes the form of a combination of uncertain returns over a period of time, it is therefore especially difficult to measure. This presents considerable difficulty to those responsible for managing the financial structure of a business and for optimising its financial

[5] For a description of the Unlisted Securities Market and the advantages it offers to growing companies see *The Unlisted Securities Market: A Guide for Growing Companies* published by Arthur Young – Chartered Accountants. Several other leading firms of Chartered Accountants publish similar guides.

[6] For an outline of the Business Expansion scheme see *The Business Expansion Scheme* published by Arthur Anderson & Co Chartered Accountants. Several similar booklets are published by major firms of Chartered Accountants.

structure. Several models have been developed to explain the cost of equity finance. The best known is Gordon's Growth model, and is expressed in the following formula:

$$K_e = \frac{d}{V_o} + g$$

The cost of equity finance (K_e) is equal to the expected dividend (d) divided by the share price (V_o) plus the expected annual growth in dividends (g). The operation of the model is best illustrated by an example.

Example

A company expects to pay a dividend of 20p and at present has a share price of £2. It is generally believed that dividends will increase by 3% per annum. The model provides a cost of capital of 13% as follows:

$$K_e = \frac{20}{200} + \frac{3}{100} = .13 \text{ or } 13\%.$$

The model suggests that investors expect a return equivalent to 13% as a result of a 10% dividend growing at 3% per annum to infinity. More complex models have been developed in order to take account of variations in dividends and growth expectations, and the impact of risk and uncertainty.[7]

Share capital plays a crucial role in the financial structure of every company because it provides the capital which can legitimately be put at risk in the commercial activities of the enterprise. If it is lost that is regrettable, but the business will not necessarily fail. Thus a business financed exclusively by share capital will enjoy considerable security. However, this is achieved at an additional cost to its shareholders. Therefore, in practice firms also make use of a wide range of alternative facilities in order to reduce the overall cost of capital.

RETAINED PROFITS

The most common form of finance used by companies is obtained by retaining profits within the business rather than using them to pay dividends to shareholders. Nevertheless, such funds are really the property of the shareholders, and have a similar basic cost. This is an important point to observe because it is often more convenient to retain funds within the business than to raise fresh share capital and the cost to shareholders may easily be overlooked. However, a firm should not retain funds for use within the business unless it can use them at least as profitably as the shareholder could in another investment.

Retained funds have a number of distinct advantages as a source of long-term finance:

[7] The best known of these models is the Capital Assets Pricing Model which is described in R. Brearly and S. Myers, *op.cit.*, Chaps. 7 and 8.

- Retention of profits avoids the payment of advanced corporation tax and possibly higher rate taxes on dividends. If funds are redeployed profitably shareholders may eventually pay capital gains tax when the shares are sold, but this tax is charged at a lower rate than income tax and is subject to considerable exemptions.
- If funds are paid to shareholders as dividends and then recovered as fresh share capital, not only will additional taxation be incurred, but considerable transaction costs associated with share issues will also be borne.

The policy a firm adopts for retaining profits is intrinsically linked with dividend policy. In theory a firm's distribution policy should be determined by the investment opportunities open to it. If it can redeploy funds in investments yielding more than the cost of capital it will be in the best interests of shareholders for the company to retain the sums, rather than to pay them away as dividends. In practice shareholders seem to have a preference for dividend payments to be consistent from year to year and most firms endeavour to pay dividends regularly, and seek to achieve a steady growth in the amount paid out.

Where a company retains a considerable amount over a period of time the balance shown as retained profits may come to exceed the balance shown for share capital. In such cases companies often convert the balance into new shares by making a *bonus or scrip issue*. This device does not increase the value of the shareholders interest in the firm, but is often associated with the payment of the previous rate of dividend on the new capital, thus increasing the amount of cash which the shareholder receives as dividend.[8] The shareholders' funds converted to share capital are locked into the company thereby strengthening the capital structure of the company as far as creditors are concerned.

PREFERENCE SHARES

In order to obtain share capital without reducing the profits available to the original shareholders some companies issue preference shares. The holders of these shares have a prior claim to receive a specified rate of dividend if the company makes a profit, and to repayment of capital in the event of a liquidation. However, unlike the equity shareholders they do not benefit from the success of the firm in increasing profits because the level of dividend is fixed. Preference shares are often issued when new businesses are incorporated or when businesses are amalgamated. They provide a useful means of preserving the interests of the affected parties. As a means of raising fresh share capital preference shares have diminished in value in recent years. The preference dividend for tax purposes is a distribution of profits, and therefore unlike payment of interest on loan stocks and debentures, is not

[8] In theory receiving higher dividends will not necessarily make the shareholder better off because the higher level of dividends will reduce the level of funds available for reinvestment within the firm.

allowed as a deduction for the purpose of calculating profit subject to corporation tax. As a result preference shares are far more expensive to the company than a loan stock offering the same nominal rate.

The basic cost to the company of issuing a perference share is found by dividing the preference dividend offered by the amount raised. Where it is proposed to make a fresh issue of preference shares the return offered must be comparable to current market yields. Thus the cost of a new preference share must be related to the yields offered by existing preference shares at current market prices. The point is illustrated by the following example.

Example

A company is considering an issue of preference shares. Its existing preference shares offer a dividend of 9% and have a market value of 75p each. The cost of a new issue of preference shares K_{ps} may be found as follows:

$$K_{ps} = \frac{\text{Preference Dividend}}{\text{Market Value of Preference Shares}} \times 100$$

$$= \frac{9}{75} \times 100 = 12\%$$

In calculating the cost of a new issue, account should be taken of the issuing costs and apportioned over the shares issued. Where the par value and market value are identical the rate of preference dividend will give the current cost.

In its simple form the preference share is a useful source of finance for a company. Non-payment of the preference dividend will not result in insolvency and preference shareholders' capital may be lost without the liabilities of the company automatically exceeding its assets. Preference shares are therefore a useful source of capital where a highly geared company does not wish to issue fresh equity shares. However, in order to attract capital in such circumstances it may be necessary to offer a rather high rate of dividend. Alternatively a number of variations exist in order to make preference shares more attractive to holders:

Cumulative preference shares provide the assurance that dividends which are not paid in a particular year because profits are inadequate, will be paid in future years when profits permit. Ordinary shareholders will receive no dividends whilst arrears of preference dividends remain outstanding.

Participating preference shares confer the right for preference shareholders to participate in equity shareholders' profits if earnings exceed a specified level.

Redeemable preference shares provide for the shares to be redeemed at a specified price and on a specified date or dates.

All of these variations in the nature of preference shares are designed to reduce the rate of dividend which must be offered or to provide greater flexibility to the company. They may be used singly or in combination. For example a company many chose to issue *9½% redeemable cumulative participating preference shares.*

LONG-TERM DEBT

Long-term debt may be regarded as money borrowed for periods in excess of 10 years, with terms of up to 25 years being common. Sums may be raised in the form of a loan provided by one institution, such as a bank or insurance company, or in the form of a stock issued to many holders and marketable through the Stock Exchange. In the case of smaller companies, the latter facility is obviously not available. The loan may be unsecured, or may be secured by a fixed or floating charge, and take the form of a debenture stock or loan. Various method exist for making loan stocks more attractive including attaching conversion rights and issuing warrants, devices which are described below.

The loan stock will generally be repayable between two specified dates and may be redeemed at a premium and issued at a discount, each device improving the return achieved by holders.

The chief advantage of loan finance is the right to set interest payments against profits for corporation tax purposes. This feature may be taken into account in calculating the cost of a loan stock, which is found by dividing the net of tax interest payment by the par value of the loan, or the market value of any stock already in issue.

Example

A company has a loan stock in issue paying interest at 9%. Corporation tax is payable at 50%. The loan stock has a market value of 75 (£75 per £100 of stock). The cost of issuing a similar stock would therefore be:

$$K_{1s} = \frac{\text{Interest}\,(1 - \text{corp. tax rate})}{\text{Market value of loan stock}} \times 100$$

$$= \frac{9(1 - 0.5)}{75} \times 100$$

$$= 6\%$$

It can be seen that the loan stock has a cost half that of a preference share offering identical returns to holders. In practice it might be expected that a loan stock would have to carry a marginally higher coupon in order to compensate for the additional risk borne by holders. The cost of non-marketable loans is calculated by using the principle sum as the denominator in the calculation shown above.

Theoretically long-term loans should always cost less than equity finance. Both forms of capital provide long-term resources, and therefore enhance liquidity, but loans impose a continuing interest burden which must be met whatever the circumstances of the company. Furthermore, the interest rate for a long-term loan is usually fixed at the outset. This has the advantage of conferring greater certainty, and of eliminating exposure to unforeseen interest rate changes. However, the borrower cannot usually benefit from a fall in interest rates without incurring penalties designed to prevent early repayment. In the case of marketable loan stock it is possible to repurchase outstanding stock and to cancel it. This may prove a useful way of improving earnings and of deploying surplus funds. Such decisions should be viewed as investment decisions and be subjected to the criteria outlined for evaluating investment decisions in Chapter 11.

A number of techniques exists for improving the position of loan stockholders, and of reducing the cost to the company.

Secured loan stocks ensure that the stockholders will be protected in the event of the failure of the firm. The stock may be secured by a fixed charge over property or by a floating charge. In each case the shareholders will achieve an advantage over unsecured shareholders as discussed in Chapter 13.

In many cases the security is arranged in the form of a *debenture stock* with a trustee appointed to act on behalf of the stockholders in matters affecting them, and especially in the appointment of a receiver should this become necessary. In the case of non-marketable loans it is extremely common for a long-term loan to be supported by security, and to take the form of a *debenture or a mortgage* over company property. The precise arrangements will depend on the strength and standing of the business.

Convertible loan stocks allow stockholders to convert their loans into equity shares in accordance with a specified formula on predetermined dates. The formula is arranged to confer benefits on the stockholders provided the company's earnings increase in accordance with projections. Conversion does not result in additional funds being received by the company, and the stockholder invariably receives ordinary shares with a nominal value lower than his holding of loan stock, the balance being treated as a share premium. However, terms are set so that upon conversion the stock holder will obtain more ordinary shares that could be obtained through the market by sale and purchase at that time. The process of conversion does not result in any transaction costs being borne by the shareholder.

Loan stock with warrants. A warrant confers the right to buy shares at a specified price and date. Thus unlike conversion rights the exercise of a warrant results in new ordinary shares being issued and new capital raised. The loan stock continues in existence in the normal way. In common with conversion rights, the formula is arranged to allow the holder to acquire shares more cheaply than through the market. Warrants may be exercised by whoever holds them, and may thus be sold by the holders for a sum reflecting their commerical value.[9]

In recent years the debt market within the UK has been relatively inactive. This situation is largely attributable to the volatility of interest rates. Few

[9] The valuation of warrants and convertible stocks is a complex subject and beyond the scope of this text. See R. Brearly and S. Myers, *op.cit.*, Chap. 23.

companies wish to raise long-term loans until it is certain that rates will not fall further; few investors wish to invest at low rates when there is the prospect of a rise in rates in the future. With the recent decline in the levels of inflation it is probable that the debt market will achieve greater levels of a activity in the future.

For companies too small to enter the loan capital market a number of institutions exist to provide long-term loans. Often loan capital is required by companies without an adequate equity base and specialist institutions offer a mixture of equity and loan finance under the title of *venture or development capital*.

MEDIUM-TERM DEBT

Medium-term finance is made available for periods of up to 10 years, and has expanded rapidly in recent years partly in order to fill the gap produced by the decline of the long-term debt market. Generally medium-term loans are made at fluctuating rates of interest often related to wholesale money market rates, in which case changes are made at periodic roll-over dates and apply for a period of 3 or 6 months. Unlike long-term debt, repayment of medium-term loans is generally made over the life of the loan but the pattern of repayments may be set to suit the firm's projected cash flow. In many cases a moritorium or repayments holiday is arranged for the early part of the loan. Sums of money are usually made available as required by the business in large round-sum amounts termed "tranches". Interest is generally paid on the amount outstanding at any one time, and additional expenses arise from legal and similar fees, including commitment fees which must be paid when the facility is agreed but undrawn. The cost of such loans to the company is therefore often greater than the basic rate of interest less tax, which constitutes the underlying charge. Such loans are an extremely flexible form of finance, and are especially useful in meeting the cost of particular projects.

In recent years the banks have encouraged companies to make increasing use of term loans, which now account for 40% of new lending by value. A number of specialist institutions have entered the market to cater for new and expanding companies, and the needs of particular industries. The leading participant in the market is Investors Industry Ltd, through its subsidiaries including the Industrial and Commercial Finance Corporation (ICFC). This company is principally owned by the clearing banks, each of which has developed special schemes to meet the needs of small companies. In addition the banks participate in the Loan Guarantee Scheme under which high risk propositions are partly guaranteed by the department of Trade and Industry. Apart from medium-term loans two further forms of finance have been important in recent years.[10]

[10] All of the banks publish leaflets dealing with their special loan schemes for small businesses, they will also provide details of the Loan Guarantee Scheme.

Leasing. Under a finance lease assets are legally owned by an institution such as the subsidiary of a bank, but operated and maintained by separate users. Lease payments are designed to cover the cost of the asset and interest, but the legal owner is entitled to the benefit of capital allowances against corporation tax. The effect of a leasing contract is to make allowances available to profitable companies thereby deferring taxation, rather than to companies which cannot utilise the allowances because of an inadequate level of taxable profits, a phenomenon know as "tax exhaustion". Because of the advantage achieved by the lessor from the use of capital alllowances the interest rate charged within the leasing payments may be lower than a comparable loan. Thus for many companies leasing is a cheaper form of finance than a term loan. Until recently leases conferred the additional advantage of not appearing on the balance sheet of the lessee, giving the impression of a stronger financial position.[11] Because of these features leasing has been the fastest growing source of finance in recent years.

Hire purchase. Under a hire purchase contract the user makes a series of payments for the use of an asset owned by the purchaser. Ultimately an extra final payment is made of a nominal sum and ownership passes to the user. Because ownership does not legally pass until the final payment is made the hirer is protected from non-payment by a right to repossess the items concerned. Hire purchase is an expensive form of finance and is mostly used by small companies seeking to expand beyond the limitation of a small capital base. Where possible it is usually preferable to obtain a medium-term loan or to arrange a finance lease rather than to acquire an asset by means of hire purchase.

SHORT-TERM FINANCE

The term "short-term finance" is generally applied to any finance which is made available for a period of less than a year, or is technically repayable on demand. In general at any time short-term finance is likely to be less expensive than new long-term money, although over a period the cost of short-term finance may rise making the long-term finance relatively cheap. Therefore, a company must take a view on the likely trend in interest rates before deciding whether to fund its requirements on a short-term or long-term basis. Despite being the cheapest form of finance short-term money lays a firm open to the greatest level of risk. Funds made available on a short-term basis may be repaid at a time when it is difficult to replace them, causing severe cash flow difficulties to the business. The dependence of a firm on short-term finance may be revealed by the liquidity ratios, and an immediate improvement in these figures will be achieved if short-term debt is refinanced with long-term or medium-term money.

[11] The position has changed with the publication of an accounting standard (SSAP 21) which requires the liability on leases to be disclosed in the balance sheet.

Overdrafts are the most significant form of short-term finance and consist of an agreement with the company's bankers to allow the firm's current account to be overdrawn to a specified extent. Technically, overdrafts are repayable on demand, although they are usually made available for periods of a year and then reviewed. In practice a bank knows that it is impossible to recover funds merely by making a demand for repayment, but a failure to make repayment gives the bank cause to seek the appointment of a receiver. Often an overdraft will be supported by security in the form of a fixed and floating charge in the form of a debenture giving power to appoint a receiver without recourse to the courts.

From a company's point of view the great advantage of an overdraft is that interest, which is allowable for tax purposes, is only charged on the outstanding balance on a day-to-day basis, thus no cost is borne as a result of borrowing more funds than are absolutely needed. Overdrafts are generally obtained with the minimum of formality, and few costs. Although no formal repayments programme is generally agreed the bank will expect to see fluctuations in the use made of the facility. If the borrowing becomes "hard core" it is generally desireable to replace the overdraft with longer-term finance. However, in practice a good deal of finance is made available by overdraft on a permanent basis to sound customers.

Trade credit is another significant source of finance for most companies, and arises because most suppliers offer an extended period for settlement of invoices as a means of encouraging trade. In general trade credit is a costless source of finance, although there may be considerable hidden costs if, as a result of taking extended credit, relationships with suppliers are damaged. Where this happens terms of sale may move against the company, deliveries may be delayed and production disrupted, and the service provided by the supplier may deteriorate generally to the disadvantage of the firm. In addition, a cost may be incurred if advantage is not taken of discounts offered by suppliers. Often the cost of loosing discounts is considerable as shown in the following example.

Example

A company usually settles its account after 60 days and foregoes the discount of 2% for settlement within 30 days.

In this case the company is effectively borrowing £98 of every £100 due at 2% for 30 days (60 days less 30 days when settlement must be made). The cost to the company is found as follows:

$$\text{cost of discount foregone} = \frac{365}{30} \times \frac{2}{98} \times 100\% = 24.8\%$$

In many cases a company is better advised to borrow on overdraft and to settle bills in time to take advantage of trade discounts.[12]

[12] In managing the level of trade debtors a company faces these issues in reverse. The cost of offering settlement discounts can be considerable but may be dictated by custom and competition. In such cases the cost should be built into any costing calculations undertaken on the product.

Factoring. Under a factoring agreement a company pays a factoring company to collect its debtors, thereby reducing the cost of maintaining a debtors ledger. For an additional fee the company is allowed to borrow a proportion of the factored debts outstanding. The finance obtained may be used for working capital within the firm. Factoring thus provides a useful source of finance for rapidly expanding companies lacking the capital base to sustain their rate of expansion. However, the cost of interest is high and in some cases the presence of a factoring company is unwelcome to the firm's customers. Furthermore, the intervention of a factoring company changes the assets covered by a floating charge. Provided the cash obtained is reinvested successfully within the business, the interests of creditors and lenders will be maintained. However, if the funds are lost in adverse trading their position will be undermined. Although still a useful form of finance factoring has not developed as rapidly as was once expected within the UK.

CALCULATING THE COST OF CAPITAL

Companies need to calculate the cost of capital for two reasons:

- in order to determine the rate which must be earned on capital investments; and
- in order to minimise it in order to obtain the best returns for shareholders.

Although the cost of capital plays a crucial role in financial management there is little agreement amongst the academic community about how it should be calculated. In the absence of guidance practising managers have had to make use of proxies which provide a workable substitute. One common approach is to calculate the weighted average cost of the various individual components of the capital structure of the firm.[13] In carrying out the calculation both the weights and the rate of return offered to holders may be based on book values or current market values. Although book values have been widely used in the past it is generally agreed that their use is unsatisfactory for the following reasons:

- the cost of capital is used in decisions involving investment and the raising of fresh capital. In these circumstances the cost of past issues of capital is of no real relevance. Instead use should be made of current rates of return which govern the cost of new issues of capital.
- there is no satisfactory way of calculating the cost of equity capital using book values.[14]

[13] This approach is rejected by supporters of the Capital Asset Pricing Model.

[14] It is important to be consistent in using either book or market values for these calculations. Thus where market values are used for weighting purposes the cost of each form of finance should be based on market prices as well. The accounting cost will be the same provided this approach is followed. Thus where a company has £100,000 of 5% debentures with a market value of £50 per £100 of stock the cost may be calculated as follows:

Book values £100,000 × 5% = £5000
Market values £50,000 × 10% = £5000

The return offered to purchasers of the stock at 50 is 5/50 × 100 giving a yield of 10% and is likely to correspond with the return which would need to be offered on a new issue.

In order to illustrate the calculation of the cost of capital use will be made of an example.

Example

Northern Chemical Industries Ltd is financed as follows:

(i) 2 million 25p ordinary shares fully paid having a mid-market value of £1.40 each.
(ii) Reserves amounting to £1,474,000.
(iii) 500,000 6% preference shares of £1 each having a market value of 60p per share.
(iv) £1 million of 15% unsecured loan stock 1992–95 quoted at 125.
(v) £500,000 of 4.5% debentures 1987–90 secured on the company's premises and quoted at 50.
(vi) A bank overdraft of £1M which generally fluctuates between £650,000 and £150,000. Interest is charged at 2% over the bank's base rate – currently 14%.

The company is profitable and considered to have good prospects. It intends to pay a dividend of 14p per share at the end of the year and has indicated that it expects to increase dividends by 5% a year for the foreseeable future.

Assume Corporate Tax at 50%.

The first step in calculating the cost of capital is to determine the cost of each individual component.

(i) *Equity.* The cost of the ordinary shares may be calculated using the dividend growth model, incorporating the expected dividend and the company's projections regarding future growth.

$$K_e = \frac{d}{p} + g = \frac{0.14}{1.40} \times 0.05 \times 100 = 15\%$$

(ii) *Reserves.* The reserves are the property of the shareholders and their value is therefore reflected in the price of the company's shares. The cost of using the reserves as a source of finance has therefore been taken into account in calculating the cost of equity finance using the market value of the ordinary shares.

(iii) *6% Preference shares.* The preference shares have a market value below par, and any future issue would have to offer a higher dividend. The cost of the preference shares is found by the following calculation.

$$K_{ps} = \frac{d}{p} = \frac{6}{60} \times 100 = 10\%$$

(iv) *Unsecured loan stock.* In contrast with the preference shares the loan stock has a market value above par, suggesting that it was issued when interest rates were higher than their present level. In the case of loan stock the cost is reduced by the effect of taxation.

$$K_{uls} = \frac{i(1-t)}{p} = \frac{0.15(1-0.5)}{1.25} \times 100 = 6\%$$

(v) *Debentures.* The cost of debentures is found by applying the same approach as was used for loan stock.

$$K_d = \frac{i(1-t)}{p} = \frac{0.045(1-0.5)}{0.50} \times 100 = 4.5\%$$

(vi) *Bank loan.* It is stated that the bank overdraft generally fluctuates between £650,000 and £150,000. It therefore seems sensible to incorporate the overdraft into the cost of capital calculation at an average figure. Where a bank overdraft does not form part of the normal capital structure of the company it should be excluded from the cost of capital calculation. The cost is found by taking the interest rate of 16% less taxation.

The weighted average cost of capital can now be found by incorporating the market value of each block of capital, as a percentage of the total market value. The cost of each component is then weighted by the appropriate proportion and aggregated to give the weighted rate, as shown below.

Northern Chemical Industries Ltd – Weighted Average Cost of Capital

	Market value £'000	*Rate* %	*Weight*	*Weighted rate* %
(i) Ordinary share capital	2800	15	0.56	8.4
(ii) Reserves	—			
(ii) 6% preference shares	300	10	0.60	0.6
(iv) 15% unsecured loan stock	1250	6	0.25	1.5
(v) 4.5% Debentures	250	4.5	0.05	0.225
(vi) Overdraft	400	8	0.08	0.640
	5,000		WACC =	11.365%

Interpretation

Northern Chemical Industries has a weighted average cost of capital of 11.365%, which may be used as a cut off rate for investment decisions. Any project earning more than this rate will enable the company to meet the cost of finance and will increase the wealth of shareholders.

However, this analysis will only be valid if no change takes place in the companies capital structure. If new finance is raised the proportions will change, and when additional borrowing takes place the cost of equity will rise to offset the additional risk. The weighted average approach is a useful device where investment is to be made from internal cash flow, and where the basic capital structure will undergo no long-term structural changes. The method does illustrate the significant role of debt in reducing the cost of capital.

CONCLUSION

The key role of equity capital within a business is to provide basic risk capital. If a company makes losses no dividends need to be paid and share capital may be lost without the company becoming insolvent. Depending on the amount of share capital available quite substantial amounts may be lost before liabilities exceed assets. Thus to ensure maximum safety a business should finance itself exclusively through share capital (and retained earnings) and some businesses are proud of the fact that they have never borrowed. However, avoidance of all risk is impossible in a competitive business environment, and there seems little reason to avoid financial risks, whilst accepting trading risk. The use of borrowed money affords considerable scope for reducing the cost of capital to the owners of a firm, and a decision to avoid borrowing is likely to conflict with the objective of maximising the shareholders interest in the firm. Thus the role of share capital is to provide an adequate base of risk capital, not to provide all of the capital requirements of the business. The use of equity finance is costly, and the minimum use should be made of it taking account of all of the circumstances of the business. Judging the appropriate balance between internal and external capital is one of the most difficult, but one of the most important, decisions that the management of a firm must take. Where the firm enjoys opportunities for rapid growth there is a strong temptation to rely excessively on borrowed money, subjecting the shareholders to considerble risk. Where opportunities are fewer there may be a tendency to play safe, and to make excessive use of shareholders capital to the detriment of their interests. Achieving the optimal balance is a matter of balancing the undoubted risks of gearing with the positive benefits, and requires the exercise of skilled professional judgement on the part of financial management.

Bankers are often asked to give their advice on the financing policies which a business should pursue. In providing an opinion it is important to remember that the objective of the firm should be to achieve the best for its proprietors. This will rarely mean following a policy of safety first. Those shareholders who wish to avoid risk will find a wide range of alternative investments. The purpose of investing in a business enterprise is to obtain a superior return from that which can be achieved from riskless investments such as government securities. The banker should advise his customers to obtain the cheapest source of finance for the purpose required, whilst accepting a suitable exposure to risk. Sometimes this will mean advising a company to use overdraft or term facilities provided by the bank or its affiliates, on other occasions a firm should be advised to seek additional long-term capital, of a debt or equity variety. In practice the banker is likely to have a far deeper knowledge of the range of available facilities, and can provide a most valuable service by directing his customers attention to the appropriate source.

FURTHER READING

There are many books dealing with the financing of business, but because of the rapidly changing nature of the commercial world these become outdated all to soon. The Bank of England publication is an extremely useful source of information, and is updated frequently. Other valuable sources include the publications of the banks and of the major firms of accountants dealing with business finance, as well as the special supplements published in *The Times* and the *Financial Times*. Of the texts shown below those by Wright and Middleton are useful basic introductions covering the whole field of financial management. The book by Brearly and Myers is much more advanced but provides a sound introduction for those who wish to pursue the subject in greater depth.

R. Brearly and S. Myers, *Principles of Corporate Finance* (McGraw-Hill, 1980).
D. R. Middleton, *Financial Decisions* (Longman, 2nd ed., 1983).
M. G. Wright, *Financial Management* (McGraw-Hill, 2nd ed., 1983).
Bank of England and City Communications Centre, *Money for Business* (4th ed., 1983).

Chapter 13
Company Valuation

INTRODUCTION

From the time it becomes necessary to value the shares in a business. Owners and potential owners require valuations in order to negotiate a reasonable price to sell or to buy, and from time to time to satisfy the revenue authorities. Bankers require valuations in order to determine how much reliance to place on assets pledged as security whether in the form of company shares or of charges on individual assets. As a result of the conventions and limitations of traditional accounting it should already be apparent to the reader that a company cannot be valued simply by reading the total from the foot of the balance sheet.

The issue is further complicated by the range of possible uses to which the acquisitions may be put. Some prospective purchasers may wish to employ the assets within a going concern, others to realise them piecemeal. Shareholdings may be obtained with a view to exercising complete control, or to receive dividend income and to benefit from appreciation of the share price whilst holding only a minority interest. Some potential investors may be able to achieve significantly better returns from particular investments by reorganisation and by integration with an existing operation. Such investors may be prepared to pay a premium to acquire control that would not be economically justified for others. Thus valuation of company shares is an art requiring considerable skill, and not a little judgement. At the outset it is essential to determine why the valuation is required in order to select a suitable method. At the end of the valuation process it is important to bear in mind that the result is at best an estimate made at a single point in time which will begin to become invalid as soon as it is made.

In this chapter a number of different techniques for valuing interests in business firms will be described and discussed. Several of the methods make use of Stock Exchange valuations as expressed in the price earnings ratios of similar firms combined with the subject's own earnings per share. Accordingly, it is necessary to begin the chapter with an outline of the way in which accountants calculate earnings per share as a basis for investment ratios. Attention will also be given to balance sheet valuation on a going and gone concern basis, and in this respect some consideration will be given to the important topic of goodwill, and its treatment in company valuation.

EARNINGS PER SHARE

The calculation of several key indicators of company performance involve the use of the earnings attributable to each equity share of a company. Therefore, it is important that a consistent approach is adopted in calculating earnings per share. Accordingly, the ASC introduced an Accounting Standard for listed companies (No. 3) on this topic in 1972 (revised 1974). Although essentially a simple calculation, it is complicated by:

- the impact of advanced corporation tax (especially if irrecoverable);
- changes in capital structure;
- the existence of contingent claims including convertible loan stocks.

Before calculating earnings per share under the imputation system, it is necessary to examine carefully the charge for taxation to be deducted in arriving at the earnings figure. The tax charge will always include some elements which are constant, in that they will not vary with the proportion of the profit distributed by way of dividend. The charge may, however, include other elements which do vary according to the amount of profit distributed and which would be absent if no distributions were made. These components may be classified as follows:

Constant

- corporation tax on income;
- tax attributable to dividends received;
- overseas tax unrelieved because the rate of overseas tax exceeds the rate of UK corporation tax.

Variable

- irrecoverable ACT;
- overseas tax unrelieved because dividend payments restrict the double tax credit available.

Two alternative methods of computing earnings per share under the imputation system have been propounded:

(i) *Net basis of calculating earnings per share.* In determining earnings per share on the net basis, the charge for taxation used in determining earnings includes:

(a) any irrecoverable advance corporation tax (ACT);
(b) any unrelieved overseas tax arising from the payment or proposed payment of dividends.

(ii) *Nil distribution basis of calculation earnings per share.* In determining earnings per share on the nil basis, the charge for taxation used in determining earnings generally excludes (a) and (b) above (except in so far as these arise in respect of preference dividends).

The standard states:

> "In the audited accounts of listed companies, the earnings per share should be shown on the face of the profit and loss account on the net basis both for the period under review and for the corresponding previous period.
>
> The basis of calculating earnings per share should be disclosed, either in the profit and loss account or in a note thereto. In particular, the amount of the earnings and the number of equity shares used in the calculation should be shown.
>
> Where a company has at the balance sheet date contracted to issue further shares after the end of the period, or where it has already issued shares which will rank for dividends later, the effect may be to dilute future earnings per share. In addition, therefore, to the basic earnings per share, as set out above, the fully diluted earnings per share should be shown on the face of the profit and loss account of quoted companies."

Although earnings per share is generally calculated on a net basis investment analysts often find it useful to ascertain the earnings per share on a nil basis as well. The distinction between the net and nil basis of calculating earnings per share and the effect of dilution may be illustrated by the following example.

Example

The profit and loss account of Blake and Co Ltd is shown below:

		£
Profit on ordinary activities before taxation		56,000
Taxation on ordinary activities		31,000
Profit on ordinary activities after taxation		25,000
Extraordinary charges	4,000	
less taxation	2,000	2,000
Profit for the year		23,000

The notes to the accounts include the following:

(1) *Taxation*

Corporation tax at 50%	
Irrecoverable ACT	£28,000
	£ 3,000
	£31,000

The company has 100,000 ordinary shares of £1 each and £50,000 of convertible loan stock which may be converted to ordinary shares on the basis of 1 ordinary share for every £5 of loan stock.

Solution

The earnings per share may be computed as follows:

	Net basis	Nil basis
Profit on ordinary activities after tax	£25,000	£25,000
Irrecoverable ACT	—	3,000
	£25,000	£28,000
Shares in issue	100,000	100,000
Earnings per share	25p	28p
Shares in issue after conversion	110,000	110,000
Fully diluted earings per share	22.7p	25.4p

It can be seen that when the irrecoverable ACT is added back to show earnings as if no dividend was paid the earnings per share is 28p. When the effect of conversion of the loan stock is taken into account, earnings per share on each basis is diluted.

INVESTMENT RATIOS

In this section we consider five important ratios which are often calculated by those seeking to investigate the value and performance of a company's shares.

THE PRICE EARNINGS RATIO

This ratio measures the relationship between the price of a share and the most recently disclosed earnings. In general similar companies might be expected to have a similiar ratio. However, if a company is believed by investors to offer the prospect of better returns in the future the increased demand for the company's shares will drive up the share price and with it the price earnings ratio. Where a company has P/E ratio higher than the norm for companies of that type it indicates an expectation of better things in the future. Conversely low expectations will lead to a lower than average P/E ratio. The ratio is calculated by dividing the latest earnings per share figure by the share price, as shown below. As the share price may change from day to day, the P/E ratio is usually shown with the share price's reported in the financial press.

Example

A company has earnings per share of 25p and a share price of £2.50.

$$\text{P/E ratio} = \frac{\text{Earnings per share}}{\text{Share price}} = \frac{25\text{p}}{250\text{p}} = 10$$

EARNINGS YIELD

The earnings yield shows the earnings of a company as a yield based on the share price, and thus shows the investor the return that he may expect from his investment based on the earnings (profits after tax) or the company. The ratio is essentially the same as the price earnings ratio, but the later has become more popular in recent years. The earnings yield is calculated by dividing the earnings per share by the share price and expressing the result as a percentage.

Example

$$\text{Earnings yield} = \frac{\text{Earnings per share}}{\text{Share price}} = \frac{25}{250} \times 100 = 10\%$$

DIVIDEND YIELD

The dividend yield shows the return which may be achieved by investing in the shares at the present price based on the dividends receivable. The ratio is calculated by dividing the last dividend by the share price, after having "grossed up" the dividend to reflect the advance corporation tax paid by the company and imputed to the shareholder. It is necessary to take this step in order to make the resulting yield comparable with the yield offered by competing investments, which is quoted "gross", such as gilt edged stocks and bank deposit interest.

Example

$$\text{Dividend yield} = \frac{\text{Dividend}\left(\dfrac{1}{1 - \text{ACT Rate}}\right)}{\text{Share price}} \times 100$$

Dividend 14p per share, Share price £2.00, Tax rate 30%.

$$\text{Dividend yield} = \frac{14\left(\dfrac{1}{0.7}\right)}{200} = 100 \times \frac{20}{200} \times 100 = 10\%$$

DIVIDEND COVER

The dividend cover ratio relates the cost of the dividend paid to shareholders to the profits available to pay the dividend. Too low a cover ratio might suggest that the dividend would be endangered if the company encountered bad times. The higher the ratio the greater the security attaching to dividend payments. In the United States the ratio is usually calculated as a payout ratio by inverting the formula to show the proportion of available profits paid as dividend.

The ratio is calculated by dividing the earnings per share by the cost of the dividend per share. There is no requirement to take account of advanced corporation tax as this is already reflected in the earnings which are shown as profits after tax.

Example

Earnings per share 25p; Dividend per share 14p.

$$\text{Dividend cover} = \frac{\text{Earnings per share}}{\text{Dividend per share}} = \frac{25}{14} = 1.78 \text{ times}$$

NET ASSETS PER SHARE

The net assets per share figure is simply found by dividing the total net assets of the company by the number of shares in issue. It is usually expressed as a net tangible asset figure, after all liabilities and intangible assets have been deducted from the total assets. A short cut to the calculation is to use the total of capital and reserves as net assets. The two figures must be the same because of the nature of the balance sheet equation. It is often interesting to compare the relationship between the share price and the net assets per share. A successful company will usually have a share price in excess of net assets. Where net assets exceed the price per share there is an apparent potential for acquiring the company and disposing of the assets for a greater sum. However, the net assets figure shown in the accounts is only as reliable as the other figures shown in the accounts, and is subject to the deficiencies of accounting referred to elsewhere in this book.

THE VALUATION OF COMPANIES: THEORETICAL AND PRACTICAL APPROACHES

In Chapter 9, which dealt with investment decisions, it was noted that the present value of an investment could be found by discounting the cash flow expected to arise therefrom. In the rare case of a company with a single investment, the value of the entire company could be found by determining the value of the investment and by deducting the present value of the cost of all outgoings which the company expects to incur until the investment reaches the end of its life. In a perfect world it would, therefore, be possible to value any company on this basis by calculating the present value of all of its future income and outgoings. In the real world such an approach is rarely possible and recourse must be made to a number of alternative methods of valuation of which the following are the most important:

- by reference to dividends;
- by capitalisation of earnings;
- by reference to the balance sheet.

Each of these three methods will be illustrated by an example.

Example

The accounts of Tayles Trading Ltd are set out below.

Profit and Loss Account for the year to 31 March 1983

	£'000
Profit before interest and tax	6,000
Interest	1,000
Profit before tax	5,000
Taxation	2,000
Profit after tax	3,000
Extraordinary item	500
	3,500
Dividends paid – interim	200
final	1,000
Profits retained	2,300

Balance Sheet as at 31 March 1983

	£'000		£'000
Ordinary share (£1 par)	20,000	Goodwill	5,000
Reserves	14,000	Freehold property	10,000
Debentures	10,000	Plant and machinery	20,000
Creditors	6,000	Investments	5,000
		Stock	3,000
		Debtors	6,000
		Cash	1,000
	£50,000		£50,000

For the year ending 31 March 1981 the profits before interest and tax were £10 million, and in the year ending 31 March 1982 they were £8 million. The basic rate of income tax is currently 30%.

The goodwill shown in the accounts was acquired for £5,000 along with the other assets of a major competitor in 1979. It has not been depreciated or revalued in the accounts since acquisition.

It has been ascertained that the current rental value of the freehold property is £1.5 million per annum, and that this could be sold to a financial institution on the basis of offering an 8% return to the freeholder.

The investments owned by the company have a current market value of £7.5 million.

There is an amount of £1 million shown in the 1980 debtors figure which is now thought to be irrecoverable.

Several companies in the same business as Tayles Trading Ltd are quoted on the Stock Market. However, most are slightly bigger than Tayles. The most recent financial data relating to the sector is given below.

P/E ratio	9.75
Net dividend per share	£0.08
Times covered	3.2
Yield gross %	4.5

DIVIDEND VALUATION MODELS

Where a company is valued on the basis of dividends paid a comparison is made with the dividend yield offered by similar companies. It is assumed that investors will set the price of the company so as to achieve a similar yield.

In the case of Tayles Trading the company pays a dividend of 6p per share before taking account of imputed tax. Similar companies offer a dividend yield of 4.5%:

$$\frac{\text{Net dividend}}{\text{No. of shares}} = \frac{1{,}200{,}000}{20{,}000{,}000} = \text{6p per share}$$

$$\text{Gross value} = 6 \times 10/7 = 8.6 \text{ per share}$$

$$\text{Share value} = 8.6 \times \frac{100}{4.5} = £1.905$$

The approach used here to value the company is only really of relevance if shares are to be acquired for the purpose of obtaining income from dividends. Where valuations are required for other purposes this model is misleadingly simplistic.

- No account is taken of the security which attaches to the dividend and of the prospect that it may not always be paid.
- No account is taken of the possibility that the dividend may grow in value over the period for which the investment is held.
- Many investors acquire shares in order to achieve capital gains by selling the shares at a higher price, thus the dividend payments may not fully explain the value of a company's shares.
- The board of directors may decide to alter dividend policy in the future, completely invalidating the assumptions on which the valuation is based. Similar discretion does not operate with regard to assets or earnings, so that this problem is avoided in valuations made by these alternative methods.

The first three factors are interrelated to the extent that the retention of profits for reinvestment will largely determine the security of the dividend, the likelihood of future growth in profits and dividends, and the prospect of appreciation in the share price. The extent of profit retention by the company may be monitored by the calculation of the dividend cover ratio described earlier in the chapter. In this case of Tayles Trading the ratio is as follows:

$$\text{Dividend cover} = \frac{\text{Profit after tax}}{\text{Dividends}} = \frac{£3{,}000{,}000}{£1{,}200{,}000} = 2.5$$

The cover for the company is lower than the figure for the sector of 3.2 times, and suggests that the valuation, based on the dividend yield might need to be reduced.

(It should be noted that in this case that the cover ratio was calculated by reference to the aggregate figures for the company rather than from dividends and earnings per share. This is a quite satisfactory alternative which produces an identical solution. It should also be observed that the extraordinary item appearing in the profit and loss account has been excluded from the calculation. Non-recurring items should obviously be eliminated from any valuation procedure.)

Although more advanced dividend valuation models incorporating a growth in the level of dividends have been developed, these are not much used by investors, who have tended to concentrate on earnings valuation methods.[1]

EARNINGS VALUATION MODELS

The most widely used valuation model is based on the price earnings ratio. If the earnings per share of a company is calculated, the ratio for similar companies may be used in order to calculate a value for the shares. Tayles Trading has 20 million shares in issue at £1 each and its latest accounts show aggregate earnings (profits after tax) of £3,000,000.

$$\text{Earnings per share} = \frac{\text{Earnings}}{\text{Shares}} = \frac{£3{,}000{,}000}{£20{,}000{,}000} = 15\text{p per share}$$

The earnings valuation method gives a lower value for the company's shares than that achieved by the use of the dividend approach. It is important to note that the earnings of the company have fallen in the last two years. The level of dividends may reflect past, rather than current, profitability thus providing a higher value. In reaching a conclusion regarding the value to be placed on the company it will be necessary to determine the exact trend in profits, and particularly whether the figure for 1983 represents a low point in a cycle. Had a valuation been made on the basis of the profits achieved in 1981 the result would have been a valuation of £2.44 per share.

[1] The best known dividend growth valuation model is associated with J. Myron Gordon, and is known as Gordon's growth model. It suggests that the value of the firm may be found by discounting the value of future dividends using the following formula where g is the expected growth rate for dividends, K the return required by investors, and n the number of years for which dividends will be received.

$$V_o = \frac{d}{(1+K)} + \frac{d(1+g)}{(1+K)^2} + \frac{d(1+g)^2}{(1+K)^3} + \dots \frac{d(1+g)^{n-1}}{(1+K)^n}$$

which simplifies to give:

$$V_o = \frac{d}{K-g}$$

More complicated versions of the model have been developed in order to deal with changes in the rate of growth of dividends.

In using the earnings valuation method three particular problems must be taken into account:

(i) *Selection of a suitable P/E Ratio for valuation.* In practice it is rarely the case that an exactly comparable company can be found on which to base a valuation, therefore use must generally be made of the ratio for the sector or an average taken of several companies. Even so a company will often be engaged in several different activities rather than just one. When a ratio is found by reference to the data on larger companies than that to be valued it must be remembered that the ratio for small companies will normally be higher than for large. (The price of the shares is lower reflecting the greater risk often associated with investing in smaller concerns, and the thinner demand for their shares.) Accordingly, it is necessary to base the valuation on a P/E ratio adjusted to (say) 80% of the sector average in such circumstances.

(ii) *Determination of the profits on which valuation is to be based.* The profit figure to be used for valuation purposes could be the most recent profits shown in the accounts, those expected for the current year or for future years, an average of profits achieved over a period of years, or a combination, possibly by weighted average, of all three. In general, the vendors of a company will wish the profit figure on which valuation is based to be as high as possible, and prospective purchasers will wish to use a low figure. It is important to remember that the value of the business to its owners will ultimately be determined by the level of future profits, which are uncertain, rather than by past profits, even though these are known with certainty. In practice the formula to be used in particular circumstances must be determined by the parties to any transaction, or by their professional advisors.

(iii) *The effect of other factors affecting valuation.* In placing a value on any business it is important to take into account any important factors which will influence future earnings but are not reflected in the figures achieved in the past. Thus account must be taken of new products or developments, the underlying assets of the company, its financing arrangements, the prospects for management development and succession, the tax position of the company, and the presence of any large holdings of shares able to influence company decisions.

BALANCE SHEET VALUATION

Three principal valuation methods are employed in order to value a company from its balance sheet on a going concern basis quite apart from the break up, or gone concern approach which is discussed later in the chapter.

Book value basis

Under this method a company is valued on the basis of the net assets or net tangible assets per share. There is little to commend this approach as it merely results in a valuation on the basis of the unexpired cost of the items shown in the books of account. In the case of Tayles Trading the following figures would apply.

$$\text{Net asset basis: } \frac{\text{Net assets}}{\text{Shares}} = \frac{34{,}000{,}000}{20{,}000{,}000} = £1.70$$

$$\text{Net tangible asset basis: } \frac{\text{Net tangible assets}}{\text{Shares}} = \frac{34{,}000{,}000}{20{,}000{,}000} = \frac{29{,}000{,}000}{20{,}000{,}000} = £1.45$$

Adjusted book value basis

The adjusted book value approach is a distinct improvement on the unadjusted method, with all current information regarding the assets and liabilities of the company being taken into account. In the case of Tayles Trading the following adjustments and balance sheet figures arise.

(i) *Goodwill.* As this item represents an unexpired balance arising from a transaction four years earlier it is eliminated from the valuation. As discussed later in the chapter a fresh valuation should be made of current goodwill and incorporated in the valuation.

(ii) *Freehold property.* Although this item is shown in the accounts at £10,000,000 its market value appears to be £18,750,000 on the basis of offering an 8% return to investors, this value is found from the following calculation.

$$\text{Value} = \text{rental value} \times \frac{1}{\text{yield}} = £1{,}500{,}000 \times \frac{1}{8\%} = 1{,}500{,}000 \times \frac{8}{100} = £18{,}750{,}000$$

(iii) *Plant and Machinery.* Shown at book value without adjustment.

(iv) *Investments.* Adjusted to current market value of £7.5m.

(v) *Stock.* Shown at book value.

(vi) *Debtors.* Adjusted to reflect the irrecoverability of a debt of £1m.

(vii) *Cash.* Shown at book value.

(viii) *Debentures and creditors.* Shown at book value.

The foregoing items produce the balance sheet and adjustments shown below:

	Adjustment	*Balance sheet*	
	£'000	£'000	
(i) Goodwill	(5,000)		
(ii) Freehold property	8,750		
(iii) Plant and Machinery		20,000)	
(iv) Investments	2,500	7,500)	18,750
(v) Stock		3,000)	
(vi) Debtors	(1,000)	5,000)	
(vii) Cash		1,000)	
		55,250)	
(viii) Debentures and Creditors	—	(16,000)	
	5,250	—	
Unadjusted net assets	34,000	—	
Adjusted net assets	39,250	39,250)	

$$\text{Value per share} = \frac{39{,}250{,}000}{20{,}000{,}000} = £1.26$$

Either the full balance sheet or summary of adjustment methods may be applied to obtain the required valuation.

Current or replacement cost basis

The third method of balance sheet valuation is to show each balance sheet item at its current or replacement value. As was noted in Chapter 7 there are a number of practical problems associated with the use of current costs.

Despite the obvious attraction of a valuation method based on figures which appear to be definitive and unbiased, the balance sheet approach has two major deficiencies:

- No account is taken of future prospects and of the significance of the intangible assets of the company, except as a result of specific and necessarily subjective valuations. In reality it is often the intangible assets of a business which make the difference between success and failure, or strongly influence its value.
- No recognition is possible of the state of the market, and of the attractiveness of alternative investments.

Because each of the principle methods used for valuing businesses have severe shortcomings it is essential to use a combination of methods with each acting as a check on the others. In each particular case one method may be more appropriate than the others. In the last resort, however, the value of a business is what someone can be persuaded to pay for it. This will be substantially determined by the circumstances of the purchaser as well as those of the vendor in each transaction. At best an accountant can estimate the value in the light of the known circumstances.

THE VALUATION OF TAYLES TRADING

The various methods used to obtain a valuation of Tayles Trading have produced the following results:

Dividends basis	£1.905 per share
Earnings basis	£1.465 per share
Balance sheet valuation (adjusted)	£1.450 per share

The dividend valuation approach provides a figure somewhat out of line with the other two results obtained. As noted above, dividend cover is low, and in view of the decline in profits, the level of dividend payments is now too high. The balance sheet valuation takes no account of any intangible assets, but in view of the decline in profitability it is possible that goodwill has declined considerably in value and may have been eliminated. Accordingly, it seems that a value of around £1.46 per share is justified. However, the future profitability of the company is a critical factor in determining its value and further information on trading prospects is required before a final conclusion is reached.

In this case a similar result is obtained from using both the earnings and balance sheet methods which are generally of most use to those wishing to acquire the company as a whole to be operated within a group or integrated with another business. The dividend approach gives a significantly different result. However, although this method is of special interest to those considering acquiring a minority interest in the share capital for dividend income and capital gains, the result obtained for Tayles must be considered unreliable in view of the profit trend and of the decline in dividend cover.

VALUATION OF PRIVATE COMPANIES AND PARTNERSHIPS

The foregoing discussion has concentrated on the techniques used to value companies where comparisons may be made with similar types of firm listed on the Stock Exchange. In many cases businesses must be valued when no suitable comparisons may be drawn with listed concerns. In such cases a number of alternative methods of valuation exist.

By reference to sales or fee income. In the case of professional partnerships it is common practice to base the valuation of the firm on its fee income. In such firms, the skill and expertise of the principals are of particular importance in determining the profitability which can be achieved from operating the business. Therefore, it would be inappropriate to base a valuation on the record of practitioners who might play no part in the management of a firm after it is sold.

Instead a value is placed on the potential offered by a body of clients as represented by recent levels of fee income. Once the basic level of income is ascertained it is necessary to apply a multiple to achieve a capitalised value. This is generally done by reference to common practice within the profession concerned. For example, it may be usual practice to pay for two years fee income. In cases such as these the tangible assets of the business may or may not form part of the sale and will be dealt with separately by reference to market values.

This approach may also be applied to the sale of a non-professional business such as a window cleaning or a delivery business. In each case the valuation will be based on the normal conventions of the trade concerned.

By reference to conventions of trade. In cases where personal skill is less relevant, as in the case of a shop, it may be appropriate to base a valuation on the level of profits. In such cases two important issues arise:

(1) Care must be exercised to determine the maintainable level of profits under new management. For example, adequate account must be taken of the staff needed to run the business in cases where services were provided by members of the vendors family. Account must also be taken of any benefits received from associated firms which do not form part of any envisaged sale.

(2) The capitalisation factor may be arrived at by reference to recent usage in the trade. However, in cases where the profits earned are not typical it is important to determine the reason and, if necessary to take this into account in the valuation.

By reference to balance sheet values with an adjustment for goodwill. Because of the inherent uncertainties in arriving at reliable capitalisation factors for use in the foregoing methods it is often the case that in valuing small companies more weight must be placed on asset values than is the case with larger companies. However, as has been found in Chapter 1–7 of this book, accounts leave a lot to be desired as a basis for valuation. One particular problem is the valuation placed on tangible assets under the historic cost convention. The following specific points must be taken into consideration:

Fixed assets. It is important in valuing any business from its balance sheet that up-to-date valuations are obtained for all fixed assets, including fixtures and fittings and plant and machinery, in order to reflect market conditions and the state of the items concerned. In the case of properties, up-to-date valuations should be obtained from qualified surveyors and full account taken of any proposed developments affecting the value of the premises.

Stocks. It will be necessary to value stocks and work-in-progress, and especially important to pay attention to slow moving, obsolete, and deteriorating items.

Debtors. Outstanding debtors should be reviewed to ensure their collectability, with special attention being paid to amounts which are overdue or in excess of credit limits.

If a small company is taken over in its entirety it is essential that all liabilities are fully taken into account.

In such cases it may be necessary to agree that a value is not placed on outstanding items until sometime after the business is taken over. An alternative approach is to agree to take over only the assets of the business with the previous owners retaining responsibility for the liabilities. However, this approach is not suitable where a value must be placed on the business as a whole. Perhaps the greatest problem with this method is the difficulty associated with placing a value on goodwill, which warrants separate consideration.

THE ACCOUNTANT'S APPROACH TO VALUING GOODWILL

Balance sheets usually contain only tangible assets or intangible assets acquired for a consideration. In reality many of the key assets which determine a firm's degree of success are intangible (viz. reputation, quality, skill and loyalty of employees, etc). Accountants argue that all balance sheet items should be given a fair value as part of the valuation process. The figure for net assets then derived may be used to calculate the notional fair return which should be achieved by the business at a reasonable rate of return. If the company earns more than this the difference may be attributed to intangible factors collectively described as goodwill.

The "super profit" figure thus found may then be capitalised at an appropriate rate and added to the adjusted balance sheet value to give the total net assets of the firm.

Example

Adjusted balance sheet value of net assets	£2,000,000
Fair return at 15%	300,000
Actual average profits earned	350,000
"Super profits"	50,000
Super profits capitalised at 15% (say multiple of 7) to give value of goodwill	350,000
Total valuation of net assets	£2,350,000

The requirement to introduce a "fair return" and a capitalisation factor for super profits renders this method highly subjective, although reference to comparable valuations may reduce this somewhat.

THE ACCOUNTANT'S REPORT

Although it would be possible to base a valuation on the latest available accounts of a company it is often unwise to do so for the following reasons:

- The accounts may be somewhat out of date and not reflect current conditions.
- The value and condition of all assets should be examined afresh.
- The annual profit figures shown in the accounts may not be fully comparable because of changes in the composition of the firm, and the need to place estimates on items shown in the accounts.
- Information concerning future prospects should be obtained from the vendor's management.

For these reasons it is prudent to commission a report by an investigating accountant, who may, but need not necessarily, be the firm's auditor. His investigation will cover the following aspects:

(1) The trading record of the firm with appropriate adjustments to ensure comparability between the figures shown over the last few years.
(2) The assets and liabilities of the company with adjustments to ensure that all items are shown at a fair value to reflect current worth and condition.
(3) The Memorandum and Articles of the company with special mention of any important or unusual features concerning the powers of the company and of its directors.

(4) An examination of future prospects including a profit forecast prepared on a basis fully consistent with the recent accounts. Special attention should be paid to the life-expectancy of the company's products, new developments, and the level of competition.
(5) The management of the company including details of contractual arrangements governing salaries and pensions.
(6) The future cash requirements of the business.

Such a report is useful whenever a business is to be sold or acquired, and is always undertaken whenever shares are offered for sale to the public by prospectus or by an offer for sale. Although lengthy, such reports are prepared so as to be useful to their recipients and are arranged in a logical and systematic format. However, it is particularly important, especially in considering a profit forecast, to pay attention to the assumptions made by the accountant which are set out in the report. These assumptions should be examined critically to ensure that they are reasonable, and that the impact of key variables is fully reflected in the results projected.

THE GONE CONCERN VALUATION

So far this chapter has dealt with the valuation of companies on the assumption that they will continue as going concerns. In some cases this is not an appropriate method of valuation and it is more suitable to value the business on a break up basis. For a banker wishing to assess the value of a floating charge over the company assets this approach is of particular importance. Clearly, the valuation cannot be obtained from the accounts without some adjustments to the figures shown.

First, as accounts are generally prepared on a going concern basis it will be necessary to estimate the realisable value of each asset in the balance sheet. Secondly, in order to assess the bank's own position it will be necessary to estimate the extent to which preferential and secured creditors are likely to obtain repayment from these assets in priority to the banks. In some cases – especially those involving groups, the position may be extremely complicated. In addition, substantial changes may occur between the balance sheet being prepared and the assets being realised – possibly involving changes in intra-group accounts. Thus the answer obtained by the banker estimating the cover available it likely to be subject to a high degree of error and must be regarded with a great deal of caution. We shall begin by considering the principal assets and the problems which are most frequently encountered in assessing and realising their value.

Stocks

As a company runs into trouble it is likely to reduce stocks to a bare minimum in order to limit the level of cash expenditure. Thus, such raw materials as remain are likely to be those items which are slow moving – and probably have little value. The amount of work-in-progress and finished goods encountered will depend upon the cause of the collapse. Where a company overtrades – or fails to control costs – these may be at the usual level. Alternatively, if the company is unable to sell all of its production, stocks may have increased, especially in unprofitable lines. Work-in-progress is likely to be of little value unless it is converted into finished goods and it is often advantageous for a liquidator or receiver to complete production if at all possible. Finished goods are likely to form the most valuable element of stocks, except where the demise of the company was caused by low sales.

Although a greater value might be achieved for stock by sales through normal channels, this may be impossible unless normal staff levels are maintained – which may be prohibitively expensive or impracticable as staff desert a "sinking ship". Furthermore, normal customers may already be seeking permanent alternative sources of supply. When a company is in dire straits word soon passes round and a receiver or liquidator will often be forced to realise the stocks in bulk at a figure far below book value.

In recent years another problem has been encountered in dealing with stocks: the use of reservation of title clauses in contracts for the supply of components. This problem was publicised by the case *Aluminium Industrie Vassen* v. *Romalpa Aluminium Limited* – generally referred to as *Romalpa*.

By the use of reservation of title clauses suppliers retain title to the goods supplied until they are paid – in some cases even though the goods may have been incorporated in finished items and sold. In such cases the seller may be able to claim sums due from debtors. In theory where the stocks of companies are covered by reserved title this fact and the amount involved should be noted in the accounts. However, to be absolutely certain of the position the banker should ask the customer for confirmation that his stocks are not covered by reserved title.[2]

The sums which may be realised by the sale of stocks varies considerably from industry to industry. Figures between 10% and 25% are more common than higher figures.

Debtors and Prepayments

Although the amounts due are fairly easy to define, it is unlikely that the full value shown in the last balance sheet will be realised after a collapse:

(1) debtors will be slow to settle where no further supplies are likely to be forthcoming;
(2) there may be counter claims for defective goods and other items as well as normal bad debts;
(3) the company will have collected sums due as promptly as possible when it encountered cash flow problems, leaving a debtors ledger of rather low quality.

[2] Since the Romalpa case, a number of judgements have considerably reduced the effect and extent of reservation of title clauses. In significant cases, legal advice should be taken regarding the strength of the reservation clauses concerned.

(4) certain sums may be covered by reservation of title clauses; and
(5) the company may have entered into a factoring agreement, realised its debtors and expended the cash.

As a general rule of thumb, where no special circumstances prevail, it is probably the best to assume that debtors will raise only 75% of book value. Prepayments are unlikely to have any value and should be disregarded.

Cash, Bank Balances, Marketable Investments and Deposits

It goes without saying that by the time a company collapses it is likely, wherever possible, to have converted all of its assets into cash in order to settle debts. Therefore, any cash balances, deposits and marketable investments are likely to have disappeared. Should any investments remain they are likely to be unmarketable – or only realisable at a figure considerable below book value.

Group Balances

Groups of companies which run into trouble inevitably tend to move funds around the group – fire fighting each emergency. When collapse finally occurs a very tangled web of inter-company indebtedness is likely to have developed, possibly further complicated by inter-company guarantees. In addition the banker may find that various assets have been effectively taken beyond his reach following their acquisition by other group companies.

Where a holding company is itself an operating company, holding the majority of group assets, it is best to assume that group balances will have a nil value in a liquidation or receivership. In looking at a larger type of group, possibly with a non-trading holding company, such an approach may render analysis meaningless. However, it must be remembered that in the liquidation of its subsidiaries, the parent company, as a shareholder, will stand behind almost all other creditors. If the banker wishes to look to the assets of the subsidiaries, appropriate guarantees must be obtained in support of the facilities. (It is worth noting that under case law such guarantees must be given for the benefit of the subsidiary concerned).

Properties. Properties are likely to be the most enduring of a company's assets and for this reason are frequently charged in support of borrowings. The figure at which properties are shown in the balance sheet may be cost or a recent valuation. Where a banker wishes to obtain an up-to-date figure he may find an indication of current value amongst the comments included in the directors' report – but ideally he should obtain an independent professional valuation. It is unwise to assume that because a property is shown in the balance sheet, it will be available for realisation should the company collapse, because, in the intervening period, the company may are disposed of the properties, possibly by arranging a sale and leaseback. Furthermore, because properties are generally realised in difficult times, with a premium on early disposal, and at a cost, it is best to assume that only 75% (say) of the market value after deducting any possible corporation tax liability will be recovered.

Plant, equipment and vehicles. Whether or not these items are likely to be realised at book value, and with reasonable promptness, varies from case to case. New machinery in the possession of a company which has over-extended itself may sometimes be realised above book value. Cars will generally be easy to dispose of but at a figure below book value. Other machinery may have to be sold at a heavily discounted figure in order to compensate for costs of removal. In some cases assets will have been financed by hire purchase and as a result will not be available to a receiver or liquidator. Except where there is a good reason to do otherwise, it is often best to assume that plant will be realised at no more than 25% of book value.

ESTIMATING REALISABLE VALUE

Drawing together the suggestions above, the following conservative basis for valuing assets emerges:

Stocks and work-in-progress	10–25%	10–25%	Book value
Debtors	75%	75%	
Cash, bank balances, investments and deposits		Nil	
Group balances		Nil	Market value
Properties		75%	Book value
Plant, equipment and vehicles		25%	

As will be appreciated these figures are very "rough and ready" and where more detailed information is available this should be substituted – subject always to a reasonable discount to cover:

(a) loss of value in adversity; and
(b) cost of realistion.

ESTIMATING PRIOR CLAIMS

It has already been noted that when a banker seeks to realise a company's assets he may find that these have effectively disappeared, or that his claim has been defeated as a result of:

(a) Hire purchase;
(b) Factoring of debtors;
(c) Sale and leaseback;
(d) Realisations.

In addition to these causes the banker must recognise that his security will be diminished by:

(a) the rights of preferential creditors;
(b) debentures and other charges (fixed and floating);
(c) assets located overseas which cannot easily be realised and the proceeds repatriated.

Some of these items will be shown in previous balance sheets. However, the banker must constantly guard against the danger that the company will give another creditor security without his knowledge. He may obtain undertakings from directors not to do so. However, these may be of little financial value. The golden rules to prevent such unpleasant surprises are:

(a) not to lend to customers one cannot trust; and
(b) to perfect the security before advancing the funds.

The list of preferential creditors will be well known to most bankers. It includes:

(a) local rates and taxes for a period of 12 months;
(b) PAYE, VAT, and National Insurance;
(c) wages and salaries to a value of £800 per employee over a period of four months;
(d) holiday pay;
(e) redundancy pay.

In addition costs of a liquidation or receivership must be met before these sums are payable.

It is extremely difficult to estimate the value of preferential debts likely to be encountered. However, a number of pointers do exist:

(1) Rates and taxes including PAYE, VAT and National Insurance contributions are always likely to assume large proportions in a failing business. The reason is simple: trade creditors will cut off supplies if they are not paid, fiscal authorities have no such lever. Therefore the proportion of the latter rises relative to trade creditors.
(2) The amount of wages and salaries accrued rarely exceeds one week or one month. Sometimes it will be possible to estimate the likely preferential credit by reference to the accounts which show total emoluments and the average number of employees in the previous year.

However, as a company encounters problems it is likely to reduce its labour force. In practice, where a company runs into trouble it is probable that its bank will have advanced funds specifically to pay wages on a separate account, and will thereby become the preferential creditor in place of the employees.

At this point it is probably useful to emphasise that only one years' corporation tax which has been assessed on the company is a preferential creditor. Where a company has made losses these may reduce or eliminate this debt – and in practice PAYE and VAT are far more likely to be found than corporation tax.

CONCLUSION

It is necessary to value a business as a going concern for a number of reasons including:

(1) Proposed sale of shares to the public.
(2) Proposed private sale (or purchase of the complete business).
(3) For the purpose of a loan from a bank.
(4) As collateral for a loan by a bank.
(5) For capital transfer tax purposes.

In each case the objectives and interests of the person seeking the valuation will be slightly different and accordingly different methods may be used in making the valuation, which will inevitably result in differing results. Obviously all such valuations will be, to some extent subjective and, because they will be related to the attraction of alternative investments, will vary over time. Although theoretical valuation is generally undertaken by accountants, in the last resort the value of a business is determined by what it will earn for its owner either in future income or by sale. Accordingly a number of non-quantitative factors must be taken into account and the practice of business valuation must be considered as an "art rather than a science".

The valuation of a business as a "gone concern" is equally subject to error, but has, nonetheless, played a major part in bank lending decisions over the years. In practice it is important to achieve a suitable balance between the going and gone concern approaches; using the information which is available in order to assess the company's prospects, whilst remembering that the company might fail, and that the bank should protect its position in the event of liquidation.

FURTHER READING

Valuation is not one of the most well documented topics in the world of business. Those texts by Clemens and Dyer and by Hutchinson contain material of particular relevance to bankers. The text by Glover is more advanced, but provides a basis for further reading in this area.

J. H. Clemens and L. S. Dyer, *Balance Sheets and the Lending Banker* (Europa 5th ed., 1977).
C. G. Glover, "The Valuation of Unlisted Shares" in *Accountants Digest Series* (ICAEW).
H. H. Hutchinson and L. S. Dyer, *Interpretation of Balance Sheets* (Institute of Bankers 5th ed., revised 1981).

Chapter 14
Accounting for Reorganisations and Reconstructions

INTRODUCTION

Over the years some businesses meet with success, others meet with failure; only a few are likely to remain unchanged. As a result it is generally the case that the basic capital structure of a company will need to change as well. This chapter is therefore devoted to considering the procedures to be followed in revising the capital structure of a company, and the issues which arise. A broad division can be made into changes associated with success where a company wishes to alter its capital structure as a prelude to fresh investment, and changes necessitated by the loss of capital which must be carried out if the company is to survive. Within the first category come the redemption of redeemable shares, the repurchase of shares, and the issue of bonus shares, whilst the latter category includes the recapitalisation of a business after certain liabilities have been extinguished, the establishment of a new business in order to take over the affairs of another, and the evaluation of various alternatives including liquidation. The contents of this chapter are largely concerned with accounting practice rather than with decision making. However this chapter is best left until the end of the book, when issues such as valuation, investment over time, and financing alternatives have been considered.

SHARE CAPITAL AND SHARE PREMIUM

Share capital may be issued at a number of times in a company's life and in return for a variety of considerations. For example, it may be allotted to the founders of the company in exchange for cash subscribed, to the shareholders of another company in exchange for their shares and control of the enterprise, to subsequent investors in return for cash to finance expansion and to the existing shareholders by conversion of the balance of profits retained. The last example is termed a scrip or bonus issue and merely results in the conversion of distributable profits into non-distributable share capital. Such a change is often made with the intention of placing the finances of a firm on a sounder footing after a period of profitable operation in which the fixed capital has become insufficient.

The authorised share capital of a company is shown in its Memorandum of Association, but may be changed by ordinary resolution of its shareholders if so provided in its Articles. A company may then issue fresh share capital up to the authorised amount. After capital is allotted it may be "called" in various stages, with the shareholders retaining a liability in respect of the amount they have agreed to subscribe which has not been called. Thus the amount of share capital shown in the balance sheet at any time may not be fully called. Where it is called, but has not been paid, the balance will be shown as an asset in the balance sheet. Shareholders who do not meet the calls may forfeit their shares.

Frequently the issue of shares is made at an in excess of par value and the excess is recognised as a share premium and credited to a separate account in the balance sheet. The balance on this account is regarded as part of the fixed capital of the company and may only be used in a limited number of ways:

- in paying up unissued shares of the company to be allotted to members of the company as fully paid bonus shares;
- in writing off preliminary expenses of the company;
- in writing off expenses, or commission paid, or discount allowed, on any issue of shares or debentures of the company;
- in providing for the premium payable on redemption of any debentures of the company; and
- in paying a premium on the purchase of its own shares by a private company.

The restrictions relating to the last two categories of usage are considered below.

REDEEMABLE SHARES

It is noted in Chapter 12 that following the Companies Act 1981, firms are allowed to issue redeemable shares of an equity type. Previously only preference shares were allowed to be redeemable. The Act introduced a number of restrictions:

- Redeemable shares may only be issued if the company has non-redeemable shares in issue; and
- The shares may be issued partly paid, but may only be redeemed if fully paid.

Payment for redemption is to be made as follows:

- *Public companies:* Out of distributable profits or out of the proceeds of fresh issue of shares made for the purposes of the redemption.
- *Private companies:* As for public companies or out of capital.

The provisions governing payment from capital also apply where a private company purchases its own shares out of capital and are therefore considered later in the chapter.

Payment of any premium on redemption must be treated as follows:

Redeemable preference shares issued prior to 15 June 1982. The premium may be paid out of distributable profits, or be charged to the share premium account.

All redeemable shares issued after 15 June 1982. Where the shares were themselves issued at a premium and a new issue of shares is made for the purpose of redemption, the premium may be charged to the share premium account if there is an adequate balance, but may not exceed the amount of the premium on the original issue. Where the shares were not themselves issued at a premium or where a new issue is not made for the purpose of redemption, the premium must be paid out of the company's distributable profits.

Where a company redeems any of its shares from profits an amount equal to the nominal value of those shares must be transferred to the capital redemption reserve. In cases where a new issue of shares is made in order to finance the redemption, the transfer to the capital redemption reserve is reduced by the aggregate amount of the proceeds.

Example

A company redeems £1 preference share issued in 1976 at a premium of 10p per share. Its balance sheet prior to the transactions includes the following items.

	£
Share capital	50,000
Ordinary shares	50,000
Preference shares	10,000
Share premium	11,400
Profit and Loss account	46,420
	£117,820

The following transactions arise:

	£	£
Dr Preference shares	10,000	
Dr Share premium account	1,000	
Cr Bank		11,000
Dr profit and loss account	10,000	
Cr Capital Redemption reserve		10,000

The balance sheet after recording the transactions is shown below:

	£
Share capital-ordinary shares	50,000
Share premium account	10,400
Other-capital redemption reserve	10,000
Profit and loss account	36,420
	£106,820

Had the company issued 5,000 ordinary £1 shares at par the transfer to redemption reserve would have been reduced by £5,000 but profit and loss account and ordinary share capital would each have been £5,000 greater.

Had the shares been issued after 15 June 1982 the premium payable on redemption would have been charged to the profit and loss account, unless a fresh issue of shares was made for the purpose of redemption and the shares redeemed had themselves been issued at a premium of at least 10p per share.[1]

PURCHASE BY A COMPANY OF ITS OWN SHARES

Companies may wish to purchase their own shares for a variety of reasons: in order to retain control in the hands of the existing ownership, in order to provide funds to shareholders other than by the payment of a dividend, in order to alter the capital structure and in order to uitilise surplus funds. In the case of a small company the retirement or death of a joint owner may give rise to the need for such a purchase. Similarly, where a company has received funds from a venture capital organisation, it may eventually wish to buy back an associated shareholding and to sever the connection. It is generally agreed that in such cases companies would benefit from the power to purchase their own shares, thus in the Companies Act 1981 the existing prohibition on a company purchasing its own shares was relaxed. However, there are two aspects which might cause concern and give rise to problems:

- the purchase of shares by a quoted company in order to boost its share price in times of difficulty, thereby depleting company funds;
- the use of the repurchase provisions in order to avoid the payment of tax on dividends.

In order to prevent abuses the Companies Act 1981 included a number of provisions designed to control and limit the uses to which the repurchase arrangement are put, and the Finance Act 1982 laid down regulations governing the tax treatment of such purchases. Where the repurchase made by a UK unquoted trading company, is for the benefit of the trade, and is not tantamount to a dividend or distribution of profits, it is not treated as a distribution on which advanced corporation tax is payable. Instead the transaction is treated as a sale by the shareholder, and, therefore, is usually subject to treatment under the capital gains tax rules. In other cases the company may be liable to pay ACT, and the sum will be treated as dividend income in the hands of the former shareholder.

REGULATIONS

Share repurchases fall into three categories:

[1] There is some uncertainty whether the aggregate amount of the proceeds of a new issue of shares should include any share premium, or be based on the par value alone. The more conservative view is to regard the nominal value of the shares issued as equivalent to the proceeds received.

Market purchases which are made on a recognised stock exchange of shares which are formally listed or for which there is a marketing agreement, for example membership of the Unlisted Market.

Off Market purchases which are not market purchases.

Contingent purchases where there is no purchase contract but the company may become entitled or obliged to purchase shares.

The last category must be treated in the same way as off market purchases.

Companies wishing to make market purchases require prior authorisation from their shareholders, specifying the maximum number of shares that may be purchased, and the maximum and minimum prices, or a formula to enable these to be calculated. The contract must be concluded within 18 months of the resolution being passed, a copy of which must be filed at the Companies Registry. In the case of off market purchases the contract itself must be approved by a special resolution of the shareholders, with a 3/4 majority, not counting those whose shares are to be purchased.[2]

PAYMENT FOR THE PURCHASE

A public company may only purchase its own shares out of distributable profits, whilst a private company may, under certain conditions, make a purchase out of capital. Where a company makes a purchase out of profits it must transfer a like amount to a capital redemption reserve, although this amount is reduced to the extent of a new share issue made for the purpose.

Example – Purchase of own shares out of profits

The company decides to purchase 1,000 shares of £1 each from one of its shareholders out of profits at a price of £1.50 each. Its capital structure is as shown below.

Allotted share capital	£
Ordinary shares	10,000
Share premium account	1,000
Revalution reserve	2,100
Profit and loss account	2,500
	£15,600

The entries are as follows:

Dr Profit and loss account	£1,500	
Cr Bank		£1,500
Dr Share capital	£1,000	
Cr Capital redemption reserve		£1,000

The revised balance sheet would appear as follows:

[2] Where shares are repurchased they must be cancelled, and not held as an investment as is sometimes the practice in the USA.

	£
Allotted share capital	
Ordinary shares	9,000
Share premium account	1,000
Revaluation reserve	2,100
Other reserves:	
Capital redemption reserve	1,000
Profit and loss account	1,000
	£14,100

If the company had made a fresh issue of shares for the purpose of purchasing the shares, the amount of the transfer to the capital redemption reserve would have been reduced by the aggregate amount of the proceeds of the fresh issue.

If the company had purchased the shares at a discount of say £100 the amount transferred to the capital redemption reserve would still have been the nominal value of the capital purchased, but the profit and loss account would have been reduced by £100 less.

THE PURCHASE OR REDEMPTION OF SHARES OUT OF CAPITAL BY PRIVATE COMPANIES

A private company may redeem or purchase its own shares out of capital. The amount which may be paid out of capital is termed the "permissible capital payment", and is equal to the price of redemption or purchase after deducting available profits of the company and the proceeds of any issue of shares made for the purpose. Where the permissible capital payment exceeds the nominal value of the shares purchased, the company may charge the premium to either unrealised profits, the capital redemption reserve, the share premium account, or to the fully paid up capital of the company. Where shares are acquired at a discount the amount of the difference is to be transferred to the capital redemption reserve.

Where a purchase is made out of capital, special provisions operate to protect other shareholders and creditors. The payment must be approved by a special resolution, and the company must complete a statutory declaration concerning the company's ability to meet its immediate and future debts. This declaration must be audited and publicity given to the proposal. There are severe penalties for failing to comply with the regulations.

Example – Purchase of own shares out of capital

The company discussed above decides to purchase 5,000 £1 ordinary shares for £2 each. The entries are as follows:

Dr Share capital	£5,000	
Dr Profit and loss account	£2,500	
Dr Share premium account	£1,000	
Dr Revaluation reserve	£1,500	
Cr Bank		£10,000

The revised balance sheet appears as follows below:

Share capital	£5,000
Revaluation reserve	£ 600
	£5,600

In this case the "permissible capital payment" amounts to £2,500 and the share premium and unrealised profits standing to the credit of the revaluation reserve are reduced by that amount. Had there been no balance on the revaluation reserve it would have been necessary to reduce the fully paid share capital by a further £1,500. In such circumstances the company would presumably have reorganised the share capital. If a new share issue had been made for the purpose of purchasing the shares, the permissible capital payment would have been reduced by the proceeds received.

RECONSTRUCTIONS, REORGANISATION AND LIQUIDATIONS

Over time a company's capital structure may become wholly inappropriate or inadequate for the business. In some cases, as we have seen, the solution may be to redeem existing company shares with surplus cash resources, or to issue new shares. However, in many cases, especially where a company has lost money, such a solution is not viable. The company may be incapable of meeting its current obligations to such an extent that an orderly liquidation of its assets is the only source of action open to it. However, in some cases it may be possible to reach an agreement between all the interested parties so that the business may continue in existence. In such cases, accounting considerations arise in evaluating the proposed scheme and in dealing with the transactions resulting from its execution.

In the main, such schemes fall into the following categories:

- Liquidation of the assets and distribution of the proceeds in the order described in Chapter 13.
- A reconstruction in which the assets and liabilities are taken over a by a new company in which most of the interested parties have a stake.
- A reorganisation in which some liabilities and share capital are extinguished and the assets and liabilities are written down to their current value.

In many cases, a receiver and manager will already have been appointed in order to run the company. Often, in order to secure acceptance of all of the interested parties, and to gain legal sanction for writing off share capital, the approval of the courts must be obtained. For the scheme to win approval and stand a chance of success, it must be devised to ensure, first, that all stand to benefit more from its execution than from an immediate liquidation, and secondly, that the parties will view the treatment they receive as reasonably fair in relation to the other parties.

The points which arise in evaluating the executing such schemes are illustrated from the following example, adapted from question set in an Institute of Bankers examination.

The balance sheet of Thornton Ltd, as at August 31 1984, is as follows:

Balance Sheet

	£		£
Share capital		Goodwill	12,000
(£1 shares)	40,000	Freehold properties	8,000
Reserves	(550)	Equipment at cost	
10% debenture, 1990	10,000	*less* depreciation	24,000
Bank overdraft	25,000	Stock	46,100
Rates & taxes	9,000	Debtors	24,700
Other creditors	31,350		
	£114,800		£114,800

The bank overdraft carries a fixed charge over the freehold property and the debenture is secured by a floating charge over the remaining assets of Thorntion Ltd.

The company was formed some years ago. After a period of profitable activity, business has steadily declined and a loss was reported for each of the last three years. The present position of the company has been further aggravated by the fact that the market for certain product lines has completely collapsed. As a result the company is now in severe financial difficulty and a meeting of the creditors is called for September 2, 1984 to consider its affairs.

The following proposals are put forward for consideration:

(1) *Immediate liquidation of the company.* In these circumstances it is estimated that the assets would realise the following amounts:

	£
Freehold property	15,000
Equipment	9,000
Stock	19,200
Debtors	24,700

It is discovered that "other creditors" includes £9,350 that would rank as preferential in a liquidation, as well as the amounts due for rates and taxes. The liquidation expenses are estimated at £8,550.

(2) *Reorganisation and capital reconstruction.* The management of Thornton Ltd have informed the creditors that a complete reorganisation is presently taking place and that the removal of unprofitable lines will reverse the present trend within a couple of months. Accordingly, the directors have prepared a scheme of capital reconstruction for consideration. The plan is to revalue tangible assets at their liquidation values, and to write off goodwill and the debit balances on reserves. The shareholders would be asked to accept shares with a nominal value of 1p each in a "one for one" exchange for shares presently held. After the exchange has taken place the shares will be consolidated into £1 shares. The bank and the non-preferential other creditors would be asked to reduced their claims to 95% and 70% of their present balances respectively. The non-preferential other creditors would obtain repayment of this revised amount in three months' time, and the bank would receive its repayment in 12 months' time. The shareholders have indicated their willingness to take up a further 20,000 £1 shares at par, to finance working capital requirements, if the proposal is adopted.

(3) *Reconstruction by the creation of a new company.* A new company will be established into which fresh capital of £20,000 will be injected in the form of cash. The company will take over the assets and liabilities of the old company, and existing shareholders will receive 400 shares of £1 each in return for each 100 shares they hold at present in order to secure their acceptance.

Immediate Liquidation

Distribution of Assets

Distribution of Assets		£
Property covered by fixed charge (at valuation)		15,000
Bank overdraft		25,000
Unsecured		10,000
Assets covered by floating charge:	£	
equipment	9,000	
stock	19,200	
debtors	24,700	52,900
Liquidation expenses		8,550
		44,350
Preferential claims		
rates and taxes	9,000	
creditors	9,350	18,350
		26,000
Debts secured by floating charge		10,000
Available for unsecured creditors		£16,000
Unsecured creditors	£	
bank	10,000	
other (31,350 + 9,350)	22,000	32,000

Dividend for unsecured creditors 50p per £

Reorganisation and Capital Reconstruction

The effect of a reorganisation on the lines proposed is shown by the following journal transactions.

	£ Dr	£ Cr
Revaluations		
freehold property	7,000	
equipment		15,000
stock		26,900
Share capital (written down)	39,600	
Bank account (5% of £25,000)	1,250	
Non preferential creditors		
(30% of £22,000)	6,600	
Reserves-written off		550
	£54,450	£54,450

Each of these transactions is passed through a reconstruction account in which the following entries appear:

Reconstruction Account

Revaluation and write offs			
	£	Revaluations	
Equipment	15,000	Freehold property	7,000
Stock	26,999	Share capital	39,600
Goodwill	12,000	Bank overdraft	1,250
Reserves	550	Creditors	6,600
	£54,450		£54,450

After the reconstruction has been completed and fresh share capital of £20,000 has been subscribed in cash the balance sheet of the company would appear as follows:

ASSETS		
Fixed assets – tangible		£
Freehold property		15,000
Equipment		9,000
		24,000
Current Assets	£	
Stock	19,200	
Debtors	24,700	
Cash	20,000	63,900
		£87,900
LIABILITIES		
Capital and reserves		
Share capital		20,400
Creditors		
10% Debenture stock	10,000	
Bank	23,750	
Rates and taxes	9,000	
Other preferential	9,350	
Other creditors	15,400	67,500
		£87,500

The balance sheet has been adapted from the requirements of the Companies Act to reflect the special circumstances of the company.

Reconstruction with a New Company

In exchange for 400 £1 shares in a new company to be allocated to the shareholders of the old company, the following assets and liabilities would be acquired.

		£
Freehold property		15,000
Equipment		9,000
Stock		19,200
Debtors		24,700
		67,900
Liabilities	£	
10% debentures	10,000	
Bank	23,750	
Rates and taxes	9,000	
Other preferential creditors	9,350	
Other creditors	15,400	67,500
		£ 400

In this case the opening balance sheet of Thornton (1984) Ltd would be identical to that achieved for Thornton Ltd under a reorganisation. However, at times when it is not possible to devise an acceptable scheme it may be preferable to set up a new company to acquire the assets and possibly some of the liabilities.

For example, in this case the receiver might have sold the assets of the company to a new firm for £67,900 in cash, and 400 £1 ordinary shares to be distributed to the shareholders. The proceeds of sale could then be used to pay off the creditors.

DEVISING A SUITABLE SCHEME

In devising and selecting a suitable scheme the following important aspects must be considered:

(1) Carrying through an effective reorganisation of the business in order to prevent future losses.
(2) Ensuring that all parties to the scheme are fairly and equitably treated, and feel themselves to be so. In practice each creditor must stand to gain more from a reconstruction than from an immediate liquidation if the scheme is to stand any chance of approval.
(3) Preserving all assets including intangible assets such as trade marks and goodwill, and making the best use of tax losses in order to maximise future profits. (This aspect is often complicated and usually requires professional advice.)
(4) Where necessary, obtaining the approval of the court for the scheme, including any writing off of share capital.

EVALUATING A SCHEME FROM THE VIEWPOINT OF THE BANKER

In evaluating any scheme the banker must usually consider the following aspects:

(1) the immediate value of any cash or assets to be received;
(2) the return offered by any continuing involvement with the company; and
(3) the risks associated with each course of action.

Where the proceeds are not to be received immediately the return offered may be judged either as a rate of interest, or by converting the sums to be received to their present value at an appropriate discount rate.

In the example above the bank was offered the following alternatives:

Under fixed charge	£15,000
Under floating charge	£ 5,000
	£20,000
Under reconstruction – in 12 months	£23,750

At first sight it might appear that the bank would be best advised to accept the reconstruction as this offers the greatest value. However, the proceeds are not to be received for 12 months, and it does not appear that any interest is payable in the meantime. Thus in present value terms the alternative is less attractive. Furthermore, the reorganisation may prove to be unsuccessful, and the proceeds may be endangered. In the circumstances, therefore, the bank would probably opt for the liquidation of the business.

THE CAUSES AND SYMPTOMS OF CORPORATE COLLAPSE

Accounts are mainly utilised by bankers in order to assess whether a company is a sound credit risk and likely to be able to repay any facilities which are made available to it. It is important therefore that a banker is aware of the causes of financial collapse and of the common symptoms of its approach. In this areas the contribution of John Argenti is worthy of note.[3] Whilst his ideas are not exclusively concerned with accounting he suggests that deficiencies in this area often play an important part in the collapse of many companies and further that some of the symptoms of approaching collapse are only evident from the accounts. Argenti suggests that corporate collapse is usually due to four main factors:

A. Poor Management

Argenti argues that six main defects may be detected whilst some successful companies also appear to suffer from one or more of these defects. For a company to be suffering from all six should be profoundly disturbing.

[3] J. Argenti, *Corporate Collapse: Causes and Symptoms* (McGraw-Hill, 1975).

1. *One man rule* – One man dominates his colleagues. This must be distinguished from the "one man band" which is often inevitably the case with small yet successful companies.

2. *Non-participating Board* – Decisions are not fully considered by the directors and certain information is suppressed before reaching them.

3. *Unbalanced top team* – A predominance of (say) engineers and an absence of accountants has often proved fatal.

4. *Weak finance function* – This may apply where the company has adequate management and cost accounts but the "key" information does not reach and influence the decision-makers.

5. *Lack of management depth* – Top managment may not be supported by adequate middle management.

6. *Chairman is also Chief Executive* – In the absence of counter-weight one man rule may develop. However, in cases where the Chief Executive does not dominate, the company may be weaker if there is no "watchdog" over his activities.

Due to the inadequacy of its management the company will:

a. have an inadequate accounting system
b. be incapable of responding to its changing environment
c. be unable to operate within the contraints of the contemporary business world.

B. Accountancy Information

Four defects most frequently contributing to collapse are:

1. Budgetary control
2. Cash flow forecasts
3. Costing systems

These may exist but be inadequate or inappropriate to the circumstances of the company

4. Valuation of assets – imprudent expansion, increased borrowing and inappropriate pricing and dividend distribution policies may result from deficiencies in the valuation of assets such as the imprudent treatment of properties and research and development expenditure.

C. Change

Change may be classified into five headings. Failure to keep abreast of each puts the company at risk.

1. *Competitive Trends* – the emergence of foreign low cost producers, the merger of two competitors, the announcement of a competitor's new range of products, the appearance of an entirely new company in the industry.

2. *Political Change* – at local, national and international level may affect markets, supplies, sources of finance and the overhead cost of operating.

3. *Economic Change* – consideration must be given to the effects of currency movements, inflation, the economic cycle, interest rates and the size and pattern of customer demand. "At this time the economies of Western nations seem to have become subject to a four or four and a half year economic cycle; it is probable therefore that any firm that is not habitually looking ahead for at least five years will not be attuned to the fundamental rhythm of the economy in which it operates."

4. *Changes in Society* – including employee attitudes and, where relevant, the life style of consumers.

5. *Changes in Technology* – equipment may render production methods obsolete and make companies uncompetitive. They may also reduce or eliminate demand for a product or service.

D. Constraints

Argenti suggests that currently companies are unable to respond to change in the most appropriate commerical fashion but are limited by the restriction of news media, trade unions, consumer organisations and other pressure groups. Such factors can contribute to and perhaps cause collapse.

As a result of these weaknesses the poor company will respond to change by making one or all of three common mistakes.

1. *Overtrading.* Companies expand faster than their capital base allows. Failure results when additional finance cannot be raised in order to meet obligations either because there is insufficient time to negotiate increased facilities or because the lenders have lost confidence and will not grant them.

2. *The Big Project.* Companies with a poor profit record often respond by putting their entire faith in one big project. Typically, revenues are over, and costs underestimated and the project is so large that the company cannot withstand its failure. Companies run by autocrats with inadequate accounting systems and inactive Boards are especially susceptible to such errors.

3. *Gearing.* Companies frequently respond to the threat of decline by taking on new business rather than cutting back. This eventually results in a need for more capital which can often only be found from further borrowings. Argenti writes: "Poorly managed companies tend to gear up their equity beyond the prudent level so that their company is vulnerable not just to massive errors or strokes of gross misfortune but even to normal business hazards." He has no time for the manager who "blames economic recession for his company's collapse" and likens him "to the ship's captain who has not heard the weather forecast." The ship which is overladen is sunk by a two-foot wave but to blame the wave is to forget the other ships which are afloat.

"There are, then, certain events which by common consent do cause the failure of companies but which, being normal hazards of any business, ought not to cause it and indeed only do so because the company is already too weak to survive the blow."

Appendix 1

Information to be given as notes to the accounts in accordance with the Companies Act

SCHEDULE 4

1. Accounting policies to be disclosed.
2. Information supplementing the balance sheet:

(a) Share capital
- authorised and allotted in each class of shares:
- earliest and latest dates for redemption of preference shares, whether at option of company, and premium payable;
- reasons for allotments during year, number, class, aggregate nominal value and consideration received for the shares allotted;
- the number, description and amount of shares over which option or conversion rights exist together with the period during which the right is exercisable and the price to be paid for the shares allotted.

(b) Debentures
- reasons for issues during year, class, amount and consideration received for issue;
- particulars of any redeemed debentures which the company has power to reissue;
- nominal amount of debentures held by a nominee or a trustee for the company, and the amount at which they are stated in the accounting records.

(c) Fixed assets
- cost or revalued amount for each category at beginning and end of financial year;
- effect on amounts shown of: revaluations, acquisitions, disposals and transfers;
- cumulative depreciation at beginning and end of year, provision made in year, adjustment for disposals and any other adjustments in respect of each category;

- in respect of revalued assets, the year in which the assets were valued and the value. In the case of valuation during the year, the names of the valuers or their qualifications, and the basis of valuation;
- land and buildings to be analysed between freehold, long and short leasehold.

(d) Investments
- analysis required between listed and other investments, with the amount of those listed on a recognised stock exchange being separately shown;
- aggregate market value of listed investments (where if differs from the book amount);
- both market value and stock exchange value where for the purpose of the accounts the former is taken as being higher than the latter.

(e) Reserves and provisions
- balance at beginning and end of financial year;
- any amounts transferred;
- the source and application respectively of any amounts transferred.

(f) Provision for taxation
- the amount of any provisions for taxation other than deferred taxation.

(g) Indebtedness
- the aggregate of amounts payable or repayable after 5 years;
  by instalments any of which fall due after 5 years;
  and in the latter case the aggregate of each such item;
- the terms of repayment and the rate of interest of all such debts or a general indication thereof if the statement would be of excessive length;
- the aggregate amount of debts in respect of which security has been given, and an indication of the nature of security;
- the amount and period of arrears of any fixed cumulative dividends and the class if more than one.

(h) Guarantees and other financial commitments
- particulars (and where practicable the amount) of any charge on the assets of the company to secure the liabilities of any other person;
- the amount or estimated amount of any contingent liability, its legal nature, and what security (if any) has been provided by the company;
- the aggregate amount of contracts for capital expenditure not provided for and the amount authorised not contracted for;
- pension commitments included in any provision shown in the balance sheet and any commitments for which no provision has been made (with separate particulars for amounts relating to pensions payable to past directors);
- details of any other financial commitment which has not been provided for and is relevant to assessing the company's state of affairs;
- commitments undertaken for the benefit of a holding company, fellow-subsidiary or subsidiary to be stated separately within each category.

(i) Miscellaneous
- particulars to be given of the first time when the cost of an asset is determined by reference to the earliest available record in the absence of a record of purchase price or production cost;
- the aggregate amount of any outstanding loans under the provisos of Section 54(1) Companies Act 1948 (financial assistance for purchase of the company's shares) shall be disclosed;
- the aggregate amount which is recommended for distribution by way of dividend shall be stated.

3. Information supplementing the profit and loss account

(a) Separate statement of certain items of income and expenditure
- interest on bank loans, overdrafts and other loans which are repayable within 5 years;
- interest on loans of any other kind (does not apply to interest or charges on group loans);
- amounts respectively provided for redemption of share capital and loans;
- income from listed investments;
- rents from land (after deduction of outgoings) if substantial;
- hire purchase charges;
- auditors remuneration (including expenses).

(b) Particulars of tax
- basis of charge for UK corporation tax and income tax;
- special circumstances affecting liability for current or succeeding years;
- separately in respect of ordinary activities and extraordinary items;
  charge for UK corporation tax;
  relief from double taxation;
  charge for UK income tax;
  overseas tax.

(c) Turnover (after deduction of trade discounts, VAT and other taxes)
- turnover attributable to each class of business (where two or more substantially different classes);
- profit or loss before tax attributable to each class;
- turnover attributable to each geographical market where markets differ substantially from each other;
  (information need not be disclosed where, in the opinion of the directors, this would be seriously prejudicial to the interest of the company, but the fact that such information has not been disclosed must be stated).

(d) Particulars of staff
- average number employed;
- average number employed within each category of persons having regard to organisation of company;
- aggregate amounts of

wages/salaries;
social security costs;
pension costs;
(save in so far as these amounts are already stated in the profit and loss account).

(e) Miscellaneous
- the effect of including any item relating to the preceding year in the profit and loss account;
- particulars to be given of any extraordinary income or charges;
- the effect of exceptional items (by virtue of size or incidence) shall be started even though they fall within the company's ordinary activities.

4. General
(a) The basis of foreign currency translation shall be stated.
(b) Comparative figures shall be stated and where the corresponding amount is not comparable, it shall be adjusted and particulars of the adjustment and the reasons for it shall be given.

SCHEDULE 5

The Companies Act requires the following information to be shown in accounts in addition to the items included in Schedule 4.

Details of transactions involving directors. See Chap. 4 p. 128 for details

Directors' emoluments. If total directors' emoluments exceed £60,000 or if holding or subsidiary company, then the following must be shown:
(a) chairman's emoluments;
(b) emoluments of highest paid director, if in excess of chairman;
(c) number of directors whose emoluments fall into each £5,000 bracket;
(d) number of directors waiving emoluments, and total amount waived.
For the purposes of this paragraph £60,000 relates to the amount required to be shown in respect of all fees, emoluments and compensations but excludes pension contributions paid on a directors behalf.

Employees emoluments. Number of employees (excluding directors) whose emoluments exceed £30,000, in bands of £5,000. In group accounts, employees of holding company only.

Investments in subsidiary companies. In respect of each subsidiary the following must be shown;
(a) name;
(country of incorporation if not Great Britain. If Great Britain state country of registration if different from that of holding company);
(b) description and proportion of nominal value of issued shares of each class held, distinguishing between direct and indirect holdings. Corresponding figures for previous year not required.
Exemption provisions apply if the statement would be of excessive length.

Details of share capital and reserves and of profits or losses are required if the company does not prepare group accounts unless exempted as a wholly owned subsidiary.

Investments in companies that are not subsidiaries. Name, country of incorporation, description and proportion of nominal value of issued share capital of each class held in excess of 10% of a class of investee's equity share capital or allotted share capital or of investors' assets.

Exemptions provisions where companies are outside UK or disclosure is harmful or information would result in statement of excessive length. Additional disclosure requirements for interests in excess of 20% not shown under equity method of valuation.

Identity of ultimate holding company.

Appendix 2

Present Value Table

Period	1%	2%	3%	4%	5%	6%	7%	8%	9%	10%	12%	14%	15%
1	0.990	0.980	0.971	0.962	0.952	0.943	0.935	0.926	0.917	0.909	0.893	0.877	0.870
2	0.980	0.961	0.943	0.925	0.907	0.890	0.873	0.857	0.842	0.826	0.797	0.769	0.756
3	0.971	0.942	0.915	0.889	0.864	0.840	0.816	0.794	0.772	0.751	0.712	0.675	0.658
4	0.961	0.924	0.889	0.855	0.823	0.792	0.763	0.735	0.708	0.683	0.636	0.592	0.572
5	0.951	0.906	0.863	0.822	0.784	0.747	0.713	0.681	0.650	0.621	0.567	0.519	0.497
6	0.942	0.888	0.838	0.790	0.746	0.705	0.666	0.630	0.596	0.564	0.507	0.456	0.432
7	0.933	0.871	0.813	0.760	0.711	0.665	0.623	0.583	0.547	0.513	0.452	0.400	0.376
8	0.923	0.853	0.789	0.731	0.677	0.627	0.582	0.540	0.502	0.467	0.404	0.351	0.327
9	0.914	0.837	0.766	0.703	0.645	0.592	0.544	0.500	0.460	0.424	0.361	0.308	0.284
10	0.905	0.820	0.744	0.676	0.614	0.558	0.508	0.463	0.422	0.386	0.322	0.270	0.247
11	0.896	0.804	0.722	0.650	0.585	0.527	0.475	0.429	0.388	0.350	0.287	0.237	0.215
12	0.887	0.788	0.701	0.625	0.557	0.497	0.444	0.397	0.356	0.319	0.257	0.208	0.187
13	0.879	0.773	0.681	0.601	0.530	0.469	0.415	0.368	0.326	0.290	0.229	0.182	0.163
14	0.870	0.758	0.661	0.577	0.505	0.442	0.388	0.340	0.299	0.263	0.205	0.160	0.141
15	0.861	0.743	0.642	0.555	0.481	0.417	0.362	0.315	0.275	0.239	0.183	0.140	0.123
16	0.853	0.728	0.623	0.534	0.458	0.394	0.339	0.292	0.252	0.218	0.163	0.123	0.107
17	0.844	0.714	0.605	0.513	0.436	0.371	0.317	0.270	0.231	0.198	0.146	0.108	0.093
18	0.836	0.700	0.587	0.494	0.416	0.350	0.296	0.250	0.212	0.180	0.130	0.095	0.081
19	0.828	0.686	0.570	0.475	0.396	0.331	0.276	0.232	0.194	0.164	0.116	0.083	0.070
20	0.820	0.673	0.554	0.456	0.377	0.312	0.258	0.215	0.178	0.149	0.104	0.073	0.061
25	0.780	0.610	0.478	0.375	0.295	0.233	0.184	0.146	0.116	0.092	0.059	0.038	0.030
30	0.742	0.552	0.412	0.38	0.231	0.174	0.131	0.099	0.075	0.057	0.033	0.020	0.015

Period	16%	18%	20%	24%	28%	32%	36%	40%	50%	60%	70%	80%	90%
1	0.862	0.847	0.833	0.806	0.781	0.758	0.735	0.714	0.667	0.625	0.588	0.556	0.526
2	0.743	0.718	0.694	0.650	0.610	0.574	0.541	0.510	0.444	0.391	0.346	0.309	0.277
3	0.641	0.609	0.579	0.524	0.477	0.435	0.398	0.364	0.296	0.244	0.204	0.171	0.146
4	0.552	0.516	0.482	0.423	0.373	0.329	0.292	0.260	0.198	0.153	0.120	0.095	0.077
5	0.476	0.437	0.402	0.341	0.291	0.250	0.215	0.186	0.132	0.095	0.070	0.053	0.040
6	0.410	0.370	0.335	0.275	0.227	0.189	0.158	0.133	0.088	0.060	0.041	0.029	0.021
7	0.354	0.314	0.279	0.222	0.178	0.143	0.116	0.095	0.059	0.037	0.024	0.016	0.011
8	0.305	0.266	0.233	0.179	0.139	0.108	0.085	0.068	0.039	0.023	0.014	0.009	0.006
9	0.263	0.226	0.194	0.144	0.108	0.082	0.063	0.048	0.026	0.015	0.008	0.005	0.003
10	0.227	0.191	0.162	0.116	0.085	0.062	0.046	0.035	0.017	0.009	0.005	0.003	0.002
11	0.195	0.162	0.135	0.094	0.066	0.047	0.034	0.025	0.012	0.006	0.003	0.002	0.001
12	0.168	0.137	0.112	0.076	0.052	0.036	0.025	0.018	0.008	0.004	0.002	0.001	0.001
13	0.145	0.116	0.093	0.061	0.040	0.027	0.018	0.013	0.005	0.002	0.001	0.001	0.000
14	0.125	0.009	0.078	0.049	0.032	0.021	0.014	0.009	0.003	0.001	0.001	0.000	0.000
15	0.108	0.084	0.065	0.040	0.025	0.016	0.010	0.006	0.002	0.001	0.000	0.000	0.000
16	0.093	0.071	0.054	0.032	0.019	0.012	0.007	0.005	0.002	0.001	0.000	0.00	
17	0.080	0.060	0.045	0.026	0.015	0.009	0.005	0.003	0.001	0.000	0.000		
18	0.089	0.051	0.038	0.021	0.012	0.007	0.004	0.002	0.001	0.000	0.000		
19	0.060	0.043	0.031	0.017	0.009	0.005	0.003	0.002	0.000	0.000			
20	0.051	0.037	0.026	0.014	0.007	0.004	0.002	0.001	0.000	0.000			
25	0.024	0.016	0.010	0.005	0.002	0.001	0.000	0.000					
30	0.012	0.007	0.004	0.002	0.001	0.000	0.000						

Note

In order to find the present value of a sum of money due in the future, multiply the amount by the factor shown for the appropriate number of years and interest rate.

Example: £650 due in 9 years time, discount factor 8%.

Present value = £650 × 0.500 = £325.

Index

MIX
Papier aus verantwortungsvollen Quellen
Paper from responsible sources
FSC® C105338

If you have any concerns about our products,
you can contact us on
ProductSafety@springernature.com

In case Publisher is established outside the EU,
the EU authorized representative is:
Springer Nature Customer Service Center GmbH
Europaplatz 3, 69115 Heidelberg, Germany

Printed by Libri Plureos GmbH
in Hamburg, Germany